INSTANT POT Cookbook @2020

600 Foolproof Recipes
for Beginners and Advanced Users

Matilda Armstrong

Contents

TURKEY, DUCK & GOOSE RECIPES 76

PORK RECIPES 85

BEEF & LAMB RECIPES 106

FISH & SEAFOOD RECIPES 130

SOUPS & STEWS 148

PASTA & SIDE DISHES 170

EGGS & VEGETABLES 194

Introduction

Thank you for choosing my Instant Pot cookbook. I've put my whole heart into it to make sure it's the only book you will ever need to start your journey with Instant Pot. I have prepared 600 recipes to give you plenty of opportunities to fall in love with this magic device.

These book's chapters are filled with easy yet tasty 600 recipes created to help you turn on your Instant Pot adventure. Designed to show you how to best use your Instant Pot to prepare simple everyday meals, most of the recipes use widely available ingredients to create incredible meals effortlessly and rich in flavors and textures.

Each recipe contains the number of servings, the cooking time it takes to prepare and cook, and nutritional info per serving. The "serve with" section of most recipes is a suggestion to help you with putting the meal together, but feel free to improvise.

My small tips for big results

To start, go through each recipe completely and prepare all the ingredients you need in advance. Measuring tools are a must have in every kitchen for optimal results in your cooking. A little prep work before, goes a long way, like everything else. It will save you time in the long run, I promise. And above all else, just have fun!

Author's note: the "Total time" provided at the beginning of each recipe does not include the time the Instant Pot pressure cooker takes to come to temperature or the time it takes for the auto release function.

Instant Pot – what do you need to know

If you're new around the block and haven't yet had fun using Instant Pot, let me quickly introduce you to it. Instant Pot is a multi-functional device that has been conquering the kitchen appliances' stage for a good decade, and it's not slowing down. It has acquired sort of a cultish status among its raving fans whose number multiplies every year.

What's the secret of Instant Pot's popularity? Well, there isn't just one. With our daily schedules getting busier and busier, we love any piece of technology that saves us time and allows us to spend it in a better way.

So if you're looking to save a few hours a week, you've made the right choice. And if you think that 2 or 3 hours a week aren't that much, then think for just a moment how you would feel if you let yourself go out for a nice dinner once a week. That's four times a month. All I'm implying is that even small improvements made daily, compound to something more significant when you look at them from a long-term perspective. In this regard sense, Instant Pot is a huge time-saver.

One of the biggest benefits of using the Instant Pot is that you can set a specific time, and cooking will automatically stop when it's over. That gives you the freedom to do other things in the meantime, not worrying about the safety of your house. You can go to the gym, go shopping or clean your home without checking the pots every ten minutes.

And, if for whatever reason, you cannot eat right after cooking, Instant Pot has got you covered. It will maintain warmth in the cooking chamber for even up to ten hours. Forget losing time rewarming your meals again.

Instant Pot is also pretty hassle-free when it comes to maintenance. As soon as you're done cooking, you just have to clean the inner port, and you're done. So, you can forget having a stack of dirty dishes in your sink.

So, are you excited yet? I would be! And I am sure you'll find plenty of flavorful recipes for you and your family in this book. There's a lot to choose from, even if you're the pickiest person out there. So, go ahead and experiment! Discover your guilty pleasures anew, and don't be afraid to tweak recipes here and there if you find it necessary. After all, eating should be all about celebrating. Let's begin!

Rice & Grains

Herbed Chicken with Rice

Total Time: 40 minutes | **Servings**: 4 | **Per Serving**: Kcal 562; Carbs 35g; Fat 25g; Protein 62g

Ingredients

1 tbsp olive oil
4 chicken breasts, skinless and boneless
Salt and black pepper to taste
1 tbsp butter
1 yellow onion, diced
2 garlic cloves, minced
2 leeks, chopped
1 ½ cups basmati rice, rinsed

½ cup white wine
1 cup chicken broth
2 tbsp chopped parsley
2 tbsp chopped dill
1 tbsp chopped scallions
1 lemon, zested and juiced
1 lemon, cut into wedges

Directions

Set your Instant Pot to Sauté and heat olive oil. Season chicken with salt and black pepper, and fry in oil until golden on both sides, 6 minutes. Transfer to a plate and set aside. Add butter to inner pot and sauté onion, garlic, and leeks until softened and leeks bright green, 4 minutes.

Mix in rice, cook for 1 minute and stir in white wine, chicken broth; return chicken. Seal the lid, select Manual/ Pressure Cook, and set cooking time to 5 minutes. Allow sitting (covered) for 10 minutes and then perform quick pressure release to let out all the steam.

Unlock the lid, use a fork to fluff, and mix in chopped parsley, chopped dill, chopped scallions, lemon zest, and lemon juice. Dish rice into serving bowls and garnish with lemon wedges. Serve warm.

Teriyaki Turkey Rice

Total Time: 45 minutes | **Servings**: 4 | **Per Serving**: Kcal 437; Carbs 32g; Fat 22g; Protein 33g

Ingredients

1 tbsp olive oil
1 lb turkey breast, cut into 1-inch cubes
Salt and black pepper to taste
1 tbsp sesame oil
1 large red bell pepper, deseeded and chopped
1 large red onion, finely chopped

1 garlic clove, minced
1 cup jasmine rice, rinsed
1 cup chicken broth
¾ cup teriyaki sauce
1 cup fresh snow peas
1 tbsp sesame seeds, for garnishing

Directions

Set your Instant Pot to Sauté and adjust to medium heat. Heat olive oil in inner pot, season turkey with salt and black pepper, and fry in oil until golden on both sides, 7 minutes. Transfer to a plate and set aside.

Add sesame oil to inner pot and sauté bell pepper and onion until softened, 4 minutes. Stir in garlic and cook until fragrant, 30 seconds. Mix in rice, allow heating for 1 minute and stir in chicken broth, teriyaki sauce, and turkey cubes.

Seal the lid, select Manual/Pressure Cook on High, and set cooking time to 5 minutes. Allow sitting (covered) for 10 minutes and then perform quick pressure release to let out all the steam. Unlock the lid and press Sauté. Mix in snow peas and cook until softened, 5 minutes. Dish rice into serving bowls and garnish with sesame seeds.

Vegetarian Taco Rice

Total Time: 35 minutes | **Servings**: 4 | **Per Serving**: Kcal 437; Carbs 65g; Fat 23g; Protein 15g

Ingredients

1 tbsp olive oil
1 yellow onion, diced
1 green bell pepper, deseeded and diced
1 red bell pepper, deseeded and diced
1 yellow bell pepper, deseeded and diced
2 garlic cloves, minced
2 tbsp taco seasoning

1 ½ cups basmati rice, rinsed
1 (20 oz) can diced tomatoes
3 green chilies, chopped
1 ¾ cups vegetable broth
1 cup frozen corn kernels, thawed
1 (15 oz) can black beans, drained and rinsed
Salt and black pepper to taste

For serving:

½ cup sour cream
¼ cup guacamole

4 tbsp chopped cilantro
1 lime, cut into wedges

Directions

Set your Instant Pot to Sauté and adjust to medium heat. Heat olive oil in inner pot and sauté onion and bell peppers until softened, 4 minutes. Stir in garlic and stir-fry until fragrant, 30 seconds. Add rice, taco seasoning, and cook for 1 minute. Pour in tomatoes, green chilies, and vegetable broth. Stir and seal the lid.

Select Manual/Pressure Cook and set cooking time to 6 minutes. Allow sitting (covered) for 10 minutes and then perform quick pressure release to let out all the steam. Unlock the lid and press Sauté.

Stir in corn, black beans, and season with salt and black pepper. Heat through for 1 to 2 minutes. Turn Instant Pot off and dish rice onto serving plates. Top with sour cream, guacamole, cilantro, and lime wedges. Serve immediately.

Cheesy Rice with Ground Beef

Total Time: 45 minutes | **Servings**: 4 | **Per Serving**: Kcal 459; Carbs 27g; Fat 25g; Protein 38g

Ingredients

1 tbsp olive oil
1 lb ground beef
Salt and black pepper to taste
1 yellow bell pepper, deseeded and diced
1 yellow onion, diced
2 garlic cloves, minced
1 cup basmati rice, rinsed

1 cup beef broth
1 tbsp Italian seasoning
¼ cup tomato sauce
2 cups chopped kale
½ cup shredded cheddar cheese, divided
¼ cup grated Parmesan cheese
2 tbsp chopped parsley

Directions

Set your Instant Pot to Sauté and adjust to medium heat. Heat olive oil in inner pot, cook beef until no longer pink, 6 minutes. Season with salt and black pepper and stir in bell pepper, onion, and garlic, stirring frequently until vegetables soften, 3 minutes.

Stir in rice, allow heating for 1 minute, and mix in beef broth, Italian seasoning, and tomato sauce. Seal the lid, select Manual/Pressure Cook, and set cooking time to 6 minutes. Allow sitting (covered) for 10 minutes and then perform quick pressure release to let out all the steam.

Unlock the lid and select Sauté. Stir in kale to wilt, 2 minutes, and then half of cheddar and Parmesan cheeses. Allow melting, 2 minutes. Turn Instant Pot off and dish rice onto serving plates. Garnish with remaining cheddar and Parmesan cheeses, and parsley. Serve warm.

Broccoli & Pea Rice

Total Time: 35 minutes | **Servings:** 4 | **Per Serving:** Kcal 281; Carbs 45g; Fat 8g; Protein 7g

Ingredients

2 tbsp olive oil
1 yellow onion, chopped
1 head broccoli, cut into small florets
2 garlic cloves, minced
Salt and black pepper to taste
1 tsp dried oregano

¼ cup white wine
1 ½ cups chicken broth
1 cup short-grain rice
½ cup frozen peas, thawed
¼ cup chopped parsley

Directions

Set your Instant Pot to Sauté mode and adjust to medium heat. Heat olive oil in inner pot and sauté onion until softened, 5 minutes. Stir in garlic and cook until fragrant, 30 seconds. Season with salt and black pepper. Pour in oregano and white wine; cook until wine reduces by one-third and mix in chicken broth, broccoli, and rice.

Seal the lid, select Manual/Pressure Cook mode on High, and set cooking time to 8 minutes. Allow sitting (covered) for 10 minutes and then perform a quick pressure release to let out remaining steam. Select Sauté mode and mix in peas; cook until warmed through, 3 to 5 minutes. Garnish with parsley and serve warm.

One-Pot Pork Rice

Total Time: 35 minutes | **Servings:** 4 | **Per Serving:** Kcal: 355; Carbs 21g; Fat 17g; Protein 35g

Ingredients

1 lb pork tenderloin, cut into 1-inch cubes
Salt and black pepper to taste
2 tbsp olive oil
½ cup chopped brown onion

½ cup chopped orange bell peppers
1 tsp smoked paprika
1 cup basmati rice
1 ¾ cups chicken broth

Directions

Set your Instant Pot to Sauté and adjust to medium heat. Heat 1 tbsp olive oil, put in pork and brown on both sides, 6 minutes. Transfer to a plate and set aside.

Heat the remaining olive oil in inner pot and sauté onion and bell peppers until softened. Season with salt, black pepper, and paprika; and cook to release flavors for 1 minute. Stir in rice and pork, cook for 1 minute, and add chicken broth. Seal the lid, select Manual/Pressure Cook, and set cooking time to 5 minutes.

After cooking, perform natural pressure release for 10 minutes, then a quick pressure release to let out the remaining steam. Unlock the lid, fluff rice and dish into serving bowls. Serve warm.

Mango Rice with Pecans

Total Time: 30 minutes | **Servings:** 4 | **Per Serving:** Kcal 212; Carbs 31g; Fat 13g; Protein 6g

Ingredients

2 tsp ghee
1 tsp cumin powder
1 tsp mustard powder
1 small brown onion, finely chopped
1 green chili, finely chopped

Salt to taste
1 large mango, peeled and finely chopped
½ tsp turmeric powder
1 cup jasmine rice
¼ cup chopped pecans

Directions

Set your Instant Pot to Sauté and adjust to medium heat. Melt ghee in inner pot and stir-fry cumin and mustard for 1 minute. Add onion and chili; cook until softened, 3 minutes. Season with salt. Add mango and turmeric, stir, and heat through for 1 minute and then mix in rice and 1 ¼ cups of water.

Seal the lid, select Manual/Pressure Cook, and set time to 5 minutes. After cooking, perform natural pressure release for 10 minutes, then quick pressure to let out remaining steam. Unlock the lid, stir in pecans and plate rice. Serve.

Thai Brown Rice Tray

Total Time: 45 minutes | **Servings**: 4 | **Per Serving**: Kcal 211; Carbs 44g; Fat 2g; Protein 5g

Ingredients

1 cup brown rice
1 ¼ cups water
Salt to taste
½ cup shredded red cabbage
½ cup shredded carrots
1 red bell pepper, deseeded and chopped
1 tbsp tamarind sauce

1 tbsp peanut butter
½ lemon, juiced
1 tsp honey
½ tsp grated ginger
1 garlic clove, minced
¼ tsp red chili flakes
2 tbsp chopped cilantro

Directions

Add rice, water, and salt to inner pot. Seal the lid, select Manual/Pressure Cook and set cooking time to 22 minutes. Allow sitting for 10 minutes, then perform a quick pressure release, and unlock the lid. Fluff and spoon rice into a medium bowl and mix in cabbage, carrots, and bell pepper.

In a bowl, mix tamarind sauce, peanut butter, lemon juice, honey, ginger, garlic, and chili flakes. Pour dressing over rice mixture, adjust taste with salt and black pepper, and spread on a serving tray. Garnish with cilantro and serve.

Shrimp & Scallop Paella

Total Time: 40 minutes | **Servings**: 4 | **Per Serving**: Kcal 493; Carbs 43g; Fat 14g; Protein 39g

Ingredients

4 tbsp butter
Salt and black pepper to taste
1 large white onion, chopped
4 garlic cloves, minced
1 tsp turmeric powder
1 tsp sweet paprika
¼ tsp red pepper flakes
1 pinch saffron threads, soaked in 2 tbsp hot water

¼ cup white wine
1 cup chicken broth
1 cup short-grain rice, rinsed
12 scallops
1 lb jumbo shrimp, peeled and deveined
½ cup frozen peas, thawed
¼ cup chopped parsley

Directions

Set your Instant Pot to Sauté and melt butter. Stir-fry onion until softened, 4 minutes. Add garlic and cook until fragrant, 1 minute. Add turmeric, paprika, salt, black pepper, and saffron liquid. Cook for 1 minute to release flavor.

Include white wine and allow reduction by one-third. Follow up with chicken broth and rice; stir well. Seal the lid, select Manual/Pressure Cook, and set cooking time to 5 minutes. Allow Instant Pot to sit uncovered for 10 minutes, then perform a quick pressure release, and unlock the lid.

Select Sauté and mix in scallops, shrimp, and peas. Cook for 5 to 7 minutes or until scallops and shrimp are opaque. Adjust taste with salt, black pepper, and stir in half of parsley. Plate paella and garnish with remaining parsley. Serve.

Kheer (Rice Pudding)

Total Time: 45 minutes | **Servings**: 4 | **Per Serving**: Kcal 230; Carbs 28g; Fat 11g; Protein 9g

Ingredients

½ cup dried cherries, chopped, soaked

<u>**For the pudding:**</u>

3 cups milk   1 tsp ground cardamom
½ cup basmati rice   ¼ cup sugar
2 large eggs

Directions

Set your Instant Pot to Sauté and place in the milk and sugar, cook for 3 minutes until the sugar dissolves. Stir in basmati rice. Seal the lid, select Manual/Pressure Cook on High, and set cooking time to 5 minutes. When done cooking, perform natural pressure release for 10 minutes: Unlock the lid.

In a bowl, whisk the eggs. Gradually pour 1 cup of the rice pudding into eggs, whisking constantly. Add the egg mixture to the remaining pudding in the pot. Select Sauté and cook for 3 minutes, moving continually with a spatula, until it thickens. Stir in cardamom and cherries. Divide between bowls and let chill for 15 minutes before serving.

Mediterranean-Style Mutton Rice

Total Time: 35 minutes | **Servings**: 4 | **Per Serving**: Kcal 371; Carbs 21g; Fat 24g; Protein 29g

Ingredients

1 tbsp butter   1 cup basmati rice, rinsed
¼ cup blended onion   ¼ cup chopped tomatoes
2 tsp fresh ginger paste   ¼ cup green peas
2 tsp fresh garlic paste   1 cup water
1 lb ground lamb   ¼ cup whole milk
Salt and black pepper to taste   1 tbsp chopped cilantro, for garnishing

Directions

Set your Instant Pot to Sauté and melt butter. Sauté onion, ginger, and garlic paste for 2 minutes. Stir in lamb, season with salt and pepper, and cook for 6 minutes or until no longer pink. Stir in rice, tomatoes, green peas, and cook for 3 minutes. Pour in water, milk and stir. Seal the lid, select Manual/Pressure Cook, and set cooking time to 5 minutes.

After cooking, perform natural pressure release for 10 minutes, then a quick pressure release to let out the remaining steam. Unlock the lid, fluff rice, and plate. Garnish with cilantro and serve.

Wild Rice Pilaf with Mixed Mushrooms

Total Time: 60 minutes | **Servings**: 4 | **Per Serving**: Kcal 232; Carbs 37g; Fat 7g; Protein 8g

Ingredients

2 tbsp olive oil   ½ tsp dried rosemary
1 medium white onion, finely chopped 1 cup wild rice
1 ½ cups sliced mixed mushrooms   3 cups vegetable broth
2 garlic cloves, minced   ½ cup sliced almonds, for topping
Salt and black pepper to taste   1 tbsp chopped parsley, for garnishing
¼ cup white wine

Directions

Set your Instant Pot to Sauté and adjust to medium heat. Heat olive oil in inner pot, stir-fry onion and mushrooms until softened, 5 minutes. Add garlic and cook until fragrant, 1 minute. Season with salt and black pepper.

Mix in white wine, rosemary, and allow reduction by one-third. Add rice, vegetable broth, and season with salt and black pepper. Seal the lid, select Manual/Pressure Cook on High, and set cooking time to 28 minutes.

After cooking, perform a natural pressure release for 15 minutes, and then a quick pressure release to let out the steam. Stir in half of the parsley and all of the almonds. Dish rice into plates and garnish with parsley to serve.

Rice Stuffed Zucchini Flowers

Total Time: 40 minutes | **Servings**: 4 | **Per Serving**: Kcal 276; Carbs 53g; Fat 4g; Protein 5g

Ingredients

1 tbsp olive oil
1 medium brown onion, finely chopped
¼ tsp coriander powder
Salt and black pepper to taste
2 tbsp chopped dill
2 tbsp chopped mint leaves

1 tbsp chopped cilantro
½ cup tomato sauce
½ cup vegetable broth
1 cup short-grain rice
20 zucchini flowers
2 cups water

Directions

Set your Instant Pot to Sauté and adjust to medium heat. Heat olive oil in inner pot and sauté onion until softened, 4 minutes. Add coriander, salt, black pepper, dill, mint, cilantro, and tomato sauce. Combine and cook for 3 to 4 minutes to allow the flavors to incorporate. Mix in vegetable broth and rice.

Seal the lid, select Manual/Pressure Cook on High, and set cooking time to 5 minutes. After cooking, perform natural pressure release for 10 minutes, then quick pressure, and unlock the lid. Prepare a large ramekin on the side. Fluff rice and spoon 2 to 3 tablespoons of rice into each zucchini flower; lay stuffed flowers side by side in ramekin.

Clean inner pot and pour in water. Fit a trivet over water and sit ramekin on top. Seal the lid, select Manual/Pressure Cook on High, and set cooking time to 2 minutes. Once done cooking, perform a quick pressure release to let out all the steam, and unlock the lid. Carefully remove ramekin and plate the food. Serve warm with hot tomato sauce.

Rice & Cannellini Beans with Bacon

Total Time: 35 minutes | **Servings**: 4 | **Per Serving**: Kcal 176; Carbs 19g; Fat 9g; Protein 6g

Ingredients

2 (15-oz) cans cannellini beans, rinsed and drained
3 bacon slices, chopped
1 cup cooked white rice
¾ cup water

½ cup canned tomatoes
1 tbsp ground mustard
1 tsp chili powder
¼ cup chopped fresh mint, for garnishing

Directions

Set your Instant Pot to Sauté mode and add the bacon. Cook for 6 minutes, flipping once, until crispy. Remove to paper towels to soak up excess fat.

To the pot, add the cannellini beans, water, tomatoes, mustard, and chili powder. Return the bacon. Seal the lid, select Manual/Pressure Cook mode on High, and set time to 8 minutes. When done, perform natural pressure release for 10 minutes, then a quick pressure release to let out the remaining steam and remove the lid. Stir in the cooked rice and garnish with mint to serve.

Coconut-Cashew Purple Rice

Total Time: 45 minutes | **Servings**: 4 | **Per Serving**: Kcal 390; Carbs 27g; Fat 34g; Protein 9g

Ingredients

1 tbsp coconut oil
½ cup raw cashews
2 garlic cloves, minced
1-inch ginger, grated

1 cup purple rice, well-rinsed
1 cup water
½ cup coconut milk
Salt to taste

Directions

Set your Instant Pot to Sauté and heat coconut oil. Fry the cashews until golden brown, 2 minutes. Set aside. Add garlic and ginger to oil and sauté until fragrant, 2 minutes. Stir in rice, water, coconut milk, and salt.

Seal the lid, select Manual/Pressure Cook, and set time to 22 minutes. After cooking, allow sitting for 10 minutes, perform a quick pressure release. Stir in cashews; allow warming on Sauté, and dish rice into plates. Serve warm with coconut curry.

Jalapeño Rice with Cilantro

Total Time: 30 minutes | **Servings**: 4 | **Per Serving**: Kcal 254; Carbs 43g; Fat 7g; Protein 4g

Ingredients

1 cup white rice
2 tbsp olive oil
1 garlic clove, minced
1 red onion, chopped
1 jalapeño pepper, minced

1 ¼ cups vegetable broth
Salt to taste
¼ cup chopped fresh cilantro
Zest and juice from 1 lemon

Directions

Set your Instant Pot to Sauté mode and heat olive oil. Cook garlic, onion, jalapeño pepper, and rice for 3 minutes until the vegetables are softened. Pour in broth and season with salt. Seal the lid, select Manual/Pressure Cook mode on High, and set time to 8 minutes. When done, perform a natural pressure release for 10 minutes.

Stir in lime juice and lime zest. Cover the pot and leave the rice to rest for a few minutes. Then, fluff the rice with a fork and sprinkle with cilantro before serving.

Creamy Coconut Rice

Total Time: 30 minutes | **Servings**: 4 | **Per Serving**: Kcal 385; Carbs 26g; Fat 33g; Protein 11g

Ingredients

1-inch piece of root ginger, finely chopped
1 cup jasmine Thai rice, rinsed and drained
¾ cup canned coconut milk
½ cup roasted unsalted cashews

½ cup water
Salt to taste
2 tbsp cilantro, roughly chopped

Directions

Mix rice, ginger, coconut milk, water, and salt in your Instant Pot. Seal the lid, select Manual/Pressure Cook mode on High, and set time to 8 minutes. When done, perform a natural pressure release for 10 minutes. Remove the lid and stir in cashews, cover, and let stand for a few minutes. After, fluff the rice with a fork and scatter cilantro over the top to serve.

Caribbean Jerk Chicken Rice

Total Time: 40 min + marinating time | **Servings**: 4 | **Per Serving**: Kcal 682; Carbs 42g; Fat 44g; Protein 39g

Ingredients

For the chicken marinade:
4 chicken thighs, boneless and skinless
½ tbsp olive oil
4 garlic cloves, pressed
1 tbsp grated ginger
2 tbsp tamarind sauce
1 tbsp balsamic vinegar
1 tbsp squeezed lemon juice

½ tbsp honey
½ tbsp allspice powder
½ tsp cinnamon powder
1 tsp dried rosemary
¼ tsp chili powder
Salt and black pepper to taste

For the rice:
½ tbsp olive oil
1 cup chopped green onions
1 cup diced red bell pepper

1 cup coconut milk
1 cup jasmine rice
1 cup fresh pineapple chunks

Directions

Place chicken in a large zipper bag and set aside. In a medium bowl, combine olive oil, garlic, ginger, tamarind sauce, vinegar, lemon juice, honey, allspice, cinnamon, rosemary, chili powder, salt, and black pepper. Pour mixture over chicken, seal bag, and massage to coat chicken with marinade. Sit in the fridge for 3 hours.

Set your Instant Pot to Sauté and heat olive oil. Remove chicken from marinade and brown in oil on both sides, 8 minutes. Transfer to a plate and set aside. Sauté onion and bell pepper for 3 minutes or until tender, and mix in coconut milk and rice. Cook for 1 minute and stir in pineapple. Place chicken thighs on top.

Seal the lid, select Manual/Pressure Cook, and set cooking time to 5 minutes. Allow pot to sit uncovered for 10 minutes, perform quick pressure release, and unlock the lid. Stir rice and dish into serving plates. Serve.

Parsley Chicken with Brown Rice

Total Time: 55 minutes + cooling time | **Servings**: 4 | **Per Serving**: Kcal 575; Carbs 44g; Fat 30g; Protein 31g

Ingredients

1 cup brown rice
1 ¼ cups water
1 tbsp coconut oil
1 lb ground chicken
Salt and black pepper to taste

½ cup frozen mixed vegetables, thawed
¼ cup soy sauce
2 eggs, beaten
1 tbsp chopped parsley

Directions

Add rice and water to inner pot. Seal the lid, select Manual/Pressure Cook, and set cooking time to 22 minutes. Allow sitting for 10 minutes, then perform a quick pressure release, and unlock the lid. Fluff and spoon rice into a medium bowl. Set aside until completely cool for 1 to 2 hours or overnight.

Set your Instant Pot to Sauté and heat coconut oil. Add chicken, season with salt and pepper, and cook until no longer pink, 6 minutes. Stir in rice, vegetables, and cook until heated through, 3 minutes.

Mix in soy sauce and create a hole at center of rice. Pour in eggs and scramble until set. Mix into rice and parsley. Spoon rice onto plates to serve.

Rice & Chorizo Stuffed Bell Peppers

Total Time: 30 minutes | **Servings**: 4 | **Per Serving**: Kcal 630; Carbs 32g; Fat 42g; Protein 31g

Ingredients

4 bell peppers, tops and seeds removed
2 tsp olive oil
¾ pound chorizo
1 onion, chopped

1 cup chopped fresh tomatoes
1 ½ cups cooked rice
½ cup shredded Mexican blend cheese

Directions

On your Instant Pot, select Sauté and heat olive oil. Cook the chorizo while breaking the meat with a spatula. Cook until just starting to brown, about 2 minutes. Add the onion and sauté for 3 more minutes. Scoop the chorizo and onion into a medium bowl. Add in the tomatoes, rice, and cheese and mix to combine well. Spoon the filling mixture into the bell peppers.

Clean the pot with paper towels. Pour in 1 cup of water and fix in a trivet. Put the peppers on the trivet and cover with foil. Seal the lid, select Manual/Pressure Cook on High, and set the time to 12 minutes. After cooking, perform a quick pressure release. Remove the foil from the peppers and let cool for a few minutes before serving.

Mexican Rice with Peas & Carrots

Total Time: 35 minutes | **Servings**: 6 | **Per Serving**: Kcal 289; Carbs 54g; Fat 5g; Protein 5g

Ingredients

3 baby carrots, chopped
2 large celery stalks, diced
2 tbsp olive oil
1 small yellow onion, chopped
2 cups hot water
2 cups white rice

2 tomatoes, peeled, seeded, and chopped
Salt to taste
1 serrano chili, seeded and minced
1 cup shredded Monterey Jack or Cheddar cheese
¼ cup chopped fresh cilantro, for garnishing

Directions

Set the Instant Pot to Sauté and heat the oil. Cook onion, baby carrots, serrano chili, and celery for 5 minutes. Add in the water, rice, tomatoes, and salt, and stir. Seal lid, select Manual/Pressure Cook on High, and cook for 10 minutes.

When done, perform a natural pressure release for 10 minutes, then a quick pressure release to let out the remaining steam. Unlock the lid and fluff the rice with a fork. Add in the cheese, stir and sprinkle with cilantro to serve.

Mascarpone & Mushroom Risotto

Total Time: 60 minutes | **Servings**: 4 | **Per Serving**: Kcal 594; Carbs 39g; Fat 23g; Protein 41g

Ingredients

4 cups vegetable stock
1 ounce dried porcini mushrooms
1 cup hot water
1 ½ pounds fresh mixed mushrooms, sliced
4 tbsp olive oil
4 tbsp butter
Salt and black pepper to taste
1 onion, chopped

2 cloves garlic, minced
1 ½ cups arborio rice
1 tbsp miso paste
3/4 cup dry white wine
¼ cup heavy cream
2 tbsp mascarpone cheese, at room temperature
1 oz grated Parmesan cheese, plus more for serving
A handful of minced chervil

Directions

Soak the porcini mushrooms in hot water for 20 minutes. Then, drain them, reserving the liquid, and roughly chop; set aside. Set your Instant Pot to Sauté mode and melt the butter and olive oil. Place in the fresh mushrooms, sprinkle with salt and pepper, and cook for 8 minutes until browned.

Add in the onion, garlic, chopped porcini, salt, and pepper, and cook for 5 minutes until onion is tender and fragrant. Stir often. Put in the rice and miso paste and cook for 3-4 minutes, until well combined. Pour in the white wine and scrape off any browned bits at the bottom of the pot and add in the stock.

Seal the lid, select Manual/Pressure Cook mode on Low, and set cooking time to 5 minutes. When done, perform a quick pressure release to let out all the steam. Unlock the lid and stir in heavy cream, mascarpone cheese, Parmesan cheese, and chervil. Serve hot topped with Parmesan cheese.

Parmesan Cinnamon Risotto

Total Time: 30 minutes | **Servings**: 4 | **Per Serving**: Kcal 829; Carbs 42g; Fat 74g; Protein 13g

Ingredients

2 tbsp butter
½ cup short vermicelli
1 cup Arborio rice
2 tsp cinnamon powder
1 cup whole milk

1 cup chicken broth
¼ cup grated Parmesan cheese + 2 tbsp for garnishing
2 oz Gouda cheese, grated
Salt and black pepper to taste

Directions

Set your Instant Pot to Sauté and adjust to medium heat. Melt butter in inner pot and fry vermicelli until light brown, 5 minutes, stirring occasionally. Stir in rice, cinnamon, and cook until transparent. Add milk and chicken broth. Seal the lid, select Manual/Pressure Cook, and set cooking time to 10 minutes.

After cooking, do a natural pressure release for 10 minutes, then a quick pressure release to release all the steam, and unlock the lid. Stir in cheeses, salt, and black pepper; and allow the cheese to melt on Sauté for 2 minutes. Stir again, and dish risotto-pilaf. Garnish with the remaining Parmesan cheese and serve warm.

Wine Risotto with White Beans

Total Time: 30 minutes | **Servings**: 4 | **Per Serving**: Kcal 302; Carbs 26g; Fat 23g; Protein 9g

Ingredients

2 tbsp olive oil
1 medium yellow onion, chopped
3 garlic cloves, minced
¼ tsp fresh thyme leaves
2 cups chicken stock
½ cup Pinot Grigio (white wine)

1 cup Arborio rice
2 tbsp butter
½ cup grated Parmesan cheese
Salt and black pepper to taste
1 (15 oz) canned white beans, drained and rinsed

Directions

Set your Instant Pot to Sauté and heat olive oil. Stir-fry onion, garlic, and thyme leaves until fragrant, 2 minutes. Add chicken stock and once simmering, stir in white wine, and pour in Arborio rice.

Seal the lid, select Manual/Pressure Cook, and set time to 10 minutes. When done cooking, perform natural pressure release for 10 minutes, then a quick pressure release to let out the remaining steam. Unlock the lid, add butter, Parmesan cheese, salt, and black pepper; vigorously stir rice until sticky and cheese melts. Fold in white beans and warm through on Sauté mode, 3 minutes. Plate risotto and serve.

Lemon Risotto with Salmon

Total Time: 35 minutes | **Servings:** 4 | **Per Serving:** Kcal 661; Carbs 22g; Fat 36g; Protein 70g

Ingredients

2 tbsp olive oil
4 salmon fillets
Salt and black pepper to taste
2 garlic cloves, minced
1 small white onion, finely chopped
1 cup Arborio rice

½ cup white wine
1 tbsp squeezed lemon juice
2 cups vegetable broth
3 tbsp butter
2 tbsp chopped parsley
2 lemons, cut into wedges

Directions

Set your Instant Pot to Sauté and heat olive oil. Season salmon with salt and black pepper on both sides, and fry in oil (skin side down) until cooked to the touch. Transfer to a plate and set aside.

Add garlic and onion to oil; stir-fry for 3 minutes. Mix in rice and cook until transparent. Add wine and cook until reduced by two-thirds. Stir in lemon juice and broth. Seal the lid, select Manual/Pressure Cook, and set time to 10 minutes. When done cooking, perform natural pressure release for 10 minutes.

Unlock the lid, add butter, half of parsley, and mix vigorously until risotto is sticky. Adjust taste with salt and pepper. Spoon onto plates, top with fried salmon, garnish with parsley, and lemon wedges, and serve.

Blue Cheese-Parmesan Risotto

Total Time: 35 minutes | **Servings:** 4 | **Per Serving:** Kcal 385; Carbs 22g; Fat 30g; Protein 14g

Ingredients

2 tbsp olive oil
1 small shallot, minced
1 cup Arborio rice
¼ cup Sauvignon Blanc
2 cups chicken stock

1 cup crumbled blue cheese
½ cup heavy cream
¼ cup grated Parmesan cheese
Salt and black pepper to taste
½ cup frozen peas, thawed

Directions

Set your Instant Pot to Sauté and adjust to medium heat. Heat olive oil in inner pot and sauté shallot until softened, 2 minutes. Mix in rice and cook until transparent. Add wine and cook until reduced by two-thirds. Stir in chicken stock. Seal the lid, select Manual/Pressure Cook, and set cooking time to 10 minutes.

When done cooking, perform natural pressure release for 10 minutes. Add in blue cheese, heavy cream, and Parmesan cheese; mix vigorously until risotto is sticky and cheese melts. Stir in peas. Turn Instant Pot off and serve risotto.

Raspberry Risotto

Total Time: 35 minutes | **Servings:** 4 | **Per Serving:** Kcal 237; Carbs 32g; Fat 14g; Protein 7g

Ingredients

2 tbsp butter
1 small carrot, chopped
1 celery stalk, chopped
A pinch salt
1 cup Arborio rice

½ cup sparkling wine
2 cups water
1 cup fresh raspberries, chopped (leave 3 for garnishing)
1 cup grated Pecorino Romano cheese

Directions

Set your Instant Pot to Sauté and adjust to medium heat. Melt butter in inner pot and sauté carrot and celery until softened, 6 minutes. Season with salt. Stir in rice and cook until transparent; add wine, cook for 1 minute, and stir in water. Pour in raspberries. Seal the lid, select Manual/Pressure Cook, and set cooking time to 10 minutes.

After cooking, do a natural pressure release for 10 minutes. Unlock the lid. Mix in cheese vigorously until risotto is sticky. Spoon risotto onto plates, garnish with remaining raspberries, and serve warm.

California Sushi Rolls

Total Time: 40 minutes | **Servings**: 4 | **Per Serving**: Kcal 465; Carbs 62g; Fat 17g; Protein 23g

Ingredients

For the rice:

1 cup short-grain Japanese rice, well-rinsed
1 ½ cups water
1 tbsp sugar

¼ cup apple cider vinegar
1 tsp salt

For assembling sushi:

Bamboo sushi mat
4 nori sheets
1 small cucumber, deseeded and julienned

1 medium avocado, peeled and julienned
3 oz crabmeat, julienned
4 tbsp black and white sesame seeds, in a plate

Directions

Combine rice and water in inner pot. Seal the lid, select Manual/Pressure Cook, and set time to 7 minutes. Perform natural pressure release for 10 minutes, then a quick pressure release to let out remaining steam, and unlock the lid.

Meanwhile, in a medium bowl, combine sugar, vinegar, and salt. Spoon rice into bowl and mix until well-coated. Spread on a wide tray and allow complete cooling.

Lay bamboo sheet on a flat surface and line with plastic wrap. Spoon a quarter of rice onto sheet and press firmly. Lay 1 nori sheet on top and arrange a quarter each of cucumber, avocado, and crabmeat at one end of nori sheet. .

Holding bamboo sheet (at the side with the cucumber topping), roll rice over the filling while compressing as you roll. Remove mat, roll sushi in sesame seeds, and set aside on a tray. Repeat assembling the remaining sushi rolls.

When done, slice each roll into 8 pieces using a sharp, knife, and plate. Serve with soy sauce, wasabi, and ginger slices.

Cherry-Choco-Walnut Oatmeal

Total Time: 20 minutes | **Servings**: 2 | **Per Serving**: Kcal 444; Carbs 72g; Fat 18g; Protein 20g

Ingredients

2 cups milk
1 cup old fashioned rolled oats
1 tbsp cocoa powder
3 tbsp maple syrup

½ cup dried cherries
Greek Yogurt for topping
¼ cup chopped walnuts

Directions

Pour milk, oats, cocoa powder, maple syrup, and cherries into inner pot. Seal the lid, select Manual/Pressure Cook on High, and set cooking time to 3 minutes.

After cooking, perform natural pressure release for 10 minutes, then a quick pressure release to let out the remaining steam. Unlock the lid, stir, and spoon oatmeal into serving bowls. Top with Greek yogurt, walnuts, and serve warm.

Mushroom & Feta Cheese Oatmeal

Total Time: 35 minutes | **Servings**: 2 | **Per Serving**: Kcal 246; Carbs 39g; Fat 13g; Protein 12g

Ingredients

1 tbsp butter

1 cup sliced cremini mushrooms

1 garlic clove, minced

1 tsp thyme leaves

Salt and black pepper to taste

1 cup chopped baby kale

1 cup old fashioned rolled oats

2 cups vegetable broth

¼ tsp red pepper flakes

¼ cup crumbled feta cheese

Directions

Set your Instant Pot to Sauté and adjust to medium heat. Melt butter in inner pot and sauté mushrooms until slightly softened, 4 to 5 minutes. Stir in garlic, thyme, salt, and black pepper. Cook until fragrant, 3 minutes.

Mix in kale to wilt; stir in oats, vegetable broth, and red pepper flakes. Seal the lid, select Manual/Pressure Cook on High, and set cooking time to 3 minutes.

After cooking, perform natural pressure release for 10 minutes. Unlock the lid, stir, and adjust taste with salt and black pepper. Dish oatmeal into serving bowls and top with feta cheese. Serve warm.

Speedy Morning Oatmeal

Total Time: 15 minutes | **Servings**: 4 | **Per Serving**: Kcal 213; Carbs 47g; Fat 9g; Protein 13g

Ingredients

1 tbsp flaxseed

3 cups rolled oats

5 cups water

1 tbsp butter

1 chocolate square, grated

Directions

Combine the butter, oats, flaxseed, and water in your Instant Pot and mix well. Seal the lid, select Manual/Pressure Cook on High, and set time to 4 minutes. After cooking, perform quick pressure to let out steam. Open the lid and divide the oatmeal between bowls. Top with grated chocolate to serve.

Corn & Scallion Oatmeal

Total Time: 25 minutes | **Servings**: 2 | **Per Serving**: Kcal 256; Carbs 55g; Fat 8g; Protein 12g

Ingredients

2 cups vegetable broth

2 tbsp soy sauce

1 cup old fashioned rolled oats

1 tsp hot sauce

1 cup fresh corn kernels

4 scallions, sliced and divided

Salt and black pepper to taste

½ tsp black sesame seeds for garnishing

Directions

Pour broth, soy sauce, oats, hot sauce, corn, and half of the scallions into inner pot. Seal the lid, select Manual/Pressure Cook mode on High, and set cooking time to 3 minutes.

After cooking, perform natural pressure release for 10 minutes, then a quick pressure release to let out the remaining steam. Unlock the lid, season with salt and black pepper, stir and spoon oatmeal into serving bowls. Garnish with sesame seeds and remaining scallions. Serve with sunny side eggs.

Strawberry-Peanut Butter Oatmeal

Total Time: 20 minutes | **Servings**: 2 | **Per Serving**: Kcal 407; Carbs 59g; Fat 18g; Protein 24g

Ingredients

1 cup old-fashioned rolled oats
2 cups milk
2 tbsp strawberry jam

3 tbsp peanut butter
¼ cup fresh strawberries to serve
2 tbsp chopped roasted peanuts

Directions

Pour oats and milk into inner pot; stir in jam and peanut butter until well mixed. Seal the lid, select Manual/Pressure Cook on High, and set cooking time to 3 minutes.

After cooking, perform natural pressure release for 10 minutes, then a quick pressure release to let out the remaining steam. Unlock the lid, stir, and spoon oatmeal into serving bowls. Top with strawberries, peanuts, and serve.

Carrot Cake Oatmeal

Total Time: 20 minutes | **Servings**: 2 | **Per Serving**: Kcal 461; Carbs 79g; Fat 17g; Protein 18g

Ingredients

2 cups milk
1 cup old fashioned rolled oats
1 cup shredded carrots + extra for garnishing
2 tbsp maple syrup
1 tsp cinnamon

¼ tsp ground ginger
1/8 tsp grated nutmeg
1 tsp vanilla extract
¼ cup chopped dates
¼ cup chopped pecans

Directions

Pour milk, oats, carrots, maple syrup, cinnamon, ginger, nutmeg, and vanilla into inner pot. Seal the lid, select Manual/Pressure Cook on High, and set cooking time to 3 minutes.

After cooking, perform natural pressure release for 10 minutes, then a quick pressure release to let out the remaining steam. Unlock lid, stir in dates and pecans, and spoon oatmeal into bowls. Garnish with remaining carrots and serve.

Asian-Style Chicken Porridge

Total Time: 40 minutes | **Servings**: 4 | **Per Serving**: Kcal 205; Carbs 12g; Fat 14g; Protein 12g

Ingredients

6 ounces ground chicken
1 ½-inch piece ginger, grated
2 garlic cloves, minced
1 tbsp rice wine
½ tsp sugar
1 ½ tbsp soy sauce

½ cup jasmine rice, rinsed
4 cups water
Salt and black pepper, to taste
Peanuts, chopped, for garnish
Spring onions, chopped for garnish

Directions

Combine all the ingredients into inner pot. Seal the lid, select Manual/Pressure Cook mode, and cook for 20 minutes on High. When done, perform a quick pressure release.

Unlock the lid and select Sauté. Cook until the desired thickness is reached (if too watery). Sprinkle with salt and pepper to taste. Top with peanuts, spring onions, and soy sauce to serve.

Raspberry-Cranberry Chia Oatmeal

Total Time: 30 minutes | **Servings:** 4 | **Per Serving:** Kcal 125; Carbs 29g; Fat 2g; Protein 3g

Ingredients

2 cups old fashioned oats
4 cups of water
¼ cup plain vinegar
½ tsp nutmeg powder
1 tbsp cinnamon powder

½ tsp vanilla extract
½ cup dried cranberries + for garnish
2 raspberries, sliced
¼ tsp salt
Honey, for topping

Directions

Combine the oats, water, vinegar, nutmeg, cinnamon, vanilla, cranberries, raspberries, and salt in your Instant Pot. Seal the lid, select Manual/Pressure Cook on High, and set the cooking time to 11 minutes.

When done, perform a natural pressure release for 10 minutes, then a quick pressure release to let off any remaining pressure, and unlock the lid. Stir the oatmeal, drizzle with honey and more dried cranberries and serve.

Easy Oatmeal Bowls with Raspberries

Total Time: 20 minutes | **Servings:** 3 | **Per Serving:** Kcal 198; Carbs 39g; Fat 6g; Protein 9g

Ingredients

1 cup steel-cut oats
1 ½ cups milk
2 tbsp honey
½ tsp vanilla extract

A pinch salt
Fresh raspberries, for topping
Toasted Brazil nuts, for topping

Directions

Add the oats, milk, honey, vanilla, and salt into inner pot. Seal the lid, select Manual/Pressure Cook mode, and set cooking time to 6 minutes on High.

When done, perform a quick pressure release to let out the steam. Unlock the lid and stir the oatmeal. Divide the porridge between serving bowls and top with raspberries and toasted Brazil nuts to serve.

Pumpkin & Pecan Buckwheat Porridge

Total Time: 25 minutes | **Servings:** 4 | **Per Serving:** Kcal 203; Carbs 21g; Fat 11g; Protein 8g

Ingredients

1 cup raw buckwheat groats
1 ½ cups milk
¼ cup pumpkin puree
A pinch of salt
1 tbsp maple syrup

1 tsp cinnamon powder
½ tsp vanilla extract
3 tbsp raisins
2 tbsp pumpkin seeds
¼ cup chopped pecans

Directions

Pour buckwheat, milk, pumpkin puree, salt, maple syrup, cinnamon, and vanilla into inner pot. Stir until pumpkin puree is well-spread. Seal the lid, select Manual/Pressure Cook on High, and set cooking time to 6 minutes.

After cooking, perform natural pressure release for 10 minutes. Unlock the lid, stir in raisins, and spoon porridge into serving bowls. Top with more milk as desired and garnish with pumpkin seeds and pecans. Serve warm.

Spinach-Barley Breakfast Bowl

Total Time: 30 minutes | **Servings**: 4 | **Per Serving**: Kcal 251; Carbs 42g; Fat 5g; Protein 11g

Ingredients

1 tbsp olive oil
1 cup pearl barley
¼ cup finely chopped red onion
1 ½ cups chicken broth
½ cup water

Salt and black pepper to taste
4 oz ham, chopped
4 oz baby spinach, chopped
2 scallions, chopped for garnishing
¼ tsp red chili flakes

Directions

Set your Instant Pot to Sauté and heat olive oil. Sauté onion and barley until fragrant. Stir in chicken broth and water; season with salt and pepper. Seal the lid, select Manual/Pressure Cook mode on High, and set time to 18 minutes.

After cooking, perform quick pressure, and select Sauté. Stir in ham and spinach. Allow spinach to wilt. Dish meal into serving bowls, garnish with scallions and chili flakes, and serve warm with hard-boiled eggs.

Banana & Oat Cups

Total Time: 25 minutes | **Servings**: 2 | **Per Serving**: Kcal 187; Carbs 43g; Fat 4g; Protein 6g

Ingredients

½ cup steel-cut oats
1 banana, mashed
1 ½ cups water

1 tsp sugar
1 tbsp walnuts, chopped

Directions

Spread the banana onto the bottom of your Instant Pot. Pour the water, steel-cut oats, and sugar over the banana. Seal the lid, select Manual/Pressure Cook mode, and cook for 6 minutes on High.

When done, perform a natural pressure release for 10 minutes, then a quick pressure release to let out the remaining steam. Unlock the lid and stir the oatmeal. Divide between cups. Top with walnuts and serve.

Dried Fruit Buckwheat Pilaf

Total Time: 25 minutes | **Servings**: 4 | **Per Serving**: Kcal 282; Carbs 46g; Fat 11g; Protein 7g

Ingredients

1 tbsp olive oil
1 red bell pepper, deseeded and diced
4 garlic cloves, minced
1 cup roasted buckwheat groats
½ cup yellow lentils
1 ¼ cups chicken broth

Salt and black pepper to taste
¾ tsp dried thyme
1 cup dried figs, chopped
½ cup dried apricots, chopped
½ cup toasted walnuts
½ cup chopped cilantro

Directions

Set your Instant Pot to Sauté and heat oil. Sauté bell pepper and garlic for 5 minutes. Mix in buckwheat, lentils, chicken broth, salt, pepper, and thyme. Seal the lid, select Manual/Pressure Cook on High, and set time to 6 minutes.

After cooking, do a natural pressure release for 10 minutes. Unlock the lid, stir in fig, apricot, walnuts, and cilantro and adjust taste with salt and black pepper. Spoon buckwheat pilaf into serving bowls and enjoy.

Mushroom Barley Risotto

Total Time: 40 minutes | **Servings**: 4 | **Per Serving**: Kcal 500; Carbs 87g; Fat 13g; Protein 18g

Ingredients

3 tbsp butter, divided
1 small red onion, finely chopped
2 garlic cloves, thinly sliced
½ lb baby Bella mushrooms, sliced
¼ tsp fresh thyme leaves + extra for garnishing

Salt and black pepper to taste
1 cup pearl barley
½ cup dry white wine
2 ½ cups beef broth, hot
¼ cup grated Parmesan cheese + extra for garnishing

Directions

Set your Instant Pot to Sauté and melt 2 tablespoons of butter. Sauté red onion and garlic until slightly softened, 4-5 minutes. Stir in mushrooms, thyme, salt, and pepper. Cook until mushrooms are tender, 4 minutes.

Mix in barley and remaining butter, cook for 1 minute, and stir in wine until absorbed, 3 to 4 minutes. Add beef broth, seal the lid, select Manual/Pressure Cook on High, and set cooking time to 7 minutes.

After cooking, perform natural pressure release for 10 minutes. Mix in Parmesan cheese to melt, adjust taste with salt and black pepper, and spoon risotto into serving bowls. Garnish with Parmesan cheese and thyme. Serve warm.

Beef Barley Soup

Total Time: 45 minutes | **Servings**: 4 | **Per Serving**: Kcal 424; Carbs 52g; Fat 11g; Protein 32g

Ingredients

1 tbsp olive oil
1 lb stewing beef, cut into ½ -inch cubes
Salt and black pepper to taste
3 celery stalks, chopped
2 carrots, chopped
1 yellow onion, diced
4 garlic cloves, minced

1 cup quartered cremini mushrooms
2 tsp Italian seasoning
1 cup pearl barley
½ cup diced tomatoes
4 cups beef broth
2 tbsp chopped parsley

Directions

Set your Instant Pot to Sauté and heat olive oil. Season beef with salt and pepper, and sear in oil until lightly brown, 4 minutes. Add celery, carrots, onion, garlic, mushrooms, and Italian seasoning; sauté until slightly softened, 4 minutes. Stir in barley, tomatoes, and beef broth. Seal the lid, select Manual/Pressure Cook on High, and cook for 20 minutes.

After cooking, do a natural pressure release for 10 minutes, then a quick pressure release to let out remaining steam. Unlock the lid, stir in parsley, and adjust taste with salt and black pepper. Spoon soup into serving bowls and serve.

Pork & Buckwheat Cabbage Roll

Total Time: 70 minutes | **Servings**: 4 | **Per Serving**: Kcal 493; Carbs 22g; Fat 30g; Protein 35g

Ingredients

2 tbsp butter
½ sweet onion, finely chopped
2 garlic cloves, minced
1 lb ground pork
Salt and black pepper to taste

1 cup buckwheat groats
1 ¾ cups beef stock
2 tbsp chopped cilantro
1 head Savoy cabbage, leaves separated (scraps kept)
1 (23 oz) canned chopped tomatoes

Directions

Set your Instant Pot to Sauté and melt butter. Sauté onion and garlic until slightly softened, 4 minutes. Stir in pork, season with salt and pepper, and cook until no longer pink, 5 minutes. Stir in buckwheat, and beef stock.

Seal the lid, select Manual/Pressure Cook on High, and set cooking time to 6 minutes. After cooking, perform a quick pressure release. Unlock the lid, add cilantro, and give buckwheat mixture a good stir.

Spread large cabbage leaves on a clean flat surface and spoon 3 to 4 tablespoons of mixture onto the center of each leave. Then, roll. Clean the pot and spread in cabbage scrap. Pour in tomatoes with liquid and arrange cabbage rolls on top. Seal the lid, select Manual/Pressure Cook on Low pressure and set cooking time to 25 minutes.

After, perform natural pressure release for 10 minutes, then a quick pressure release to let out the remaining steam. Using a slotted spoon, remove cabbage rolls onto serving plates and serve.

Milk & Honey Corn on the Cob

Total Time: 25 minutes | **Servings**: 4 | **Per Serving**: Kcal 529; Carbs 69g; Fat 26g; Protein 10g

Ingredients

2 cups whole milk
4 cups water
1 stick butter, sliced thinly

3 tbsp Creole seasoning
¼ cup honey
6-8 ears corn, shucked

Directions

Set your Instant Pot to Sauté and adjust to medium heat. Add milk, water, and butter, and begin warming with frequent stirring until butter melts, 3 minutes. Pour in Creole seasoning and honey; mix again until evenly combined. Place in corn pieces. Seal the lid, select Manual/Pressure Cook on High, and set cooking time to 4 minutes.

After cooking, perform natural pressure release for 10 minutes, then a quick pressure release to let out the remaining steam. Unlock lid, stir, and using tongs, lift corn onto serving plates and allow slight cooling. Serve warm as a snack.

Zucchini-Artichoke Corn Risotto

Total Time: 40 minutes | **Servings**: 4 | **Per Serving**: Kcal 388; Carbs 46g; Fat 22g; Protein 15g

Ingredients

4 cups vegetable stock
2 tbsp olive oil
2 large white onion, chopped
4 garlic cloves, minced
1 medium zucchini, chopped
Salt and black pepper to taste
1 cup Arborio rice

½ cup white wine
2 cups corn kernels
3 ½ cups chicken stock
1 (6 oz) can artichokes, drained and chopped
1 cup grated Parmesan cheese
1 lemon, 1 tbsp zest, and 3 tbsp juice
½ cup chopped basil

Directions

Set your Instant Pot to Sauté and adjust to medium heat. Heat olive oil and sauté onion, garlic, and zucchini until softened, 5 minutes. Season with salt and black pepper. Stir in rice and cook until translucent, 3 minutes.

Mix in white wine and allow reduction by one-third. Add corn, chicken stock, salt, and black pepper. Seal the lid, select Manual/Pressure Cook on High, and set cooking time to 6 minutes.

After cooking, perform natural pressure release for 15 minutes, then a quick pressure release to let out the remaining steam. Unlock the lid, add artichokes, Parmesan cheese, lemon zest, and lemon juice, and stir vigorously until risotto is sticky. Mix in half of basil and spoon risotto into serving bowls. Garnish with remaining basil and serve warm.

Chicken & Corn Chowder with Potatoes

Total Time: 28 minutes | **Servings**: 4 | **Per Serving**: Kcal 555; Carbs 76g; Fat 19g; Protein 26g

Ingredients

8 bacon strips, chopped
4 garlic cloves, minced
1 medium white onion, finely chopped
2 jalapeño peppers, deseeded and minced
2 medium potatoes, peeled and chopped
3 cups frozen sweet corn kernels
1 chicken breast, cut into 1-inch cubes

2 cups chicken broth
1 tsp dried thyme
1 tsp smoked paprika
Salt and black pepper to taste
¾ cup heavy cream
3 tbsp all-purpose flour
¼ cup chopped chives

Directions

Set your Instant Pot to Sauté and adjust to medium heat. Place bacon in inner pot and cook in rendering fat until brown and crispy, 5 minutes. Transfer to a paper towel-lined plate and set aside.

Add chicken, garlic, onion, and jalapeño peppers; sauté for 5 to 6 minutes. Pour in potatoes, corn, chicken broth, thyme, paprika, salt, and black pepper and mix well.

Seal the lid, select Manual/Pressure Cook on High, and set cooking time to 10 minutes.

Meanwhile, in a medium bowl, combine heavy cream with flour and set aside. After cooking, perform a quick pressure release to let out all the steam. Unlock the lid and stir in heavy cream mixture and half of the bacon.

Cook on Sauté for 5 minutes or until chowder thickens. Mix in chives, spoon soups into serving bowls, top with the remaining bacon, and serve warm.

Beef Taco Quinoa Lunch

Total Time: 18 minutes | **Servings**: 4 | **Per Serving**: Kcal 582; Carbs 60g; Fat 21g; Protein 41g

Ingredients

1 tbsp olive oil
1 lb ground beef
Salt and black pepper to taste
1 onion, finely diced
2 garlic cloves, minced
1 red bell pepper, deseeded and chopped
1 jalapeño pepper, minced
1 cup corn, fresh or frozen
1 tsp ground cumin

1 tbsp chili seasoning
1 (8 oz) can black beans, rinsed and drained
1 cup quick-cooking quinoa
1 (14 oz) can diced tomatoes
2 ½ cups chicken broth
1 cup grated cheddar cheese, grated
2 tbsp chopped cilantro
2 limes, cut into wedges for garnishing

Directions

Set your Instant Pot to Sauté and adjust to medium heat. Heat olive oil in inner pot and cook beef until no longer pink, 5 minutes. Season with salt and black pepper; add onion, garlic, red bell pepper, jalapeño pepper, and corn. Cook until bell pepper softens, 5 minutes.

Season with ground cumin, chili seasoning, and add black beans, quinoa, tomatoes, and chicken broth, and stir. Seal the lid, select Manual/Pressure Cook on High, and set cooking time to 1 minute.

After cooking, do a quick pressure to release steam, and unlock the lid. Select Sauté and sprinkle the food with cheddar cheese and half of cilantro. Cook until cheese melts, 3 to 4 minutes. Spoon quinoa into serving bowls and garnish with remaining cilantro and lime wedges. Serve warm.

Bacon & Corn Bundt Casserole

Total Time: 50 minutes | **Servings**: 4 | **Per Serving**: Kcal 447; Carbs 46g; Fat 27g; Protein 13g

Ingredients

8 bacon strips, chopped
2 eggs, beaten
1 cup shredded cheddar cheese
3 tbsp finely chopped habanero chilies
1 (15 oz) can corn, drained

1 (8.5 oz) pack corn muffin mix
1 (10.5 oz) cream of sweet corn
¼ cup salted butter, melted
¾ cup heavy cream
2 cups water

Directions

Set your Instant Pot to Sauté and adjust to medium heat. Place bacon in inner pot and cook until crispy and brown, 5 minutes. Fetch bacon into a large bowl and clean inner pot. Return pot to the base.

In the bowl, add eggs, cheddar cheese, habanero chilies, corn, muffin mix, corn cream, butter, and heavy cream. Pour mixture into a greased bundt pan, safe for the Instant Pot, and cover with aluminum foil.

Pour water into the inner pot, fit in a trivet, and sit bundt pan on top. Seal the lid, select Manual/Pressure Cook on High, and set cooking time to 20 minutes.

When done cooking, perform natural pressure release for 10 minutes, then a quick pressure release to let out the remaining steam. Unlock the lid and carefully remove the bundt pan. Take off foil and turn the casserole over onto a plate. Garnish with parsley, slice, and serve.

Cajun-Style Grits with Sausage & Shrimp

Total Time: 45 minutes | **Servings**: 4 | **Per Serving**: Kcal 544; Carbs 47g; Fat 24g; Protein 39g

Ingredients

1 tbsp olive oil
6 oz andouille sausage, diced
1 yellow onion, diced
2 garlic cloves, minced
1 cup white wine
1 cup corn grits
1 cup chicken broth
1 cup whole milk

1 (8 oz) canned diced tomatoes
1 tbsp Cajun seasoning
1 tsp cayenne pepper or to taste
1 tbsp butter
¼ cup chopped chives
1 tbsp chopped parsley
1 lb jumbo shrimp, peeled and deveined
¼ cup heavy cream

Directions

Set your Instant Pot to Sauté and adjust to medium heat. Heat olive oil in inner pot and fry sausage until light brown on all sides, 5 minutes. Add onion and garlic; cook until softened and fragrant. Stir in white wine and allow reducing by one-third, 3 minutes.

Meanwhile, in a medium heatproof bowl, mix grits with chicken broth and milk. Stir in tomatoes, Cajun seasoning, and cayenne pepper. Fit a trivet over the sausage mixture and place grit bowl on top of the trivet. Seal the lid, select Manual/Pressure Cook on High, and set cooking time to 10 minutes.

After cooking, do a natural pressure release for 10 minutes, then a quick pressure release to let out remaining steam. Unlock the lid, take out grits bowl, mix in butter, and set aside for serving. Take out the trivet also. Select Sauté and stir in chives, parsley, and shrimp.

Cook for 5 minutes and mix in heavy cream. Allow cooking for 2 minutes and turn off Instant Pot. Spoon grits into serving bowls and top with shrimp and sauce. Serve warm.

South American Style Quinoa

Total Time: 35 minutes | **Servings**: 4 | **Per Serving**: Kcal 405; Carbs 75g; Fat 4g; Protein 19g

Ingredients

1 cup dried black beans, soaked overnight and rinsed
4 cups vegetable broth
3 sweet potatoes, peeled and cut into ½ -inch cubes
1 cup white quinoa, rinsed
1 cup frozen corn kernels, thawed
½ tsp dried thyme

1 tsp cumin powder
1 tsp coriander powder
1 tsp cayenne pepper
1 tsp garlic powder
Salt and black pepper to taste
½ cup chopped scallions for garnish

Directions

Pour beans and vegetable broth into inner pot. Seal the lid, select Manual/Pressure Cook on High, and cook for 5 minutes. After cooking, perform a quick pressure release. Unlock the lid and mix in potatoes and quinoa.

Seal the lid again, and cook further 10 minutes on Manual/Pressure Cook. When done, perform a quick pressure release. Select Sauté. Stir in the remaining ingredients and cook for 5 minutes. Garnish with scallions and serve warm.

Delicious Shrimp Quinoa

Total Time: 25 minutes | **Servings**: 4 | **Per Serving**: Kcal 451; Carbs 52g; Fat 12g; Protein 34g

Ingredients

2 tbsp butter
1 medium white onion, finely diced
1 red bell pepper, deseeded and chopped
4 garlic cloves, minced
2 tsp smoked paprika
1 ½ cups quick-cooking quinoa

3 cups chicken broth
2 cups broccoli florets
Salt and black pepper to taste
1 lb jumbo shrimp, peeled and deveined
1 lemon, zested and juiced
3 scallions, chopped

Directions

Set your Instant Pot to Sauté and melt butter. Sauté onion and bell pepper for 4 minutes. Add garlic, paprika, and cook for 1 minute. Stir in quinoa and pour chicken broth all over; season with salt and pepper. Seal the lid, select Manual/Pressure Cook on High, and set cooking time to 1 minute. After cooking, perform a quick pressure release.

Mix in shrimp and broccoli, season with lemon zest and juice and continue cooking on Sauté until shrimp are pink, 5 minutes. Adjust taste with salt and pepper; spoon food into serving bowls. Garnish with scallions and serve warm.

Black Currant-Coconut Rye Porridge

Total Time: 20 minutes | **Servings**: 2 | **Per Serving**: Kcal 607; Carbs 67g; Fat 37g; Protein 10g

Ingredients

1 cup rye flakes
A pinch of salt
1 ¼ cups coconut milk

1 tsp vanilla extract
2 tbsp maple syrup
¾ cup frozen black currants

Directions

In inner pot, combine rye flakes, salt, coconut milk, water, vanilla, and maple syrup. Seal the lid, select Manual/Pressure Cook on High, and set time to 5 minutes. After cooking, perform natural pressure release for 10 minutes. Stir and spoon porridge into serving bowls. Top with black currants and serve warm.

Parmesan Chicken Quinoa

Total Time: 15 minutes | **Servings**: 4 | **Per Serving**: Kcal 835; Carbs 63g; Fat 39g; Protein 58g

Ingredients

2 tbsp butter
2 leeks, sliced
3 garlic cloves, minced
1 ½ cups quick-cooking quinoa
1 tbsp chopped rosemary
2 ¾ cups chicken broth
2 chicken breasts, cut into bite-size pieces

1 tsp dried basil
Salt and black pepper to taste
1 ½ cups frozen green peas, thawed
1 cup ricotta cheese
1 lemon, 2 tbsp zest, and juice
¼ cup fresh parsley, chopped
1 cup grated Parmesan cheese

Directions

Set your Instant Pot to Sauté and adjust to medium heat. Melt butter in inner pot and sauté leeks until bright green and softened, 3 minutes. Mix in garlic and sauté until fragrant, 2 minutes. Add quinoa, rosemary, chicken broth, chicken, basil, salt, and black pepper; give ingredients a good stir.

Seal the lid, select Manual/Pressure Cook on High, and set time to 1 minute. Perform a quick pressure release to let out all the steam and unlock lid. Stir in ricotta cheese, green peas, lemon zest, lemon juice, half of parsley, and Parmesan cheese.

Press Sauté and continue cooking until cheese melts and chicken cooks through, 6 minutes. Adjust taste with salt and black pepper. Spoon quinoa into serving bowls and garnish with remaining parsley.

Taco Beef Quinoa

Total Time: 30 minutes | **Servings**: 4 | **Per Serving**: Kcal 641; Carbs 84g; Fat 18g; Protein 41g

Ingredients

1 lb beef stew meat, sliced
1 cup sweet onion, chopped
¾ cup poblano pepper, chopped
1 cup frozen corn kernels
¾ cup mixed bell peppers, chopped
1 (15 oz) can black beans, drained and rinsed
1 (15 oz) can tomatoes, chopped
½ cup beef broth
1 (15 oz) can red enchilada sauce

3 garlic cloves, minced
1 pack taco seasoning
1 ½ cups quinoa, rinsed
For topping:
½ cup grated cheddar cheese
½ cup pico de gallo
3 tbsp cilantro leaves
1 avocado, halved, pitted and sliced
1 jalapeño pepper, sliced into rings and deseeded

Directions

Season beef with salt and black pepper and add to inner pot. Top with onion, poblano pepper, corn kernels, mixed bell peppers, black beans, tomatoes, beef broth, enchilada sauce, garlic, and taco seasoning.

Seal the lid, select Manual/Pressure Cook mode on High, and set cooking time to 10 minutes.

After cooking, perform a natural pressure release for 10 minutes, then a quick pressure release to let out remaining steam. Unlock the lid.

Stir in quinoa and cook to Sauté mode until quinoa softens and cooking liquid reduces, 5 minutes. Adjust taste with salt and black pepper. Top with cheddar cheese, pico de gallo, cilantro, avocado, and jalapeño pepper. Serve warm.

Beans & Legumes

Sausage & Bean Cassoulet

Total time: 55 minutes | **Servings**: 4 | **Per Serving**: Kcal 46; Carbs 4g; Fat 3g; Protein 2g

Ingredients

2 tbsp olive oil
2 shallots, chopped
1 lb white beans, soaked overnight
1 green bell pepper, chopped
1 tsp dried oregano
1 bay leaf

2 smoked sausages, sliced
1 (14-oz) can diced tomatoes, drained
4 cups vegetable broth
¼ cup white wine vinegar
Salt to taste

Directions

Select Sauté on your Instant Pot and heat olive oil. Cook the smoked sausages for 5 minutes, stirring occasionally; set aside. Add in the bell pepper and shallots and cook for 4 minutes, until tender. Pour in broth, tomatoes, oregano, beans, and bay leaf. Return the smoked sausages and stir to combine.

Seal the lid, select Manual/Pressure Cook mode on High, and set time to 25 minutes. When done, perform natural pressure release for 10 minutes, then a quick pressure release to let out the remaining steam. Remove and discard the bay leaf. Taste and adjust the seasonings; drizzle with the vinegar and serve.

Brazilian Black Beans with Smoked Bacon

Total Time: 60 minutes | **Servings**: 4 | **Per Serving**: Kcal 391; Carbs 27g; Fat 32g; Protein 8g

Ingredients

1 pound dried black beans, soaked overnight
4 dried Guajillo chilies, soaked, liquid reserved
¼ cup avocado oil
4 oz smoked bacon, cooked and crumbled
1 yellow onion, chopped
5 cloves garlic
1 ½ tsp ground cumin

Salt to taste
½ tsp dried oregano
1 bay leaf
3 cups fresh tomatoes, chopped
4 cups vegetable broth
1 bell pepper, chopped

Directions

Cut the stems of the Guajillo chilies and deseed. Put in a blender along with garlic and onion, and process until finely chopped. Mix all the spices in a bowl.

Set your Instant Pot to Sauté mode and heat avocado oil. Place in the chili mixture and sauté for 5 minutes, stirring frequently. Pour in the spices and cook for 30 seconds until everything is well combined.

Pour in the reserved chili liquid, beans, tomatoes, broth, and bell pepper, and stir to combine. Seal the lid, select Bean/Chili on High, and set cooking time to 30 minutes.

When done cooking, perform natural pressure release for 10 minutes, then a quick pressure release to let out the remaining steam. Unlock the lid and discard the bay leaf. Stir in the bacon. Serve immediately.

Chili Corn Chips with Beans & Avocado Sauce

Total Time: 25 min + cooling time | **Servings**: 6 | **Per Serving**: Kcal 553; Carbs 83g; Fat 23g; Protein 13g

Ingredients:

For the corn fritters:

2 ½ cups canned yellow corn, drained
2 tbsp olive oil + extra for frying
3 garlic cloves, crushed
2 tbsp ginger powder
Salt and black pepper to taste

2 tbsp chopped parsley
1 fresh red chili, deseeded and minced
½ cup freshly chopped oregano
¼ cup water
Plain flour for dusting

For the avocado sauce:

2 ripe avocados, pitted
2 tomatoes, ripe
½ lemon, juiced
3 garlic cloves, crushed
6 green onions, chopped

1 tsp maple syrup
3 tbsp canned pinto beans
1 celery stick, chopped
1 tbsp freshly chopped parsley

Directions:

In a food processor, add the corn, 2 tablespoons of olive oil, garlic, ginger, salt, black pepper, parsley, red chili, oregano, and water. Blend the ingredients until evenly combined. Form 2-inch patties out of the batter using your hands, place on a paper towel-lined plate, and refrigerate for 20 minutes.

Set your Instant Pot to Sauté mode and heat 3 tbsp of olive oil. Dust the patties with a little flour and fry in batches until golden brown on both sides, 15 minutes. Remove the patties onto a wire rack to drain the oil.

In a blender, add avocados, tomatoes, lemon juice, garlic, green onions, maple syrup, pinto beans, celery stick, and parsley. Process the ingredients until smooth. Serve patties with the sauce.

Jalapeño Bean Soup with Tomato-Avocado Topping

Total Time: 55 minutes | **Servings**: 4 | **Per Serving**: Kcal 457; Carbs 48g; Fat 22g; Protein 21g

Ingredients

2 tbsp olive oil
1 medium yellow onions, chopped
2 garlic cloves, minced
1 cup dried pinto beans, soaked and rinsed
1 jalapeño pepper, chopped
2 bay leaves
¼ cup pureed onion
2 tbsp chicken bouillon, crumbled

5 cups water
1 tsp pureed green chilies
Salt to taste
2 large tomatoes, chopped
¼ cup chopped cilantro
2 avocados, halved, pitted, and chopped
3 oz grated mozzarella cheese

Directions

Set your Instant Pot to Sauté and adjust to medium heat. Heat olive oil in inner pot and stir-fry chopped onion and garlic until softened, 3 minutes. Stir in pinto beans, jalapeño pepper, bay leaves, pureed onion, chicken bouillon, water, green chilies, and salt. Seal the lid, select Manual/Pressure Cook on High, and set cooking time to 30 minutes.

When done cooking, perform natural pressure release for 10 minutes, then a quick pressure release to let out the remaining steam. Unlock the lid, discard bay leaf, and press Sauté. Allow bean sauce to thicken. In a small bowl, combine the tomatoes, cilantro, avocado, and mozzarella cheese. Dish beans and top with tomato-avocado mixture. Serve with tortillas.

Bean & Fennel Tempeh Chops

Total Time: 30 min | **Servings**: 4 | **Per Serving**: Kcal 648; Carbs 50g; Fat 34.9g; Protein 46.9g

Ingredients:

2 tbsp olive oil
2 lb tempeh, chopped
1 large yellow onion, chopped
1 small fennel bulb, chopped
3 carrots, cubed
3 large garlic cloves, roughly chopped
1 cinnamon stick

1 bay leaf
1 ½ tsp ground allspice
1 tsp ras el hanout
½ tsp ginger paste
6 large tomatoes, chopped
2 ½ cups vegetable broth
1 (15-oz) can white beans

Directions:

Add the oil to your Instant Pot and select Sauté. Pour in the tempeh and fry until golden brown on all sides. Remove to a plate. Put onion, fennel, carrots, and garlic into the pot and sauté for 6 minutes. Drop in cinnamon stick, followed by bay leaf, allspice, ras el hanout, and ginger paste. Stir-fry for 2 minutes. Pour in tomatoes and broth and stir.

Seal the lid, select Manual/Pressure Cook on High, and set time to 2 minutes. Once the pot beeps, naturally release the pressure until all the steam escapes, for 15 minutes, and open the lid. Select Sauté. Stir in the tempeh and white beans; cook to warm both through, 3 minutes. Serve with pita bread.

Spicy Kidney Bean Dip

Total Time: 45 minutes | **Servings**: 4 | **Per Serving**: Kcal 266; Carbs 34g; Fat 6g; Protein 12g

Ingredients

1 tbsp coconut oil
1 red onion, finely chopped
4 garlic cloves, minced
Salt and black pepper to taste
2 tbsp tomato paste
1 tbsp curry paste

1 cup dried kidney beans, soaked overnight and rinsed
4 cups vegetable stock
1 tbsp Sriracha sauce
1 lemon, juiced
1 tsp honey

Directions

Set your Instant Pot to Sauté and adjust to medium heat. Heat coconut oil and stir-fry onion and garlic until softened, 3 minutes. Season with salt and black pepper. Add tomato paste and curry paste; cook for 2 minutes, stirring frequently. Mix in kidney beans, vegetable stock, and Sriracha sauce.

Seal the lid, select Manual/Pressure Cook on High, and set cooking time to 30 minutes. After cooking, perform a quick pressure release. Unlock the lid. Mix in lemon juice, honey, and using an immersion blender, puree ingredients until very smooth. Spoon bean dip into small ramekins and serve with julienned vegetables.

Cheesy Bean Spread

Total Time: 50 minutes | **Servings**: 4 | **Per Serving**: Kcal 279; Carbs 28g; Fat 6g; Protein 17g

Ingredients

1 cup kidney beans, soaked overnight and drained
4 cups chicken broth
Salt and black pepper to taste
¼ cup grated mozzarella cheese

¼ cup grated Gouda cheese
¼ cup grated Parmesan cheese + extra for topping

Directions

Pour beans and chicken broth in inner pot. Seal the lid, select Manual/Pressure Cook on High, and set cooking time to 30 minutes. After cooking, perform a natural pressure release for 10 minutes. Unlock the lid.

Stir in cheeses until melted, 2 minutes. Turn Instant Pot off. Spoon cheesy beans over toasts and top with Parmesan cheese. Serve for breakfast.

Black Bean Tofu Scramble

Total Time: 25 minutes | **Servings**: 2 | **Per Serving**: Kcal 510; Carbs 54g; Fat 21g; Protein 36g

Ingredients

1 cup canned black beans
2 cups vegetable broth
1 tbsp ghee
1 small red onion, finely chopped
3 garlic cloves, minced
3 tomatoes, chopped

1 (14 oz) extra-firm tofu, pressed and crumbled
1 tsp smoked paprika
1 tsp turmeric powder
1 tsp cumin powder
Salt and black pepper to taste

Directions

Pour beans and vegetable broth in inner pot. Seal the lid, select Manual/Pressure Cook on High, and set cooking time to 10 minutes.

After cooking, perform a quick pressure release. Unlock the lid and transfer the beans to a medium bowl. Drain excess liquid and wipe inner pot clean.

Select Sauté and adjust to medium heat. Melt ghee in inner pot and sauté onion, garlic, and tomatoes until softened, 4 minutes. Crumble tofu into pan and cook for 5 minutes. Season with paprika, turmeric, cumin, salt, and black pepper. Cook for 1 minute. Add black beans, stir, and allow heating for 3 minutes. Dish scramble and enjoy for breakfast.

Go Green Navy Bean Soup

Total Time: 40 minutes | **Servings**: 4 | **Per Serving**: Kcal 336; Carbs 43g; Fat 13g; Protein 15g

Ingredients

3 tbsp olive oil
3 garlic cloves, minced
1 medium yellow onion, diced
1 cup chopped asparagus
1 cup dried navy beans, soaked overnight and drained
4 cups chicken broth
5 slices sun-dried tomatoes, chopped

1 bay leaf
Salt to taste
1 cup baby spinach
1 cup baby kale
2 tbsp chopped parsley
¼ cup grated Parmesan cheese, for topping

Directions

Set your Instant Pot to Sauté and adjust to medium heat. Heat olive oil in inner pot and cook garlic, onion, and asparagus until softened, 3 minutes. Add navy beans, chicken broth, sun-dried tomatoes, bay leaf, and season with salt. Seal the lid, select Manual/Pressure Cook on High, and set cooking time to 20 minutes.

After cooking, perform a quick pressure release to release all the steam and unlock the lid. Remove bay leaf and set pot to Sauté. Add spinach, and kale and allow wilting for 5 minutes. Stir in parsley and adjust taste with salt. Serve bean soup topped with Parmesan cheese.

Braised Soybeans with Sesame Seeds

Total Time: 50 minutes | **Servings**: 4 | **Per Serving**: Kcal 240; Carbs 24g; Fat 12g; Protein 11g

Ingredients

1 cup dried soybeans, soaked overnight and drained
4 cups water
½ cup soy sauce
¼ cup brown sugar

1 tsp sesame oil
1 tbsp rice vinegar
2 garlic cloves, minced
2 tsp sesame seeds, for garnishing

Directions

Pour soybeans and water in inner pot. Seal the lid, select Manual/Pressure Cook on High, and set cooking time to 20 minutes. After cooking, perform a natural pressure release for 10 minutes, then a quick pressure release to let out remaining steam. Unlock the lid.

Meanwhile, in a bowl, combine soy sauce, brown sugar, sesame oil, rice vinegar, and garlic. Set aside.

On the Instant Pot, press Sauté and adjust to medium heat. Add soy sauce mixture, stir and cook for 15 minutes. Spoon beans onto a serving platter and garnish with sesame seeds. Serve warm.

Pork & Pinto Bean Casserole

Total Time: 35 minutes | **Servings**: 4 | **Per Serving**: Kcal 579; Carbs 56g; Fat 20g; Protein 45g

Ingredients

2 tbsp olive oil
1 lb pork roast, cubed
Salt and black pepper to taste
1 cup dried pinto beans, soaked overnight and rinsed
2 cups chicken broth
1 small red onion, chopped

1 cup tomato sauce
2 green chilies, chopped
1 tsp garlic powder
1 tsp chili powder
¼ cup chopped parsley

Directions

Set your Instant Pot to Sauté and adjust to medium heat. Heat olive oil in inner pot, season pork with salt and black pepper, and fry in oil until brown, 4 minutes. Add beans, chicken broth, red onion, tomato sauce, green chilies, garlic powder, and chili powder.

Seal the lid, select Manual/Pressure Cook on High, and set cooking time to 10 minutes. After cooking, perform natural pressure release for 10 minutes, then a quick pressure release to let out the remaining steam. Unlock the lid, stir in parsley and adjust taste with salt and black pepper. Serve stew.

Rosemary Navy Beans with Mushrooms & Spinach

Total Time: 35 minutes | **Servings**: 2 | **Per Serving**: Kcal 239; Carbs 37g; Fat 9g; Protein 10g

Ingredients

1 tbsp olive oil
1 medium white onion, diced
1 lb white button mushrooms, quartered
1 medium butternut squash, peeled and chopped
Salt and black pepper to taste
¼ tsp dried rosemary

1 cup chopped tomatoes
2 cups chicken broth
2 cups baby spinach
1 (15 oz) can navy beans, drained and rinsed
1 lemon, juiced

Directions

Set your Instant Pot to Sauté and heat olive oil. Sauté onion, mushroom, and squash until softened, 6 minutes. Season with salt, black pepper, rosemary, and cook further for 1 minute. Stir in tomato and chicken broth.

Seal the lid, select Manual/Pressure Cook on High, and set cooking time to 3 minutes. After cooking, perform natural pressure release for 10 minutes, and then quick pressure to release steam, and unlock the lid. Press Sauté, add spinach, navy beans, and allow spinach to wilt, 3 minutes. Top with lemon juice, adjust taste with salt and black pepper and serve.

Italian Bean Chowder with Crispy Prosciutto

Total Time: 45 minutes | **Servings**: 4 | **Per Serving**: Kcal 369; Carbs 57g; Fat 9g; Protein 18g

Ingredients

6 prosciutto slices, chopped
1 celery stalk, chopped
1 medium carrot, chopped
1 cup chopped white onion
1 small Yukon gold potato, cubed

1 tsp mixed dried herbs
1 cup dried navy beans, soaked overnight and drained
3 cups chicken broth
Salt and black pepper to taste
4 tbsp heavy cream

Directions

Set your Instant Pot to Sauté and adjust to medium heat. Add prosciutto to inner pot and cook until brown and crispy, 5 minutes. Transfer to a paper towel-lined plate and set aside.

Sauté celery, carrots, onion, and potatoes in prosciutto grease until slightly tender, 5 minutes. Stir in mixed herbs, navy beans, chicken broth, salt, and black pepper.

Seal the lid, select Manual/Pressure Cook on High, and set cooking time to 25 minutes. Perform a quick pressure release to let out all the steam and unlock the lid. Turn Instant Pot off and stir in heavy cream. Serve chowder and top with prosciutto pieces.

Moroccan Chickpea Curry

Total Time: 30 minutes | **Servings**: 4 | **Per Serving**: Kcal 554; Carbs 88g; Fat 12g; Protein 28g

Ingredients

2 ½ cups canned chickpeas, drained
2 medium carrots, chopped
1 celery stalk, chopped
4 garlic cloves, minced
1 large yellow onion, finely chopped
1 green bell pepper, deseeded and chopped
1 red bell pepper, deseeded and chopped
½ cup chopped tomatoes

2 cups vegetable broth
2 tbsp ras el hanout
½ tsp turmeric powder
Salt and black pepper to taste
2 tsp dried thyme
2 red chilies, minced
2 tbsp chopped parsley
2 tbsp chopped scallions, for garnishing

Directions

In inner pot, combine chickpeas, carrots, celery, garlic, onion, bell peppers, tomatoes, vegetable broth, ras el hanout, turmeric, salt, black pepper, thyme, and red chilies. Seal the lid, select Manual/Pressure Cook on High, and set cooking time to 10 minutes.

After cooking, perform natural pressure release for 10 minutes, then a quick pressure release to let out the remaining steam. Unlock the lid and stir half of parsley into curry. Adjust taste with salt and black pepper. Spoon curry into serving bowls and garnish with scallions. Serve chickpea curry with cooked white rice.

Mexican Black Beans with Cotija Cheese

Total Time: 25 minutes | **Servings**: 2 | **Per Serving**: Kcal 477; Carbs 70g; Fat 11g; Protein 27g

Ingredients

1 tsp olive oil
1 large white onion, chopped
1 tsp grated garlic
1 cup dried black beans, soaked overnight and rinsed
2 cups vegetable broth

1 tsp Mexican seasoning
¼ cup chopped cilantro + more for topping
Salt to taste
½ cup Cotija cheese, for topping

Directions

Set your Instant Pot to Sauté and adjust to medium heat. Heat olive oil and sauté onion and garlic until softened, 3 minutes. Add beans, broth, Mexican seasoning, cilantro, and salt.

Seal the lid, select Manual/Pressure Cook on High, and set cooking time to 12 minutes. After cooking, perform a quick pressure release. Unlock the lid. Spoon beans into plates, top with Cotija cheese and cilantro, and serve.

Beet & Pinto Bean Hummus

Total Time: 16 minutes | **Servings**: 4 | **Per Serving**: Kcal 357; Carbs 51g; Fat 14g; Protein 9g

Ingredients

3 large beets, peeled and chopped
2 cups canned pinto beans, drained and rinsed
¼ cup vegetable stock
1 tsp garlic powder

Salt to taste
½ lemon, juiced
¼ cup olive oil

Directions

Combine beets, pinto beans, vegetable stock, garlic powder, and salt into inner pot. Seal the lid, select Manual/Pressure Cook on High, and set cooking time to 13 minutes.

After cooking, do a quick pressure to release steam, and unlock the lid. Transfer mixture to a blender and process until smooth. Add lemon juice and olive oil and blend again to combine. Pour mixture into serving bowls and serve.

Pinto Beans with Pancetta

Total time: 65 minutes | **Servings**: 6 | **Per Serving**: Kcal 517; Carbs 79g; Fat 8g; Protein 33g

Ingredients

4 oz pancetta, chopped
1 tbsp olive oil
1 onion, finely chopped
1 garlic clove, minced
1 lb dry pinto beans, soaked overnight

4 cups water
½ tsp ground cumin
Salt and black pepper to taste
3 tbsp parsley, chopped

Directions

Select Sauté on your Instant Pot and heat olive oil. Add in pancetta, onion, and garlic and cook for 5 minutes. Stir in beans, water, cumin, salt, and pepper. Seal the lid, select Manual/Pressure Cook on High, and set time to 40 minutes.

When done, perform natural pressure release for 10 minutes, then a quick pressure release to let out the remaining steam and remove the lid. Garnish with parsley and serve.

Chickpea & Avocado Burritos

Total Time: 30 minutes | **Servings**: 3 | **Per Serving**: Kcal 675; Carbs 92g; Fat 25g; Protein 27g

Ingredients

1 tbsp coconut oil
1 medium red onion, finely chopped
1 red bell pepper, deseeded and chopped
1 garlic clove, minced
1 tsp cumin powder
1 ½ cups canned chickpeas, drained
½ cup vegetable broth

Salt and black pepper to taste
3 corn tortillas
1 large avocado, halved, pitted, and chopped
½ cup shredded red cabbage
3 tbsp chopped cilantro
3 tbsp tomato salsa
½ cup sour cream

Directions

Set your Instant Pot to Sauté and adjust to medium heat. Heat coconut oil in inner pot and sauté onion and bell pepper until softened, 4 minutes. Add garlic, cumin, and cook for 1 minute or until fragrant.

Mix in chickpeas, heat through for 1 minute with frequent stirring, and pour in vegetable broth. Season with salt and black pepper. Seal the lid, select Manual/Pressure Cook on High, and set cooking time to 8 minutes.

After cooking, perform natural pressure release for 10 minutes, then a quick pressure release to let out the remaining steam. Unlock the lid, stir, and adjust taste with salt and black pepper. Turn Instant Pot off.

Lay tortillas on a flat surface and divide chickpea filling at the center. Top with avocados, cabbage, cilantro, salsa, and sour cream. Wrap, tuck ends, and slice in halves. Serve for lunch.

Brown Lentils with Goat Cheese & Rice

Total Time: 60 minutes + 2h chilling time | **Servings**: 4 | **Per Serving**: Kcal 318; Carbs 51g; Fat 9g; Protein 8g

Ingredients

1 cup brown rice, uncooked
2 cups vegetable broth
1 cup brown lentils, picked
4 cups water
1 bay leaf
4 green onions, chopped
1 red bell pepper, deseeded and chopped

1 medium cucumber, chopped
½ cup crumbled goat cheese
2 tbsp olive oil
2 tbsp red wine vinegar
½ tsp dried thyme
Salt and black pepper to taste
1 lemon, cut into wedges

Directions

Pour water and brown rice into inner pot. Seal the lid, select Manual/Pressure Cook, and set cooking time to 22 minutes. After cooking, perform quick pressure to let out steam and transfer rice to a large salad bowl; set aside.

Pour lentils, water, and bay leaf in inner pot. Seal the lid, select Manual/Pressure Cook on High, and set cooking time to 10 minutes. Do a natural pressure release for 10 minutes, then a quick pressure release, and unlock the lid.

Remove bay leaf and add lentils to rice bowls and combine with green onions, bell pepper, cucumber, half of goat cheese, olive oil, vinegar, thyme, salt, and black pepper. Toss until well-coated and refrigerate for 1 to 2 hours. Plate, top with remaining goat cheese, and serve immediately with lemon wedges.

Homemade Chickpea Spread

Total Time: 65 minutes | **Servings:** 4 | **Per Serving:** Kcal 288; Carbs 39g; Fat 11g; Protein 12g

Ingredients

1 cup dried chickpeas, soaked
2 cups water
1 onion, chopped
Salt and black pepper to taste
1 garlic clove
¼ tsp ground cumin

½ lemon, juiced
2 tbsp tahini
1 tbsp olive oil
¼ tsp ground cumin
A pinch of paprika
2 tbsp parsley, chopped

Directions

Place the chickpeas, water, salt, onion, and black pepper into inner pot. Seal the lid, select Manual/Pressure Cook mode, and set cooking time to 45 minutes on High. When done, perform a quick pressure release to let out the steam. Unlock the lid and drain the chickpeas. Set aside.

In a food processor, puree the chickpeas, lemon juice, tahini, olive oil, 2 tbsp of water, garlic, and cumin until smooth. Season with salt. Sprinkle with paprika and parsley and serve.

Red Lentil Dhal with Kale & Cilantro

Total Time: 35 minutes | **Servings:** 4 | **Per Serving:** Kcal 328; Carbs 54g; Fat 5g; Protein 19g

Ingredients

1 tbsp ghee
1 tsp mustard seeds
1 tbsp turmeric powder
1 tbsp cumin seeds
½ tsp cayenne powder
1 onion, thinly sliced
3 garlic cloves, minced

1 tbsp grated ginger
1 ½ cups dried red lentils, washed, drained
2 cups chopped tomatoes
1 cup vegetable broth
1 tsp sugar
2 cups chopped kale
2 tbsp chopped cilantro

Directions

Set your Instant Pot to Sauté and melt ghee. Stir-fry mustard seeds, turmeric, cumin seeds, and cayenne powder. Cook for 1 minute or until fragrant. Stir in onion, garlic, and ginger. Cook for 2 minutes and mix in lentils, tomatoes, and sugar. Seal the lid, select Manual/Pressure Cook on High, and set time to 10 minutes.

Once done cooking, perform natural pressure release for 10 minutes, then a quick pressure release to let out the remaining steam. Unlock the lid, stir in kale and half of cilantro, and adjust taste with salt and black pepper. Select Sauté and allow kale to wilt, 3 to 4 minutes. Spoon dhal into bowls and serve with mango chutney and bread.

Yellow Lentil-Arugula Pancake

Total Time: 45 minutes | **Servings:** 2 | **Per Serving:** Kcal 277; Carbs 19g; Fat 16g; Protein 17g

Ingredients

1 cup split yellow lentils, soaked overnight and drained
2 garlic cloves, whole
½ tsp smoked paprika
1 pinch turmeric
¼ tsp coriander powder

¼ tsp cumin powder
Salt to taste
3 eggs, cracked into a bowl
1 ¼ cups water
2 cups chopped arugula

Directions

Line a cake pan with parchment paper, grease with cooking spray, and set aside. In a blender, process lentils, garlic, paprika, turmeric, coriander, cumin, salt, eggs, and 1/3 cup of water until smooth. Pour mixture into cake pan and mix arugula through the batter. Cover with foil. Pour remaining water into the pot, fit in a trivet, and place cake pan on top. Seal the lid, select Manual/Pressure Cook on High, and set cooking time to 35 minutes.

After cooking, do a quick pressure release to let out steam, and unlock the lid. Carefully remove the pan, take off foil, and release pancake onto a plate. Slice and serve with Greek yogurt.

Zucchini & Beluga Lentil Sauté

Total Time: 12 minutes | **Servings**: 4 | **Per Serving**: Kcal 139; Carbs 17g; Fat7g; Protein 5g

Ingredients

2 tbsp olive oil
2 large zucchinis, chopped
4 garlic cloves, minced
½ tbsp dried oregano
½ tbsp curry powder
1 tbsp brown sugar
Salt and black pepper to taste

2 cups canned beluga lentils, drained
¼ cup chopped parsley
½ cup chopped basil
1 small red onion, diced
2 tbsp balsamic vinegar
1 tsp Dijon mustard

Directions

Set your Instant Pot to Sauté and adjust to medium heat. Add oil to heat and stir-fry zucchinis until tender. Mix in garlic and cook until fragrant, 30 seconds. Top with oregano, curry powder, brown sugar, salt, and black pepper. Allow flavors to combine, 1 minute, stirring frequently. Pour in lentils, heat through for 3 minutes, and stir in half of parsley, basil, and onion. Sauté until onion softens, 5 minutes. Adjust taste with salt and black pepper.

Meanwhile, in a small bowl, combine vinegar with Dijon mustard and pour mixture onto lentils. Plate and garnish with remaining parsley. Serve warm.

Coconut Green Lentil Curry

Total Time: 35 minutes | **Servings**: 4 | **Per Serving**: Kcal 201; Carbs 18g; Fat 14g; Protein 4g

Ingredients

1 cup dried green lentils, rinsed and drained
2 tbsp coconut oil
1 large carrot, finely chopped
1 leek, chopped
1 medium onion, finely chopped
Salt to taste
2 garlic cloves

2 tsp turmeric powder
1 cup chopped tomatoes
½ cup coconut milk
2 cups vegetable stock
½ lemon, juiced
2 tbsp chopped cilantro

Directions

Set your Instant Pot to Sauté and adjust to medium heat. Heat coconut oil in inner pot and stir-fry carrots, leek, onion, and salt until softened, 5 minutes. Mix in garlic, turmeric, and tomatoes. Allow tomatoes to soften for 3 minutes and add coconut milk and vegetable stock.

Seal the lid, select Manual/Pressure Cook on High, and set cooking time to 5 minutes. After cooking, perform natural pressure release for 10 minutes, then a quick pressure release to let out the remaining steam. Unlock the lid, add lemon juice and stir. Serve the lentil curry garnished with cilantro.

Chicken Recipes

Lemony Chicken with Garlic Sauce

Total Time: 35 minutes | **Servings**: 4 | **Per Serving**: Kcal 456; Carbs 8g; Fat 23g; Protein 43g

Ingredients

2 tbsp olive oil
4 chicken breasts, skinless and boneless
Salt and black pepper to taste
3 tbsp butter
1 small white onion, finely chopped

5 garlic cloves, minced
1 cup milk
½ cup chicken broth
½ lemon, juiced + 1 lemon, sliced
2 tbsp chopped parsley

Directions

Set your Instant Pot to Sauté and adjust to medium heat. Heat olive oil in inner pot, season chicken with salt and black pepper, and fry in oil until golden brown on both sides, 4 minutes. Set aside.

Melt butter in inner pot and sauté onion until softened, 3 minutes. Add garlic and cook until fragrant, 30 seconds. Stir in milk, chicken broth, and place chicken in sauce. Seal the lid, select Manual/Pressure Cook on High, and set cooking time to 4 minutes.

After cooking, perform a natural pressure release for 10 minutes. Unlock the lid, stir in lemon juice, stick in lemon slices, and simmer on Sauté mode for 2 minutes. Adjust taste with salt and black pepper. Dish chicken with sauce into serving bowls, garnish with parsley and serve warm with mashed potatoes.

West Country Chicken Thighs with Vegetables

Total Time: 35 minutes | **Servings**: 4 | **Per Serving**: Kcal 415; Carbs 24g; Fat 27g; Protein 23g

Ingredients

2 tbsp olive oil
1 lb chicken thighs
Salt and black pepper to taste
½ lb asparagus, stems removed
2 large carrots, chopped
½ lb baby russet potatoes, quartered
½ lb radishes, halved

1 cup chicken broth
2 tbsp smoked paprika
1 tsp garlic powder
1 tsp onion powder
3 fresh rosemary sprigs
1 tbsp chopped parsley to garnish

Directions

Set your Instant Pot to Sauté and adjust to medium heat. Heat olive oil in inner pot, season chicken on both sides with salt and black pepper, and fry in oil until golden brown on both sides, 6 minutes. Set aside.

Sweat asparagus and carrots for 1 minute and add potatoes, radishes, chicken broth, paprika, garlic powder, onion powder, rosemary sprigs, and chicken. Seal the lid, select Manual/Pressure Cook on High, and set time to 4 minutes.

After cooking, perform natural pressure release for 10 minutes, then quick pressure release to let out the remaining steam. Unlock the lid, discard rosemary sprigs, stir, and adjust taste with salt and black pepper. Spoon chicken and vegetables onto serving plates and set aside for serving.

Select Sauté mode and cook remaining sauce until reduced and thickened, 2 minutes. Drizzle sauce over chicken and vegetables, garnish with parsley and serve warm.

Chicken & Noodle One Pot

Total Time: 20 minutes | **Servings**: 4 | **Per Serving**: Kcal 470; Carbs 44g; Fat 18g; Protein 31g

Ingredients

2 tbsp butter
1 lb chicken breasts, sliced into strips
Salt and black pepper to taste
1 small onion, chopped
1 garlic clove, minced
16 oz bag frozen mixed vegetables

12 oz frozen egg noodles
4 cups chicken stock
1 tsp chicken seasoning
½ tsp dried thyme
1 tbsp cornstarch
1 tsp dried parsley

Directions

Set your Instant Pot to Sauté mode and adjust to medium heat. Melt butter in inner pot, season chicken with salt and black pepper, and fry in oil until golden brown, 4 minutes. Add onion and cook until softened, 3 minutes. Stir in garlic and cook until fragrant, 30 seconds.

Pour in mixed vegetables, top with noodles, chicken stock, chicken seasoning, and thyme; stir. Seal the lid, select Manual/Pressure Cook mode on High, and set cooking time to 3 minutes.

After cooking, perform a quick pressure release, and unlock lid. Stir in cornstarch, select Sauté, and allow sauce to thicken for 1 minute. Adjust taste with salt and pepper. Spoon into bowls, garnish with parsley and serve warm.

Drumsticks in Adobo Sauce

Total Time: 35 minutes + marinating time | **Servings**: 4 **Per Serving**: Kcal 536; Carbs 44g; Fat 32g; Protein 32g

Ingredients

1 lb chicken drumsticks
½ cup plain vinegar
½ cup soy sauce
1 bay leaf
2 tbsp olive oil
10 Ancho dried chilies, seeds removed
5 Guajillo dried chilies, seeds removed
8 garlic cloves, peeled

½ tsp Mexican oregano
½ tsp cumin powder
A pinch clove powder
Salt and black pepper to taste
¼ cup apple cider vinegar
½ cup water
2 tbsp chopped cilantro to garnish

Directions

In a medium bowl, combine chicken, vinegar, soy sauce, and bay leaf. Cover the bowl with a plastic wrap and marinate chicken in the fridge for 1 hour.

Set your Instant Pot to Sauté and adjust to medium heat. Remove chicken from fridge and marinade (while shaking off extra marinade), and fry in olive oil on both sides until golden brown, 6 minutes. Transfer to a paper towel-lined plate and set aside to drain fat.

Meanwhile, in a blender, grind chilies, garlic, oregano, cumin powder, and clove powder until smooth paste forms. Pour mixture into the oil in inner pot and stir-fry until fragrant, 3 minutes. Add salt, black pepper, vinegar, and water; stir and arrange chicken in the sauce.

Seal the lid, select Manual/Pressure Cook mode on High, and set cooking time to 4 minutes. After cooking, perform natural pressure release for 10 minutes, then quick pressure release to let out the remaining steam.

Unlock the lid, stir, and adjust taste with salt and black pepper. Spoon chicken with sauce into serving bowls and garnish with cilantro. Serve warm with rice.

Moroccan Chicken with Pomegranate

Total Time: 45 minutes | **Servings**: 4 | **Per Serving**: Kcal 630; Carbs 31g; Fat 41g; Protein 36g

Ingredients

2 tbsp olive oil
4 chicken thighs, bone-in
Salt and black pepper to taste
2 large carrots, peeled and chopped
1 large onion, chopped
1 tsp fresh ginger puree
3 garlic cloves, minced
15 oz canned diced tomatoes with juice
1 tbsp balsamic vinegar

2 tbsp ras el hanout
1 tsp smoked paprika
1 tsp cumin powder
½ tsp cinnamon powder
1 cup chicken broth
½ lemon, juiced
½ cup frozen peas
1 tbsp fresh parsley leaves to garnish
1 tbsp pomegranate to garnish

Directions

Set your Instant Pot to Sauté and adjust to medium heat. Heat olive oil in the inner pot, season chicken with salt and black pepper, and cook until brown on both sides, 6 minutes. Transfer to a plate and set aside.

Stir-fry carrots and onion until softened, 3 minutes. Add ginger, garlic, and cook until fragrant, 30 seconds. Mix in tomatoes, vinegar, ras el hanout, paprika, cumin, cinnamon, and cook until tomatoes begin to soften 3 minutes. Add chicken broth, lemon juice, salt, black pepper, and the chicken.

Seal the lid, select Manual/Pressure Cook mode on High, and set cooking time to 10 minutes. After cooking, perform natural pressure release for 10 minutes, then quick pressure release to let out the remaining steam.

Unlock the lid, stir in peas and parsley, and adjust taste with salt and black pepper. Cook on Sauté mode to warm the peas, 2 minutes. Spoon tagine into serving bowls, garnish with pomegranate and serve warm with pita bread.

Chicken Cacciatore with Kale, Rice & Mushrooms

Total Time: 35 minutes | **Servings**: 4 | **Per Serving**: Kcal 534; Carbs 30g; Fat 17g; Protein 55g

Ingredients

2 tbsp olive oil
4 chicken breasts
Salt and black pepper to taste
1 medium white onion, chopped
1 cup sliced white button mushrooms
¼ tsp ginger paste

½ cup short-grain rice
15 oz can diced tomatoes
½ cup chicken broth
1 tbsp Italian seasoning
¼ cup grated Parmesan cheese
2 cups kale, steamed

Directions

Set your Instant Pot to Sauté and adjust to medium heat. Heat olive oil in inner pot, season chicken with salt and black pepper, and sear in oil on both sides until golden brown, 4 minutes. Remove onto a plate and set aside.

Add onion and mushrooms to oil and cook until softened, 4 minutes. Add ginger and allow releasing of fragrance, 1 minute. Stir in rice, tomatoes, chicken broth, and Italian seasoning. Adjust taste with salt and black pepper and return chicken to pot.

Seal the lid, select Manual/Pressure Cook on High, and set cooking time to 10 minutes. After cooking, perform natural pressure release for 10 minutes, then quick pressure release to let out the remaining steam.

Unlock the lid, adjust taste with salt and black pepper, and spoon cacciatore over a bed of steamed kale. Garnish with Parmesan cheese and serve warm.

Hot Chicken Dirty Rice

Total Time: 35 minutes | **Servings**: 4 | **Per Serving**: Kcal 732; Carbs 32g; Fat 52g; Protein 43g

Ingredients

For marinade:

½ tsp dried minced onion
½ tsp cayenne pepper
1 tsp salt
1 tsp garlic powder
1 ½ tsp paprika
½ tsp chili pepper

½ tsp dried basil
¼ tsp red pepper flakes
1 tsp lemon juice
1 tbsp olive oil
4 chicken thighs

For chicken and rice:

2 tbsp olive oil
1 link of andouille sausages, sliced
1 jalapeño pepper, deseeded and diced
1 medium yellow onion, diced
2 celery stalks, diced
A pinch red pepper flakes

¼ tsp cayenne pepper
1 cup basmati rice
2 ¼ cups chicken broth
Salt and black pepper to taste
2 tbsp scallions, for garnishing
2 tbsp chopped parsley

Directions

In a medium bowl, combine onion, cayenne pepper, salt, garlic powder, paprika, chili pepper, basil, red pepper flakes, lemon juice, and olive oil. Place in chicken, coat in marinade, cover with plastic wrap and chill in the fridge for 1 hour.

Set your Instant Pot to Sauté mode. Heat olive oil in inner pot, remove chicken from marinade and sear in oil on both sides until golden brown, 6 minutes. Place on a plate and set aside.

Brown sausages in the pot for 5 minutes and spoon to side of chicken. To the pot, add jalapeño pepper, onion, celery, and sauté until softened, 3 minutes. Stir in red pepper flakes, cayenne pepper, rice, chicken broth, salt, and pepper. Place chicken and sausages on top. Seal the lid, select Manual/Pressure Cook on High, and set time to 5 minutes.

Allow sitting (covered) for 10 minutes and then perform a quick pressure release to let out remaining steam. Unlock the lid, stir rice, and spoon into serving plates. Garnish with scallions and parsley; serve.

Spicy Mango-Glazed Chicken

Total Time: 25 minutes | **Servings**: 4 | **Per Serving**: Kcal 345; Carbs 16g; Fat 15g; Protein 32g

Ingredients

1 tbsp butter
1 lb chicken breasts, halved
Salt and black pepper to taste
1 medium mango, chopped

1 small red chili, minced
2 tbsp spicy mango chutney
½ cup chicken broth
2 scallions, thinly sliced

Directions

Set your Instant Pot to Sauté mode and adjust to medium heat. Melt butter in inner pot, season chicken with salt and black pepper, and cook in fat until cooked through and golden brown, 6 to 8 minutes. Plate chicken and set aside for serving. To the pot, add mango, red chili, mango chutney, and broth.

Seal the lid, select Manual/Pressure Cook mode on High, and set cooking time to 1 minute. After cooking, perform natural pressure release for 10 minutes, and then quick pressure release to let out remaining steam. Unlock the lid, stir sauce, and season to taste. Spoon sauce over chicken, garnish with scallions and serve with steamed spinach.

Chicken Gruyere with Bell Peppers

Total Time: 40 minutes | **Servings**: 4 | **Per Serving**: Kcal 613; Carbs 26g; Fat 36g; Protein 43g

Ingredients

1 tbsp olive oil
1 large white onion, chopped
2 red bell peppers, deseeded and chopped
2 green bell peppers, deseeded and chopped
Salt and black pepper to taste
2 garlic cloves, minced
¾ cup marinara sauce

2 tbsp basil pesto
4 chicken breasts, skinless and boneless
1 cup chicken broth
1 cup sliced baby Bella mushrooms
1 cup grated Gruyere cheese
4 flatbreads, warmed for serving
2 tbsp chopped parsley

Directions

Set your Instant Pot to Sauté mode. Heat olive oil in inner pot and sauté onion, bell peppers, salt, and pepper until softened, 3 minutes. Stir in garlic and cook until fragrant, 30 seconds. Add marinara sauce, basil pesto, chicken, and chicken broth. Seal the lid, select Manual/Pressure Cook mode on High, and set cooking time to 12 minutes.

After cooking, perform a natural pressure release for 5 minutes, then a quick pressure release to let out remaining steam. Unlock the lid and remove chicken onto a plate and shred into strands. Fetch out two-thirds cup of liquid in inner pot, making sure to leave in vegetables.

Select Sauté mode and mix in mushrooms. Cook until softened, 2 to 3 minutes. Stir in chicken, adjust taste with salt, black pepper, and mix in Gruyere cheese to melt. Spoon mixture onto flatbread, garnish with parsley, and serve.

Onion Chicken with Salsa Verde

Total Time: 35 minutes | **Servings**: 4 | **Per Serving**: Kcal 422; Carbs 8g; Fat 29g; Protein 32g

Ingredients

1 large yellow onion, chopped
1 cup salsa verde
½ cup chicken broth

Salt and black pepper to taste
4 chicken breasts, cut into 1-inch cubes

Directions

In inner pot, combine onion, salsa verde, chicken broth, salt, black pepper, and chicken. Seal the lid, select Manual/Pressure Cook on High, and set cooking time to 12 minutes.

After cooking, perform a natural pressure release for 10 minutes, then a quick pressure release to let out remaining steam. Unlock the lid and remove chicken onto a plate and serve warm over salad.

Chicken with Asparagus & Jasmine Rice

Total Time: 40 minutes | **Servings**: 4 | **Per Serving**: Kcal 646; Carbs 22g; Fat 25g; Protein 88g

Ingredients

1 tbsp olive oil
4 chicken breasts
1 tsp garlic salt
½ cup onion, finely diced
2 garlic cloves, minced
1 cup jasmine rice

1 lemon, zested and juiced
2 ¼ cups chicken broth
1 cup asparagus, chopped
1 tbsp parsley for garnish
Black pepper to taste
Lemon slices to garnish

Directions

Set your Instant Pot to Sauté mode and adjust to medium heat. Heat olive oil in inner pot, season chicken with garlic salt and black pepper, and sear chicken on both sides until golden brown, 6 minutes. Place on a plate and set aside.

Add onion and cook until softened, 3 minutes. Stir in garlic, allow to release fragrant for 30 seconds. Stir in rice and cook until translucent, 2 to 3 minutes. Add lemon zest, lemon juice, chicken broth, asparagus, salt, black pepper, and place chicken on top.

Seal the lid, select Manual/Pressure Cook mode on High, and set cooking time to 5 minutes. After cooking, perform natural pressure release for 15 minutes, then quick pressure release to let out the remaining steam. Unlock the lid, fluff rice, and plate. Garnish with parsley and lemon slices; serve warm.

Chicken with Rotini, Mushrooms & Spinach

Total Time: 30 minutes | **Servings**: 4 | **Per Serving**: Kcal 687; Carbs 35g; Fat 32g; Protein 63g

Ingredients

2 tbsp butter
4 chicken breasts, cut into cubes
Salt and black pepper to taste
1 small yellow onion, diced
4 cups sliced white mushrooms
1 garlic clove, minced

1 lb rotini pasta
1 cup chicken broth
1 tsp chopped oregano
4 cups chopped baby spinach
½ cup crumbled goat cheese

Directions

Set your Instant Pot to Sauté mode and adjust to medium heat. Melt butter in inner pot, season chicken with salt and black pepper, and sear in oil until golden brown, 4 minutes. Place in a plate and set aside.

Add onion and mushroom and cook until softened, 4 minutes. Stir in garlic, allow to release fragrant for 30 seconds. Return chicken to pot, stir in rotini, chicken broth, and oregano.

Seal the lid, select Manual/Pressure Cook on High, and set cooking time to 3 minutes. After cooking, do a natural pressure release for 10 minutes, then a quick pressure release to let out remaining steam.

Select Sauté mode and unlock the lid. Stir in spinach, allow wilting, and mix in goat cheese until properly incorporated. Adjust taste with salt, black pepper, and serve warm.

Teriyaki Chicken with Brussels Sprouts & Scallions

Total Time: 40 minutes | **Servings**: 4 | **Per Serving**: Kcal 429; Carbs 14g; Fat 27g; Protein 34g

Ingredients

1 tbsp honey
1 cup teriyaki sauce
¼ cup chicken broth

4 chicken breasts, skinless and boneless
1 cup Brussels sprouts, halved
2 tbsp chopped scallions

Directions

In inner pot, mix honey and teriyaki sauce until evenly combined. Stir in chicken broth and place in chicken. Seal the lid, select Manual/Pressure Cook mode on High, and set cooking time to 12 minutes.

After cooking, perform a natural pressure release for 10 minutes, then a quick pressure release to let out remaining steam. Unlock the lid and remove chicken onto a plate and shred into strands.

Fetch out two-thirds of cooking liquid and return chicken with Brussels sprouts to inner pot. Select Sauté mode and cook until Brussels sprouts soften, 5 minutes. Stir in scallions and serve warm.

Thai Chicken Curry Rice

Total Time: 35 minutes | **Servings:** 4 | **Per Serving:** Kcal 715; Carbs 38g; Fat 48g; Protein 43g

Ingredients

4 chicken thighs
Salt and black pepper to taste
1 tbsp olive oil
2 medium carrots, julienned
1 red bell pepper, deseeded and thinly sliced
2 tbsp red curry paste
1 garlic clove, minced

1 tsp ginger paste
2 cups basmati rice
3 cups chicken broth
1 cup coconut milk
2 tbsp chopped cilantro to garnish
1 lime, cut into wedges to garnish

Directions

Set your Instant Pot to Sauté and adjust to medium heat. Heat olive oil in inner pot, season chicken with salt and black pepper, and sear in oil until golden brown on both sides, 6 minutes. Place on a plate and set aside.

Add carrots and bell pepper to oil and cook until softened, 4 minutes. Stir in curry paste, garlic, and ginger; sauté for 1 minute. Add rice, broth, coconut milk and give ingredients a good stir. Arrange chicken on top. Seal the lid, select Manual/Pressure Cook mode on High, and set cooking time to 10 minutes.

After cooking, do a natural pressure release for 10 minutes, then quick pressure release to let out remaining steam. Unlock the lid, fluff rice, and adjust taste with salt and black pepper. Garnish with cilantro, lime wedges, and serve.

Rich Louisiana Chicken with Quinoa

Total Time: 20 minutes | **Servings:** 4 | **Per Serving:** Kcal 523; Carbs 32g; Fat 17g; Protein 37g

Ingredients

2 tbsp olive oil
4 chicken breasts, thinly sliced
1 tsp Creole seasoning
2 green bell peppers, deseeded and sliced
1 cup dry rainbow quinoa

2 cups chicken broth
Salt to taste
1 lemon, zested and juiced
2 chives, chopped
2 tbsp chopped parsley

Directions

Set your Instant Pot to Sauté and adjust to medium heat. Heat olive oil in inner pot, season chicken with Creole seasoning, and fry with bell peppers in oil until chicken is golden brown on both sides, 5 minutes and peppers soften. Stir in quinoa, chicken broth, and salt.

Seal the lid, select Manual/Pressure Cook mode on High, and set cooking time to 1 minute. After cooking, perform quick pressure to let out steam, and select Sauté mode. Unlock the lid, fluff quinoa, and stir in lemon zest, lemon juice, chives, and parsley. Dish meal into serving bowls and serve warm with hard-boiled eggs.

Holiday BBQ Chicken

Total Time: 40 minutes | **Servings:** 4 | **Per Serving:** Kcal 447; Carbs 12g; Fat 27g; Protein 32g

Ingredients

1 ½ cups chopped sweet pineapple
¼ cup chicken broth
¼ tsp salt

¾ cup BBQ sauce
4 chicken breasts, cut into 1-inch cubes

Directions

In inner pot, combine pineapples, chicken broth, salt, BBQ sauce, and chicken. Seal the lid, select Manual/Pressure Cook on High, and set cooking time to 12 minutes.

After cooking, perform a natural pressure release for 10 minutes, then a quick pressure release to let out remaining steam, and unlock the lid. Remove chicken onto a plate and select Sauté mode. Cook sauce until boiled down by half, 4 minutes, and stir in chicken. Serve chicken and sauce with rice.

Spicy Chicken Manchurian

Total Time: 35 minutes | **Servings**: 4 | **Per Serving**: Kcal 722; Carbs 14g; Fat 46g; Protein 61g

Ingredients

½ cup olive oil
4 tbsp cornstarch, divided
2 eggs, beaten
2 tbsp soy sauce, divided
Salt and black pepper to taste
4 chicken breasts, cubed
2 tbsp sesame oil

1 tbsp fresh garlic paste
1 tbsp fresh ginger paste
1 red chili, sliced
2 tbsp hot sauce
½ tsp honey
½ cup chicken broth
2 scallions, sliced for garnishing

Directions

Set your Instant Pot to Sauté and adjust to medium heat. Heat olive oil in inner pot. Meanwhile, in a medium bowl, whisk cornstarch, eggs, soy sauce, salt, and black pepper. Pour chicken into mixture and stir to coat well.

Fry coated chicken in oil until cooked through and golden brown on all sides, 6 to 8 minutes. Transfer to a paper towel-lined plate to drain grease. Empty inner pot, wipe clean with a paper towel and return to base.

Heat in sesame oil and sauté garlic, ginger, and red chili until fragrant and chili softened, 1 minute. Stir in hot sauce, honey, chicken broth, and arrange chicken in sauce.

Seal the lid, select Manual/Pressure Cook mode on High, and set cooking time to 3 minutes. After cooking, perform natural pressure release for 10 minutes, then quick pressure release to let out the remaining steam.

Unlock the lid, stir, and adjust taste with salt and black pepper. Spoon into serving bowls and garnish generously with scallions. Serve warm with rice.

Maple Balsamic & Thyme Chicken

Total Time: 40 minutes | **Servings**: 4 | **Per Serving**: Kcal 464; Carbs 14g; Fat 25g; Protein 32g

Ingredients

¼ cup balsamic vinegar
2 tbsp maple syrup
1 tbsp Dijon mustard
½ cup chicken broth

1 medium brown onion, chopped
2 garlic cloves, minced
½ tsp dried thyme
4 chicken breasts

Directions

In inner pot, mix balsamic vinegar, maple syrup, Dijon mustard, chicken broth, onion, garlic, thyme, and chicken. Seal the lid, select Manual/Pressure Cook on High, and set cooking time to 12 minutes.

After cooking, perform a natural pressure release for 10 minutes, then a quick pressure release to let out remaining steam. Unlock the lid and remove chicken onto a plate and select Sauté mode. Shred chicken with two forks and return to sauce. Cook until sauce thickens, 5 minutes. Serve immediately.

Sweet & Saucy Chicken

Total Time: 25 minutes | **Servings**: 4 | **Per Serving**: Kcal 521; Carbs 8g; Fat 39g; Protein 33g

Ingredients

2 tbsp olive oil
4 chicken thighs, bone-in
Salt and black pepper to taste
3 tbsp Dijon mustard
1 tbsp tamarind sauce

1 tbsp honey
½ cup chicken broth
3 garlic cloves, minced
1 tbsp chopped parsley

Directions

Set your Instant Pot to Sauté mode and heat olive oil. Season chicken with salt and black pepper, and sear in oil until golden brown on both sides, 6 minutes.

Meanwhile, in a bowl, combine mustard, tamarind sauce, honey, chicken broth, and pour into pot along with garlic. Seal the lid, select Manual/Pressure Cook mode on High, and set cooking time to 2 minutes.

After cooking, do a natural pressure release for 10 minutes, then quick pressure release to let out remaining steam. Unlock the lid, stir in parsley, and adjust taste with salt and black pepper. Dish chicken with sauce and serve.

Thyme Chicken with Asiago Sauce

Total Time: 35 minutes | **Servings**: 4 | **Per Serving**: Kcal 523; Carbs 11g; Fat 37g; Protein 55g

Ingredients

2 tbsp olive oil
4 chicken breasts, boneless and skinless
Salt and black pepper to taste
1 small white onion, diced

2 tbsp all-purpose flour
1 ½ cups chicken broth
2 tsp chopped thyme leaves
½ cup grated Asiago cheese

Directions

Set your Instant Pot to Sauté mode and heat olive oil. Season chicken with salt and black pepper, and sear in oil until golden brown, 4 minutes. Place in a plate and set aside.

Add onion to oil and sauté until softened, 3 minutes. Stir in flour until light brown and mix in chicken broth and thyme. Allow reduction by one-third and stir in cheese to melt. Place chicken in sauce and turn over 3 to 4 times until chicken is well-coated.

Seal the lid, select Manual/Pressure Cook mode on High, and set cooking time to 3 minutes. After cooking, perform natural pressure release for 10 minutes, then quick pressure release to let out the remaining steam. Unlock the lid, stir, and place chicken on serving plates. Spoon sauce all over and serve with mashed potatoes.

Honey-Lime Chicken Drumsticks

Total Time: 30 minutes | **Servings**: 4 | **Per Serving**: Kcal 366; Carbs 26g; Fat 18g; Protein 25g

Ingredients

1 tbsp olive oil
4 chicken drumsticks
Salt and black pepper to taste
¼ cup honey
3 limes, juiced

¼ cup soy sauce
2 garlic cloves, minced
1 tsp freshly grated ginger
½ cup water
2 scallions, thinly sliced to garnish

Directions

Set your Instant Pot to Sauté mode and adjust to medium heat. Heat olive oil in inner pot, season chicken with salt and black pepper, and sear chicken on both sides until golden brown, 6 minutes. Place on a plate and set aside.

Pour honey, lime juice, soy sauce, garlic, water, and ginger into inner pot and place chicken in sauce. Seal the lid, select Manual/Pressure Cook mode on High, and set cooking time to 5 minutes.

After cooking, perform natural pressure release for 10 minutes, then quick pressure release to let out remaining steam. Unlock the lid, baste chicken with sauce, and plate. Garnish with scallions and serve over a bed of rice.

Sesame Orange Chicken

Total Time: 45 minutes | **Servings**: 4 | **Per Serving**: Kcal 563; Carbs 46g; Fat 35g; Protein 33g

Ingredients

2 tbsp olive oil
4 chicken breasts, cut into 1-inch cubes
Salt and black pepper to taste
1 cup orange juice
6 garlic cloves, minced
2 tbsp ginger puree
1 tbsp dry white wine
¼ cup honey

¼ cup brown sugar
¼ cup coconut aminos
1 tbsp hot sauce
¼ cup chicken broth
1 orange, zested
2 tbsp cornstarch mixed with 2 tbsp orange juice
4 scallions, chopped for garnishing
1 tbsp sesame seeds for garnishing

Directions

Set your Instant Pot to Sauté and adjust to medium heat. Heat olive oil in inner pot, season chicken with salt, black pepper, and sear in oil until golden, 5 minutes.

Meanwhile, in a bowl, mix orange juice, garlic, ginger, white wine, honey, brown sugar, coconut aminos, hot sauce, chicken broth, and orange zest. Pour mixture onto chicken and stir. Seal the lid, select Manual/Pressure Cook on High, and set cooking time to 12 minutes.

After cooking, perform a natural pressure release for 10 minutes, then a quick pressure release to let out remaining steam, and unlock the lid. Mix in cornstarch mixture and cook in Sauté mode until syrupy, 3 minutes. Dish food onto serving plates, garnish with scallions, and sesame seeds, and serve.

Creamy Ranch Chicken

Total Time: 40 minutes | **Servings**: 4 | **Per Serving**: Kcal 548; Carbs 6g; Fat 40g; Protein 36g

Ingredients

2 bacon slices, chopped
1 oz pack ranch seasoning
1 cup chicken broth

4 chicken breasts
4 oz light cream cheese, softened
2 tbsp chopped scallions

Directions

Set your Instant Pot to Sauté mode and adjust to medium heat. Add bacon and cook until crispy and brown, 5 minutes. Stir in ranch seasoning, broth, and chicken. Seal the lid, select Manual/Pressure Cook on High, and set cooking time to 12 minutes. After cooking, perform a natural pressure release for 10 minutes, then a quick pressure release to let out remaining steam.

Unlock the lid and remove chicken onto a plate and select Sauté mode. Shred chicken with two forks and return to sauce. Stir in cream cheese until melted and mix in scallions. Dish and serve warm.

Chicken Piccata with Capers

Total Time: 25 minutes | **Servings**: 4 | **Per Serving**: Kcal 486; Carbs 4g; Fat 25g; Protein 39g

Ingredients

4 chicken breasts, boneless and skinless
Salt and black pepper to taste
3 tbsp butter, room temperature
1 ½ tbsp all-purpose flour + ½ cup for dipping
2 tbsp olive oil

¼ cup dry white wine
¼ cup chicken broth
2 lemons, juiced
¼ cup drained capers
¼ cup chopped cilantro

Directions

Place chicken between two plastic wraps and using a meat pounder, lightly pound chicken until about ¼-inch thickness. Take off the plastic wrap and season chicken with salt and black pepper.

In a medium bowl, combine 1 tbsp butter with 1 ½ tbsp flour until smooth. Pour remaining flour on a plate. Set your Instant Pot to Sauté on medium heat. Heat olive oil in inner pot, dip chicken in flour, and fry in oil until golden brown on both sides and cooked through, 8 minutes. Plate and set aside.

Pour white wine, chicken broth, and lemon juice into inner pot, allow boiling, and stir in butter mixture. Stir in capers, remaining butter, parsley, and cook until sauce thickens, 2 minutes. Adjust taste with salt and black pepper. Plate chicken and spoon sauce all over. Serve warm with mashed potatoes.

Avocado Chicken Dip

Total Time: 25 minutes | **Servings**: 4 | **Per Serving**: Kcal 366; Carbs 6g; Fat 23g; Protein 35g

Ingredients

2 chicken breasts, boneless and skinless
¼ cup chicken broth
Salt and black pepper to taste
1 large avocado, peeled, pitted, and diced
1 shallot, finely chopped
2 tbsp chopped cilantro

1 tbsp lemon juice
2 tbsp sour cream
½ tsp garlic powder
¼ tsp cumin powder
¼ tsp hot sauce

Directions

Add chicken, broth, salt, and black pepper to inner pot. Seal the lid, select Manual/Pressure Cook on High, and set cooking time to 10 minutes. After cooking, perform a quick pressure release, and unlock the lid. Using two forks, shred chicken into small strands.

Add avocado, shallot, cilantro, lemon juice, sour cream, garlic powder, cumin powder, hot sauce, salt, and black pepper. Stir ingredients until well-combined. Adjust taste and spoon food into serving bowls. Serve with pretzel chips.

Lemongrass Garlic Chicken

Total Time: 40 minutes | **Servings**: 4 | **Per Serving**: Kcal 427; Carbs 6g; Fat 27g; Protein 33g

Ingredients

2 lemongrass stalks, chopped
2 garlic cloves, minced
Salt and black pepper to taste

1 cup chicken broth
4 chicken breasts
1 lemon, juiced

Directions

In inner pot, combine lemongrass, garlic, salt, pepper, chicken broth, and chicken. Seal the lid, select Manual/Pressure Cook on High, and set cooking time to 12 minutes.

After cooking, perform a natural pressure release for 10 minutes, then a quick pressure release to let out remaining steam, and unlock the lid. Select Sauté and remove chicken onto a plate. Take out lemongrass and discard. Shred chicken into strands and return to sauce. Stir in lemon juice and cook further for 5 minutes. Serve warm.

Chicken Taco Bowls

Total Time: 45 minutes | **Servings**: 4 | **Per Serving**: Kcal 678; Carbs 43g; Fat 54g; Protein 42g

Ingredients

2 tbsp olive oil
4 chicken breasts, cut into 1-inch cubes
1 tbsp taco seasoning
1 ½ cups salsa
½ cup sweet corn kernels, drained
1 (15 oz) can black beans, rinsed and drained
1 ¼ cups basmati rice, rinsed and drained
2 ½ cups chicken broth

Salt and black pepper to taste
For topping:
½ cup grated cheddar cheese
2 scallions, chopped
½ cup chopped cilantro
1 large avocado, pitted and chopped
1 cup sour cream

Directions

Set your Instant Pot to Sauté and adjust to medium heat. Heat olive oil in inner pot, season chicken breasts with taco seasoning sauce, and sear in oil on both sides until golden, 5 minutes. Mix in salsa, corn kernels, black beans, rice, and chicken broth and season with salt and black pepper.

Seal the lid, select Manual/Pressure Cook mode on High, and set time to 8 minutes. Allow sitting (covered) for 10 minutes and then perform a quick pressure release to let out remaining steam, and unlock the lid. Stir, adjust taste with salt, pepper, and spoon into serving bowls. Top with cheddar cheese, scallions, cilantro, avocado, and sour cream, to serve.

Bourbon Chicken with Broccoli

Total Time: 17 minutes | **Servings**: 4 | **Per Serving**: Kcal 397; Carbs 45g; Fat 11g; Protein 27g

Ingredients

1 lb chicken breasts, cubed
2 cups broccoli florets
½ cup bourbon
½ cup teriyaki sauce
2 tbsp honey
1 Dijon mustard

1 tsp garlic powder
2 tsp onion powder
1/8 tsp ginger powder
½ cup brown sugar
1 tbsp cornstarch
1 tbsp water

Directions

Pour chicken and broccoli into inner pot of your Instant Pot.

In a medium bowl, mix bourbon, teriyaki sauce, honey, mustard, garlic powder, onion powder, ginger powder, and brown sugar. Pour mixture all over chicken and broccoli and stir. Seal the lid, select Manual/Pressure Cook mode on High, and set cooking time to 6 minutes. Perform a quick pressure release to let out all the steam and unlock the lid.

Combine cornstarch and water in a small bow. On the Instant Pot, select Sauté, and pour cornstarch mixture over chicken. Stir and allow thickening for a minute. Spoon chicken over rice and serve warm.

Asian Peanut Chicken

Total Time: 45 minutes | **Servings**: 4 | **Per Serving**: Kcal 427; Carbs 8g; Fat 31g; Protein 32g

Ingredients

1 tbsp olive oil
1 small red onion, chopped
½ red bell pepper, deseeded and chopped
1 cup peanut sauce

2 tsp soy sauce
½ tsp miso paste
½ cup chicken broth
4 chicken breasts

Directions

Set your Instant Pot to Sauté mode and adjust to medium heat. Heat olive oil in inner pot and sauté onion and bell pepper until softened, 3 minutes. Mix in peanut sauce, soy sauce, miso paste, and chicken broth. Boil for 1 minute and stir in chicken. Seal the lid, select Manual/Pressure Cook on High, and set cooking time to 12 minutes.

After cooking, perform a natural pressure release for 10 minutes, then a quick pressure release to let out remaining steam, and unlock the lid. Remove chicken onto a plate and select Sauté mode. Shred chicken with two forks and return to sauce. Cook until sauce thickens, 5 minutes. Serve chicken and sauce with rice.

Mexican Jalapeño Chicken

Total Time: 40 minutes | **Servings**: 4 | **Per Serving**: Kcal 467; Carbs 13g; Fat 22g; Protein 33g

Ingredients

1 tbsp olive oil
1 white onion, chopped
1 red bell pepper, deseeded and chopped
1 green bell pepper, deseeded and chopped
Salt and black pepper to taste
2 tsp cumin powder
½ tsp chili powder

2 jalapeño peppers, deseeded and chopped
2 tsp garlic powder
1 (10 oz) can diced tomatoes
1 cup chicken broth
4 chicken breasts, cut into 1-inch cubes
1 lemon, juiced

Directions

Set your Instant Pot to Sauté mode and adjust to medium heat. Heat olive oil in inner pot and sauté onion, bell peppers, and season with salt until vegetables soften, 3 minutes. Mix in black pepper, cumin powder, chili powder, jalapeño peppers, garlic powder, tomatoes, broth, and chicken breasts.

Seal the lid, select Manual/Pressure Cook on High, and set time to 12 minutes. After cooking, perform a natural pressure release for 10 minutes, then a quick pressure release to let out remaining steam. Unlock the lid, select Sauté and stir in lemon juice. Cook further for 3 minutes and adjust taste with salt and pepper. Dish food and serve warm.

Chicken Cordon Blue Casserole

Total Time: 30 minutes | **Servings**: 4 | **Per Serving**: Kcal 661; Carbs 23g; Fat 44g; Protein 59g

Ingredients

10 oz rotini pasta
2 ½ cups chicken broth
4 chicken breasts, cut into strips
1 lb ham, cubed
1 tbsp Dijon mustard
1 tsp garlic powder

Salt and black pepper to taste
¼ cup shredded Gouda cheese
¼ cup shredded Parmesan cheese
½ cup heavy cream
2 tbsp unsalted butter, melted
1 cup crushed pork rinds

Directions

In inner pot, add rotini, chicken broth, and arrange chicken and ham on top. Top with Dijon mustard, garlic powder, salt, and black pepper. Seal the lid, select Manual/Pressure Cook on High, and set cooking time to 10 minutes.

After cooking, perform a quick pressure release, and unlock the lid. Mix in cheeses and heavy cream. Cook on Sauté mode until cheeses melt, 5 minutes. Spoon cordon blue onto serving plates and set aside. In a medium bowl, mix butter with pork rinds and drizzle on cordon blue. Serve immediately.

Chicken Pozole

Total Time: 40 minutes | **Servings**: 4 | **Per Serving**: Kcal 696; Carbs 44g; Fat 42g; Protein 37g

Ingredients

1 tbsp olive oil
1 medium onion, chopped
6 garlic cloves, minced
1 tbsp tomato paste
2 green chilis, minced
2 tsp cumin powder
1 tbsp chili powder
2 tsp dried oregano
½ tsp chipotle paste
Salt and black pepper to taste

2 chicken thighs, skinless and boneless
4 cups chicken broth
3 cups cooked hominy
1 lime, juiced
For topping:
½ cup shredded red cabbage
1 cup sour cream
1 large avocado, pitted and sliced
1 lime, cut into wedges
½ cup grated cheddar cheese

Directions

Set your Instant Pot to Sauté and adjust to medium heat. Heat olive oil in inner pot and sauté onion, garlic, tomato paste, and green chilies. Cook until softened, 3 minutes. Mix in cumin powder, chili powder, oregano, chipotle paste, salt, and black pepper; cook until fragrant, 30 seconds. Add chicken, broth, and hominy.

Seal the lid, select Manual/Pressure Cook on High, and set cooking time to 12 minutes. After cooking, perform a natural pressure release for 10 minutes, then a quick pressure release to let out remaining steam, and unlock the lid.

Remove chicken onto a plate, shred into strands, return to sauce, and stir in lime juice. Adjust taste with salt and black pepper. Dish soup into serving bowls and top with cabbage, sour cream, avocado, lime wedges, and cheddar cheese.

Hunter's chicken

Total Time: 30 minutes | **Servings**: 4 | **Per Serving**: Kcal 513; Carbs 35g; Fat 31g; Protein 36g

Ingredients

2 cups tomato sauce
4 chicken breasts, cut into bite-size pieces
1 medium onion, thinly sliced
3 red bell peppers, deseeded and chopped
½ tsp cayenne pepper
Salt and black pepper to taste

1 tsp garlic powder
½ cup chicken broth
1 cup sliced oyster mushrooms
1 cup Kalamata olives, pitted
2 tbsp chopped parsley to garnish

Directions

In inner pot, add tomato sauce, chicken, onion, bell peppers, cayenne pepper, salt, black pepper, garlic powder, chicken broth, and mushrooms. Seal the lid, select Manual/Pressure Cook mode on High, and set time to 10 minutes.

After cooking, perform a natural pressure release for 5 minutes, then a quick pressure release to let out remaining steam. Unlock the lid, stir in olives, and adjust taste. Garnish with parsley and serve.

Easy Chicken Poblano Pot

Total Time: 35 minutes | **Servings**: 4 | **Per Serving**: Kcal 474; Carbs 21g; Fat 19g; Protein 43g

Ingredients

2 tbsp olive oil
4 chicken breasts
Salt and black pepper to taste
2 medium red onions, chopped
3 poblano peppers, deseeded and thinly sliced

3 garlic cloves, minced
2 tbsp coriander powder
1 ½ cups orange juice
1 ½ cups chicken broth

Directions

Set your Instant Pot to Sauté and heat olive oil. Season chicken with salt and black pepper, and sear chicken on both sides until golden brown, 6 minutes. Stir in onion, poblano peppers, garlic, coriander, orange juice, and chicken broth.

Seal the lid, select Manual/Pressure Cook mode on High, and set cooking time to 6 minutes. After cooking, perform natural pressure release for 10 minutes, then a quick pressure release, and unlock the lid. Stir and adjust taste with salt and black pepper. Spoon food into serving bowls and serve with tortilla chips, salsa, and taco toppings.

Greek Chicken with Dill-Lemon Pilaf

Total Time: 35 minutes | **Servings**: 4 | **Per Serving**: Kcal 543; Carbs 21g; Fat 32g; Protein 37g

Ingredients

1 tbsp olive oil
4 chicken breasts, cut into 1-inch cubes
1 tbsp Greek seasoning
1 small white onion, chopped
3 garlic cloves, minced
1 tbsp dried dill

2 lemons, 1 tbsp zest and all juiced
1 cup jasmine rice
1 ¼ cups chicken broth
Salt and black pepper to taste
1 tbsp fresh chopped dill to garnish

Directions

Set your Instant Pot to Sauté and adjust to medium heat. Heat olive oil in inner pot, season chicken with Italian seasoning and sear in oil until golden on the outside, 5 minutes. Mix in onion, garlic, and cook for 3 minutes or until fragrant. Stir in dill, lemon zest, rice, chicken broth, salt, and black pepper.

Seal the lid, select Manual/Pressure Cook mode on High, and set cooking time to 5 minutes. Allow sitting (covered) for 10 minutes and then perform quick pressure release to let out steam. Mix in lemon juice and dish food onto serving plates. Garnish with dill and serve warm.

Chicken Parmigiana

Total Time: 40 minutes | **Servings**: 4 | **Per Serving**: Kcal 652; Carbs 41g; Fat 42g; Protein 36g

Ingredients

4 chicken thighs, boneless and skinless
5 cups tomato pasta sauce
1 cup chicken broth
Salt and black pepper to taste
¼ tsp red chili flakes
1 tsp dried thyme
1 tsp garlic powder

1 tsp dried oregano
10 oz rigatoni
1 cup grated Parmesan cheese
2 cups grated mozzarella cheese

Directions

Cut chicken into 1-inch cubes and add to inner pot. Top with pasta sauce, chicken broth, salt, black pepper, red chili flakes, thyme, garlic powder, and oregano.

Seal the lid, select Manual/Pressure Cook on High, and set cooking time to 12 minutes. After cooking, perform a quick pressure release. Unlock the lid and stir in rigatoni.

Seal the lid again, select Manual/Pressure Cook mode on High, and set cooking time to 5 minutes. After cooking, perform a quick pressure release and unlock the lid. Stir in Parmesan cheese to melt and dish food onto serving plates. Top with mozzarella cheese and serve warm.

Thai Sweet Chili Chicken

Total Time: 40 minutes | **Servings**: 4 | **Per Serving**: Kcal 495; Carbs 22g; Fat 32g; Protein 36g

Ingredients

4 chicken breasts
¼ cup soy sauce
2 tbsp teriyaki sauce
¼ cup ketchup
2 tbsp sweet chili sauce
2 ½ tbsp brown sugar

3 garlic cloves, minced
1 tbsp freshly grated ginger
½ tsp onion powder
1 ½ tbsp cornstarch
¼ cup chicken broth
Salt and black pepper to taste

Directions

Place chicken in inner pot. In a bowl, combine soy sauce, teriyaki sauce, ketchup, sweet chili sauce, brown sugar, garlic, ginger, onion powder, cornstarch, broth, salt, and black pepper. Pour mixture over chicken.

Seal the lid, select Manual/Pressure Cook on High, and set cooking time to 12 minutes. After cooking, perform a natural pressure release for 10 minutes, then a quick pressure release to let out remaining steam, and unlock the lid.

Remove chicken onto a plate and shred with two forks. Return chicken to sauce, top with cornstarch mixture, and stir. Select Sauté mode and cook until sauce is syrupy. Dish food and serve warm.

Balsamic Rosemary Chicken

Total Time: 50 minutes | **Servings**: 4 | **Per Serving**: Kcal 412; Carbs 15g; Fat 18g; Protein 41g

Ingredients

1 tbsp fresh rosemary leaves
6 garlic cloves, minced
Salt and black pepper to taste
½ tsp smoked paprika
3 lb whole chicken, cleaned and rinsed

2 tbsp olive oil
4 tbsp balsamic vinegar
1 lemon, zested and juiced
1 cup chicken broth
1 large white onion, diced

Directions

In a medium bowl, mix rosemary, garlic, salt, black pepper, and paprika. Rub spice mixture all over chicken. Set your Instant Pot to Sauté. Heat olive oil in inner pot and sear chicken all around until golden, 7 minutes. Remove to a plate.

Pour balsamic vinegar, lemon zest, lemon juice, and chicken broth into the pot. Using a spatula, scrape the stuck bits at the bottom of the pot. Place onion and then chicken in inner pot.

Seal the lid, select Manual/Pressure Cook on High, and set cooking time to 18 minutes. After cooking, perform a natural pressure release for 10 minutes, then a quick pressure release to let out remaining steam. Unlock the lid and remove chicken onto a plate and cover with foil for 5 minutes before slicing. Serve warm.

Cajun Chicken with Rice & Vegetables

Total Time: 40 minutes | **Servings**: 4 | **Per Serving**: Kcal 556; Carbs 26g; Fat 32g; Protein 36g

Ingredients

1 tbsp olive oil
4 chicken breasts, cut into 1-inch cubes
1 tbsp Cajun seasoning
1 small white onion, chopped
3 garlic cloves, minced

1 tbsp tomato paste
1 cup basmati rice
1 ¼ cups chicken broth
1 cup frozen mixed vegetables, thawed

Directions

Set your Instant Pot to Sauté and heat olive oil. Season chicken with Cajun seasoning and sear in oil until golden on the outside, 5 minutes. Mix in onion, garlic, and cook for 3 minutes or until fragrant. Stir in tomato paste, rice, and cook for 1 minute. Stir in broth.

Seal the lid, select Manual/Pressure Cook mode on High, and set cooking time to 5 minutes. Once ready, perform a quick pressure release to let out steam. Select Sauté mode and mix in vegetables; cook until warmed through, 3 to 5 minutes. Dish food and serve warm.

Chili Drumsticks in Cilantro-Lime Sauce

Total Time: 30 minutes | **Servings**: 4 | **Per Serving**: Kcal 346; Carbs 4g; Fat 20g; Protein 37g

Ingredients

1 tbsp olive oil
4 large drumsticks
Salt and black pepper to taste
4 garlic cloves, minced
1 tsp chili powder

1 tsp red chili flakes
2 limes, juiced
¼ chopped cilantro
1 cup chicken broth

Directions

Set your Instant Pot to Sauté and adjust to medium heat. Heat olive oil in inner pot, season chicken with salt, black pepper, and sear in oil until golden on the outside, 5 minutes. Stir in garlic, chili powder, red chili flakes, lime juice, cilantro, and chicken broth.

Seal the lid, select Manual/Pressure Cook on High, and set cooking time to 10 minutes. After cooking, perform a natural pressure release for 5 minutes, and then a quick pressure release to let out remaining steam. Unlock the lid, stir, and dish food onto serving plates. Serve warm.

Chicken & Artichoke Soup with Vermicelli

Total Time: 45 minutes | **Servings**: 4 | **Per Serving**: Kcal 429; Carbs 22g; Fat 23g; Protein 35g

Ingredients

2 tbsp olive oil
1 yellow onion, chopped
2 celery stalks, chopped
2 large carrots, chopped
5 garlic cloves, minced
2 chicken breasts, cut into ½-inch cubes
4 cups chicken stock

2 tsp Italian seasoning
2 bay leaves
Salt and black pepper to taste
½ tsp chili powder
½ lemon, juiced
3 cups chopped artichoke hearts
¼ cup vermicelli

Directions

Set your Instant Pot to Sauté mode. Heat olive oil in inner pot, sauté onion, celery, carrots, and cook until softened, 3 minutes. Stir in garlic until softened, 3 minutes. Mix in chicken breasts, stock, Italian seasoning, bay leaves, salt, pepper, and chili powder. Seal the lid, select Manual/Pressure Cook on High, and set time to 10 minutes.

After cooking, perform a natural pressure release for 10 minutes, then a quick pressure release to let out remaining steam, and unlock the lid. Mix in lemon juice, artichoke, and vermicelli and cook further 5 minutes on Sauté. Dish soup and serve warm.

Hainanese Chicken Rice

Total Time: 35 minutes | **Servings**: 4 | **Per Serving**: Kcal 553; Carbs 63g; Fat 25g; Protein 29g

Ingredients

2 tbsp sesame oil
2 lb boneless, skinless chicken breasts
½ cup Thai sweet chili sauce
3 tbsp soy sauce
1 ½ tsp minced fresh ginger
1 garlic clove, minced
1 lime, juiced

1 tsp habanero hot sauce
1 tbsp peanut butter
1 cup white rice
1 cup chicken broth
1 cup coconut milk
1 bunch of fresh cilantro, chopped

Directions

Set your Instant Pot to Sauté and warm sesame oil, place in the chicken, and brown for 6 minutes on all sides. Remove to a plate.

In a bowl, mix sweet chili sauce, soy sauce, ginger, garlic, lime juice, habanero sauce, and peanut butter. Stir to combine. Place the rice in the pot, top with the chicken, and pour the sauce over. Add in broth and coconut milk. Seal the lid, select Manual/Pressure Cook on High, and set time to 10 minutes.

When done, perform a natural pressure release for 10 minutes. Unlock the lid and remove the chicken to a plate. Shred-it with a fork. Fluff the rice and ladle it into four bowls. Top with the chicken, sprinkle with cilantro, and serve.

Bombay Chicken Tikka Masala

Total Time: 40 minutes | **Servings**: 4 | **Per Serving**: Kcal 511; Carbs 7g; Fat 39g; Protein 34g

Ingredients

1 (14 oz) can diced tomatoes
2 tsp ginger puree
1 tsp turmeric powder
½ tsp cayenne powder
1 tsp sweet paprika
Salt to taste
1 tsp garam masala

1 tsp cumin powder
4 chicken thighs, boneless and cut into bite-size pieces
2 tbsp butter
½ cup chicken broth
2 tbsp coconut milk
¼ chopped cilantro

Directions

In inner pot of your Instant, add tomatoes, ginger, turmeric powder, cayenne powder, sweet paprika, salt, garam masala, cumin powder, chicken, butter, broth, and coconut milk. Seal the lid, select Manual/Pressure Cook on High, and set cooking time to 12 minutes.

After cooking, perform a natural pressure release for 10 minutes, then a quick pressure release to let out remaining steam. Unlock lid and stir and adjust taste with salt. Ladle into serving bowls, garnish with cilantro and serve warm.

Pecorino-Romano Chicken with Potatoes

Total Time: 40 minutes | **Servings:** 4 | **Per Serving:** Kcal 527; Carbs 26g; Fat 38g; Protein 36g

Ingredients

4 chicken breasts
1 lb baby russet potatoes, cleaned
3 tbsp olive oil
3 tbsp ranch seasoning
Salt and black pepper to taste
½ tsp dried basil

½ tsp dried oregano
1 tsp garlic powder
1 tsp dried rosemary
1 cup chicken broth
3 tbsp grated Pecorino Romano cheese

Directions

In a large bowl, add chicken, potatoes, olive oil, 2 tablespoons of ranch seasoning, salt, black pepper, basil, oregano, garlic powder, and rosemary. Toss well. Pour broth into inner pot, add potatoes, and place chicken on top. Seal the lid, select Manual/Pressure Cook on High, and set cooking time to 15 minutes.

After cooking, perform a natural pressure release for 10 minutes, then a quick pressure release to let out remaining steam. Unlock the lid. Plate chicken and potatoes, sprinkle with remaining ranch seasoning and scatter Pecorino cheese on top. Serve.

Cheesy Macaroni with Chicken & Bacon

Total Time: 35 minutes | **Servings:** 4 | **Per Serving:** Kcal 878; Carbs 76g; Fat 47g; Protein 73g

Ingredients

4 bacon slices, chopped
2 tbsp olive oil
4 chicken breasts
1 tbsp ranch dressing mix
16 oz macaroni

3 cups chicken broth
Salt and black pepper to taste
4 oz cream cheese, softened
1 cup grated Monterey Jack cheese

Directions

Set your Instant Pot to Sauté and adjust to medium heat. Cook bacon in inner pot until brown and crispy. Remove onto a plate and set aside. Heat olive oil in bacon fat, season chicken with ranch dressing mix, and sear in oil until golden, 5 minutes. Return bacon to pot and top with macaroni and chicken broth. Season with salt and pepper.

Seal the lid, select Manual/Pressure Cook on High, and set cooking time to 6 minutes. After cooking, perform a quick pressure release to let out remaining steam, and unlock the lid. Select Sauté and mix in cream cheese and Monterey Jack cheese until melted, 3 minutes. Dish food and serve warm.

Thyme Chicken & Cannellini Bean Soup

Total Time: 40 minutes | **Servings:** 4 | **Per Serving:** Kcal 399; Carbs 17g; Fat 23g; Protein 32g

Ingredients

2 tbsp olive oil
1 white onion, chopped
1 celery stalk, chopped
6 garlic clove, minced
2 tbsp thyme leaves
1 cup dried cannellini beans

2 chicken breasts, cut into 1-inch cubes
4 cups chicken stock
Salt and black pepper to taste
1 lemon, juiced
2 tbsp chopped parsley to garnish

Directions

Set your Instant Pot to Sauté and adjust to medium heat. Heat olive oil in inner pot and sauté onion, celery, and garlic until softened, 3 minutes. Mix in thyme, beans, chicken breasts, stock, salt, and black pepper. Seal the lid, select Manual/Pressure Cook on High, and set cooking time to 13 minutes.

After cooking, perform a natural pressure release for 10 minutes, then a quick pressure release to let out remaining steam, and unlock the lid. Stir in lemon juice and adjust taste with salt and black pepper. Ladle soup into serving bowls and garnish with parsley.

Mediterranean Chicken with Capers & Olives

Total Time: 55 minutes | **Servings**: 4 | **Per Serving**: Kcal 451; Carbs 28g; Fat 28g; Protein 33g

Ingredients

1 lb chicken thighs, with the bone, skin removed
Salt and black pepper to taste
1 bay leaf
2 tbsp olive oil
2 red bell peppers, cut into strips
1 red onion, diced
1 garlic clove, minced

¼ cup dry white wine
1 ½ cups canned passata
½ cup chicken stock
2 tbsp black olives, pitted
½ tbsp capers, drained
½ tsp dried rosemary
Fresh parsley, for garnish

Directions

Set your Instant Pot to Sauté and heat olive oil. Season chicken with salt and pepper. Add to the pot and cook for 8 minutes until golden brown. Remove to a plate. Pour in bell peppers, onion, and garlic.

Cook for 6 minutes until the vegetables are softened. Pour in white wine, passata, chicken stock, bay leaf, and rosemary and cook for another 2 minutes. Return the chicken to the pot.

Seal the lid, select Manual/Pressure Cook, and cook for 15 minutes on High. When done, perform a natural pressure release for 10 minutes, then a quick pressure release to let out the remaining steam. Unlock the lid, remove and discard the bay leaf. Stir in olives and capers and adjust the seasoning. Garnish with parsley and serve.

Creamy Basil Chicken Breasts

Total Time: 45 minutes | **Servings**: 4 | **Per Serving**: Kcal 463; Carbs 5g; Fat 31g; Protein 32g

Ingredients

4 chicken breasts
1 cup chicken broth
1 tsp Italian seasoning
3 garlic cloves, minced
Salt and black pepper to taste

¼ cup chopped roasted red peppers
¼ cup heavy cream
1 ½ tbsp cornstarch
1 tbsp basil pesto

Directions

In inner pot, add chicken, broth, Italian seasoning, garlic, salt, black pepper, and roasted peppers; stir. Seal the lid, select Manual/Pressure Cook on High, and set cooking time to 10 minutes. After cooking, perform a natural pressure release for 10 minutes, then a quick pressure release to let out remaining steam, and unlock the lid.

Select Sauté mode and remove chicken onto a plate. Into sauce, mix heavy cream, cornstarch, and pesto. Cook for 3 to 4 minutes or until sauce thickens. Return chicken to pot, coat with sauce, and cook for 2 minutes. Dish chicken and serve warm with sauce.

Smoky Chicken Pilaf

Total Time: 50 minutes | **Servings**: 4 | **Per Serving**: Kcal 292; Carbs 24g; Fat 16g; Protein 23g

Ingredients

2 tbsp olive oil
½ lb boneless chicken thighs, skin on
1 leek, chopped
1 cup rice, rinsed
Salt and black pepper to serve
¼ tsp ground smoked paprika

¼ tsp ground coriander
1 bay leaf
1 ½ cups chicken stock
1 carrot, chopped
1 celery stick, chopped
2 garlic cloves, minced

Directions

Set your Instant Pot to Sauté and heat the olive oil. Cook chicken for 5 minutes per side or until golden brown; reserve. Put in leek, carrot, celery, and garlic and cook for 3 minutes. Stir in the rice, salt, black pepper, cumin, paprika, coriander, and bay leaf. Cook for 2 minutes. Pour in the stock and add stir.

Return the chicken. Seal the lid, select Manual/Pressure Cook and set cooking time to 15 minutes on High. When done, perform a natural pressure release for 10 minutes, then a quick pressure release to let out the remaining steam. Unlock the lid and remove the bay leaf. Fluff the rice with a fork and serve.

Parmesan Chicken Meatballs with Tomato Sauce

Total Time: 25 minutes | **Servings**: 4 | **Per Serving**: Kcal 268; Carbs 10g; Fat 16g; Protein 23g

Ingredients

1 pound ground chicken
3 tbsp breadcrumbs
2 ¼ tbsp whole milk
1 garlic clove, minced
1 egg, beaten
2 tbsp fresh basil, chopped

2 ¼ tbsp Parmesan cheese, grated
2 tbsp olive oil
2 tbsp white wine
½ can (14.5-oz) tomato sauce
Salt and black pepper, to taste

Directions

In a bowl, mix chicken, breadcrumbs, garlic, black pepper, salt, egg, and Parmesan cheese with your hands. Shape the mixture into medium-size balls.

Set your Instant Pot to Sauté and heat oil. Add in the meatballs and cook for 8 minutes; reserve. Pour in the white wine to scrape up any browned bits from the bottom of the pot. Stir in the tomato sauce and meatballs.

Seal the lid, select Manual/Pressure Cook mode, and set cooking time to 5 minutes. When done, perform a quick pressure release to let out the steam. Garnish with parsley and serve.

Peanut Chicken with Rice Noodles

Total Time: 30 minutes | **Servings**: 4 | **Per Serving**: Kcal 584; Carbs 17g; Fat 28g; Protein 63g

Ingredients

4 chicken breasts
¾ cup chicken broth
1 cup peanut sauce
Salt and black pepper to taste

5 oz rice noodles
1 cup green beans, trimmed and halved
1 tbsp chopped peanuts to garnish
1 tsp chopped cilantro to garnish

Directions

In inner pot, add chicken, broth, peanut sauce, and salt. Seal the lid, select Manual/Pressure Cook on High, and set time to 12 minutes. After cooking, perform a quick pressure release to let out steam, and unlock the lid.

Meanwhile, in a bowl, pour the rice noodles and top with 2 cups of hot water. Allow sitting for 4 minutes. Strain noodles through a colander and divide between serving plates. Select Sauté and add green beans. Cook for 3 minutes and adjust taste with salt and pepper. Top with chicken and sauce, garnish with peanuts, and cilantro, and serve.

Chicken Fajitas with Avocado & Cherry Tomatoes

Total Time: 30 minutes | **Servings**: 4 | **Per Serving**: Kcal 444; Carbs 30g; Fat 24g; Protein 28g

Ingredients

1 lb chicken breasts
8 corn tortilla shells

1 avocado, sliced
½ cup cherry tomatoes, halved

Filling

½ yellow onion, chopped
1 garlic clove, minced
1 tbsp olive oil
1 can (10-oz) fire-roasted tomatoes, chopped
½ cup chicken broth

½ tbsp chili powder
1 tbsp taco seasoning
Salt and black pepper to serve
¼ tsp ground coriander

Directions

Add the chicken to your Instant Pot. In a bowl, mix together all filling ingredients. Pour the mixture over the chicken. Seal the lid, select Poultry on High, and cook for 15 minutes.

When done, perform a quick pressure release. Unlock the lid and remove the chicken to a cutting board and let it cool for a few minutes before shredding it. Then, return to the pot and stir to combine.

Warm the tortilla in the microwave. To serve, divide the chicken mixture between the tortilla and top with cherry tomatoes and avocado.

Chicken with Mushrooms & Pancetta

Total Time: 40 minutes | **Servings**: 4 | **Per Serving**: Kcal 689; Carbs 48g; Fat 43g; Protein 27g

Ingredients

2 pancetta slices, chopped
¼ cup flour
1 pound bone-in, skinless chicken thighs
Salt and black pepper to taste
4 tbsp olive oil
1 cup mushrooms, sliced

2 leeks, white part only, chopped
2 garlic cloves, minced
1 cup chicken broth
1 cup tomato sauce
1 (10-oz) can condensed cream of mushroom soup

Directions

Rub chicken thighs with salt and pepper and brush with half of the oil. Roll them in flour until evenly coated. Set your Instant Pot to Sauté, heat the remaining oil and brown chicken for 3 minutes per side. Add in pancetta, mushrooms, leeks, and garlic and cook for 5 minutes. Stir in broth and tomato sauce.

Seal the lid, select Manual/Pressure Cook on High, and cook 15 minutes. When done, perform a natural pressure release for 10 minutes, then a quick pressure release to let out the remaining steam. Unlock the lid and select Sauté. Add in the cream of mushroom soup and cook an additional 3 minutes. Serve.

Classic Chicken Caesar Salad

Total Time: 25 minutes | **Servings:** 4 | **Per Serving:** Kcal 395; Carbs 12g; Fat 24g; Protein 33g

Ingredients

2 boneless, skinless chicken breasts
Salt and black pepper to taste
1 cup water
1 bay leaf
1 lemon, quartered
1 head Iceberg lettuce, torn into bite-sized pieces
¼ cup croutons

½ cup grated Parmesan cheese
1 garlic clove, minced
1 tsp Worcestershire sauce
¼ tsp grated lemon zest
2 tbsp white wine vinegar
3 tbsp mayonnaise
4 tbsp olive oil

Directions

Season the chicken with salt and pepper. Place it in your Instant Pot; add in water, bay leaf and lemon, and stir. Seal the lid, select Manual/Pressure Cook, and set time to 10 minutes. When done, perform a quick pressure to let out steam and unlock the lid. Remove the chicken to a plate to cool slightly and slice it into strips.

Place the lettuce in a bowl and toss with the croutons and half of the cheese. In another bowl, to make the dressing, whisk the garlic, Worcestershire sauce, lemon zest, remaining cheese, vinegar, mayonnaise, oil, and salt to taste. Split the lettuce mixture into bowls, top with the chicken, and drizzle with the dressing to serve.

Sriracha Chicken Drumsticks

Total Time: 30 minutes | **Servings:** 4 | **Per Serving:** Kcal 272; Carbs 15g; Fat 13g; Protein 22g

Ingredients

1 lb chicken drumsticks
1 lime, juiced
4 tbsp soy sauce
2 tbsp Sriracha sauce
1 ½ tbsp honey

1/8 tsp ginger powder
1 garlic clove, minced
½ tsp crushed red pepper
1 tbsp cornstarch
1 green onion, chopped

Directions

In a bowl, combine sriracha sauce, soy sauce, honey, ginger powder, garlic, and red pepper and mix well. Place in chicken and toss to coat. Transfer to your Instant Pot. Seal the lid, select Poultry on High, and cook for 15 minutes.

When done, perform a quick pressure release. Select Sauté. In a bowl, combine the cornstarch and 2 tbsp of water. Pour into the pot and stir. Cook for 2 minutes until the sauce thickens. Top with green onions to serve.

Chinese Noodles with Chicken & Mushrooms

Total Time: 25 minutes | **Servings:** 4 | **Per Serving:** Kcal 625; Carbs 81g; Fat 23g; Protein 22g

Ingredients

1 tbsp olive oil
1 ½ lb boneless, skinless chicken breasts, sliced
1 garlic clove, minced
8 oz Chinese egg noodles
1 cup snap peas
½ cup shiitake mushrooms, sliced
1 carrot, sliced

1 ½ cups chicken broth
1 tbsp soy sauce
1 tbsp fish sauce
1 tbsp rice wine
1 tsp grated fresh ginger
1 tbsp brown sugar

Directions

Set your Instant Pot to Sauté mode and heat the olive oil. Add in the chicken and garlic and cook for 5 minutes, until the chicken is browned. Add in the snap peas, mushrooms, and carrot, and stir.

In a bowl, combine broth, soy sauce, fish sauce, rice wine, ginger, and brown sugar. Whisk until the sugar is dissolved. Pour the mixture in the pot. Seal the lid, select Manual/Pressure Cook on High, and set time to 5 minutes.

When done, perform a quick pressure to let out steam. Unlock the lid and stir in the noodles. Select Sauté and cook for 4 minutes. Ladle into individual bowls and serve.

Traditional Arroz con Pollo

Total Time: 35 minutes | **Servings**: 4 | **Per Serving**: Kcal 579; Carbs 51g; Fat 22g; Protein 47g

Ingredients

1 onion, chopped
4 tbsp olive oil
3 boneless, skinless chicken breasts, cubed
Salt and black pepper to taste
1 red bell pepper, chopped
2 garlic cloves, minced
1 cup white rice
2 tsp ground cumin

1 ½ cups chicken broth
½ cup dry white wine
2 tbsp drained Spanish capers
1 (14-oz) can crushed tomatoes
1 cup frozen peas
½ cup green olives
¼ cup chopped parsley, for garnishing

Directions

Set your Instant Pot to Sauté and heat the olive oil. Sprinkle the chicken with salt and pepper and add it to the pot. Cook for 3 minutes per side, until browned. Remove to a plate.

In the pot, warm the remaining oil and sauté the onion, bell pepper, and garlic for 3 minutes. Add in the rice and stir. Pour in the broth, wine, cumin, Spanish capers, tomatoes, frozen peas, and olives. Return the chicken. Seal the lid, select Manual/Pressure Cook on High, and set time to 10 minutes.

When done, perform a natural pressure release for 10 minutes, then a quick pressure release to let out the remaining steam. Unlock the lid and fluff the rice with a fork. Garnish with parsley to serve.

Dijon Chicken with Rosemary & Potatoes

Total Time: 30 minutes | **Servings**: 4 | **Per Serving**: Kcal 638; Carbs 40g; Fat 45g; Protein 43g

Ingredients

2 lb chicken thighs
Salt and black pepper to taste
2 tbsp olive oil
1 ¼ cups chicken broth
Lemon juice from 1 lemon

2 tbsp Dijon mustard
2 tsp rosemary, chopped
3 garlic cloves, crushed
2 lb red potatoes, quartered

Directions

Rub the chicken with salt and pepper. Set your Instant Pot to Sauté mode, warm olive oil, and sear the chicken for 6 minutes on all sides until golden brown.

In a bowl, place broth, lemon juice, mustard, rosemary, and garlic and mix to combine. Pour into the pot and add the potatoes. Seal the lid, select Manual/Pressure Cook mode on High, and set time to 15 minutes. When done, perform a quick pressure to let out steam. Serve.

Roman-Style Chicken

Total Time: 30 minutes | **Servings**: 4 | **Per Serving**: Kcal 533; Carbs 42g; Fat 33g; Protein 30g

Ingredients

2 lb boneless, skinless chicken breasts, halved lengthwise
1 tbsp Italian seasoning
Salt and black pepper to taste
1 tbsp garlic powder
2 tbsp butter
¾ cup chicken broth

¾ cup heavy cream
¾ cup Parmesan cheese, grated
½ cup sun-dried tomatoes, chopped
2 cups fresh spinach, chopped
Fresh parsley, chopped for garnish

Directions

Flatten the chicken breasts with a meat mallet. Season with the Italian seasoning, salt, black pepper, and garlic powder. Set your Instant Pot to Sauté and melt the butter, place in the chicken, and brown for 4 minutes on all sides. Pour in the broth, seal the lid, select Manual/Pressure Cook on High, and set time to 10 minutes.

When done, perform a quick pressure to let out steam. Unlock the lid and remove the chicken to a plate. Select Sauté and add in the heavy cream. Cook for 2 minutes, stirring often. Pour in the cheese and sun-dried tomatoes, stir until the cheese is melted. Add in the spinach and stir until the spinach is wilted. Serve the chicken topped with parsley.

Pulled Chicken Carnitas

Total Time: 25 minutes | **Servings**: 4 | **Per Serving**: Kcal 563; Carbs 36g; Fat 35g; Protein 36g

Ingredients

2 tbsp soy sauce
1 tbsp rice vinegar
1 tsp sugar
½ head white cabbage, shredded
1 large carrot, shredded
1 bell pepper, sliced
3 spring onions, chopped

2 garlic cloves, minced
1 tsp fresh ginger, grated
1 tbsp olive oil
½ cup chicken broth
4 chicken breast halves, cut into 1-inch strips
4 tortillas, warmed

Directions

Mix the soy sauce, vinegar, and sugar in your Instant Pot. Stir in cabbage, carrot, bell pepper, spring onions, garlic, ginger, and olive oil. Place the chicken on top and pour the broth. Seal the lid, select Manual/Pressure Cook on High, and set time to 12 minutes.

When ready, do a quick pressure release. Unlock the lid and remove the chicken to a plate. Allow cooling and shred it into small pieces. Put it back in the pot, select Sauté and cook until the liquid has reduced by half. Divide the filling between tortillas with a perforated spoon. Roll up and serve immediately.

Agave & Tamari Chicken

Total Time: 30 minutes | **Servings**: 2 | **Per Serving**: Kcal 330; Carbs 11g; Fat 22g; Protein 23g

Ingredients

½ pound bone-in, skin-on chicken thighs
1 tbsp tamari sauce
1 tsp lemon pepper seasoning
3 tbsp agave nectar

1 lemon, juiced and zested
1 tbsp olive oil
2 cloves garlic, peeled and minced
½ cup water

Directions

Rub chicken with lemon pepper seasoning. Set your Instant Pot to Sauté and heat olive oil. Place in chicken and cook for 4-5 minutes on all sides, until lightly browned. Add in the garlic and cook for 1 minute, stirring often.

In a bowl, combine lemon juice, lemon zest, agave nectar, water, and tamari sauce. Pour over the chicken. Seal the lid, select Poultry, and set cooking time to 15 minutes. When done, perform a quick pressure release to let out all the steam. Serve hot with rice.

Mango Chicken with Teriyaki Sauce

Total Time: 35 minutes | **Servings**: 4 | **Per Serving**: Kcal 588; Carbs 13g; Fat 59g; Protein 13g

Ingredients

1 lb bone-in, skin-on chicken thighs
Salt to taste
2 tbsp sesame oil
½ cup chicken broth
¼ cup teriyaki sauce

2 tbsp soy sauce
1 large red bell pepper, chopped
1 cup canned mango chunks, drained
1 tsp sesame seeds for garnish

Directions

Season the chicken with salt. Set your Instant Pot to Sauté mode and warm the sesame oil. Cook the chicken for 4 minutes, until golden brown. Remove to a plate.

Pour in the broth to scrape up any browned bits from the bottom. Stir in 2 tbsp of teriyaki sauce and soy sauce. Add in the pepper and return the chicken. Seal the lid, select Manual/Pressure Cook on High, and set time to 10 minutes.

When done, perform a natural pressure release for 10 minutes. Transfer the chicken to a baking sheet. Drizzle with the remaining teriyaki sauce and place under the broiler for 4 minutes, until golden brown.

Add mango chunks to the pot. Press Sauté and cook for 3 minutes until the sauce is thickened. Divide chicken among plates, top with bell pepper and mango, and spoon the sauce over the top. Sprinkle with sesame seeds before serving.

Sweet Chili Chicken Strips

Total Time: 25 minutes | **Servings**: 4 | **Per Serving**: Kcal 563; Carbs 23g; Fat 27g; Protein 55g

Ingredients

¼ cup maple syrup
2 tbsp cornstarch, divided
Salt to taste
1 lb chicken tenders, sliced
2 tbsp sesame oil
½ cup soy sauce

2 tbsp sweet chili sauce
¼ tsp red pepper flakes
2 tbsp water
2 tsp sesame seeds
3 scallions, chopped for garnish

Directions

Mix 1 tbsp of cornstarch with salt in a bowl. Add in the chicken and toss to coat. Set your Instant Pot to Sauté and heat 1 tbsp of the sesame oil, cook the chicken for 4 minutes, until golden brown.

In a separate bowl, mix the soy sauce, chili sauce, and red pepper flakes. Pour the mixture over the chicken. Seal the lid, select Manual/Pressure Cook on High, and set time to 5 minutes.

When done, perform a quick pressure. Stir in the remaining sesame oil and maple syrup. Set to Sauté. In a bowl, combine the remaining cornstarch with water. Pour the slurry in the pot and cook for 2 minutes, stirring frequently until it reaches the desired consistency. Top with sesame seeds and scallions to serve.

Parsley Chicken & Vegetable Rice

Total Time: 30 minutes | **Servings**: 4 | **Per Serving**: Kcal 178; Carbs 19g; Fat 3g; Protein 19g

Ingredients

4 chicken breast halves
1 bunch parsley
2 cups water
½ tbsp butter
1 cup pearl onions, halved
2 cloves garlic, minced

1 carrot, chopped
1 cup rice
1 cup celery, chopped
1 cup red bell peppers, chopped
Salt and black pepper to taste
1 cup frozen peas

Directions

Rub the chicken with salt and pepper on all sides. Set aside. Set your Instant Pot to Sauté and melt the butter. Place in onions and garlic and sauté for 3 minutes, until slightly brown, stirring occasionally.

Pour in rice, salt, pepper, frozen peas, and water and stir. Put in the chopped vegetables and top with the chicken. Seal the lid, select Manual/Pressure Cook on High, and set time to 8 minutes. When done, perform natural pressure release for 10 minutes, then a quick pressure release to let out the remaining steam. Unlock the lid and remove the chicken to shred it using two forks. Then, return it to the pot and mix well. Serve immediately topped with parsley.

Cilantro & Lime Chicken Pilaf

Total Time: 40 minutes | **Servings**: 4 | **Per Serving**: Kcal 545; Carbs 23g; Fat 28g; Protein 32g

Ingredients

2 tbsp avocado oil
1 red onion, chopped
1 yellow bell pepper, chopped
1 tbsp cayenne powder
1 tsp ground cumin
1 tsp Italian herb mix
Salt to taste

1 cup basmati rice
1 ¼ cups chicken broth
½ cup tomato sauce
1 pound bone-in, skin-on chicken thighs
Chopped fresh cilantro, for garnish
Lime wedges, for serving

Directions

Select Sauté mode on your Instant Pot. Heat avocado oil and cook onion, chicken thighs, bell pepper, cayenne pepper, cumin, herb mix, and salt, for 5 minutes, stirring occasionally. Pour in the rice, chicken broth, and tomato sauce.

Seal the lid, select Manual/Pressure Cook on High, and set the cooking time to 25 minutes. When the time is over, perform a quick pressure release and unlock the lid. Garnish with cilantro and serve with lime wedges.

Southwestern Chicken in Green Chile Salsa

Total Time: 25 minutes | **Servings**: 4 | **Per Serving**: Kcal 451; Carbs 44g; Fat 20g; Protein 31g

Ingredients

30 oz canned roasted bell peppers, drained
1 pound bone-in, skin-on chicken legs
1 (15-oz) jar green chile salsa
1 cup chopped canned green chiles
1 chopped serrano pepper

1 onion, chopped
4 tsp minced garlic
Salt and black pepper to taste
2 tbsp fresh cilantro, chopped for garnish

Directions

Mix the chicken, salsa verde, bell peppers, green chiles, serrano, onion, garlic, cumin, and salt in your Instant Pot; stir to combine. Seal the lid, select Manual/Pressure Cook on High, and set time to 15 minutes.

When done, perform a quick pressure to let out steam. Remove the chicken to a plate. Discard the bones and skin and let cool before cutting into small pieces. Bring the chicken back to the pot and stir. Serve with scattered cilantro.

Jalapeño & Serrano Peppered Chicken

Total Time: 35 minutes | **Servings**: 4 | **Per Serving**: Kcal 349; Carbs 26g; Fat 9g; Protein 41g

Ingredients

1 tbsp olive oil
12 oz, baby plum tomatoes, halved
¾ cup chicken stock
Salt to taste
½ tsp ground cumin
1 tsp Mexican seasoning mix
1 ½ lb boneless skinless chicken breasts

2 jalapeño peppers, seeded and chopped
2 large serrano pepper, seeded chopped
2 garlic cloves, minced
1 onion, sliced
¼ cup minced fresh cilantro
½ cup shredded cheddar cheese
½ lime, juiced

Directions

Select Sauté on your Instant Pot and heat the olive oil. Add the plum tomatoes; cook without turning, for 3-4 minutes. Add in the chicken stock while scraping the bottom of the pot to dissolve any browned bits. Stir in cumin, Mexican seasoning, and salt. Add chicken, jalapeños, serrano peppers, garlic, and onion.

Seal the lid, select Manual/Pressure Cook on High, and set the cooking time to 15 minutes. After cooking, perform a natural pressure release for 5 minutes. Take out the chicken and set aside.

With an immersion blender, purée the vegetables. Shred the chicken with two forks and return the pieces to sauce. Add the lime juice. Serve the chili in bowls sprinkled with cheddar cheese and cilantro.

Tandoori Chicken Thighs

Total Time: 25 min + marinating time | **Servings**: 4 | **Per Serving**: Kcal 725; Carbs 49g; Fat 43g; Protein 37g

Ingredients

1 ½ lb chicken thighs
Salt and black pepper to taste
1 cup plain Greek yogurt
1 ½ tsp garlic puree
1 tbsp ginger puree
1 tsp sweet paprika
½ tsp chili pepper powder

½ tsp garam masala
½ tsp ground cumin
1 tsp turmeric powder
1 cup long-grain rice
¾ cup coconut milk
½ cup lima beans
1 tbsp chopped fresh parsley

Directions

In a bowl, mix the yogurt, salt, garlic, ginger, paprika, chili pepper, garam masala, cumin, turmeric, and black pepper. Pour the marinade with the chicken in a plastic zipper bag. Seal the bag and rub the marinade on the chicken to coat. Refrigerate for 2-3 hours.

Pour rice into the Instant Pot's inner pot and mix in coconut milk, lima beans, 1 cup of water, and salt. Place a trivet over the rice. Remove chicken from the marinade and arrange it on the greased trivet in a single layer. Seal the lid, select Manual/Pressure Cook on High, and set time to 12 minutes. After cooking, perform natural pressure release for 10 minutes. Serve garnished with parsley.

Chicken & Broccoli Bulgur

Total Time: 20 minutes | **Servings**: 2 | **Per Serving**: Kcal 543; Carbs 33g; Fat 39g; Protein 43g

Ingredients

1 cup basmati bulgur
1 head broccoli, cut into florets
2 tbsp butter
Salt and black pepper to taste

4 boneless, skinless chicken tenders
1 tbsp sesame seeds, for garnish
2 tbsp sliced green onions, for garnish

Directions

On your Instant Pot, select Sauté. Melt the butter and cook the chicken for 5 minutes in total. Add in the bulgur and stir for 2 minutes, then pour in 2 cups of water. Season with salt and pepper.

Seal the lid, select Manual/Pressure Cook on High, and set the cooking time to 5 minutes. When done cooking, perform a quick pressure release, and unlock the lid.

Place a trivet over the rice and arrange the broccoli on top. Seal the lid, select Manual/Pressure Cook, and cook for 3 minutes on High. Once ready, do a quick pressure release. Spoon the dish into serving plates and top with broccoli. Top with the sesame seeds and green onions and serve.

Korean Spicy Chicken

Total Time: 50 minutes | **Servings**: 4 | **Per Serving**: Kcal 536; Carbs 59g; Fat 22g; Protein 24g

Ingredients

2 tbsp olive oil
2 lb boneless, skinless chicken thighs
½ cup chili sauce
½ cup chicken broth
2 tbsp vinegar

1 tsp kimchi spice
Salt and black pepper to taste
1 onion, chopped
4 green onions, sliced
2 tbsp sesame seeds

Directions

Set your Instant Pot to Sauté and heat olive oil. Place in the chicken and cook for 3 per side minutes until browned. Season with kimchi, salt, and pepper. In a bowl, mix onion, chili sauce, broth, and vinegar and pour over the chicken.

Seal the lid, select Manual/Pressure Cook on High, and set cooking time to 25 minutes. When done cooking, perform natural pressure release for 10 minutes, then a quick pressure release to let out the remaining steam. Unlock the lid and garnish with green onions and sesame seeds. Serve immediately.

Hot Crispy Chicken with Carrots & Potatoes

Total Time: 35 minutes | **Servings**: 4 | **Per Serving**: Kcal 411; Carbs 25g; Fat 24g; Protein 25g

Ingredients

4 bone-in skin-on chicken thighs
Salt to taste
2 tbsp melted butter
2 tsp Worcestershire sauce
2 tsp turmeric powder
1 tsp dried oregano
½ tsp dry mustard

½ tsp garlic powder
¼ tsp sweet paprika
2 dashes hot sauce
½ cup chicken stock
1 tbsp olive oil
1 lb potatoes, quartered
2 carrots, sliced into rounds

Directions

In a small bowl, mix the melted butter, Worcestershire sauce, turmeric, oregano, dry mustard, garlic powder, sweet paprika, and hot sauce until well combined and stir in the chicken stock.

On the Instant Pot, select Sauté. Heat olive oil and add the chicken thighs to fry for 4-5 minutes or until browned. Season with salt. Remove from the pot. Add the potatoes and carrots.

Pour in about half of the hot sauce and mix to coat. Put the chicken thighs on top and drizzle with the remaining sauce. Seal the lid, select Manual/Pressure Cook on High, and set the cooking time to 15 minutes. After cooking, do a quick pressure release and unlock the lid. Serve.

Wine Chicken with Mushrooms & Brussel Sprouts

Total Time: 35 minutes | **Servings**: 4 | **Per Serving**: Kcal 546; Carbs 6g; Fat 41g; Protein 37g

Ingredients

4 chicken thighs, bone-in skin-on
1 tbsp olive oil
½ small onion, sliced
½ cup dry white wine
½ cup chicken stock
1 cup halved Brussel sprouts

1 bay leaf
¼ tsp dried rosemary
Salt and black pepper to taste
1 cup mushrooms
¼ cup heavy cream

Directions

Season the chicken on both sides with salt. On the Instant Pot, select Sauté and heat olive oil. Add the chicken thighs and fry for 5 minutes or until browned. Remove to a plate. Sauté the onion for about 2 minutes to soften. Stir in the white wine and bring to a boil for 2 to 3 minutes or until reduced by half.

Mix in chicken stock, Brussel sprouts, mushrooms, bay leaf, rosemary, salt, and pepper. Arrange chicken thighs on top. Seal the lid, select Manual/Pressure Cook on High, and set time to 15 minutes. When ready, perform a quick pressure release; remove bay leaf. Stir in heavy cream and serve.

BBQ Chicken & Kale Quesadillas

Total Time: 20 minutes | **Servings**: 4 | **Per Serving**: Kcal 521; Carbs 36g; Fat 33g; Protein 21g

Ingredients

¼ cup butter
2 cups baby kale, chopped
1 jalapeño pepper, minced
1 onion, chopped
3 oz cottage cheese, at room temperature

2 tsp Mexican seasoning mix
1 cup shredded cooked chicken
6 oz shredded cheddar cheese
4 medium flour tortillas
¼ cup grated Pecorino Romano cheese

Directions

On your Instant Pot, select Sauté and melt 1 tbsp of butter. Add the kale, jalapeño pepper, and onion, and cook for 3-4 minutes, stirring occasionally, until the vegetables soften. Mix in the cottage cheese to melt and add the Mexican seasoning and chicken. Stir to combine. Spoon the filling into a large bowl and stir in cheddar cheese. Set aside.

Place a tortilla on a clean flat surface. Brush the top with olive oil and sprinkle 1 tsp of Pecorino Romano cheese on top. Press the cheese down with the palm of your hand to stick to the tortilla.

Spread about a 1/3 cup of filling over half the tortilla. Fold the other half over the filling and press gently. Repeat the process with the remaining tortillas. Serve with guacamole.

Chicken Shawarma Wraps

Total Time: 30 minutes + marinating time | **Servings**: 4 | **Per Serving**: Kcal 329; Carbs 8g; Fat 14g; Protein 41g

Ingredients

1 ½ lb boneless skinless chicken breasts
2 tbsp olive oil, divided
2 tbsp yogurt
2 tbsp freshly squeezed lemon juice
3 garlic cloves, minced
1 tsp ground cumin

¼ tsp cinnamon powder
1 tsp smoked paprika
¼ tsp turmeric
Salt and black pepper to taste
¼ tsp cayenne pepper
4 lettuce leaves

For the Sauce

½ cup yogurt
Salt to taste
1 tsp olive oil

1 small garlic clove, minced
2 tbsp Italian herb mix
1 tbsp chopped fresh cilantro

To Assemble

2 large tomatoes, sliced

½ medium cucumber, sliced

Directions

In a bowl, evenly mix the olive oil, yogurt, lemon juice, garlic, cumin, cinnamon, paprika, turmeric, black pepper, and cayenne pepper. Pour the marinade with the chicken in a plastic zipper bag. Seal the bag and massage to coat the chicken thoroughly with the marinade. Refrigerate for 1 hour to marinate.

Pour 1 cup water in the Instant Pot and insert a trivet. Place chicken on top, seal the lid, select Manual/Pressure Cook on High, and set the cooking time to 15 minutes. When ready, do a quick pressure release. Let chicken cool slightly before shredding it with 2 forks.

To prepare the sauce: whisk the sauce ingredients in a bowl until combined. Spread 1 to 2 tbsp of yogurt sauce onto one half of a lettuce leaf. Spoon in some chicken and add the tomato and cucumber slices. Wrap the leaf over the filling, repeat the assembling process for the remaining leaves and serve.

Chicken with Rosemary Dumplings

Total Time: 35 minutes | **Servings**: 4 | **Per Serving**: Kcal 296; Carbs 16g; Fat 13g; Protein 28g

Ingredients

1 tbsp coconut oil
1 white onion, chopped
2 carrots, chopped
2 celery stalks, chopped
1 lb skinless, boneless chicken breasts, cubed
2 cups chicken stock

Salt to taste
½ cup half-and-half
1 cup flour
½ cup butter, softened
2 tbsp rosemary, chopped

Directions

Select Sauté to preheat your Instant Pot. Melt the coconut oil and sauté onion, carrots, celery, and chicken and cook for 5 minutes, stirring frequently. Pour in the stock and season with salt. Seal the lid, select Manual/Pressure Cook on High, and set the cooking time to 6 minutes.

Whisk together the flour, rosemary, 2 tbsp of water, butter, and salt in a bowl. Mix with a wooden spoon until well combined. Shape the mixture into balls and set aside. When done cooking, perform a quick pressure release, and unlock the lid. Stir in the half-and-half. Drop the dumpling over the top and cook for 10 minutes on Sauté. Serve.

Mayan Enchilada Chicken

Total Time: 20 minutes | **Servings**: 4 | **Per Serving**: Kcal 436; Carbs 5g; Fat 29g; Protein 31g

Ingredients

½ cup chicken broth

4 chicken breasts, cut into 1-inch cubes

1 ½ tsp dried oregano

1 ½ tsp cumin powder

1 ½ cups red enchilada sauce

Directions

In inner pot, combine broth, chicken, oregano, cumin powder, and enchilada sauce. Seal the lid, select Manual/Pressure Cook on High, and set cooking time to 10 minutes. After cooking, perform a natural pressure release for 5 minutes, then a quick pressure release to let out remaining steam. Unlock the lid, stir, and serve chicken with sauce.

Herbed Chicken & Biscuit Chili

Total Time: 25 minutes | **Servings**: 6 | **Per Serving**: Kcal 324; Carbs 17g; Fat 12g; Protein 22g

Ingredients

1 tbsp olive oil

1 onion, chopped

2 garlic cloves, minced

1 ½ lb ground chicken

1 tbsp ground cilantro

1 tbsp dried oregano

4 cups chicken broth

Salt and black pepper to taste

1 package refrigerated biscuits

Directions

Select Sauté on your Instant Pot. Heat the olive oil and add the ground chicken, onion, and garlic; sauté until the onion is softened, about 3 minutes. Add in cilantro, oregano, broth, salt, and black pepper. Spread the biscuits in a single layer over the chili.

Seal the lid, select Manual/Pressure Cook on High, and set the cooking time to 10 minutes. When the time is over, perform a quick pressure release, and unlock the lid. Serve.

Quick Chicken Fried Rice with Vegetables

Total Time: 35 minutes | **Servings**: 4 | **Per Serving**: Kcal 487; Carbs 32g; Fat 12g; Protein 18g

Ingredients

1 tbsp canola oil

1 onion, chopped

4 garlic cloves, minced

1 lb boneless, skinless chicken breasts, chopped

Salt and black pepper to taste

2 cups chicken broth

¼ cup coconut aminos

1 cup long-grain rice

1 (16-oz) bag frozen mixed vegetables

Directions

Set Sauté mode on your Instant Pot. Heat oil and cook the onion and garlic for 3 minutes, until fragrant. Put chicken in the pot and season with the salt and black pepper. Cook for 5 minutes, until browned.

Pour in chicken broth, coconut aminos, and rice. Seal the lid, select Manual/Pressure Cook on High, and set cooking time to 8 minutes. When done, perform a quick pressure release. Pour in the frozen vegetables. Select Sauté and cook for 5 minutes, stirring occasionally. Serve immediately.

Classic Coq Au Vin

Total Time: 45 minutes | **Servings**: 4 | **Per Serving**: Kcal 407; Carbs 5g; Fat 15g; Protein 56g

Ingredients

4 chicken leg quarters, skin on
1 tbsp olive oil
4 serrano ham slices, cut into thirds
1 onion, sliced
1 ¼ cups dry red wine
½ cup chicken stock

1 ½ tsp tomato puree
½ tsp brown sugar
Salt and black pepper to taste
½ cup mushrooms
¾ cup shallots, sliced

Directions

On your Instant Pot, select Sauté and heat the olive oil. Place the ham in the pot in a single layer and cook for 4 minutes or until browned. Remove to a plate. Add in the chicken.

Cook for 5 minutes or until the skin is golden brown. Set aside. Stir in onion, mushrooms and shallots and cook until the onion begins to brown, about 4 minutes.

Add ½ cup of red wine, stir, and scrape the bottom of the pot to let off any browned bits. Boil the mixture until the wine reduces by about 1/3, about 2 minutes. Pour in the remaining red wine, stock, tomato puree, brown sugar, and black pepper. Boil the sauce for 1 minute.

Return in the chicken pieces with skin-side up. Seal the lid, select Manual/Pressure Cook on High, and set the cooking time to 12 minutes. After cooking, perform a natural pressure release for 10 minutes. Plate the dish and crumble the reserved ham on top.

Buffalo-Blue Cheese Chicken

Total Time: 40 minutes | **Servings**: 4 | **Per Serving**: Kcal 521; Carbs 19g; Fat 32g; Protein 34g

Ingredients

1 large white onion, chopped
2 celery stalks, chopped
½ cup buffalo sauce

½ cup chicken broth
4 chicken breasts
¼ cup crumbled blue cheese

Directions

In inner pot, combine onion, celery, buffalo sauce, broth, and chicken. Seal the lid, select Manual/Pressure Cook on High, and set cooking time to 12 minutes. After cooking, perform a natural pressure release for 10 minutes, then a quick pressure release to let out remaining steam, and unlock the lid.

Select Sauté mode and remove chicken onto a plate. Shred chicken into strands and return to sauce. Stir in blue cheese and cook further for 3 minutes. Dish food and serve warm.

Restaurant-Style Chicken with Frijoles

Total Time: 45 minutes | **Servings**: 4 | **Per Serving**: Kcal 368; Carbs 18g; Fat 21g; Protein 28g

Ingredients

4 chicken thighs, bone-in skin-on
Salt and black pepper to taste
2 pancetta slices, cut into thirds
1 medium carrot, chopped

½ small onion, chopped
½ cup dry red wine
1 cup pinto beans Frijoles, soaked
3 cups chicken stock

Directions

Season the chicken on both sides with salt and black pepper. On the Instant Pot, select Sauté and add the pancetta slices; cook for 5 minutes or until browned. Remove pancetta to a paper towel-lined plate. Put the thighs in the pot and fry for about 6-7 minutes or until golden brown on both sides. Set aside.

Sauté carrot and onion in the same fat for 3 minutes. Stir in the wine while scraping off the brown bits at the bottom. Allow boiling until the wine reduces by one-third and stir in the beans and chicken stock. Return the chicken.

Seal the lid, select Manual/Pressure Cook on High, and set the time to 25 minutes. When done, do a quick pressure release. Scatter the pancetta over the cassoulet and serve.

Easy Chicken Stroganoff with Fettucini

Total Time: 35 minutes | **Servings**: 4 | **Per Serving**: Kcal 412; Carbs 18g; Fat 18g; Protein 43g

Ingredients

2 boneless skinless chicken breasts
Salt to taste
2 tbsp butter
½ cup sliced onion
1 tbsp flour
½ cup dry white wine

2 cups chicken stock
8 oz fettucini
½ tsp Worcestershire sauce
1 cup white mushrooms, sliced
¼ cup heavy cream
2 tbsp chopped dill to garnish

Directions

Select Sauté on your Instant Pot and melt the butter. Sauté onion until brown, about 3 minutes. Mix in flour to make a roux, about 2 minutes, and gradually pour in the dry white wine while stirring and scraping the bottom of the pot to release any browned bits.

Allow the white wine to reduce by two-thirds. Pour in 1 ½ cups of water, stock, salt, fettucini, and mushrooms. Arrange the chicken on top and season with salt.

Seal the lid, select Manual/Pressure Cook on High, and set the time to 15 minutes. When done, perform a quick pressure release. Transfer chicken to a cutting board to cool slightly and then cut into bite-size chunks.

Then, return the chicken to the pot and stir in the Worcestershire sauce and mushrooms. Add heavy cream and cook until the mixture stops simmering. Ladle the stroganoff into bowls and garnish with dill.

Sweet Sesame Chicken Wings

Total Time: 25 minutes | **Servings**: 4 | **Per Serving**: Kcal 326; Carbs 10g; Fat 14g; Protein 39g

Ingredients

24 chicken wings
2 tbsp sesame oil
2 tbsp hot garlic sauce

2 tbsp honey
2 garlic cloves, minced
1 tbsp toasted sesame seeds

Directions

Pour 1 cup of water into your Instant Pot and put in a trivet. Place the chicken wings on the trivet.

Seal the lid, select Manual/Pressure Cook on High, and set the cooking time to 10 minutes. After cooking, perform a quick pressure release, and unlock the lid. Remove the trivet and discard the water.

In a large bowl, whisk the sesame oil, hot garlic sauce, honey, and garlic. Toss the wings in the sauce and put them in the pot. Press Sauté and cook for 5 minutes. Sprinkle with the sesame seeds to serve.

Turkey, Duck & Goose Recipes

Turkey Thighs in Dijon Gravy

Total Time: 60 minutes | **Servings**: 4 | **Per Serving**: Kcal 312; Carbs 7g; Fat 14g; Protein 37g

Ingredients

1 tbsp avocado oil
1 ½ lb turkey thighs, boneless and skinless
Salt and black pepper to taste
2 white onions, thinly sliced
3 garlic, minced
½ cup white wine

½ cup chicken broth
2 tbsp Dijon mustard
1 tsp dried rosemary
1 tbsp all-purpose flour
1 tbsp chopped parsley for garnishing

Directions

Set your Instant Pot to Sauté mode and adjust to medium heat. Heat avocado oil in inner pot, season turkey with salt and black pepper, and sear turkey on both sides until golden brown, 6 minutes. Plate and set aside.

Cook onion and garlic until softened and stir in white wine, chicken broth, Dijon mustard, and rosemary. Once simmering, lay in turkey. Seal the lid, select Manual/Pressure Cook mode on High, and set cooking time to 30 minutes.

After cooking, perform natural pressure release for 10 minutes, then quick pressure release to let out all the steam. Unlock the lid and choose Sauté mode. Remove turkey onto serving plates and set aside for serving.

Mix flour into sauce and cook until thickened, 1 minute. Adjust taste with salt and black pepper if needed. Stir in parsley and spoon gravy all over turkey. Serve food warm with mashed potatoes, or rice.

Ground Turkey Lentil Chili

Total Time: 50 minutes | **Servings**: 4 | **Per Serving**: Kcal 728; Carbs 29g; Fat 57g; Protein 30g

Ingredients

1 lb ground turkey
1 medium yellow onion, diced
2 garlic cloves, minced
2 tbsp tomato paste
Salt and black pepper to taste
1 cup dry green lentils
2 cups chicken broth

1 (8 oz) can tomato sauce
1 (14.5 oz) can chopped tomatoes
1 (4 oz) can green chilies, chopped
1 tsp cumin powder
2 tsp chili powder
¼ cup grated cheddar cheese

Directions

Set your Instant Pot to Sauté mode and adjust to medium heat. Brown turkey in inner pot for 6 minutes and top with onion, garlic, tomato paste, salt, and black pepper. Stir and cook until onions soften, 3 minutes.

Mix in lentils, chicken broth, tomato sauce, tomatoes, green chilies, and cumin. Seal the lid, select Manual/Pressure Cook mode on High, and set cooking time to 15 minutes.

Allow Instant Pot to sit uncovered for 10 minutes, perform natural pressure release for 10 minutes and then a quick pressure release, and unlock the lid. Stir in chili, adjust taste with salt and black pepper, and dish. Top with cheddar cheese and serve warm.

Hungarian Turkey Goulash

Total Time: 40 minutes | **Servings**: 4 | **Per Serving**: Kcal 549; Carbs 28g; Fat 24g; Protein 55g

Ingredients

2 tbsp olive oil
1 lb turkey breast, cubed
Salt and black pepper to taste
3 yellow onions, chopped
2 carrots, peeled and diced
3 red bell peppers, deseeded and chopped
2 yellow bell peppers, deseeded and chopped
2 garlic cloves, minced
2 tbsp tomato paste
1 tsp cumin powder

2 tbsp paprika powder
1 tsp caraway powder
1 tbsp dried mixed herbs
2 cups vegetable stock
1 ½ cups Guinness stout
2 tbsp all-purpose flour
2 tbsp tomato ketchup
¼ tsp chili powder
2 tbsp chopped parsley

Directions

Set your Instant Pot to Sauté mode and adjust to medium heat. Heat olive oil in inner pot, season turkey with salt and black pepper, and sear in the oil on both sides until golden brown, 6 minutes. Plate and set aside.

Sauté onions, carrots, and bell peppers until softened, 5 minutes. Add garlic and allow releasing of fragrance, 30 seconds. Stir in tomato paste, cumin, paprika, and caraway powder. Allow flavors to combine, 1 minute while frequently stirring. Add mixed herbs, turkey, stock, and Guinness stout.

Seal the lid, select Manual/Pressure Cook on High, and set time to 4 minutes. After cooking, perform natural pressure release for 10 minutes, a quick pressure release, and unlock the lid. Mix in flour, tomato ketchup, chili powder, and adjust taste with salt and black pepper. Select Sauté and cook until sauce thickens. Stir in parsley and serve over rice.

Hot Turkey in Orange-Ginger Sauce

Total Time: 35 min + marinating time | **Servings**: 4 | **Per Serving**: Kcal 484; Carbs 22g; Fat 25g; Protein 40g

Ingredients

1 ¼ cups orange juice
¼ cup soy sauce
3 tbsp grated ginger
3 tbsp olive oil
2 tbsp garlic paste
1 ½ tbsp plain vinegar
2 tsp orange zest

2 tsp honey
¼ tsp white pepper
2 tbsp hot sauce
1 lb turkey breast fillets
1 cup chicken broth
1 tbsp cornstarch
3 scallions, thinly sliced

Directions

In a medium bowl, combine orange juice, soy sauce, ginger, half of olive oil, garlic, vinegar, orange zest, honey, white pepper, and hot sauce. Place turkey in marinade, cover with plastic wrap and marinate in refrigerator for 1 hour.

Set your Instant Pot to Sauté mode and adjust to medium heat. Heat remaining olive oil in inner pot, remove turkey from fridge and marinade (shaking off as much marinade as possible) and sear in oil until golden brown on both sides, 6 minutes. Pour in remaining marinade and chicken broth. Stir.

Seal the lid, select Manual/Pressure Cook mode on High, and set cooking time to 4 minutes. After cooking, allow sitting for 5 minutes, then perform natural pressure release for 10 minutes.

Unlock the lid, stir in cornstarch, and set to Sauté mode. Cook until sauce thickens, 1 minute. Spoon turkey with sauce over beds of rice, garnish with scallions, and serve warm.

Macaroni with Turkey Meatballs in Tomato Sauce

Total Time: 20 minutes | **Servings**: 4 | **Per Serving**: Kcal 717; Carbs 89g; Fat 16g; Protein 46g

Ingredients

2 cups chicken broth

4 tbsp tomato paste

¼ cup chopped basil

1 tsp oregano

1 tsp onion powder

¼ tsp red chili flakes

5 garlic cloves, minced

24 frozen turkey meatballs

10 oz macaroni

1 (25 oz) jar tomato sauce

Salt and black pepper to taste

¼ cup grated Parmesan cheese

Directions

In inner pot, add chicken broth and stir in tomato paste until properly combined. Add basil, oregano, onion powder, chili flakes, garlic, meatballs, macaroni, and tomato sauce. Stir, making sure not to break the meatballs.

Seal the lid, select Manual/Pressure Cook mode, and set cooking time to 3 minutes. After cooking, perform natural pressure release for 10 minutes, then quick pressure release to let out remaining steam. Unlock the lid, gently stir and adjust taste with salt and black pepper. Garnish with Parmesan cheese and serve warm.

Basil Fettuccine Turkey Bolognese

Total Time: 25 minutes | **Servings**: 4 | **Per Serving**: Kcal 592; Carbs 20g; Fat 32g; Protein 53g

Ingredients

1 tbsp olive oil

1 lb ground turkey

Salt and black pepper to taste

1 large yellow onion, chopped

1 celery stalk, chopped

1 large carrot, peeled and chopped

1 garlic clove, minced

1 (25 oz) jar marinara sauce

2 cups chicken broth

8 oz fettuccine pasta

¼ cup grated Parmesan cheese for topping

2 tbsp basil, chopped

Directions

Set your Instant Pot to Sauté mode and adjust to medium heat. Heat olive oil in inner pot, season turkey with salt and black pepper, and cook with frequent stirring until brown, 5 minutes. Add onion, celery, carrot, and garlic; cook until vegetables soften, 3 minutes.

Stir in marinara sauce, chicken broth, salt, black pepper, and fettuccine. Seal the lid, select Manual/Pressure Cook mode, and set cooking time to 4 minutes. After cooking, perform a quick pressure release to let out steam. Unlock the lid, stir, and plate. Top with Parmesan cheese and basil to serve.

Bell Peppers Stuffed with Turkey & Cauliflower Rice

Total Time: 35 minutes | **Servings**: 4 | **Per Serving**: Kcal 413; Carbs 34g; Fat 13g; Protein 42g

Ingredients

1 lb ground turkey

¾ cup cauliflower rice

¼ cup seasoned breadcrumbs

¾ cup tomato sauce

¼ cup finely chopped yellow onion

¼ cup grated Parmesan cheese

3 tbsp chopped parsley

Salt and black pepper to taste

4 mixed bell peppers, top removed and deseeded

¼ cup grated mozzarella cheese

½ cup water

Directions

In a medium bowl, combine turkey, cauliflower rice, breadcrumbs, tomato sauce, yellow onion, Parmesan cheese, parsley, salt, and black pepper. Stuff peppers with the mixture and cover with mozzarella cheese.

Pour water into inner pot, fit in a trivet, and carefully place bell peppers on top. Seal the lid, select Manual/Pressure Cook mode, and set cooking time to 15 minutes.

Perform natural pressure release for 10 minutes, then quick pressure release to let out remaining steam. Unlock the lid and carefully remove peppers. Plate and serve warm.

Flavorful Turkey & Spinach Chowder

Total Time: 30 minutes | **Servings**: 4 | **Per Serving**: Kcal 444; Carbs 43g; Fat 16g; Protein 30g

Ingredients

2 tbsp olive oil
1 link turkey sausages, thinly sliced
½ cup chopped green onions
2 tbsp red chili flakes
1 cup short-grain rice

2 cups chicken broth
1 tbsp Old Bay Seasoning
Salt and black pepper to taste
2 cups baby spinach
2 tbsp chopped basil

Directions

Set your Instant Pot to Sauté mode and adjust to medium heat. Heat olive oil in inner pot and fry sausages until brown on both sides, 5 minutes. Stir in onions and red chili flakes; cook until onions soften, 3 minutes.

Mix in rice, allow heating for 1 minute and stir in chicken broth, Old Bay seasoning, salt, and black pepper. Seal the lid, select Manual/Pressure Cook mode on High, and set cooking time to 5 minutes.

After cooking, allow sitting (covered) for 5 minutes and then perform a quick pressure release to let out steam. Unlock the lid and select Sauté mode. Mix in spinach and cook until softened, 5 minutes. Dish chowder into serving bowls and garnish with basil. Serve warm.

Jamaican-Style Turkey Tacos

Total Time: 35 minutes | **Servings**: 4 | **Per Serving**: Kcal 497; Carbs 49g; Fat 15g; Protein 42g

Ingredients

2 tbsp Jamaican jerk seasoning
¼ cup mayonnaise
2 tbsp honey
2 tbsp lime juice
1 tsp ginger puree
1 tsp dried thyme
¼ cup chicken broth

2 turkey breasts, cubed
½ cup celery, thinly sliced
1 cup chopped pineapple
4 flour tortillas
2 limes, cut into wedges for serving
1 tbsp chopped cilantro for serving

Directions

In inner pot, mix Jamaican seasoning, mayonnaise, honey, lime juice, ginger puree, thyme, and chicken broth. Place in turkey, celery, and pineapple. Coat well with sauce. Seal the lid, select Manual/Pressure Cook mode on High, and set cooking time to 10 minutes.

After cooking, allow sitting for 5 minutes, perform natural pressure release for 10 minutes, and then quick pressure to let out remaining steam. Unlock the lid, stir and spoon taco filling into tortillas. Garnish with cilantro and serve warm with lime wedges.

Mediterranean Turkey Soup

Total Time: 35 minutes | **Servings**: 4 | **Per Serving**: Kcal 561; Carbs 31g; Fat 33g; Protein 36g

Ingredients

1 pound hot turkey sausage
2 tbsp olive oil
3 celery stalks, chopped
3 garlic cloves, chopped
1 red onion, chopped
Salt to taste
½ cup dry white wine

4 cups chicken broth
½ tsp fennel seeds
1 (15-oz) can cannellini beans, rinsed
9 oz refrigerated tortellini
1 Parmesan cheese rind
2 cups chopped spinach
½ cup grated Parmesan cheese

Directions

On your Instant Pot, select Sauté and heat olive oil; cook the sausage for 4 minutes, until golden brown. Stir in the celery, garlic, and onion, season with salt, and cook for 3 minutes. Pour in the wine. Scrape the bottom of the pot to let off any browned bits. Add the chicken broth, fennel seeds, tortellini, Parmesan rind, cannellini beans, and spinach.

Seal the lid, select Manual/Pressure Cook on High, and set the cooking time to 10 minutes. Once done, perform a natural pressure release for 10 minutes. Ladle the soup into bowls and sprinkle with the grated cheese and serve.

Terrific Holiday Turkey with Cranberry Gravy

Total Time: 55 minutes | **Servings**: 4 | **Per Serving**: Kcal 447; Carbs 9g; Fat 22g; Protein 51g

Ingredients

2 tbsp butter, melted
2 pounds bone-in turkey breast
4 tsp poultry seasoning
Salt and black pepper to taste

1 cup chicken broth
2 tbsp flour
½ cup white wine
2 tbsp cranberry sauce

Directions

In a bowl, combine the poultry seasoning, salt, and black pepper. Use about half of the seasoning to rub the turkey. In your Instant Pot, pour chicken broth and fit in a trivet. Lay the turkey on the trivet. Seal the lid, select Manual/Pressure Cook on High, and cook for 15 minutes. When done, perform a natural pressure release for 10 minutes.

Preheat the oven to 400 °F.

Combine the remaining seasoning mix with the butter. Transfer the turkey to a baking sheet and brush with the butter mix. Bake for 10 minutes, until brown.

Take out the trivet from the pot and press Sauté. In a bowl, combine the flour, wine, cranberry sauce, and the ½ cup of the cooking juices from the pot and stir well. Throw the mixture into the pot and cook for 3-5 minutes, until the sauce has thickened. Remove the turkey from the oven and let sit for 10 minutes before slicing. Serve with the sauce.

Cheesy Turkey Pearl Barley

Total Time: 20 minutes | **Servings**: 4 | **Per Serving**: Kcal 414; Carbs 42g; Fat 12g; Protein 35g

Ingredients

1 cup pearl barley
4 cups chicken broth
Salt and black pepper to taste

1 pound turkey breasts, cubed
1 broccoli head, cut into florets
1 ½ cups shredded gouda cheese

Directions

Place the broth, pearl barley, salt, pepper, and turkey in your Instant Pot. Seal the lid, select Manual/Pressure Cook mode on High, and set time to 10 minutes.

When done, perform a quick pressure to let out steam and unlock the lid. Press Sauté and add the broccoli; cook for 4 minutes. Scatter shredded gouda cheese over the top and serve.

Turkey & Brown Rice Salad with Peanuts

Total Time: 35 minutes | **Servings:** 4 | **Per Serving:** Kcal 407; Carbs 24g; Fat 21g; Protein 31g

Ingredients

1 cup brown rice
1 lb turkey breast tenderloin
3 tsp peanut oil
3 tbsp apple cider vinegar
Salt and black pepper to taste

¼ tsp celery seeds
A pinch of sugar
½ cup peanuts, toasted
3 celery stalks, thinly sliced
1 apple, cored and cubed

Directions

Pour the 2 cups of water into the inner pot. Stir in brown rice and salt. Seal the lid, select Manual/Pressure Cook on High, and set the cooking time to 8 minutes. After cooking, perform a natural pressure release for 10 minutes. Unlock the lid and spoon the rice into a large bowl to cool completely. Season the turkey on both sides with salt; set aside.

Wipe inner pot clean with a napkin and set Instant Pot to Sauté. Heat 2 teaspoons of the peanut oil and put in the turkey. Cook for 7-8 minutes. Pour the remaining peanut oil and the vinegar into a jar with a tight-fitting lid.

Add black pepper, celery seeds, salt, and sugar. Close the jar and shake until the ingredients are properly combined. Transfer the turkey to a plate to cool for several minutes. Cut it into bite-size chunks and add to the rice along with the peanuts, celery stalks, and apple. Pour the dressing over the salad and toss gently to coat. Serve.

Juicy Turkey with Green Peas

Total Time: 60 minutes | **Servings:** 4 | **Per Serving:** Kcal 478; Carbs 11g; Fat 23g; Protein 53g

Ingredients

2 tbsp olive oil
1 (1 oz) package onion soup mix
2 lb turkey breast, sliced
2 ribs celery, chopped
1 onion, chopped

1 cup chicken broth
2 tbsp water
1 tbsp cornstarch
1 cup green peas

Directions

Set your Instant Pot to Sauté and heat olive oil. Add in celery, onion, salt, and pepper, and cook for 3 minutes, until softened. Rub the turkey breast with the onion soup mix and add to the pot; cook for 5 minutes, stirring occasionally. Pour in the chicken broth. Seal the lid, select Poultry, and set cooking time to 30 minutes.

When done cooking, perform natural pressure release for 15 minutes, then a quick pressure release to let out the remaining steam. Unlock the lid and remove the turkey onto a plate.

In a bowl, combine water, cornstarch, and some hot liquid from the pot. Stir until dissolved. Set your pot to Sauté, pour in the cornstarch mixture, and cook for 3 minutes until reduced to a thick consistency. Stir in the green peas and cook for 3-4 minutes. Top the turkey with green peas gravy to serve.

Creamy Turkey & Corn Casserole

Total Time: 35 minutes | **Servings**: 6 | **Per Serving**: Kcal 545; Carbs 30g; Fat 23g; Protein 26g

Ingredients

1 tbsp butter
1 yellow onion, chopped
2 garlic cloves, minced
1 lb boneless, skinless turkey breast
2 cups enchilada sauce

Salt and black pepper to taste
1 (15-oz) can pinto beans, drained
8 tortillas, each cut into 8 pieces
1 (16-oz) bag frozen corn
2 cups shredded Monterey Jack cheese

Directions

Select Sauté to preheat your Instant Pot. Melt the butter and cook the onion and garlic for 3 minutes, stirring occasionally. Put in the turkey and enchilada sauce and season with salt and black pepper. Stir to combine.

Seal the lid, select Manual/Pressure Cook on High, and set time to 15 minutes. When done cooking, perform a quick pressure release and unlock the lid. Shred the turkey with two forks. Mix in the pinto beans, tortilla pieces, corn, and half of the cheese. Serve topped with the remaining cheese.

Buffalo Turkey Sandwiches

Total Time: 30 minutes | **Servings**: 4 | **Per Serving**: Kcal 323; Carbs 37g; Fat 7g; Protein 15g

Ingredients

1 lb turkey breasts, boneless
¼ cup chicken broth
2 tbsp ranch seasoning
½ cup buffalo sauce

Salt and white pepper to taste
4 hamburger buns
¼ cup coleslaw

Directions

In inner pot, add turkey, chicken broth, ranch seasoning, buffalo sauce, salt, and white pepper. Seal the lid, select Manual/Pressure Cook mode on High, and set cooking time to 10 minutes.

After cooking, perform natural pressure release for 10 minutes, then quick pressure release to let out remaining steam, and unlock the lid. Using two forks, shred turkey and give food a good stir. Fill burger buns with turkey accompanied with coleslaw. Serve burgers immediately.

Chinese-Style Duck with Cashew

Total Time: 35 minutes | **Servings**: 4 | **Per Serving**: Kcal 768; Carbs 32g; Fat 44g; Protein 59g

Ingredients

2 tbsp sesame oil
½ cup soy sauce
3 tbsp ketchup
3 tbsp balsamic vinegar
1 tbsp brown sugar
1 tbsp honey
1 tbsp minced ginger
1 tbsp minced garlic
½ tsp Chinese Five Spice powder
½ tsp red chili flakes, or to taste

2 cups chopped smoked duck
1 medium red onion, quartered
2 cups broccoli florets
2 tbsp chicken broth
Salt and black pepper to taste
2 tbsp cornstarch
1 cup cashews
2 tbsp parsley
½ celery cup, chopped

Directions

In a medium bowl, whisk 1 tbsp of sesame oil, soy sauce, ketchup, vinegar, brown sugar, honey, ginger, garlic, Five Spice, and red chili flakes. Set aside.

Set your Instant Pot to Sauté and heat the remaining sesame oil. Cook duck to take on flavor of sesame oil. Stir in onion, celery, and broccoli and cook for 3 minutes. Mix in ketchup mixture and chicken broth. Seal the lid, select Manual/Pressure Cook on High, and set time to 3 minutes. When done, do natural pressure release for 10 minutes.

Unlock the lid; adjust taste with salt and black pepper, and stir in cornstarch and cashews. Select Sauté mode and allow sauce thickening for 1 to 2 minutes. Spoon stew over rice and serve warm.

Smoked Duck Soup

Total Time: 45 minutes | **Servings**: 4 | **Per Serving**: Kcal 602; Carbs 65g; Fat 20g; Protein 34g

Ingredients

2 tbsp melted duck fat
1 lb cremini mushrooms, sliced
¼ cup finely chopped green onions
2 garlic cloves, minced
1 lb smoked duck, cut into small pieces

3 cups chicken broth
1 ½ cups short-grain rice
Salt and black pepper to taste
¾ cup mustard greens, chopped
1 lemon, juiced

Directions

Set your Instant Pot to Sauté mode and adjust to medium heat. Heat duck fat in inner pot and sauté mushrooms and green onions until softened, 3 minutes. Add garlic and cook until fragrant, 30 seconds. Toss duck in vegetables; allow releasing of flavor, and pour chicken broth on top. Add rice, salt, and black pepper.

Seal the lid, select Manual/Pressure Cook mode on High, and set cooking time to 10 minutes. Allow sitting for 10 minutes, perform natural pressure release for 10 minutes, and then a quick pressure release.

Unlock the lid; set to Sauté mode and mix in mustard greens. Allow wilting for 1 to 2 minutes; adjust taste with salt and black pepper and stir in lemon juice. Spoon soup into serving bowls and serve sprinkled with parsley.

Herby Duck with Lemon Gravy

Total Time: 35 minutes | **Servings**: 4 | **Per Serving**: Kcal 232; Carbs 10g; Fat 17g; Protein 11g

Ingredients

2 tbsp duck fat
1 pound duck breast, cut into 1-inch cubes
½ tsp mixed herbs
Salt and black pepper to taste
1 yellow onion, chopped
2 celery stalks, chopped

8 garlic cloves, minced
1 fresh rosemary sprig
1 tbsp tomato paste
1 cup chicken stock
2 lemon, juiced
2 tbsp chopped parsley

Directions

Set your Instant Pot to Sauté mode and adjust to medium heat. Melt duck fat in inner pot, season duck with mixed herbs, salt, and black pepper, and fry in the oil until golden brown on both sides, 8 minutes. Set aside.

Add onion and celery to oil and sauté until softened, 3 minutes. Stir in garlic, rosemary, and cook until fragrant, 30 seconds. Mix in tomato paste and pour in chicken stock. Allow simmering for 1 minute and return duck to pot.

Seal the lid, select Manual/Pressure Cook on High, and set time to 5 minutes. After cooking, perform a quick pressure release. Stir in lemon juice and parsley, and serve duck with gravy. Serve warm with mashed potatoes.

Mushroom Goose Soup

Total Time: 40 min + marinating time | **Servings**: 4 | **Per Serving**: Kcal 649; Carbs 51g; Fat 28g; Protein 47g

Ingredients

¼ cup coconut aminos
2 tsp olive oil
2 tsp freshly squeezed lime juice
1 tsp garlic powder
1 tsp Worcestershire sauce
1 lb cubed goose breast

1 cup all-purpose flour
¼ cup butter, cubed
4 cups chicken broth
1 pack onion soup mix
16 oz egg noodles
2 tbsp chopped oregano

Directions

In a medium bowl, combine coconut aminos, olive oil, lime juice, garlic powder, and Worcestershire sauce. Toss goose in marinade, cover the bowl with plastic wrap, and marinate in refrigerator for at least 4 hours.

Set your Instant Pot to Sauté mode and adjust to medium heat. Melt butter in inner pot; meanwhile, pour flour in a plate, remove goose from marinade (discard marinade), toss in flour, and fry in butter until brown on both sides, 8 minutes. Fetch out most of butter and discard. On goose, pour chicken broth, onion soup mix, and egg noodles.

Seal the lid, select Manual/Pressure Cook mode on High, and set cooking time to 7 minutes. After cooking, perform a natural pressure release for 15 minutes and then a quick pressure release to let out remaining steam and unlock the lid. Stir in oregano and serve warm with braised green beans.

French-Style Goose Choucroute Garnie

Total Time: 35 minutes | **Servings**: 6 | **Per Serving**: Kcal 523; Carbs 32g; Fat 28g; Protein 26g

Ingredients

4 bacon slices, chopped
2 tbsp rendered goose fat
2 yellow onions, thinly sliced
½ head savoy cabbage, thinly sliced
4 garlic cloves, minced
1 lb sauerkraut, drained
1 lb Yukon Gold potatoes, pricked all over with a fork
1 tsp ground caraway powder

Salt and black pepper to taste
3 bay leaves
1 lb goose breast, cubed
1 lb cooked knockwurst sausages, cubed
1 cup Riesling wine
1 cup chicken broth
1 tbsp whole-grain mustard

Directions

Set your Instant Pot to Sauté mode and adjust to medium heat. Cook bacon in inner pot until brown and crispy, 5 minutes. Plate and set aside.

Melt in goose fat and sauté onion and cabbage until softened, 4 minutes. Stir in garlic for 30 seconds. Add sauerkraut, potatoes, caraway powder, salt, bay leaves, and bacon. Place goose on top and season with salt and pepper.

Prick sausages all over with a fork, arrange on goose, and pour Riesling wine and chicken broth all over. Seal the lid, select Manual/Pressure Cook mode on High, and set cooking time to 13 minutes.

When done cooking, perform a quick pressure release to let out steam. Unlock the lid, spoon sauerkraut and potatoes onto serving plates and top with meat. Garnish with mustard and serve warm.

Pork Recipes

Thyme Pork in Wine & Cream Sauce

Total Time: 35 minutes | **Servings**: 4 | **Per Serving**: Kcal 482; Carbs 11g; Fat 27g; Protein 47g

Ingredients

1 tsp onion powder
1 tsp garlic powder
2 tsp dried mixed herbs
¼ cup + 1 tbsp all-purpose flour
Salt and black pepper to taste
4 tbsp butter
4 boneless pork chops

2 garlic cloves, minced
½ cup dry white wine
½ cup chicken stock
½ lemon, juiced
½ cup heavy cream
4 fresh thyme sprigs, leaves extracted

Directions

In a medium bowl, combine onion powder, garlic powder, mixed herbs, ¼ cup of flour, salt, and black pepper. Dredge pork lightly in mixture.

Set your Instant Pot to Sauté mode and adjust to medium heat. Melt 2 tbsp of butter in inner pot and sear pork on both sides until golden brown and cooked, 10 minutes. Add in chicken stock and seal the lid. Cook for 15 minutes on Manual/Pressure Cook on High. When ready, do a quick pressure release. Transfer pork with cooking liquid to a bowl, cover with foil, and set aside.

Clean inner pot with paper towel and melt in remaining butter. Add garlic and cook for 2 minutes until fragrant and stir in remaining flour. Pour in white wine, cook for 1 minute, and stir in cooking liquid and lemon juice. Cook further for 2 minutes. Stir in heavy cream and thyme, season with salt and black pepper, and simmer for 2 to 3 minutes. Plate pork and drizzle sauce all over. Serve warm.

Braised Pork Ragu

Total Time: 45 minutes | **Servings**: 4 | **Per Serving**: Kcal 415; Carbs 30g; Fat 21g; Protein 36g

Ingredients

8 oz fettuccine
1 ½ cups water
1 lb pork shoulder, cubed
1 white onion, chopped
2 large carrots, chopped
2 garlic cloves, minced

2 tbsp tomato paste
2 (15 oz) tomatoes with juice, chopped
1 tsp dried oregano
1 tsp dried rosemary
Salt and black pepper to taste
¼ grated Parmesan cheese for garnishing

Directions

Pour fettuccine and water into inner pot. Seal the lid, select Manual/Pressure Cook on High, and set time to 2 minutes. After cooking, perform a quick pressure release to let out steam, and unlock lid. Drain pasta and set aside.

Into inner pot, add pork, onion, carrots, garlic, tomato paste, tomatoes with juice, oregano, rosemary, salt, and pepper. Stir to coat the pork. Seal the lid, select Manual/Pressure Cook on High, and set cooking time to 30 minutes.

After cooking, perform a quick pressure release to let out steam, and unlock the lid. Stir in fettuccine and adjust taste with salt and black pepper. Garnish with Parmesan cheese and serve warm.

Veggie & Pork Rice

Total time: 55 minutes | **Servings**: 6 | **Per Serving**: Kcal 534; Carbs 32g; Fat 32g; Protein 45g

Ingredients

2 tbsp olive oil
1 onion, finely chopped
1 garlic clove, minced
2 lb pork loin filet, cut into ½-inch pieces
Salt and black pepper to taste
3 cups water

2 cups rice
1 large egg, beaten
3 tbsp soy sauce
1 carrot, chopped
1 cup green beans, chopped
2 scallions, finely chopped

Directions

Set your Instant Pot to Sauté and heat 1 tbsp of olive oil. Stir-fry onion and garlic for 3 minutes. Sprinkle pork with salt and pepper and cook in the pot for 8-10 minutes with a splash of water.

Pour 1 cup of water in the pot to scrape up any browned bits from the bottom. Place in rice and the remaining water. Seal the lid, select Manual/Pressure Cook mode, and cook for 8 minutes on High.

When done, perform a natural pressure release for 10 minutes, then a quick pressure release to let out the remaining steam. Unlock the lid and fluff the rice with a fork.

In a bowl, mix in the remaining oil and beaten egg. Add in the soy sauce and pork mixture and stir. Put in the green beans and carrots. Stir the resulting mixture in the rice and let sit until heated through, for about 6 minutes on Sauté mode. Sprinkle with the scallions to serve.

Juicy Meatballs with Tagliatelle

Total time: 30 minutes | **Servings**: 6 | **Per Serving**: Kcal 343; Carbs 58g; Fat 12g; Protein 8g

Ingredients

2 tbsp olive oil
1 lb pork meatballs
1 lb dried tagliatelle
1 (24-oz) tomato & basil pasta sauce

3 cups water
½ cup dry white wine
1 cup shredded Parmesan cheese
Fresh parsley, for garnish

Directions

Set your Instant Pot to Sauté mode and heat the olive oil. Add in the pork meatballs and cook for 5-6 minutes on all sides. Add in the tagliatelle on top and pour in the tomato sauce. Pour the water and white wine over the top.

Seal the lid, select Manual/Pressure Cook mode on High, and set time to 10 minutes. When done, perform a quick pressure to let out steam. Add in Parmesan cheese and stir. Serve topped with parsley.

Maple Glazed Pork Chops

Total Time: 20 minutes | **Servings**: 4 | **Per Serving**: Kcal 502; Carbs 46g; Fat 28g; Protein 40g

Ingredients

4 pork chops
Salt and black pepper to taste
1 tbsp olive oil
2 tbsp butter
1 ½ cups maple syrup

3 tbsp ketchup
2 tsp garlic powder
1 tsp grated ginger
2 tbsp soy sauce
1 tsp thyme leaves

Directions

Pat pork dry with a paper towel and season with salt and black pepper.

Set your Instant Pot to Sauté mode and adjust to medium heat. Heat olive oil in inner pot and brown pork chops until golden brown on both sides and cooked through, 10 minutes. Transfer to a plate and set aside for serving.

Melt butter in oil and stir in maple syrup, ketchup, garlic powder, ginger, soy sauce, and thyme; simmer for 1 minute. Spoon sauce all over pork and serve warm.

Agave BBQ Pulled Pork

Total Time: 60 minutes | **Servings**: 4 | **Per Serving**: Kcal 831; Carbs 51g; Fat 42g; Protein 64g

Ingredients

2 lb pork shoulder, cut into 4 chunks
1 can root beer
¼ cup agave syrup
2 ½ cups BBQ sauce

½ lemon, juiced
2 tsp garlic powder
1 tsp onion powder
4 hamburger buns for serving

Directions

Place pork in inner pot and pour beer all over. In a medium bowl, whisk agave syrup, 2 cups of BBQ sauce, lemon juice, garlic powder, and onion powder. Pour mixture all over meat.

Seal the lid, select Manual/Pressure Cook mode on High, and set cooking time to 45 minutes. After cooking, perform a natural pressure release for 10 minutes, then quick pressure release to let out remaining steam, and unlock the lid.

Using two forks, shred pork into small pieces. Using tongs or slotted spoon, transfer to a serving bowl and stir in remaining BBQ sauce. Spoon pulled pork into burger buns, top with coleslaw, mayonnaise, if desired, and serve.

Three-Pepper Pork Chili

Total Time: 40 minutes | **Servings**: 4 | **Per Serving**: Kcal 466; Carbs 21g; Fat 26g; Protein 45g

Ingredients

2 tbsp olive oil
2 lb pork shoulder, cubed
Salt and black pepper to taste
2 jalapeño peppers
2 poblano peppers
2 Anaheim peppers
4 garlic cloves

6 tomatillos, husk removed
1 large white onion, quartered
1 bunch cilantro
½ tsp cumin powder
½ tsp dried basil
1 cup chicken broth

Directions

Preheat the oven to 350°F.

Set your Instant Pot to Sauté mode and adjust to medium heat. Heat olive oil in inner pot, season pork with salt and black pepper, and sear in oil until golden brown on both sides, 8 minutes.

Meanwhile, as pork cooks, align the peppers, garlic, tomatillos, and onion on a baking sheet. Roast in the oven for 3 to 5 minutes or until slightly charred. Quickly blend roasted vegetables with cilantro, in a blender, and pour all over pork inside the Instant Pot. Add cumin, basil, and chicken broth.

Seal the lid, select Manual/Pressure Cook mode on High, and set cooking time to 15 minutes. Once done cooking, perform natural pressure release for 10 minutes, then a quick pressure release until remaining steam is out; unlock the lid. Stir sauce, adjust taste with salt and black pepper, and dish into serving bowls. Serve warm with tortillas.

Bacon & Sausage Frittata

Total Time: 25 minutes | **Servings**: 4 | **Per Serving**: Kcal 315; Carbs 7g; Fat 26g; Protein 12g

Ingredients

4 bacon slices, chopped
¼ cup chopped pork sausages
1 large yellow onion, chopped
1 red bell pepper, deseeded and chopped

¼ cup chopped spinach
1 cup water
12 eggs, beaten with ¾ cup milk
Salt and black pepper to taste

Directions

Set your Instant Pot to Sauté mode. Add bacon and sausages to inner pot and cook until crisp and brown, 5 minutes. Plate and set aside. Sauté onion and bell pepper in bacon grease until softened, 5 minutes. Add spinach to wilt for 2 minutes. Plate on one side of bacon and set aside. Clean up inner pot, pour in water, and fit in a trivet.

Grease an 8-inch cake pan with cooking spray and pour in eggs. Top with bacon, sausages, vegetable mixture, and season with salt and black pepper. Cover pan with foil and place on trivet.

Seal the lid, select Manual/Pressure Cook mode on High, and set cooking time to 15 minutes.

After cooking, perform a quick pressure release steam, and unlock the lid. Remove cake pan, aluminum foil, and brown top of eggs under a broiler for 1 to 2 minutes. Transfer frittata onto a plate, slice, and serve.

Russian-Style Pork Stew with Rice

Total time: 40 minutes | **Servings**: 6 | **Per Serving**: Kcal 443; Carbs 41g; Fat 19g; Protein 26g

Ingredients

3 cups beef broth
3 tbsp olive oil
1 lb pork tenderloin, cut into thin strips
1 onion, sliced
1 garlic cloves, minced
1 (10-oz) can condensed cream of mushroom soup

Salt and black pepper to taste
1 tbsp flour
1 ½ cups brown rice
1 cup crème fraiche
2 tsp yellow mustard

Directions

Set your Instant Pot to Sauté mode and heat the olive oil. Cook pork, onion, and garlic for 8 minutes, with a couple of splashes water, until the meat is tender.

Pour in the broth, cream of mushroom soup, salt, pepper, and flour, stir until smooth. Place in the rice. Seal the lid, select Manual/Pressure Cook mode on High, and set time to 10 minutes.

When done, perform a natural pressure release for 10 minutes, then a quick pressure release to let out the remaining steam. Unlock the lid and pour in the crème fraîche and mustard and stir. Let it rest for a few minutes and serve.

Apple Cider Pork Chops

Total Time: 20 minutes | **Servings**: 4 | **Per Serving**: Kcal 490; Carbs 21g; Fat 27g; Protein 41g

Ingredients

4 pork chops
Salt and black pepper to taste
1 tbsp olive oil
2 tbsp butter

1 ½ cups apple cider vinegar
2 tbsp honey
1 tbsp Dijon mustard

Directions

Pat pork chops dry with a paper towel and season with salt and black pepper. Set your Instant Pot to Sauté mode and adjust to medium heat. Heat olive oil in inner pot and brown pork until golden brown on both sides and cooked through, 8 minutes. Transfer to a plate and set aside for serving.

Add butter to oil and allow melting while stirring. Pour in apple cider vinegar, honey, and mustard. Continually stir until well-combined and simmering, 1 minute. Spoon sauce all over pork and serve warm.

English Breakfast Pork Shakshuka

Total Time: 45 minutes | **Servings**: 4 | **Per Serving**: Kcal 271; Carbs 12g; Fat 16g; Protein 21g

Ingredients

1 tbsp olive oil
½ lb ground pork
1 small white onion, chopped
1 garlic clove, minced
1 small red bell pepper, chopped
2 tbsp tomato paste

4 cups tomatoes, chopped
1 tsp smoked paprika
1 tsp chili powder
Salt and black pepper to taste
4 large eggs, cracked into a bowl
1 tbsp chopped parsley

Directions

Set your Instant Pot to Sauté mode and heat olive oil. Add and cook pork until brown, 5 minutes. Add onion, garlic, and red bell pepper. Stir-fry until softened, 3 minutes. Stir in tomato paste, tomatoes, paprika, chili powder, salt, and black pepper.

Seal the lid, select Manual/Pressure Cook on Low, and set cooking time to 15 minutes. Perform natural pressure release for 10 minutes, then a quick pressure release to let out remaining steam and unlock the lid.

Select Sauté mode, stir, create four holes in sauce, and pour each egg into each hole. Allow egg setting for 1 to 2 minutes. Spoon shakshuka into serving bowls, garnish with parsley and serve warm.

Sweet & Savory Corn Pork Chowder

Total Time: 40 minutes | **Servings**: 4 | **Per Serving**: Kcal 284; Carbs 12g; Fat 12g; Protein 31g

Ingredients

1 tbsp olive oil
1 lb pork tenderloin, cubed
2 shallots, chopped
2 garlic cloves, minced
1 (8 oz) can sweet corn kernels, drained
½ tsp mustard powder

4 cups chicken stock
½ lemon, juiced
Salt and black pepper to taste
3 tbsp heavy cream
3 tbsp chopped chives

Directions

Set your Instant Pot to Sauté mode and adjust to medium heat. Heat olive oil in inner pot, season pork with salt and black pepper, and sear in oil until golden brown, 8 minutes. Plate and set aside.

Sauté shallots until softened, 2 minutes. Stir in garlic, cook for 30 seconds, follow up with corn kernels, mustard, and cook for 1 minute. Stir in chicken stock and pork. Seal the lid, select Manual/Pressure Cook on High, and set time to 10 minutes. Perform natural pressure release for 10 minutes. Spoon pork meat into bowls and set aside.

Using an immersion blender, puree soup until smooth, and stir in lemon juice. Adjust taste with salt and black pepper. Mix in heavy cream and spoon soup over pork. Garnish with chives and serve warm.

Bacon & Ham Split Pea Soup

Total Time: 25 minutes | **Servings**: 4 | **Per Serving**: Kcal 314; Carbs 19g; Fat 21g; Protein 13g

Ingredients

8 bacon slices, chopped
16 oz dried split peas
1 onion, diced
1 celery stalk, chopped
2 carrots, diced

2 cups ham, diced
1 tsp dried rosemary
4 cups chicken stock
Salt and black pepper to taste

Directions

Set your Instant Pot to Sauté mode and adjust to medium heat. Add bacon to inner pot and cook until roasted and crisp, 5 minutes. Top with split peas, onion, celery, carrots, ham, rosemary, chicken stock, salt, and black pepper. Seal the lid, select Manual/Pressure Cook mode on High, and set cooking time to 5 minutes.

Once done, perform natural pressure release for 10 minutes, then quick pressure release; unlock the lid. Whip soup continually until creamy. Spoon into serving bowls and serve warm.

Smoky Pulled Pork Shoulder with Lemon

Total Time: 35 minutes | **Servings**: 4 | **Per Serving**: Kcal 588; Carbs 11g; Fat 35g; Protein 48g

Ingredients

2 lb pork shoulder
2 tbsp olive oil
1 ½ cups chicken broth
1 orange, juiced
1 lemon, juiced
1 lime, juiced

1 tbsp dried oregano
1 tbsp smoked paprika
10 garlic cloves, minced
Salt and black pepper to taste
1 white onion, cut into rounds
Lime wedges to garnish

Directions

Place pork in inner pot. In a small bowl, combine olive oil, chicken broth, orange juice, lemon juice, lime juice, oregano, smoked paprika, garlic, salt, and black pepper. Pour mixture all over meat and top with onions.

Seal the lid, select Manual/Pressure Cook mode on High, and set cooking time to 30 minutes.

After cooking, perform a quick pressure release until steam is out and unlock the lid. Using two forks, shred meat and stir well. Adjust taste with salt and black pepper, and plate. Garnish with lime wedges and serve warm.

Pancetta & Potato Marsala Pork

Total Time: 65 minutes | **Servings**: 4 | **Per Serving**: Kcal 674; Carbs 47g; Fat 31g; Protein 53g

Ingredients

6 pieces pancetta, chopped
1 tbsp olive oil
4 boneless pork chops
Salt and black pepper to taste
1 medium red onion, chopped
2 garlic cloves, minced
1 red chili pepper, deseeded and minced

½ cup marsala wine
2 cups chicken broth
1 ½ cups sweet corn kernels
2 small Yukon Gold potatoes, peeled and diced
2 tsp chopped chives
3 tbsp heavy cream
¼ cup chopped parsley

Directions

Set your Instant Pot to Sauté. Fry pancetta in inner pot until brown and crispy, 5 minutes. Transfer to a paper towel-lined plate to drain grease and set aside.

Heat olive oil in inner pot, season pork with salt and black pepper, and sear in oil on both sides until golden, 6 minutes. Transfer to a plate and set aside. Sauté onion, garlic, and red chili pepper in oil until fragrant, 2 minutes. Add marsala wine and cook until reduced by one-third. Pour in chicken broth, corn kernels, potatoes, pork, and pancetta.

Seal the lid, select Manual/Pressure Cook mode on High, and set cooking time to 30 minutes. After cooking, perform a natural pressure release for 10 minutes, then a quick pressure release to let out remaining steam. Unlock the lid. Fetch out pork onto serving plates and adjust masala's taste with salt and black pepper. Mix in chives, heavy cream, and spoon masala all over pork. Garnish with parsley and serve warm.

Pork in Corn Field

Total Time: 40 minutes | **Servings**: 4 | **Per Serving**: Kcal 574; Carbs 10g; Fat 48g; Protein 28g

Ingredients

8 slices bacon, chopped
6 half ears of corn
5 small potatoes, chopped
1 medium yellow onion, chopped
4 boneless pork chops

1 (21 oz) can cream of mushroom soup
½ cup whole milk
Salt and black pepper to taste
¾ tsp dried rosemary

Directions

Set your Instant Pot to Sauté mode and adjust to medium heat. Add bacon to inner pot and cook until brown and crispy, 5 minutes. Spoon onto a paper towel-lined plate to drain grease; set aside.

In inner pot, arrange corn, potatoes, onion, and pork. Pour mushroom soup on top followed by milk, salt, black pepper, rosemary, and bacon.

Seal the lid, select Manual/Pressure Cook mode on High, and set cooking time to 20 minutes. Once done cooking, perform natural pressure release for 10 minutes, then a quick pressure release until remaining steam is out. Unlock the lid and stir food. Serve warm.

Chili Pork with Zucchini

Total Time: 30 minutes | **Servings**: 4 | **Per Serving**: Kcal 424; Carbs 6g; Fat 31g; Protein 31g

Ingredients

2 tbsp olive oil
1 lb ground pork
1 yellow onion, chopped
3 cloves garlic, chopped
Salt and black pepper to taste

½ tsp dried thyme
2 large zucchinis, sliced into 1-inch coins
1 tsp red chili powder
1 handful parsley, chopped

Directions

Set your Instant Pot to Sauté mode and heat olive oil. Add and cook pork until brown, 10 minutes. Add in onion, garlic, cook until softened, 3 minutes. Season with salt, black pepper, chili powder, thyme, and stir in 1 cup of water. Seal the lid, select Manual/Pressure Cook, and set time to 15 minutes on High.

When done, perform a quick pressure release until steam is out. Unlock the lid and stir in zucchinis. Press Sauté and cook until zucchinis soften, 7-10 minutes. Garnish with parsley and serve warm.

Spice-Rubbed Baby Back Ribs

Total Time: 45 min + marinating time | **Servings**: 4 | **Per Serving**: Kcal 720; Carbs 38g; Fat 42g; Protein 49g

Ingredients

Seasoning
1 tbsp salt
2 tbsp smoked paprika
1 tbsp black pepper
1 tbsp garlic powder
1 tbsp onion powder
1 tbsp chili powder

1 tbsp white sugar
½ tbsp ground mustard
½ tsp cayenne pepper
½ tsp cumin
½ tsp ground fennel seeds
½ tsp dried rosemary

Ribs
1 rack (2 pounds) baby back ribs, quartered
1 tbsp oil

Hoisin sauce

Directions

In a bowl, combine all the seasoning ingredients. Coat the ribs with the mixture. Cover the ribs with plastic wrap and let sit to marinate in the fridge overnight.

Set your Instant Pot to Sauté and heat the oil. Cook the ribs meat-side down for 5 minutes, until browned. Remove to a plate. Pour 1 cup of water in your Instant Pot and fit in a trivet. Arrange the ribs on the trivet. Seal the lid, select Manual/Pressure Cook mode, and cook for 20 minutes on High.

When done, perform a quick pressure release. Unlock the lid and transfer the ribs to a foil-lined baking dish. Brush with hoisin sauce and set under the broiler approximately 5-10 minutes, until a nice crust is formed.

Pork Meatballs the Swedish Way

Total Time: 25 minutes | **Servings**: 4 | **Per Serving**: Kcal 537; Carbs 15g; Fat 38g; Protein 33g

Ingredients

1 pound ground pork
½ cup breadcrumbs
1 onion, chopped
1 garlic clove, minced
¼ tsp coriander seeds, chopped
¼ tsp allspice
¼ tsp ground nutmeg
Salt and black pepper to taste
1 egg, beaten

1 tbsp butter
2 tbsp olive oil
2 tbsp flour
1 cup vegetable broth
½ tbsp Tabasco sauce
½ tsp mayonnaise
¼ cup heavy cream
2 tbsp parsley, chopped

Directions

Combine the ground pork, breadcrumbs, onion, garlic, coriander seeds, allspice, nutmeg, black pepper, salt, and egg. Mix well. Shape the mixture into small balls.

Set your Instant Pot to Sauté and heat the olive oil. Place in the meatballs and cook them in batches for about 5 minutes per side or until golden brown; reserve. Stir in the butter and flour and whisk until it is fully combined, about 2 minutes. Add in the broth, Tabasco sauce, and mayonnaise and mix. Return the meatballs to inner pot.

Seal the lid, select Manual/Pressure Cook, and set time to 5 minutes. When done, perform a quick pressure release. Stir in heavy cream until well mixed. Adjust the seasoning. Sprinkle with parsley and serve with mashed potatoes.

Pork Bean Dip

Total Time: 27 minutes | **Servings**: 4 | **Per Serving**: Kcal 225; Carbs 6g; Fat 12g; Protein 25g

Ingredients

1 tbsp olive oil
½ lb ground pork
Salt and black pepper to taste
2 cups black beans, soaked overnight, rinsed

4 tbsp chicken broth
1 tbsp coriander powder
1 tbsp cumin powder
¼ cup grated cheddar cheese

Directions

Set your Instant Pot to Sauté and heat olive oil. Season pork with salt and black pepper, and sear until brown, 10 minutes. Plate and set aside. Pour black beans, chicken broth, coriander powder, and cumin powder into inner pot.

Seal the lid, select Manual/Pressure Cook mode on High, and set cooking time to 15 minutes. After cooking, perform a quick pressure release until steam is out and unlock the lid. Using an immersion blender, puree ingredients and stir in pork. Adjust taste with salt and black pepper. Dish, top with cheddar cheese and serve.

Authentic Mississippi Pork

Total Time: 50 minutes | **Servings**: 4 | **Per Serving**: Kcal 479; Carbs 5g; Fat 28g; Protein 51g

Ingredients

1 lb pork shoulder
1 pack ranch dressing mix

16 oz deli sliced pepperoncini peppers with ½ cup juices
Salt and black pepper to taste

Directions

Combine pork, ranch dressing mix, and pepperoncini with juices in inner pot. Seal the lid, select Manual/Pressure Cook mode on High, and set cooking time to 30 minutes.

After cooking, perform a natural pressure release for 10 minutes, then a quick pressure release until remaining steam is out, and unlock the lid. Using two forks, shred meat into small strands, adjust taste with salt and black pepper, and dish. Serve warm over rice or with potatoes.

Pork with Spicy Red Sauce

Total Time: 35 minutes | **Servings**: 4 | **Per Serving**: Kcal 556; Carbs 32g; Fat 32g; Protein 39g

Ingredients

1 lb ground pork
2 tbsp chili powder
Salt and black pepper to taste
½ tsp dried oregano
2 tsp garlic, minced
¼ cup cilantro, chopped

1 cup diced red onion
2 (15-oz) cans stewed tomatoes
1 (19-oz) can enchilada sauce
1 cup chicken broth
2 (15-oz) cans red kidney beans, drained

Directions

Into inner pot, add pork, chili powder, salt, black pepper, oregano, garlic, cilantro, onion, tomatoes, enchilada sauce, chicken broth, and kidney beans. Seal the lid, select Manual/Pressure Cook on High, and set time to 15 minutes.

Perform natural pressure release for 10 minutes, then a quick pressure release until remaining steam is out, and unlock the lid. Stir, adjust taste with salt and pepper, and dish the chili. Serve warm with tortillas and cheddar cheese.

Sriracha Lemon Pork Chops

Total Time: 50 minutes + marinating time | **Servings**: 4 | **Per Serving**: Kcal 379; Carbs 3g; Fat 21g; Protein 43g

Ingredients

4 boneless pork chops
2 tbsp hot sauce
2 tbsp sesame oil
1 lemon, juiced
1 tbsp soy sauce

1 ½ tsp sriracha sauce
2 tbsp olive oil
1 cup chicken broth
Salt to taste

Directions

Place pork chops in a plastic zipper bag. In a small bowl, mix hot sauce, sesame oil, lemon juice, soy sauce, and sriracha sauce. Pour mixture over pork, close bag, and massage marinade into the meat. Marinate in refrigerator for 30 minutes to 1 hour.

Set your Instant Pot to Sauté mode and adjust to medium heat. Heat olive oil in inner pot, take pork out of the fridge and marinade, and sear in oil on both sides until brown, 6 minutes. Pour in chicken broth and season with salt.

Seal the lid, select Manual/Pressure Cook mode on High, and set cooking time to 20 minutes. After cooking, perform a natural pressure release for 10 minutes, then a quick pressure release to let out remaining steam. Unlock the lid. Remove pork onto serving plates, baste with a little sauce, and serve warm.

Rosemary Lemon Pork Chops

Total Time: 55 minutes | **Servings**: 4 | **Per Serving**: Kcal 373: Carbs 4g; Fat 21g; Protein 41g

Ingredients

1 tbsp olive oil
4 bone-in pork chops
Salt and black pepper to taste
2 tsp garlic powder

½ cup chicken broth
1 lemon, zested and juiced
4 rosemary sprigs
½ tsp Dijon mustard

Directions

Set your Instant Pot to Sauté mode and adjust to medium heat. Heat olive oil in inner pot, season pork with salt, black pepper, garlic powder, and sear in oil on both sides until golden brown, 6 minutes. Pour in chicken broth, lemon zest, lemon juice, rosemary sprigs, and mix in Dijon mustard.

Seal the lid, select Manual/Pressure Cook mode on High, and set cooking time to 25 minutes. After cooking, perform a natural pressure release for 10 minutes, then a quick pressure release to let out remaining steam. Unlock the lid. Remove pork onto serving plates, allow sitting for 2 minutes, and serve warm.

Instant BBQ Baby Back Ribs

Total Time: 55 minutes | **Servings**: 4 | **Per Serving**: Kcal 895; Carbs 8g; Fat 62g; Protein 78g

Ingredients

2 tbsp brown sugar
¼ tsp onion powder
½ tsp garlic powder
Salt and black pepper to taste
½ tsp smoked paprika

1 rack baby back ribs
1 cup chicken broth
½ cup bbq sauce + more for serving
2 tsp hickory liquid smoke

Directions

In a small bowl, combine brown sugar, onion powder, garlic powder, salt, black pepper, and paprika. Cut ribs into four pieces each and rub generously with spice mixture. Place in inner pot. Top with chicken broth, bbq sauce, and liquid smoke. Seal the lid, select Manual/Pressure Cook mode on High, and set cooking time to 35 minutes.

Once done cooking, perform natural pressure release for 10 minutes, then a quick pressure release until remaining steam is out. Unlock the lid. Using tongs, remove ribs into serving plates, brush with bbq sauce, and serve warm.

Pork Cheeseburger Soup

Total Time: 20 minutes | **Servings**: 4 | **Per Serving**: Kcal 858; Carbs 51g; Fat 52g; Protein 47g

Ingredients

2 tbsp olive oil
1 lb ground pork
Salt and black pepper to taste
2 russet potatoes, chopped
3 celery stalks, chopped
2 carrots, chopped

1 white onion, chopped
2 tsp dried tarragon
½ tsp garlic powder
4 cups chicken broth
8 oz Velveeta cheese
8 oz cream cheese, room temperature

Directions

Set your Instant Pot to Sauté mode and heat olive oil. Cook pork until brown, 5 minutes, season with salt and black pepper. Add potatoes, celery, carrots, onion, tarragon, garlic powder, and chicken broth. Seal the lid, select Manual/Pressure Cook mode on High, and set cooking time to 3 minutes.

After cooking, perform a quick pressure release until steam is out. Select Sauté mode and stir in Velveeta and cream cheese until melted and well combined. Adjust taste with salt and black pepper. Dish soup and serve.

Pork in Creamy Sauce

Total Time: 60 minutes | **Servings**: 4 | **Per Serving**: Kcal 484; Carbs 12g; Fat 34g; Protein 28g

Ingredients

1 tbsp olive oil
1 tbsp butter
1 pork shoulder, cut into 2-inch cubes
1 tsp dried thyme
Salt and black pepper to taste
½ tsp dried mustard powder
1 small yellow onion, diced

3 garlic cloves, minced
1 ½ cups chicken broth
¾ cup heavy cream
1 tbsp cornstarch
1 tsp dried parsley
1 tsp dried basil

Directions

Set your Instant Pot to Sauté mode and adjust to medium heat. Heat olive oil and butter in inner pot, season pork with thyme, salt, black pepper, and mustard powder. Sear in oil until golden on the outside, 7 minutes. Transfer to a plate. Sauté onion until softened, 3 minutes. Stir in garlic and cook until fragrant, 30 seconds. Pour in chicken broth and return meat to inner pot.

Seal the lid, select Manual/Pressure Cook mode on High, and set cooking time to 20 minutes. After cooking, perform a natural pressure release for 10 minutes, then a quick pressure release to let out remaining steam. Unlock the lid. Transfer pork to a plate and select Sauté mode.

Into sauce, whisk heavy cream, cornstarch, basil, and parsley. Cook for 2 minutes and return pork to sauce. Allow heating through for 3 minutes. Spoon pork with sauce onto plates and serve warm.

Salsa Verde Pork with Velveeta Cheese

Total Time: 30 minutes | **Servings**: 4 | **Per Serving**: Kcal 739; Carbs 30g; Fat 27g; Protein 51g

Ingredients

2 tbsp olive oil
1 lb ground pork
Salt and black pepper to taste
1 cup milk

2 lb white Velveeta cheese
1 (16 oz) jar salsa verde
16 oz sour cream
2 jalapeño peppers, sliced

Directions

Set your Instant Pot to Sauté mode and heat olive oil. Cook pork until brown, 5 minutes. Season with a little salt and black pepper. Add in milk and seal the lid. Select Manual/Pressure Cook, and set time to 15 minutes. When ready, do a quick pressure release.

Press Sauté, mix in Velveeta cheese, salsa verde, sour cream, and jalapeño peppers. Cook with frequent stirring until cheese melts. Dish into serving bowls and serve warm.

Pork Chops with Caramelized Apples

Total Time: 55 minutes | **Servings**: 4 | **Per Serving**: Kcal 766; Carbs 59g; Fat 41g; Protein 43g

Ingredients

2 tbsp olive oil
4 bone-in pork chops
Salt and black pepper to taste
2 garlic cloves, minced
2 tbsp chopped sage
1 lb honey crisp apples, peeled, cored and sliced in
¼-inch slices

3 tbsp butter
4 tbsp honey
½ cup apple cider vinegar
½ cup chicken broth
½ cup heavy cream
2 tbsp chopped parsley

Directions

Set your Instant Pot to Sauté mode. Heat olive oil, season pork with salt and pepper, and sear in oil until golden brown on the outside, 6 minutes. Set aside. Add garlic and sage to oil and stir-fry until fragrant, 30 seconds. Pour in apples, butter, and honey; cook until apples caramelize, 5 minutes. Top with apple cider vinegar, broth, and pork.

Seal the lid, select Manual/Pressure Cook mode on High, and set cooking time to 20 minutes. After cooking, perform a natural pressure release for 10 minutes. Unlock the lid and stir in heavy cream. Simmer in Sauté mode for 2 to 3 minutes. Spoon food into serving plates with a generous topping of sauce. Garnish with parsley and serve warm.

Broccoli & Cabbage Pork Ramen

Total Time: 50 minutes | **Servings**: 4 | **Per Serving**: Kcal 425; Carbs 44g; Fat 12g; Protein 34g

Ingredients

2 (3 oz) packs ramen noodles
¼ cup soy sauce
2 tbsp Worcestershire sauce
2 tbsp ketchup
2 tsp granulated sugar
¼ tsp red chili flakes
3 tsp olive oil, divided

1 lb boneless pork chops, cut in ½ inch strips
1 cup broccoli florets
1 cup shredded red cabbage
1 cup shredded green cabbage
4 garlic cloves, minced
1 ½ cups chicken broth

Directions

In inner pot, add ramen noodles (discard seasoning), 2 ½ cups of water, and salt. Seal the lid, select Manual/Pressure Cook mode on High, and set cooking time to 1 minute. After cooking, perform a quick pressure release to let out steam and unlock the lid. Drain noodles through a colander, set aside, and clean inner pot.

Select Sauté mode and adjust to medium heat. In a small bowl, mix soy sauce, Worcestershire sauce, ketchup, sugar, red chili flakes, and 2 teaspoons of olive oil. Pour mixture into inner pot, allow heating for 1 minute, and add pork; cook until no longer pink. Using a slotted spoon, strain pork and transfer to a plate.

In the pot, add broccoli, cabbages, garlic, and chicken broth. Cook for 2 minutes and return pork to inner pot. Seal the lid, select Manual/Pressure Cook on High, and set time to 15 minutes. After cooking, perform a natural pressure release for 10 minutes. Stir in ramen. Press Sauté and heat noodles for 2 minutes. Spoon into serving plates and serve.

Tuscan Pork Chops

Total Time: 45 minutes | **Servings**: 4 | **Per Serving**: Kcal 517; Carbs 18g; Fat 35g; Protein 33g

Ingredients

1 tbsp olive oil
4 pork chops, fat trimmed
Salt and black pepper to taste
1 large red onion, chopped
5 garlic cloves, minced

1 ½ chopped tomatoes
2 tsp dried oregano
1 tsp dried basil
1 tsp dried sage
½ cup chicken broth

Directions

Set your Instant Pot to Sauté mode. Heat olive oil, season pork with salt, pepper, and sear in oil until golden brown on both sides, 6 to 8 minutes. Stir in onion and garlic until softened and fragrant, 2 minutes. Add tomatoes, oregano, basil, sage, and cook for 2 minutes, turn meat halfway. Pour in chicken broth and season with salt and pepper.

Seal the lid, select Manual/Pressure Cook mode on High, and set cooking time to 15 minutes. After cooking, perform a natural pressure release for 10 minutes, then a quick pressure release to let out remaining steam. Unlock the lid, stir, and plate. Serve warm.

Pork Egg Roll Bowls

Total Time: 20 minutes | **Servings**: 4 | **Per Serving**: Kcal 539; Carbs 18g; Fat 33g; Protein 36g

Ingredients

1 tbsp olive oil
1 lb ground pork
Salt and black pepper to taste
1 garlic clove, minced
1 tbsp freshly grated ginger
1 tbsp sesame oil
½ medium red onion, thinly sliced

1 cup shredded carrots
1 small green cabbage, thinly sliced
¼ cup soy sauce
1 tbsp hot sauce
¼ cup chicken broth
1 scallion, thinly sliced
1 tbsp sesame seeds

Directions

Set your Instant Pot to Sauté mode and adjust to medium heat. Heat olive oil in inner pot, add pork, season with salt, black pepper, and cook until brown, 5 minutes. Add garlic, ginger, and cook until fragrant, 1 minute. Mix in sesame oil, onion, carrots, cabbage, soy sauce, hot sauce, and broth.

Seal the lid, select Manual/Pressure Cook on High, and set time to 1 minute. After cooking, perform a quick pressure. Stir in scallion and adjust taste with salt and pepper. Dish food into serving bowls and garnish with sesame seeds.

Shallot & Mushroom Pork Stew

Total Time: 55 minutes | **Servings**: 4 | **Per Serving**: Kcal 402; Carbs 11g; Fat 19g; Protein 44g

Ingredients

2 tbsp olive oil
2 tbsp butter
4 boneless pork chops
Salt and black pepper to taste
2 shallots, thinly sliced
2 garlic cloves, minced
1 cup sliced cremini mushrooms

½ cup Marsala wine
½ cup chicken stock
1 tsp garlic powder
1 tsp thyme leaves
¼ cup plain flour
2 tbsp chopped parsley

Directions

Set your Instant Pot to Sauté mode and adjust to medium heat. Heat olive oil and butter in inner pot, season pork with salt, black pepper, and sear in oil until golden brown on both sides, 6 to 8 minutes. Transfer to a plate.

Stir in shallots and garlic until softened and fragrant, 2 minutes. Add mushrooms, cook for 2 minutes. Pour in marsala wine, allow reduction by one-third, and add chicken stock, garlic powder, and thyme. Return pork to inner pot.

Seal the lid, select Manual/Pressure Cook mode on High, and set cooking time to 20 minutes. After cooking, perform a natural pressure release for 10 minutes, then a quick pressure release to let out remaining steam.

Stir in flour and cook sauce further in Sauté mode until slightly thickened. Spoon pork and sauce onto serving plates and garnish with parsley.

Carcamusa (Spanish-Style Chili)

Total time: 40 minutes | **Servings**: 6 | **Per Serving**: Kcal 332; Carbs 12g; Fat 22g; Protein 22g

Ingredients

1 tbsp olive oil
1 pound ground pork
1 cup frozen green peas
2 yellow onions, chopped
2 garlic cloves, minced

2 (14-oz) cans tomatoes, drained
2 tbsp chili powder
½ tsp salt
2 tbsp parsley, chopped

Directions

Set your Instant Pot to Sauté mode and heat the olive oil. Brown the ground pork for 5-6 minutes, crumbling with a spatula. Add in peas, onions, and garlic and continue cooking for 5 minutes, stirring often. Add in the tomatoes, chili powder, and salt. Stir and allow simmering for 2 minutes.

Seal the lid, select Manual/Pressure Cook mode on High, and set time to 15 minutes. When done, perform a quick pressure to let out steam and unlock the lid. Serve garnished with parsley.

Calzone with Pork Sausage & Mozzarella

Total Time: 30 minutes | **Servings**: 4 | **Per Serving**: Kcal 464; Carbs 23g; Fat 18g; Protein 20g

Ingredients

2 tbsp olive oil
1 green bell pepper, chopped
2 Italian pork sausages, sliced

1 pound frozen bread dough, thawed
¼ cup tomato sauce
1 cup shredded mozzarella cheese

Directions

On your Instant Pot, select Sauté, and heat 1 tbsp of olive oil. Sauté the bell pepper for 3 minutes. Set aside. Brown the sausages for 5 minutes on both sides.

Use your hands to press each bread dough into a circle about 7 inches in diameter. One after the other spread 1 tbsp of tomato sauce over half of a dough circle. Arrange the sausage in a single layer and sprinkle a quarter of the green peppers over the top. Top with a quarter cup of cheese. Fold the uncovered half of each circle over the filling and pinch the edges together to seal. Brush the calzones with the remaining oil. Transfer the calzones to a baking dish.

Put a trivet in the pot and pour 1 cup water. Place baking dish on the trivet. Seal the lid, select Manual/Pressure Cook on High, and set the time to 6 minutes. After cooking, perform a quick pressure release, and unlock the lid. Serve.

Chinese-Style Pork Chili

Total Time: 35 minutes | **Servings**: 4 | **Per Serving**: Kcal 632; Carbs 26g; Fat 44g; Protein 39g

Ingredients

1 lb ground pork
2 large brown onions, finely chopped
4 jalapeño peppers, deseeded and minced
1 green bell pepper, deseeded and chopped
1 tbsp olive oil
1 tbsp grated ginger
4 garlic cloves, minced
1 tbsp five-spice powder
1 tbsp Sichuan peppercorns, crushed

¼ cup hoisin sauce
¼ cup soy sauce
2 cups chicken broth
12 oz amber colored beer
1 cup chopped tomatoes
1 tbsp rice wine vinegar
2 tsp Sriracha sauce
3 tbsp chopped cilantro

Directions

Set your Instant Pot to Sauté mode and adjust to medium heat. In inner pot, add pork, onions, jalapeño peppers, bell pepper, and olive oil. Cook until pork is brown, 5 minutes. Stir in ginger, garlic, five-spice powder, peppercorns, hoisin sauce, soy sauce, broth, beer, tomatoes, vinegar, and Sriracha sauce.

Seal the lid, set on Manual/Pressure Cook mode on High, and set cooking time to 10 minutes. After cooking, do a natural pressure release for 10 minutes. Stir in cilantro, adjust taste with salt, pepper, and dish chili into bowls. Serve.

Teriyaki Pork Noodles

Total Time: 30 minutes | **Servings**: 4 | **Per Serving**: Kcal 392; Carbs 19g; Fat 19g; Protein 36g

Ingredients

8 oz egg noodles
1 pound green beans, trimmed
1 tbsp olive oil
Salt and black pepper to taste

1 pork tenderloin, trimmed and cubed
1 cup teriyaki sauce
Sesame seeds, for garnish

Directions

Pour the egg noodles and cover with enough water in the pot. In a large bowl, toss the green beans with olive oil, salt, and black pepper. Seal the lid, select Manual/Pressure Cook on High, and set the cooking time to 3 minutes. When ready, perform a quick pressure release, and unlock the lid. Drain the noodles and set aside.

In the Instant Pot, toss the tenderloin with the teriyaki sauce. Add in 1/2 cup of water. Seal the lid, select Manual/Pressure Cook on High, and set the cooking time to 12 minutes. When ready, perform a quick pressure release, and unlock the lid. Serve the pork with green beans over the egg noodles and garnish with sesame seeds.

Juicy Barbecue Pork Chops

Total Time: 45 minutes | **Servings**: 4 | **Per Serving**: Kcal 442; Carbs 18g; Fat 22g; Protein 43g

Ingredients

3 tbsp brown sugar
1 ½ tbsp smoked paprika
2 tsp garlic powder
Salt and black pepper to taste

4 bone-in pork chops
1 tbsp olive oil
1 ½ cups chicken broth
4 tbsp barbecue sauce

Directions

In a small bowl, mix the brown sugar, salt, paprika, garlic powder, and black pepper. Season the pork with the rub. Select Sauté on your Instant Pot and heat the oil. Sear the pork chops, one at a time, on both sides, about 5 minutes. Pour in the chicken broth and barbecue sauce.

Seal the lid, select Manual/Pressure Cook on High, and set the cooking time to 5 minutes. When done, perform a natural pressure release for 10 minutes, then a quick pressure release, and unlock the lid. Serve.

Pork Sausage Ragu with Capers

Total Time: 40 minutes | **Servings**: 4 | **Per Serving**: Kcal 465; Carbs 61g; Fat 12g; Protein 32g

Ingredients

1 pound pork sausages, sliced
2 tbsp olive oil
1 onion, chopped
2 garlic cloves, minced
1 tbsp red wine vinegar
Salt and black pepper to taste

6 oz canned tomatoes
½ tsp dried oregano
1 bay leaf
2 tbsp capers
8 oz spirals pasta

Directions

Set your Instant Pot to Sauté and heat the olive oil. Place in the onion, garlic, salt, and black pepper and sauté for 5 minutes, stirring often. Add in the sausages and brown on all sides, about 5-6 minutes. Pour in the red wine vinegar, spirals pasta, canned tomatoes, oregano, bay leaf, and 2 cups water.

Seal the lid, select Manual/Pressure Cook mode on High, and set cooking time to 8 minutes. When done cooking, perform natural pressure release for 6 minutes, then a quick pressure release to let out the remaining steam. Unlock the lid and stir in the capers. Serve hot.

Cheesy BBQ Pulled Pork

Total Time: 50 minutes | **Servings**: 4 | **Per Serving**: Kcal 622; Carbs 36g; Fat 34g; Protein 42g

Ingredients

1 tsp onion powder
2 tsp garlic powder
¼ tsp cayenne powder
2 tsp chili powder
1 tsp dry mustard
Salt and freshly ground black pepper
1 tbsp brown sugar
1 tbsp smoked paprika

1 ½ tsp cumin powder
2 tbsp olive oil
1 lb pork shoulder, cut into 2-inch pieces
1 cup bbq sauce
1 cup ketchup
2 tbsp Worcestershire sauce
1 ½ cups chicken broth
½ cup grated cheddar cheese

Directions

In a medium bowl, mix onion powder, garlic powder, cayenne powder, chili powder, mustard, salt, black pepper, brown sugar, paprika, and cumin powder.

Set your Instant Pot to Sauté and heat olive. Season pork with dry rub on all sides, and sear the meat in oil until golden brown, 10 minutes. Pour in bbq sauce, ketchup, Worcestershire sauce, and chicken broth. Seal the lid, select Manual/Pressure Cook mode on High, and set cooking time to 15 minutes.

After cooking, do a natural pressure release for 10 minutes, then a quick pressure release to let out steam, and unlock the lid. Using two forks, shred pork into strands. Select Sauté mode, mix in cheddar cheese, and cook until cheese melts and is evenly combined onto meat. Dish food and serve.

Chinese-Style Braised Pork

Total Time: 80 minutes | **Servings**: 4 | **Per Serving**: Kcal 445; Carbs 15g; Fat 32g; Protein 23g

Ingredients

1 lb pork belly, cut into 2-inch cubes	1 star anise
Salt to taste	2 tsp granulated sugar
2 tbsp olive oil	1 ½ cups chicken broth
2 tbsp freshly grated ginger	1 tbsp regular soy sauce
2 leeks, chopped	1 tbsp dark soy sauce
1 long red chili	2 scallions, chopped
2 bay leaves	1 tbsp sesame seeds

Directions

Pour 3 cups of water and add pork and salt into inner pot. Seal the lid, set on Manual/Pressure Cook mode on High, and set cooking time to 30 minutes. After cooking, perform a natural pressure release for 10 minutes, then a quick pressure release to let out remaining steam. Unlock the lid. Drain pork through a colander and set aside.

Clean inner pot and press Sauté. Heat olive oil and stir-fry ginger, leeks, red chili, bay leaves, star anise, until fragrant, 3 minutes. Add pork. In a medium bowl, mix sugar, chicken broth, and soy sauces. Pour mixture over pork. Seal the lid, set on Manual/Pressure Cook mode on High, and set cooking time to 10 minutes.

After cooking, perform a natural pressure release for 10 minutes, then a quick pressure release to let out remaining steam. Unlock the lid. Stir food and spoon into serving plates. Garnish with scallions, sesame seeds, and serve warm.

Pork Bolognese-Style Pizza

Total Time: 20 minutes | **Servings**: 4 | **Per Serving**: Kcal 479; Carbs 34g; Fat 26g; Protein 26g

Ingredients

1 pizza crust	1 cup shredded mozzarella cheese
½ cup canned crushed tomatoes	1 tsp red chili flakes, divided
1 yellow bell pepper, sliced, divided	1 tbsp chopped fresh basil, for garnish
½ lb ground pork, meat cooked and crumbled	

Directions

Grease one side of a pizza crust with cooking spray and lay on a baking pan. Top the crust with crushed tomatoes, bell pepper, ground pork, mozzarella cheese, and red chili flakes.

Pour 1 cup of water in Instant Pot and place in a trivet. Lay the pan on top. Seal the lid, select Manual/Pressure Cook on High, and set the time to 10 minutes. When done, perform a quick pressure release. Top with basil to serve.

Primavera Risotto with Crispy Bacon

Total Time: 30 minutes | **Servings**: 4 | **Per Serving**: Kcal 290; Carbs 20g; Fat 21g; Protein 13g

Ingredients

2 tbsp butter
4 spring onions, sliced
1 cup Arborio rice
1 ½ cups mushrooms, sliced
¼ cup white wine

2 cups chicken broth
1 cup capers
¼ cup bacon, chopped
1 cup Pecorino Romano cheese, grated
Salt and black pepper to taste

Directions

Set your Instant Pot to Sauté and melt the butter. Add in the bacon and capers and stir-fry for 5 minutes, until the bacon is crispy. Set aside. Add in spring onions and mushrooms and cook for 5 minutes, stirring often. Place in rice and cook for 2 minutes. Pour in the white wine and chicken broth and stir. Season with salt and black pepper.

Seal the lid, select Manual/Pressure Cook mode, and set time to 7 minutes on High. When done, perform a quick pressure release to let out the remaining steam. Unlock the lid and stir in the Pecorino Romano cheese until melted. Serve risotto topped with the capers and bacon.

Mexican Pork Burritos

Total Time: 55 minutes | **Servings**: 4 | **Per Serving**: Kcal 513; Carbs 47g; Fat 24g; Protein 46g

Ingredients

2 pounds pork shoulder
1 cup beef stock
1 tsp ground coriander
4 garlic cloves, crushed
1 onion, chopped
2 bay leaves
1 tsp cinnamon powder

Salt and black pepper to taste
1 tbsp soy sauce
½ cup enchilada sauce
12 corn tortilla wraps, warm
1 lime, juiced
Spicy pico de gallo for garnish

Directions

Mix pork, garlic, onion, ground coriander, cinnamon powder, bay leaves, soy sauce, enchilada sauce, salt, and black pepper in a bowl and marinate for 20 minutes, covered. Next, place the mixture in your Instant Pot along with the beef stock. Seal the lid, select Manual/Pressure Cook mode on High, and set cooking time to 30 minutes.

When done cooking, perform natural pressure release for 10 minutes, then a quick pressure release to let out the remaining steam. Unlock the lid and transfer the meat to a cutting board to cool. Shred with a fork and return it to the pot. To serve, fill the tortillas with the pork and top with pico de gallo and lime juice. Serve immediately.

BBQ Sticky Pork Baby Pork Baby Ribs

Total Time: 60 minutes | **Servings**: 4 | **Per Serving**: Kcal 890; Carbs 11g; Fat 59g; Protein 76g

Ingredients

1 rack pork baby back ribs
1 tbsp garlic powder
1 tsp dried oregano
1 tsp New Mexico chili powder

1 tsp mustard powder
4 tbsp BBQ sauce
Salt and black pepper to taste

Directions

Rub the back ribs with garlic powder, oregano, chili powder, mustard powder, salt, and black pepper. Pour 1 cup of water into the pot and fit in a trivet. Place the ribs on the trivet. Seal the lid, select Manual/Pressure Cook mode on High, and set cooking time to 25 minutes.

When done cooking, perform natural pressure release for 10 minutes, then a quick pressure release to let out the remaining steam. Unlock the lid and remove the ribs to a lined baking sheet. Brush with BBQ sauce and set under the broiler for approximately 10-15 minutes, until the ribs are sticky and charred.

Gingered Pork & Cucumber Salad

Total Time: 40 minutes | **Servings**: 4 | **Per Serving**: Kcal 414; Carbs 7g; Fat 29g; Protein 31g

Ingredients

1 tbsp olive oil
1 lb ground pork
1 small red chili, minced
2 ½ tbsp grated ginger
2 garlic cloves, minced
2 tbsp soy sauce
2 limes, juiced

1 tsp brown sugar
½ cup chicken broth
1 medium cucumber, thinly sliced
2 scallions, thinly sliced
1 cup chopped cilantro
½ cup chopped mint leaves

Directions

Set your Instant Pot to Sauté mode and adjust to medium heat. Heat olive oil in inner pot and cook pork until brown, 5 minutes. Add red chili, ginger, garlic, and cook until softened, 3 minutes.

In a medium bowl, mix soy sauce, lime juice, brown sugar, and chicken broth. Pour mixture onto pork and stir. Seal the lid, set on Manual/Pressure Cook mode on High, and set cooking time to 10 minutes.

After cooking, perform a natural pressure release for 10 minutes. Unlock the lid. Stir and spoon pork into a serving bowl. Top with cucumber, scallions, cilantro, and mint leaves. Serve immediately.

Hominy & Pork Soup

Total Time: 35 minutes | **Servings**: 4 | **Per Serving**: Kcal 503; Carbs 28g; Fat 29g; Protein 32g

Ingredients

1 lb ground pork
Salt and black pepper to taste
½ tsp chili powder
1 tsp cumin powder
1 tsp coriander powder
1 tbsp olive oil
1 white onion, thinly sliced

½ bunch cilantro, leaves chopped
4 cups chicken broth
1 cup chopped tomatoes
1 (28 oz) can hominy, rinsed
1 lemon, juiced
4 radishes, sliced for topping

Directions

Place pork in a medium bowl and season well with salt, pepper, chili powder, cumin powder, and coriander powder. Set your Instant Pot to Sauté mode and adjust to medium heat. Heat olive oil in inner pot and cook pork until brown, 5 minutes. Add onion, cilantro, and cook until softened, 3 minutes.

Pour in chicken broth, tomatoes, hominy, and stir. Seal the lid, set on Manual/Pressure Cook on High, and set time to 10 minutes. After cooking, perform a quick pressure release. Stir in lemon juice and adjust taste with salt and pepper. Dish food into serving bowls and top with radishes. Serve warm.

Soy-Marinated Pork Chops with Red Sauce

Total Time: 75 minutes | **Servings:** 4 | **Per Serving:** Kcal 366; Carbs 16g; Fat 14g; Protein 44g

Ingredients

4 boneless pork loin chops
1 onion, sliced
4 garlic cloves, minced
8 mushrooms, sliced
¼ cup tomato paste
2 tbsp ketchup

1 tbsp peanut oil
1 tbsp sugar
1 tsp tabasco sauce
1 cup water
Salt and black pepper to taste
1 ½ tbsp cornstarch mixed with 2 tbsp water

Marinade

½ tsp brown sugar
¼ tsp salt
2 tbsp sambal oelek ground fresh chili paste

¼ tsp sesame oil
1 ½ tbsp soy sauce
2 tbsp light soy sauce

Directions

Using a meat mallet, flatten the pork chops. In a bowl, combine the brown sugar, salt, soy sauce, sesame oil, and chili paste. Stir in the pork chops, cover, and marinate for at least 30 minutes.

Set your Instant Pot to Sauté and heat peanut oil. Place in marinated pork chops and cook for 2 minutes per side. Remove to a plate. Add in onion, garlic, mushrooms, salt, and pepper. Cook for 2-3 minutes until tender. Pour in 1 cup of water to scrape up any browned bits from the bottom of the pot. Place in the ketchup, sugar, tabasco sauce, and tomato paste and stir. Return the chops to the pot along with the meat juice.

Seal the lid, select Manual/Pressure Cook mode on High, and set cooking time to 15 minutes. When done cooking, perform natural pressure release for 10 minutes, then a quick pressure release to let out the remaining steam. Unlock the lid and remove the chops. Select Sauté and stir in the cornstarch slurry. Cook until you have a thick sauce. Adjust the seasoning and serve.

Pork with Sweet Pepper Sauce & Potatoes

Total Time: 50 minutes | **Servings:** 4 | **Per Serving:** Kcal 639; Carbs 42g; Fat 29g; Protein 52g

Ingredients

1 ¼ lb pork tenderloin, cut into 2 pieces
Salt and black pepper to taste
2 tbsp olive oil
4 potatoes, quartered
½ cup dry white wine
1 cup chicken stock

1 thyme sprig
2 garlic cloves, minced
1 roasted red bell pepper, cut into strips
6 pickled pimientos, stemmed and quartered
2 tsp pickling liquid from the peppers
2 tbsp butter

Directions

Season the beef with salt and pepper on all sides. On your Instant Pot, select Sauté and heat oil. Add the beef, sear for 6 minutes or until browned. Remove to a plate. Pour in wine and scrape off any browned bits at the bottom. Let the wine cook until reduced by one-third. Stir in potatoes, stock, thyme, and garlic. Return the beef to the pot.

Seal the lid, select Manual/Pressure Cook on High, and set the time to 20 minutes. After cooking, perform a natural pressure release for 10 minutes. Remove the pork and allow resting. Remove and discard the thyme. Select Sauté and stir in the roasted pepper, pimientos, and the pickling liquid. Taste and adjust the seasoning.

Right before serving, stir in the butter. Slice the tenderloin and lay the pieces on a platter. Ladle the peppers and potatoes around the pork and spoon the sauce over.

Braised Pork Shoulder Ragu with Rigatoni

Total Time: 50 minutes | **Servings:** 6 | **Per Serving:** Kcal 304; Carbs 20g; Fat 15g; Protein 24g

Ingredients

1 pound boneless pork shoulder
Salt to taste
2 tbsp olive oil
4 oz Italian sausage, casings removed
1 medium onion, chopped
2 garlic cloves, minced or pressed
1 medium carrot, peeled and chopped
1 celery stalk, chopped

½ cup dry red wine
¼ tsp red pepper flakes
1 (28-oz) can crushed tomatoes
2 tbsp tomato paste
2 tsp dried Italian herb mix
12 oz rigatoni
½ cup grated Parmesan cheese + for serving

Directions

On your Instant Pot, select Sauté and heat the olive oil. Season the pork with salt and sear it for 4 minutes or until browned. Add in sausage, onion, garlic, carrot, and celery. Sauté for 2 minutes or until softened.

Stir in the wine, use a wooden spoon to scrape the bottom of any browned bits. Cook for 2 to 3 minutes until the wine has reduced by half. Add the red pepper flakes, tomatoes, tomato paste, remaining salt, and Italian herbs. Stir to combine. Seal the lid, select Manual/Pressure Cook on High, and set the cooking time to 20 minutes.

After cooking, perform a natural pressure release for 10 minutes, then a quick pressure release. Unlock the lid. Shred the pork with two forks and break the sausage apart. Add 2 cups of water and the rigatoni.

Seal the lid again, choose Manual/Pressure Cook on High for 4 minutes. After cooking, do a quick pressure release. Sprinkle Parmesan cheese over the sauce and pasta, and serve.

Tropical Pineapple Pork Pot

Total Time: 40 minutes | **Servings:** 4 | **Per Serving:** Kcal 581; Carbs 46g; Fat 14g; Protein 66g

Ingredients

1 (20 oz) can pineapple chunks in juice
2 tbsp water
1 tbsp cornstarch
3 tbsp maple syrup
2 tbsp coconut aminos
2 tbsp brown sugar
1 tbsp grated ginger
3 garlic cloves, minced

2 tbsp olive oil, separated
2 lb pork stew meat, boneless and cubed
Salt and black pepper to taste
1 onion, chopped
1 medium red bell pepper, chopped
1 medium green bell pepper, chopped
1 tsp dried oregano
2 tbsp chopped parsley

Directions

In a small bowl, drain pineapple juice, and set aside pineapple chunks. In a medium bowl, combine water, cornstarch, maple syrup, coconut aminos, brown sugar, ginger, and garlic. Set aside.

Set your Instant Pot to Sauté mode and adjust to medium heat. Heat olive oil in inner pot, season pork with salt and black pepper, and sear in oil until golden brown on all sides, 5 minutes. Stir in onion, bell peppers, oregano, and cook until softened, 5 minutes. Add pineapple chunks and juice.

Seal the lid, select Manual/Pressure Cook on High, and set cooking time to 10 minutes. When done cooking, perform a natural pressure release for 10 minutes, then a quick pressure release until all the steam is out, and unlock the lid.

Stir food and adjust taste with salt and pepper. Garnish with parsley and serve warm with cooked basmati rice.

Beef & Lamb Recipes

Sticky Beef with Snap Peas

Total Time: 25 minutes | **Servings**: 4 | **Per Serving**: Kcal 422; Carbs 28g; Fat 23g; Protein 25g

Ingredients

¼ cup soy sauce
2 tbsp sesame oil
2 tbsp maple syrup
½ tsp hot sauce
1 tsp balsamic vinegar
½ cup chicken stock

½ cup + 2 tsp cornstarch, divided
1 lb beef sirloin, sliced against the grain
2 cups snow peas
3 garlic cloves, minced
3 scallions, thinly sliced

Directions

In a medium bowl, combine soy sauce, 1 tbsp of sesame oil, maple syrup, hot sauce, balsamic vinegar, chicken stock, and 2 tbsp of cornstarch. Set aside.

Pour remaining cornstarch on a plate. Season beef with salt, black pepper, and toss lightly in cornstarch. Set your Instant Pot to Sauté mode and adjust to medium heat. Heat remaining sesame oil in inner pot and fry beef in batches until brown and crispy, 5 minutes. Plate and set aside.

Discard oil, wipe inner pot clean with a paper towel, and pour in soy sauce mixture. Return meat to sauce; add snow peas and garlic. Seal the lid, select Manual/Pressure Cook mode on High and set cooking time to 3 minutes.

When done cooking, perform natural pressure release for 10 minutes, then quick pressure release to let out remaining steam. Unlock the lid, stir and adjust taste with salt and black pepper. Garnish with scallions and serve warm.

BBQ Beef Sloppy Joes

Total time: 25 minutes | **Servings**: 4 | **Per Serving**: Kcal 412; Carbs 20g; Fat 21g; Protein 35g

Ingredients

1 onion, chopped
2 tbsp olive oil
1 pound ground beef
1 red pepper, chopped
1 celery stick, chopped
¼ cup beef broth
1 garlic clove, minced
¾ cup tomato purée

1 tbsp yellow mustard
2 tsp brown sugar
2 tsp BBQ sauce
Salt to taste
½ tsp hot sauce
4 seeded burger buns, halved
4 lettuce leaves

Directions

Set your Instant Pot to Sauté and warm olive oil. Brown the beef for 4 minutes, breaking the meat with a wooden spatula. Stir in onion, red pepper, and celery. Pour in the beef broth, garlic, tomato puree, mustard, brown sugar, BBQ sauce, and salt and stir. Seal the lid, select Manual/Pressure Cook on High, and set time to 12 minutes. When done, perform a quick pressure to let out steam. Stir in the hot sauce.

To assemble the sloppy joes, arrange the lettuce leaves on the bottom bun halves, top with the meat and sauce, and finish with the other half of the bun.

Steaks in Berry Gravy

Total Time: 50 minutes | **Servings**: 4 | **Per Serving**: Kcal 529; Carbs 21g; Fat 16g; Protein 69g

Ingredients

For steaks:
1 tbsp butter
4 round beef steaks
Salt and black pepper to taste

¼ tsp dried thyme
1 tsp garlic powder
1 tsp onion powder

For berry sauce:
2 cups frozen mixed berries
4 tbsp granulated sugar
½ lemon, juiced and zested
1 fresh sprig rosemary + extra for garnishing

3 tbsp water
¼ cup red wine
½ tbsp cornstarch mixed with 1 tbsp of water

Directions

For steaks: set your Instant Pot to Sauté mode and adjust to medium heat. Melt butter in inner pot; season beef with salt, black pepper, thyme, garlic powder, and onion powder. Fry in butter until brown on both sides and almost cooked, 7 to 8 minutes. Transfer meat to plate and set aside.

For berry sauce: discard fat from inner pot, wipe clean with paper towel, and select Sauté. Pour in berries, sugar, lemon juice, rosemary, and water. Cook with frequent stirring until sugar dissolves. Add red wine, half cup water, and meat; baste meat with sauce. Seal the lid, select Manual/Pressure Cook on High, and set cooking time to 15 minutes.

After cooking, perform natural pressure release for 10 minutes, then quick pressure release to let out remaining steam. Unlock the lid and place meat on serving plates. Set to Sauté mode and stir cornstarch into sauce. Cook until thickens, 1 to 2 minutes. Spoon sauce all over meat, garnish with rosemary sprigs and serve immediately.

South Indian Spicy Beef

Total Time: 30 minutes | **Servings**: 4 | **Per Serving**: Kcal 353; Carbs 27g; Fat 18g; Protein 31g

Ingredients

1 tbsp olive oil
1 lb beef stew meat, cubed
Salt and black pepper to taste
1 cup grated carrots
2 white onions, sliced
2 garlic cloves, minced
½ tsp ginger puree
1 tbsp cilantro leaves

½ tsp garam masala powder
½ tsp red chili powder
¼ tsp turmeric powder
1 tsp cloves powder
1 tsp cumin powder
1 cup basmati rice
2 cups beef broth
¼ cup cashew nuts

Directions

Set your Instant Pot to Sauté mode and adjust to medium heat. Heat olive oil in inner pot, season beef with salt and black pepper, and brown in oil on both sides, 5 minutes. Plate and set aside.

Into oil, mix onions, garlic, ginger, cilantro, garam masala, red chili, turmeric, cloves, cumin, salt, and black pepper. Frequently stir while cooking until fragrance combines, 1 minute. Stir in rice, carrots, beef, and pour beef broth all over. Seal the lid, select Manual/Pressure Cook mode, and set cooking time to 6 minutes.

After cooking, allow sitting for 10 minutes, then do a quick pressure release to let out steam, and unlock the lid. Fluff rice and stir in cashews. Serve rice with coconut yogurt.

Saucy Honey Short Ribs

Total Time: 60 minutes | **Servings**: 4 | **Per Serving**: Kcal 368; Carbs 15g; Fat 21g; Protein 31g

Ingredients

1 ½ pounds large beef short ribs
2 tbsp olive oil
1 medium onion, finely chopped
3 garlic cloves, minced
½ cup apple cider vinegar

1 cup beef broth
1 tbsp honey
2 tbsp tomato paste
1 tbsp cornstarch
2 tbsp chopped parsley to garnish

Directions

Select Sauté mode and adjust to medium heat. Heat olive oil in inner pot, season ribs with salt and black pepper, and fry until brown on both sides, 8 minutes. Plate and set aside.

Sauté onion, garlic, and cook until soft and fragrant, 4 minutes. Stir in apple cider vinegar, beef broth, honey, tomato paste, and once simmering, add ribs. Seal the lid, select Manual/Pressure Cook on High, and set time to 25 minutes.

Once done cooking, perform natural pressure release for 10 minutes, then quick pressure release to let out remaining steam. Unlock the lid, transfer ribs to serving plates, and stir cornstarch into sauce. Cook on Sauté mode until thickened, 1 minute. Spoon sauce over ribs, garnish with parsley and serve warm.

Beef & Tofu Soup

Total Time: 35 minutes | **Servings**: 4 | **Per Serving**: Kcal 323; Carbs 13g; Fat 20g; Protein 27g

Ingredients

1 tbsp coconut oil
½ lb ground beef
Salt and black pepper to taste
1 medium onion, diced
2 garlic cloves, minced
1 green bell pepper, deseeded and diced
1 cup chopped shiitake mushrooms

½ cup kimchi + extra for serving
1 lb extra-firm tofu, pressed and cubed
4 cups beef broth
2 tbsp coconut aminos
1 tbsp mirin
2 tsp lemon juice

Directions

Set your Instant Pot to Sauté mode and adjust to medium heat. Heat coconut oil, add beef, season with salt and black pepper, and cook until brown, 5 minutes. Add onion, garlic, bell pepper, and mushrooms; cook until softened, 3 minutes. Stir in kimchi, tofu, cook for 1 minute, and pour in beef broth, coconut aminos, mirin, and lemon juice.

Seal the lid, select Manual/Pressure Cook mode on High, and set cooking time to 5 minutes. Perform natural pressure release for 10 minutes, then quick pressure release to let out remaining steam, and unlock the lid. Adjust taste with salt and black pepper and dish soup. Serve warm.

Rosemary Sauced Beef

Total Time: 35 minutes | **Servings**: 4 | **Per Serving**: Kcal 163; Carbs 7g; Fat 5g; Protein 23g

Ingredients

1 lb chuck roast
¼ cup red chili puree
½ cup beef broth

Salt and black pepper to taste
1 tsp dried rosemary

Directions

In inner pot, combine chuck roast, red chili puree, beef broth, salt, black pepper, and rosemary. Seal the lid, select Manual/Pressure Cook mode on High, and set cooking time to 15 minutes.

Once done, perform natural pressure release for 10 minutes, then quick pressure release to let out remaining steam, and unlock the lid. Shred beef with two forks, stir and adjust taste with salt and black pepper. Dish and serve as a condiment for rice and bread dishes.

Classic French Onion Beef Soup

Total Time: 65 minutes | **Servings**: 4 | **Per Serving**: Kcal 508; Carbs 35g; Fat 28g; Protein 31g

Ingredients

2 tbsp olive oil
1 ½ lb short ribs
Salt and black pepper to taste
1 tsp dried rosemary
1 tsp dried tarragon
1 tsp dried oregano
2 tbsp butter

6 medium onions, thinly sliced
½ tsp dried thyme
¼ cup dry white wine
4 cups hot beef stock
4 cups grated Gruyere cheese
8 slices toasted baguettes for topping

Directions

Set your Instant Pot to Sauté mode and adjust to medium heat. Heat olive oil in inner pot, season meat with salt, black pepper, rosemary, tarragon, oregano, and sear in oil until brown on both sides, 8 minutes. Plate and set aside.

Melt butter in inner pot and cook onions with frequent stirring until caramelized, 30 minutes. Pour in thyme, wine, and stock. Once boiling, place in beef. Seal the lid, select Manual/Pressure Cook on High, and set time to 15 minutes.

After cooking, perform natural pressure release for 10 minutes. Unlock the lid, stir and adjust taste with salt and black pepper. Spoon soup into four serving bowls, place two baguette slices in each bowl and cover with Gruyere cheese. Place soup bowls under a broiler and melt cheese, 3 to 4 minutes. Remove soup and serve warm.

Rich Beef Gumbo

Total Time: 35 minutes | **Servings**: 4 | **Per Serving**: Kcal 271; Carbs 24g; Fat 8g; Protein 28g

Ingredients

1 tbsp butter
1 lb beef stew meat, cubed
Salt and black pepper to taste
2 bell peppers, deseeded and diced
1 large onion, chopped
2 garlic cloves, minced
1 tbsp all-purpose flour

2 cups beef broth
1 cup canned whole tomatoes
1 cup sliced okras
¼ cup short-grain rice
¼ tsp dried rosemary
1 bay leaf
½ tsp hot sauce

Directions

Set your Instant Pot to Sauté mode and adjust to medium heat. Melt butter in inner pot, season beef with salt and black pepper, and brown on both sides, 5 minutes. Pour in bell peppers, onion, garlic, flour, beef broth, tomatoes, okras, rice, rosemary, bay leaf, hot sauce, and 2 cups of water.

Seal the lid, select Manual/Pressure Cook mode on High, and set cooking time to 15 minutes. Do a quick release. Unlock the lid, adjust taste with salt and black pepper, stir, and serve beef gumbo hot.

Irish Beef Shepherd's Pie

Total Time: 55 minutes | **Servings**: 4 | **Per Serving**: Kcal 654; Carbs 70g; Fat 22g; Protein 43g

Ingredients

3 russet potatoes, cubed
2 cups water, divided
1 tsp salt
2 tbsp butter
1 egg, cracked into a bowl
Black pepper to taste
1 lb ground beef
1 tsp garlic powder

1 tbsp Worcestershire sauce
2 medium white onion
1 cup mushrooms, chopped
3 carrots, chopped
¼ cup Guinness stout
1 cup beef broth
2 tbsp all-purpose flour
1 cup grated cheddar cheese

Directions

Pour potatoes, 1 cup water, and salt into inner pot. Seal the lid, select Manual/Pressure Cook mode on High, and set cooking time to 8 minutes.

After cooking, perform a natural pressure release for 10 minutes and then a quick pressure release to let out remaining steam. Unlock the lid and drain potatoes. Transfer to a medium bowl and add butter, egg, salt, and black pepper. Mash using a masher until smooth. Set aside.

Wipe inner pot clean with paper towels and select Sauté. Add beef to inner pot and brown for 5 to 6 minutes. Add garlic powder, Worcestershire sauce, onion, mushrooms, carrots, and stout. Cook until vegetables soften, 4 minutes.

In a medium bowl, mix beef broth with flour and pour into beef mixture. Cook until sauce thickens, 3 minutes. Turn Instant Pot off. Spoon beef filling into four ramekins, spread potato mixture on top, and cover with aluminum foil.

Clean inner pot, return to base, and pour in 1 cup water. Fit in a trivet and place ramekins on top. You may place two ramekins on trivet and fit remaining ramekins on the rims of the other two.

Seal the lid, select Manual/Pressure Cook mode on High, and set cooking time to 10 minutes. After cooking, perform a quick pressure release to let out steam. Unlock the lid and remove ramekins, take off aluminum foil, and top with cheddar cheese. Serve warm.

Coconut-Saffron Beef with Rice

Total Time: 36 minutes | **Servings**: 4 | **Per Serving**: Kcal 520; Carbs 25g; Fat 32g; Protein 43g

Ingredients

1 tbsp olive oil
1 lb ground beef
Salt and black pepper to taste
3 garlic cloves, minced
1 cup basmati rice

½ cup coconut milk
1 ½ cups chicken broth
20 saffron threads
2 scallions, thinly sliced

Directions

Set your Instant Pot to Sauté mode and adjust to medium heat. Heat olive oil in inner pot, add beef, season with salt and pepper, and cook until brown, 5 minutes. Add garlic and cook until fragrant, 30 seconds. Stir in rice until transparent, 3 minutes, and pour in coconut milk, broth, and saffron threads. Stir.

Seal the lid, select Manual/Pressure Cook mode, and set cooking time to 6 minutes. When done cooking, perform natural pressure release for 10 minutes, then quick pressure release to let out remaining steam. Unlock the lid, fluff rice, and plate. Garnish with scallions and serve warm with curry sauce.

Macaroni & Beef Casserole

Total Time: 35 minutes | **Servings**: 4 | **Per Serving**: Kcal 763; Carbs 96g; Fat 19g; Protein 48g

Ingredients

1 tbsp olive oil
1 lb ground beef
Salt and black pepper to taste
1 tsp garlic powder
2 large celery stalks, chopped

1 medium brown onion, chopped
16 oz raw macaroni
3 cups chicken broth
2 cups chopped tomatoes
3 cups grated cheddar cheese

Directions

Set your Instant Pot to Sauté. Heat olive oil, add beef and cook until brown, 5 minutes. Season with salt, pepper, and garlic powder. Mix in celery, onion, and cook until softened, 3 minutes. Pour in chicken broth and tomatoes.

Seal the lid, select Manual/Pressure Cook on High, and set time to 15 minutes. After cooking, do a quick pressure release. Stir in macaroni, seal the lid again and cook on Manual/Pressure Cook for 4 minutes. Do a quick pressure release. Spoon into bowls and serve sprinkle with cheddar cheese.

Simple Beef Chili

Total Time: 35 minutes | **Servings**: 4 | **Per Serving**: Kcal 408; Carbs 31g; Fat 14g; Protein 40g

Ingredients

2 tbsp butter
1 lb ground beef
Salt and black pepper to taste
1 white onion, chopped
1 red bell pepper, chopped

2 garlic cloves, minced
2 cups canned black beans, drained and rinsed
1 ½ cups chopped tomatoes
2 cups chicken broth
2 tbsp chili powder

Directions

Set your Instant Pot to Sauté mode and melt butter. Add in beef, season with salt and black pepper, add onion, bell pepper, garlic, and cook for 5 minutes. Stir in black beans, tomatoes, chicken broth, and chili powder.

Seal the lid, select Manual/Pressure Cook mode on High, and set time to 10 minutes. After cooking, perform natural pressure release for 10 minutes. Serve warm with rice or bread.

Sweet Short Ribs with Garlic & Rosemary

Total Time: 65 minutes | **Servings**: 4 | **Per Serving**: Kcal 583; Carbs 16g; Fat 45g; Protein 34g

Ingredients

4 bone-in beef short ribs, silver skin
Salt and black pepper to taste
2 tbsp olive oil
1 onion, chopped

2 tbsp honey
½ cup beef broth
2 tbsp minced fresh rosemary
3 garlic cloves, minced

Directions

Season the ribs on all sides with salt and pepper. Select Sauté on your Instant Pot and heat 1 tbsp of olive oil. Brown the ribs on all sides, about 6 minutes in total. Stir in onion, honey, broth, half of the rosemary, and garlic. Seal the lid, select Manual/Pressure Cook on High, and set the time to 40 minutes. When done, do a quick pressure release. Serve the ribs sprinkled with the remaining rosemary.

Beef Meatballs in Orange-Honey Sauce

Total Time: 45 minutes | **Servings:** 4 | **Per Serving:** Kcal 690; Carbs 26g; Fat 41g; Protein 53g

Ingredients

For beef meatballs:
1 cup quick-cooking oats
½ cup crushed graham crackers
2 large eggs, lightly beaten
1 (5 oz) can evaporated milk
1 tbsp dried minced onion
Salt and black pepper to taste

1 tsp garlic powder
1 tsp cumin powder
1 tsp honey
1 ½ lb ground beef
2 tbsp olive oil

For sauce:
3 tbsp brown sugar
¼ cup orange marmalade
2 tbsp cornstarch
2 tbsp soy sauce

2 tbsp hot sauce
1 tbsp Worcestershire sauce
¼ cup chicken broth

Directions

In a large bowl, combine oats, graham crackers, eggs, milk, onion, salt, black pepper, garlic, cumin, honey, and beef. Mix and form mixture into 1 ½ - inch balls. Set your Instant Pot to Sauté mode and adjust to medium heat. Heat olive oil in inner pot and fry meatballs until golden brown, 5 minutes. Set aside.

In the pot, mix brown sugar, orange marmalade, cornstarch, soy sauce, hot sauce, Worcestershire sauce, and chicken broth. Allow simmering for 5 minutes. Return meatballs to inner pot and coat with sauce.

Seal the lid, select Manual/Pressure Cook mode on High, and set cooking time to 10 minutes. After cooking, do a natural pressure release for 10 minutes, then quick pressure release to let out remaining steam. Unlock the lid. Dish meatballs into plates and spoon sauce over meatballs.

Korean-Style Beef with Rice & Scallions

Total Time: 30 minutes | **Servings:** 4 | **Per Serving:** Kcal 635; Carbs 52g; Fat 24g; Protein 53g

Ingredients

2 tbsp olive oil
1 lb ground beef
3 garlic cloves, minced
¼ cup tamarind sauce
¼ cup packed brown sugar
2 tsp sesame oil
¼ tsp ground ginger

¼ tsp red chili flakes
Black pepper to taste
1 cup brown rice
2 cups beef broth
2 scallions, thinly sliced
½ tsp sesame seeds for garnishing

Directions

Set your Instant Pot to Sauté mode and heat olive oil. Fry beef until brown, 5 minutes and add garlic; cook until fragrant, 30 seconds. In a small bowl, whisk tamarind sauce, brown sugar, sesame oil, ginger, red chili flakes, and black pepper. Pour mixture all over beef, stir in rice, and beef broth.

Seal the lid, select Manual/Pressure Cook mode, and set cooking time to 10 minutes. When done cooking, perform natural pressure release for 10 minutes, then quick pressure release to let out remaining steam. Unlock the lid, fluff rice, and plate. Garnish with scallions and sesame seeds. Serve warm.

Lemongrass-Ginger Beef Pot

Total Time: 35 min + marinating time | **Servings**: 4 | **Per Serving**: Kcal 370; Carbs 25g; Fat 20g; Protein 33g

Ingredients

1 lb beef stew meat, cut into 1-inch cubes
1 tbsp soy sauce
½ tsp miso paste
1 tsp garlic puree
1 tsp cumin powder
1 tsp chili powder
1 tsp + ½ tbsp ginger paste
A pinch five-spice
Salt and black pepper to taste
1 tbsp rice wine

½ tsp sesame oil
2 tbsp olive oil
1 onion, chopped
1 red bell pepper, deseeded and chopped
1 green bell pepper, deseeded and chopped
1 lemongrass stalk, thinly sliced
2 garlic cloves, minced
1 cup jasmine rice
1 ¾ cups chicken broth
2 tbsp chopped parsley to garnish

Directions

In a bowl, add beef and top with soy sauce, miso paste, garlic puree, cumin powder, chili powder, 1 tsp of ginger paste, five-spice, salt, black pepper, rice wine, and sesame oil. Mix and marinate meat for 30 minutes.

Set your Instant Pot to Sauté mode and adjust to medium heat. Heat olive oil in inner pot, drain beef from marinade and cook in oil until brown, 5 minutes. Stir in onion, bell peppers, lemongrass, and garlic. Cook until vegetables soften and are fragrant, 3 minutes. Stir in rice, cook for 1 minute and top with chicken broth.

Seal the lid, select Manual/Pressure Cook mode on High, and set cooking time to 5 minutes. Allow sitting (covered) for 10 minutes, and then perform quick pressure release to let out remaining steam. Unlock the lid, stir and adjust taste with salt and black pepper. Dish food onto serving plates and garnish with parsley.

Quick Thai Basil Beef

Total Time: 20 minutes | **Servings**: 4 | **Per Serving**: Kcal 269; Carbs 16g; Fat 14g; Protein 22g

Ingredients

¼ cup soy sauce
1 tsp honey
1 tbsp fish sauce
1 tsp chili paste
1 tbsp oyster sauce
1 tsp fresh garlic puree
1 tsp cornstarch
1 tbsp sesame oil
2 cups thinly sliced beef steak

1 yellow onion, thinly sliced
1 large green pepper, thinly sliced
1 large red pepper, thinly sliced
3 garlic cloves, minced
1 tsp freshly grated ginger
1 cup Thai basil
1 tsp sesame seeds for garnishing
Salt and black pepper to taste

Directions

In a medium bowl, whisk soy sauce, honey, fish sauce, chili paste, oyster sauce, garlic paste, and cornstarch. Set aside.

Set your Instant Pot to Sauté mode and adjust to medium heat. Heat sesame oil and cook beef until brown on both sides, 5 to 6 minutes. Top with onion, bell peppers, and allow softening for 3 minutes. Add garlic and ginger; cook until fragrant, 1 minute.

Pour sauce mixture all over, stir and cook until sauce is syrupy, 1 minute. Stir in Thai basil and allow slight wilting, 45 seconds. Adjust taste with salt and black pepper as needed. Spoon stir-fry over bowls of cooked white rice, garnish with sesame seeds and serve warm.

Beef with Cabbage & Bell Pepper

Total Time: 17 minutes | **Servings:** 4 | **Per Serving:** Kcal 373; Carbs 11g; Fat 22g; Protein 33g

Ingredients

1 tbsp olive oil
1 lb ground beef
Salt and black pepper to taste
1 tbsp grated ginger
3 garlic cloves, minced
1 medium red cabbage, shredded
1 medium green cabbage, shredded

1 red bell pepper, deseeded and chopped
2 tbsp tamarind sauce
1 tbsp hot sauce
½ tbsp honey
1 tbsp sesame oil
2 tbsp walnuts
1 tsp toasted sesame seeds, for garnishing

Directions

Set your Instant Pot to Sauté mode and adjust to medium heat. Heat olive oil in inner pot, add beef, season with salt, black pepper, ginger, garlic, and cook until beef is no longer pink, 5 minutes. Add red and green cabbage, bell pepper, and stir-fry until softened, 5 minutes.

Meanwhile, in a medium bowl, combine tamarind sauce, hot sauce, honey, and sesame oil. Pour over stir-fry, add walnuts, and cook for 1 to 2 minutes. Dish, garnish with sesame seeds and serve warm.

Mongolian Beef

Total Time: 35 minutes | **Servings:** 4 | **Per Serving:** Kcal 421; Carbs 26g; Fat 23g; Protein 26g

Ingredients

1 lb flank steak, sliced into thin strips
Salt and black pepper to taste
¼ cup cornstarch
¼ cup olive oil
1 medium broccoli, cut into small florets
2 tsp grated ginger

1 tbsp garlic cloves, minced
½ cup soy sauce
½ cup water
½ cup dark brown sugar
4 scallions, thinly sliced

Directions

Season steak with salt and pepper. Pour cornstarch onto a plate and dredge meat in cornstarch. Set your Instant Pot to Sauté mode and adjust to medium heat. Heat olive oil in inner pot and cook beef until brown on all sides, 5 minutes. Stir in ginger, garlic, and cook until softened, 5 minutes. Pour in soy sauce, water, and brown sugar.

Seal the lid, select Manual/Pressure Cook mode on High, and set cooking time to 20 minutes. After cooking, perform a natural pressure release for 10 minutes. Unlock the lid, adjust taste with salt, black pepper, and stir in broccoli, and cook for 5 minutes on Sauté. Sprinkle with scallions to serve.

Greek-Style Beef with Feta & Ravioli

Total Time: 35 minutes | **Servings:** 4 | **Per Serving:** Kcal 439; Carbs 3g; Fat 29g; Protein 40g

Ingredients

1 cup cheese ravioli
1 tbsp olive oil
1 lb ground beef
Salt and black pepper to taste
1 cup canned diced tomatoes

1 tbsp dried mixed herbs
½ cup chicken broth
1 cup baby spinach
¼ cup Kalamata olives, pitted and sliced
¼ cup crumbled feta cheese

Directions

Pour ravioli, 3 cups of water, and salt in inner pot. Seal the lid, select Manual/Pressure Cook on High, and set time to 3 minutes. After cooking, perform a quick pressure release. Drain pasta through a colander and set aside.

Set your Instant Pot to Sauté mode and adjust to medium heat. Heat olive oil in inner pot, add beef, season with salt, black pepper, and cook until brown, 5 minutes. Mix in tomatoes, mixed herbs, and chicken broth. Seal the lid, select Manual/Pressure Cook mode on High, and set cooking time to 10 minutes.

After cooking, perform a quick pressure release to let out steam and unlock the lid. Select Sauté mode. Mix in pasta, spinach, olives, and cook until spinach wilts. Stir in feta cheese and dish food.

Beef & Sweet Potato Pot

Total Time: 35 minutes | **Servings**: 4 | **Per Serving**: Kcal 410; Carbs 20g; Fat 21g; Protein 35g

Ingredients

2 tbsp olive oil
1 lb ground beef
1 small onion, finely chopped
1 carrot, peeled and chopped
1 celery stick, chopped
¾ cup chopped baby Bella mushrooms

1 garlic clove, minced
2 tbsp tomato paste
1 tbsp Worcestershire Sauce
1 tsp cinnamon powder
2 cups beef stock
2 medium-sized sweet potatoes, chopped

Directions

Set your Instant Pot to Sauté mode. Heat olive oil in inner pot and cook beef until brown, 5 minutes. Mix in onion, carrot, celery, mushrooms, and garlic. Cook until vegetables soften, 5 minutes. Mix in tomato paste, Worcestershire sauce, and cinnamon powder. Cook further for 1 minute. Pour in beef stock and potatoes; stir.

Seal the lid, select Manual/Pressure Cook on High, and set time to 10 minutes. After cooking, perform a natural pressure release and unlock the lid. Stir and adjust taste with salt and black pepper. Dish food and serve warm.

Short Ribs in Fig-Tomato Chutney

Total Time: 50 minutes | **Servings**: 4 | **Per Serving**: Kcal 844; Carbs 31g; Fat 50g; Protein 76g

Ingredients

3 bacon slices, chopped
1 tsp olive oil
4 lb beef short ribs
Salt and black pepper to taste
1 lb cherry tomatoes, halved
1 medium white onion, chopped

3 garlic cloves, minced
2 cups beef broth
1 cup Marsala wine
¼ cup fig preserves
3 tbsp thyme leaves

Directions

Set your Instant Pot to Sauté mode and adjust to medium heat. Cook bacon in inner pot until brown and crispy, 5 minutes. Place on a paper towel-lined plate and set aside.

Heat olive oil in inner pot, season beef ribs with salt, black pepper, and cook on both sides until brown. Transfer next to bacon. Add tomatoes, onion, and garlic to inner pot; cook until softened, 5 minutes. Stir in beef broth, Marsala wine, fig preserves, and thyme. Return beef and bacon to pot.

Seal the lid, select Manual/Pressure Cook mode on High, and set cooking time to 20 minutes. After cooking, perform a natural pressure release for 10 minutes, then a quick pressure release to let out steam. Unlock the lid. Stir and serve.

Lentil & Beef Chili

Total Time: 35 minutes | **Servings:** 4 | **Per Serving:** Kcal 282; Carbs 15g; Fat 14g; Protein 26g

Ingredients

1 tbsp oil
12 ounces ground beef
¼ tsp lemon pepper seasoning
1 onion, chopped
2 garlic cloves, minced
1 can (14.5 ounces) crushed tomatoes
1 tbsp chili powder

1 tbsp ground cumin
1 tsp dried oregano
¼ tsp crushed red pepper
½ cup beef broth
1 cup canned lentils
Salt and black pepper to taste
Chives, chopped for garnish

Directions

Set your Instant Pot to Sauté and heat the oil. Add in the ground beef, salt, and lemon pepper. Cook for 8 minutes, stirring often until browned. Put in the onion and garlic and cook for another 2 minutes. Pour in tomatoes, remaining spices, broth, and lentils and stir.

Seal the lid, select Manual/Pressure Cook, and set the time to 10 minutes on High. When done, perform a quick pressure release. Adjust the seasoning with salt and black pepper, top with chopped chives and serve.

One-Pot Spinach Beef Tagliatelle

Total Time: 35 minutes | **Servings:** 4 | **Per Serving:** Kcal 452; Carbs 39g; Fat 17g; Protein 34g

Ingredients

1 tbsp olive oil
1 lb ground beef
1 small yellow onion, chopped
1 cup sliced cremini mushrooms
2 garlic cloves, minced
2 (26-oz) jars tomato pasta sauce

3 cups water
16 oz tagliatelle
1 tbsp Italian seasoning
1 tsp dried basil
Salt and black pepper to taste
1 cup baby spinach

Directions

Set your Instant Pot to Sauté and heat oil. Cook beef for 5 minutes. Add onion, mushrooms, garlic, and cook until vegetables soften, 3 minutes. Stir in tomato sauce, water, tagliatelle, Italian seasoning, basil, salt, and pepper.

Seal the lid, select Manual/Pressure Cook mode on High, and set cooking time to 5 minutes. After cooking, perform a quick pressure release to let out steam, and unlock the lid. Select Sauté mode and mix in spinach. Allow wilting for 5 minutes and adjust taste with salt and black pepper. Dish food and serve warm.

Ground Beef Stuffed Empanadas

Total Time: 35 minutes | **Servings:** 2 | **Per Serving:** Kcal 418; Carbs 35g; Fat 32g; Protein 33g

Ingredients

1 cup olive oil
1 garlic clove, minced
½ white onion, chopped
¼ pound ground beef
6 green olives, pitted and chopped
¼ tsp cumin powder

¼ tsp paprika
¼ tsp cinnamon powder
2 small tomatoes, chopped
8 square wonton wrappers
1 egg, beaten

Directions

Select Sauté on your Instant Pot and heat 1 tbsp of the olive oil. Cook the garlic, onion, and ground beef for 5 minutes, stirring occasionally, until fragrant and the beef is no longer pink. Stir in the olives, cumin, paprika, and cinnamon, and cook for an additional 3 minutes. Add the tomatoes and 1 cup water, and cook for 1 more minute.

Seal the lid, select Manual/Pressure Cook on High, and set time to 8 minutes. After cooking, perform a natural pressure release for 10 minutes. Spoon the beef mixture into a plate and allow cooling for a few minutes.

Lay the wonton wrappers on a flat surface. Place 2 tbsp of the beef mixture in the middle of each wrapper. Brush the edges of the wrapper with egg and fold in half to form a triangle. Pinch the edges together to seal.

Wipe out the inner pot. Heat the remaining oil and fry the empanadas in a single layer, about 20 seconds per side. Remove to paper towels to soak up excess fat before serving.

Malaysian Beef

Total Time: 50 minutes | **Servings**: 4 | **Per Serving**: Kcal 453; Carbs 31g; Fat 17g; Protein 38g

Ingredients

1 tbsp olive oil
1 ½ pounds beef shanks, cross-cut
½ tsp ginger, grated
1 garlic clove, minced
¼ cup water
½ cup coconut milk

¾ cup brown sugar
1 tbsp cornstarch
1 ½ tbsp cold water
Cilantro, chopped for garnish
1 red chili, finely sliced for garnish

Directions

Set your Instant Pot to Sauté, heat olive oil, and cook meat for 5 minutes on all sides until browned. Stir in the ginger, garlic, water, and coconut milk. Seal the lid, select Meat/Stew mode, and cook for 35 minutes on High.

When done, perform a quick pressure release to let out the steam. Unlock the lid and select Sauté. Add in brown sugar and stir. In a bowl, mix the cornstarch with cold water and stir until making a slurry. Pour in the pot and mix well. Cook until the sauce thickens. Top with cilantro and red chili to serve.

Mexican Shredded Beef

Total Time: 50 minutes | **Servings**: 4 | **Per Serving**: Kcal 484; Carbs 9g; Fat 23g; Protein 62g

Ingredients

2 lb tender chuck roast, cut into half
1 (8 oz) can tomato sauce
3 tbsp chipotle sauce
½ cup beef broth
½ cup chopped cilantro
1 lime, zested and juiced

1 tsp cayenne pepper
2 tsp cumin powder
Salt and black pepper to taste
½ tsp garlic powder
1 tbsp olive oil

Directions

In inner pot, add beef, tomato sauce, chipotle sauce, beef broth, cilantro, lime zest, lime juice, cayenne pepper, cumin powder, salt, pepper, and garlic powder. Seal the lid, select Manual/Pressure Cook on High, and cook for 30 minutes.

After cooking, do a natural pressure release for 10 minutes, then a quick pressure release to let out remaining steam. Unlock the lid and using two forks, shred beef into strands. Adjust taste with salt, black pepper, and stir in olive oil. Dish and serve warm with tortilla bread.

Beef & Ripe Plantain Chili

Total Time: 30 minutes | **Servings**: 4 | **Per Serving**: Kcal 468; Carbs 25g; Fat 23g; Protein 34g

Ingredients

3 tbsp palm oil
1 lb ground beef
1 medium red onion, chopped
2 garlic cloves, minced
2 tbsp chopped parsley
1 ½ cups tomato sauce

1 cup chicken stock
2 large ripe plantains, peeled and diced
1 scotch bonnet pepper, deseeded and chopped
1 tbsp mixed herbs
Salt and black pepper to taste
2 cups baby spinach

Directions

Set your Instant Pot to Sauté mode. Heat 1 tbsp of palm oil in inner pot and cook beef until brown, 5 minutes. Add onion, garlic, parsley, and cook until fragrant, 1 minute. Mix in tomato sauce, chicken stock, plantains, scotch bonnet pepper, mixed herbs, salt, and pepper. Seal the lid, select Manual/Pressure Cook on High, and set time to 10 minutes.

After cooking, perform a quick pressure release to let out steam and unlock the lid. Select Sauté mode and stir in spinach. Cook until wilted, 3 minutes. Adjust taste with salt and black pepper. Dish food into bowls and serve warm.

Beef Niçoise Sandwiches

Total time: 2 hours | **Servings**: 6 | **Per Serving**: Kcal 695; Carbs 28g; Fat 32g; Protein 74g

Ingredients

1 onion, chopped
1 garlic clove, minced
1 tbsp olive oil
3 pounds beef chuck roast
Salt and black pepper to taste
1 tbsp soy sauce

1 (10-oz) can condensed onion soup
1 ½ cups beef broth
2 bay leaves
6 small French Baguettes, halved lengthwise
6 Fontina cheese slices
2 tbsp Dijon mustard

Directions

Set your Instant Pot to Sauté mode and warm the olive oil. Rub the roast with salt and pepper and put it in the pot. Brown for 5 minutes per side. Add in garlic, onion, soy sauce, onion soup, broth, and bay leaves. Seal the lid, select Manual/Pressure Cook and cook for 80 minutes.

When done, perform a natural pressure release for 10 minutes, then a quick pressure release to let out the remaining steam. Unlock the lid and transfer the roast to a plate. Let it cool slightly before shredding with a fork. Divide the cheese and mustard among the baguettes, top with shredded meat, and serve with the cooking sauce.

Winter Beef Pot Roast with Pearl Onions

Total Time: 50 minutes | **Servings**: 6 | **Per Serving**: Kcal 361; Carbs 16g; Fat 13g; Protein 44g

Ingredients

2 tbsp olive oil
1 (3-pound) chuck roast
½ cup dry red wine
1 cup beef broth
1 tsp dried oregano leaves
1 bay leaf

Salt and black pepper to taste
1 small red onion, quartered
1-pound butternut squash, chopped
2 carrots, chopped
¾ cup pearl onions

Directions

On your Instant Pot, select Sauté and heat the oil. Season the beef with salt and cook in the pot for 3 minutes per side or until deeply browned. Add the wine to the pot and stir with a wooden spoon, scraping the bottom of the pot to let off any browned bits. Bring to a boil and cook for 2 minutes or until the wine has reduced by half.

Mix in beef broth, butternut squash, pearl onions, oregano, bay leaf, carrots, black pepper, and red onion. Stir to combine and add the beef with its juices. Seal the lid, select Manual/Pressure Cook on High, and set time to 35 minutes. After cooking, perform a quick pressure release. Remove the beef to slice. Spoon over the sauce and vegetables to serve.

Juicy Beef with Vegetables

Total Time: 35 minutes | **Servings:** 4 | **Per Serving:** Kcal 388; Carbs 44g; Fat 10g; Protein 32g

Ingredients

3 cups boiled water
3 cups rice noodles
¼ cup tamarind sauce
1 tbsp hoisin sauce
1 tsp maple syrup
1 tsp grated ginger
3 garlic cloves, minced
1 tbsp sesame oil

1 lb ground beef
2 cups sliced shitake mushrooms
1 yellow onion, thinly sliced
½ cup julienned carrots
1 cup shredded green cabbage
¼ cup sliced scallions
Sesame seeds for garnish

Directions

In a medium bowl, whisk tamarind sauce, hoisin sauce, maple syrup, ginger, and garlic. Set aside. Pour boiling water into a bowl and add rice noodles. Cover bowl with a napkin and allow softening for 5 minutes. Drain and set aside.

Set your Instant Pot to Sauté and heat sesame oil. Cook beef until brown, 5 minutes. Stir in mushrooms, onion, carrots, and cabbage; cook until softened, 3 to 5 minutes. Add in noodles. Top with sauce and mix well. Cook further for 1 minute to allow the flavors to incorporate. Garnish with scallions and sesame seeds and serve immediately.

Beef Steaks with Mushroom Sauce

Total Time: 40 minutes | **Servings:** 2 | **Per Serving:** Kcal 513; Carbs 15g; Fat 27g; Protein 52g

Ingredients

2 beef steaks, boneless
Salt and black pepper to taste
2 tbsp olive oil
4 ounces mushrooms, sliced
½ onion, chopped

1 garlic clove, minced
1 cup vegetable stock
1 tsp parsley, chopped
1 ½ tbsp cornstarch
1 tbsp half and half

Directions

Rub the beef steaks with salt and pepper. Set your Instant Pot to Sauté and warm the oil. Place in the beef and sear it for 2 minutes per side. Remove to a plate. Put in the mushrooms and cook for 5 minutes. Add in onion and garlic and cook for 2 minutes, until fragrant and aromatic. Return the steaks to the pot and pour in the stock.

Seal the lid, select Manual/Pressure Cook mode, and set cooking time to 15 minutes on High. When done, perform a quick pressure release to let out the steam. Unlock the lid and transfer the chops to a plate. Select Sauté made.

In a bowl, combine the cornstarch and half and half and mix well. Pour the slurry into the pot and cook until the sauce reaches the desired consistency. Serve topped with parsley.

Spicy Beef Pitas

Total Time: 45 minutes | **Servings:** 4 | **Per Serving:** Kcal 315; Carbs 26g; Fat 11g; Protein 31g

Ingredients

1 tbsp olive oil
1 lb beef stew meat, cut into strips
Salt and black pepper to taste
1 small white onion, chopped
3 garlic cloves, minced
1 tsp dried oregano
2 tsp hot sauce

½ cup beef broth
1 medium tomato, chopped
1 cucumber, deseeded and chopped
4 whole pita bread, warmed
1 cup Greek yogurt
1 tsp chopped dill

Directions

Set your Instant Pot to Sauté. Heat olive, season beef with salt, pepper, and cook until brown on the outside, 5 minutes. Set aside. Add onion and garlic to oil and sauté until softened, 3 minutes. Return beef to pot, stir in oregano, hot sauce, and beef broth. Seal the lid, select Manual/Pressure Cook mode on High, and set time to 20 minutes.

After cooking, perform a natural pressure release, then a quick pressure release to let remaining steam, and unlock the lid. Stir beef and spoon into a bowl. Mix in tomatoes, cucumber, and spoon beef mixture into pita bread. In a medium bowl, mix yogurt and dill. Top beef with yogurt mixture and serve immediately.

Sweet Ginger Beef & Broccoli

Total Time: 40 minutes | **Servings:** 4 | **Per Serving:** Kcal 585; Carbs 24g; Fat 27g; Protein 34g

Ingredients

1 tbsp olive oil
2 pounds skirt steak, cut into strips
4 garlic cloves, minced
½ cup coconut aminos
½ cup dark brown sugar

½ tsp ginger puree
2 tbsp cornstarch
1 head broccoli, cut into florets
3 scallions, thinly sliced

Directions

Select Sauté on your Instant Pot and heat the olive oil. Brown the steak on both sides, about 5 minutes in total. Set aside. Add in the garlic and cook for 1 minute or until fragrant. Stir in the coconut aminos, ½ cup water, brown sugar, and ginger. Mix, and return the beef. Seal the lid, select Manual/Pressure Cook on High, and set time to 20 minutes.

In a small bowl, whisk the cornstarch and 3 tbsp of water. When done cooking, perform a quick pressure release. Open the lid and pour in the cornstarch mixture and stir continuously until the sauce becomes syrupy on Sauté. Add the broccoli, stir to coat in the sauce, and cook for another 5 minutes. Garnish scallions and serve.

Colby Cheese Beef Carnitas

Total Time: 45 minutes | **Servings:** 4 | **Per Serving:** Kcal 621; Carbs 10g; Fat 25g; Protein 43g

Ingredients

2 ½ pounds bone-in country ribs
Salt to taste
¼ cup orange juice
½ cup beef stock
1 tbsp lime juice

1 onion, cut into wedges
2 garlic cloves, smashed and peeled
1 tsp chili powder
4 flour tortillas, warmed
1 cup shredded colby cheese

Directions

Season the ribs with salt. In your Instant Pot, combine the orange juice, stock, and lime juice. Drop in the onion and garlic; stir. Put the ribs in the pot, seal the lid, select Manual/Pressure Cook on High, and cook for 25 minutes.

After cooking, do a natural pressure release for 10 minutes. Transfer beef to a plate to cool. Remove and discard the bones. Shred the meat with two forks. Stir into the sauce. Serve the carnitas on tortillas sprinkled with cheese.

Beef Mushroom Soup

Total Time: 40 minutes | **Servings**: 4 | **Per Serving**: Kcal 329; Carbs 19g; Fat 17g; Protein 27g

Ingredients

1 tbsp coconut oil
½ lb ground beef
1 lb sliced baby Portobello mushrooms
½ lb oyster mushrooms, sliced
1 oz dried shiitake mushrooms
2 medium carrots, halved
1 celery ribs, halved
1 medium onion, quartered

2 tbsp soy sauce
5 cups chicken broth
2 bay leaves
2 tsp dried thyme
1 tbsp lemon juice
¼ tsp cayenne pepper
Salt and black pepper to taste

Directions

Set your Instant Pot to Sauté mode and adjust to medium heat. Heat coconut oil in inner pot, add beef and cook until brown, 5 minutes. Add oyster and dried mushrooms, carrots, celery, and onion. Stir and cook until softened, 5 minutes. Mix in soy sauce, chicken broth, bay leaves, thyme, lemon juice, cayenne pepper, salt, and black pepper.

Seal the lid, select Manual/Pressure Cook mode on High, and set cooking time to 10 minutes. After cooking, do a natural pressure release for 10 minutes, and then a quick pressure release to let out the steam. Unlock the lid. Stir soup and adjust taste with salt and black pepper. Dish into serving bowls and serve warm.

Spicy Tex-Mex Chili

Total time: 35 minutes | **Servings**: 6 | **Per Serving**: Kcal 485; Carbs 28g; Fat 23g; Protein 43g

Ingredients

2 tbsp olive oil
1 ½ pounds lean ground beef
3 garlic cloves, minced
2 onions, chopped
1 red bell pepper, chopped
1 tsp ground cumin
Salt and black pepper to taste
1 tbsp chili powder

2 jalapeño peppers, minced
2 cups beef broth
1 (14.5-oz) can fire-roasted tomatoes, undrained
1 (15-oz) can pinto beans, rinsed and drained
2 tbsp cornmeal
½ cup shredded cheddar cheese
¼ cup fresh cilantro, chopped for garnish

Directions

Set your Instant Pot to Sauté and heat olive oil. Cook the ground beef for 5 minutes, until slightly browned. Add in garlic, onions, cumin, bell pepper, chili powder, and jalapeño peppers; sauté for 5 minutes, until everything is thoroughly cooked. Stir in broth and tomatoes. Seal the lid, select Manual/Pressure Cook on High, and set time to 15 minutes.

When done, perform a quick pressure. Unlock the lid and press Sauté. Put in pinto beans and cornmeal. Stir and cook for another 3 minutes until the chili is thickened. Serve in bowls topped with cheddar cheese and cilantro.

Classic Carbonnade à la Flamande

Total Time: 60 minutes | **Servings**: 4 | **Per Serving**: Kcal 378; Carbs 8g; Fat 15g; Protein 39g

Ingredients

2 pounds brisket, cut into 3 pieces
Salt to taste
1 tbsp olive oil
1 large onion, sliced
8 oz Ale beer

¼ tsp dried rosemary leaves
¼ cup beef broth
½ tsp Dijon mustard
½ tsp brown sugar to taste
2 tbsp chopped fresh chervil

Directions

Season the brisket with salt. On your Instant Pot, select Sauté and heat olive oil. Sear the brisket for 4 minutes. Move the beef to the side. Add onion on the other side. Cook, stirring, for 2 minutes. Pour in beer, scraping off any browned bits from the bottom of the pot. Cook until the beer has reduced by half. Stir in the rosemary and broth.

Seal the lid, select Manual/Pressure Cook on High, and set time to 35 minutes. After cooking, perform a natural pressure release for 10 minutes. Remove beef onto a cutting board. Stir in the mustard and brown sugar. Select Sauté and cook for 5 minutes to reduce the liquid. Slice beef and return to the sauce to reheat. Serve garnished with chervil.

Baked Rigatoni with Beef Tomato Sauce

Total Time: 35 minutes | **Servings**: 4 | **Per Serving**: Kcal 634; Carbs 43g; Fat 20g; Protein 29g

Ingredients

1 tbsp butter
2 pounds ground beef
2 (24-oz) cans tomato sauce
1 cup dry red wine
16 oz dry rigatoni

½ tsp garlic powder
Salt to taste
1 cup cottage cheese
1 cup shredded mozzarella cheese
½ cup chopped fresh parsley

Directions

Select Sauté on your Instant Pot and melt the butter. Add the ground beef and cook for 5 minutes, or until browned and cooked well. Stir in the tomato sauce, 1 cup of water, wine, and rigatoni; season with the garlic powder and salt.

Seal the lid, select Manual/Pressure Cook on High, and set the cooking time to 10 minutes. When done, perform a natural pressure release for 10 minutes, then a quick pressure release, and unlock the lid. Stir in the cottage cheese and sprinkle the top of the pasta with the mozzarella cheese. Garnish with parsley and serve.

Cuban Beef Picadillo

Total Time: 50 minutes | **Servings**: 4 | **Per Serving**: Kcal 380; Carbs 12g; Fat 22g; Protein 33g

Ingredients

1 lb ground beef
1 tbsp cumin powder
¼ tsp chili powder
2 tbsp olive oil
1 large yellow onion, chopped
1 small red bell pepper, chopped
6 garlic cloves, minced
1 sweet potato, chopped

Salt and black pepper to taste
½ cup Marsala wine
1 ½ cups tomatoes, chopped
3 tbsp raisins
¼ cup capers, drained
½ cup green olives with pimento stuffing
1 tbsp chopped cilantro

Directions

Set your Instant Pot to Sauté and heat oil. Add beef, season with half tbsp of cumin, chili powder, and brown for 5 minutes. Place on a plate and set aside. Add in onion, garlic, and bell pepper and sauté until softened, 5 minutes. Mix in potatoes, remaining cumin, salt, and pepper; cook for 5 minutes. Return beef, wine, tomatoes, and raisins; stir.

Seal the lid, select Manual/Pressure Cook mode on High, and set time to 10 minutes. After cooking, perform a natural pressure release for 10 minutes. Stir in capers and olives. Garnish with cilantro and serve warm.

Creamy Shells with Beef & Mustard Greens

Total Time: 30 minutes | **Servings**: 4 | **Per Serving**: Kcal 634; Carbs 29g; Fat 38g; Protein 45g

Ingredients

2 cups water
Salt and black pepper to taste
8 oz medium pasta shells
1 tbsp olive oil
1 lb ground beef
½ medium brown onion, diced
2 garlic cloves, minced

1 ½ tsp dried mixed herbs
2 tbsp all-purpose flour
2 cups beef stock
1 (15-oz) can tomato sauce
¾ cup heavy cream
1 cup mustard greens, chopped
6 oz Monterey Jack cheese, shredded

Directions

Make salted water in inner pot and add pasta. Seal the lid, select Manual/Pressure Cook on High, and set cooking time to 5 minutes. After cooking, perform a quick pressure release to let out steam, and drain pasta. Set aside.

Set the pot to Sauté mode. Heat olive oil and cook beef until brown, 5 minutes. Add onion and cook for 3 minutes, then top with garlic, mixed herbs; cook for 1 minute. Gradually, mix in flour, beef stock, and tomato sauce.

Seal the lid, select Manual/Pressure Cook on High, and set time to 5 minutes. Perform a quick pressure release. Select Sauté. Stir in pasta, heavy cream, mustard greens, salt, pepper, and cheese. Cook until cheese melts and greens wilt.

Delicious Beef & Cheese Quiche

Total time: 50 minutes | **Servings**: 6 | **Per Serving**: Kcal 549; Carbs 22g; Fat 34g; Protein 37g

Ingredients

1 pound ground beef
3 tbsp taco seasoning
1 ½ cups water
1 ½ cups canned refried beans
½ cup salsa
3 tbsp olive oil

4 flour tortillas
¼ cup habanero hot sauce
2 ½ cups shredded Monterrey Jack cheese
1 red onion, sliced for topping
1 large tomato, sliced

Directions

Set your Instant Pot to Sauté and warm the olive oil. Add in the beef and brown for 7 minutes; scatter with the taco seasoning and stir. Remove to a plate. Wipe the inner pot clean with a paper towel, pour in water, and fit in a trivet.

In a bowl, mix together refried beans and salsa. In a greased baking pan, lay one flour tortilla, ½ cup of the bean mixture, 1 cup of the ground beef, a little bit of habanero sauce, and one fourth cup of cheese. Repeat these steps for the 3 layers. Top with the fourth tortilla and cover with foil.

Place the pan on the trivet. Seal the lid, select Manual/Pressure Cook on High, and set time to 15 minutes. Perform a natural pressure release for 10 minutes. Remove the foil. Serve topped with the remaining cheese, onion, and tomato.

Homemade Sloppy Joes

Total Time: 45 minutes | **Servings**: 4 | **Per Serving**: Kcal 679; Carbs 31g; Fat 36g; Protein 56g

Ingredients

1 tbsp olive oil
1 ½ lb ground beef
1 medium onion, chopped
1 red bell pepper, deseeded and chopped
3 garlic cloves, minced
1 tbsp light soy sauce
1 tbsp Worcestershire sauce
¾ cup ketchup

1 tbsp tomato paste
1 tbsp brown sugar
1 tsp Dijon mustard
½ cup chicken broth
Salt and black pepper to taste
2 drops liquid smoke
4 burger buns, halved

Directions

Set your Instant Pot to Sauté mode and adjust to medium heat. Heat olive oil in inner pot and cook beef until brown while breaking the lumps that form, 5 minutes. Add onion, bell pepper, and garlic. Cook until softened, 3 minutes.

In a medium bowl, whisk soy sauce, Worcestershire sauce, ketchup, tomato paste, brown sugar, and mustard. Stir mixture into beef mix and top with chicken broth, salt, black pepper, and liquid smoke.

Seal the lid, select Manual/Pressure Cook mode on High, and set cooking time to 15 minutes. After cooking, perform a natural pressure release for 10 minutes, then a quick pressure release to let out steam, and unlock the lid. Spoon food into burger buns and serve warm.

Beef Spaghetti Bolognese

Total Time: 35 minutes | **Servings**: 4 | **Per Serving**: Kcal 590; Carbs 56g; Fat 20g; Protein 30g

Ingredients

½ pound ground beef
1 pound spaghetti
1 carrot, grated
3 cloves garlic, minced
1 celery, chopped
1 onion, chopped

¼ cup red wine
1 tsp dried oregano
2 tbsp fresh basil, chopped
Salt and black pepper to taste
2 tbsp olive oil
Parmesan cheese, shredded to serve

Pasta Sauce:

1 cup beef stock
2 cups water

½ cup canned passata tomato
2 tbsp Worcestershire sauce

Directions

Set your Instant Pot to Sauté mode and warm olive oil. Place in the ground beef, salt, and pepper. Cook until browned, about 5-6 minutes. Set aside. Add in garlic, onion, carrot, celery, oregano, basil, salt, and pepper and sauté for 5 minutes, until softened. Add in 1/4 cup of red wine to scrape up any browned bits from the bottom of the pot.

Pour in beef stock, water, and Worcestershire sauce and return the ground beef; stir to combine. Mix in spaghetti and passata tomato and season with salt and pepper. Add in more water, if needed.

Seal the lid, select Manual/Pressure Cook mode on High, and set cooking time to 4 minutes. When done cooking, perform natural pressure release for 5 minutes, then a quick pressure release to let out the remaining steam. Unlock the lid and stir. Serve immediately topped with Parmesan cheese.

Beef & Veggie Mix with Rice

Total Time: 50 minutes | **Servings**: 4 | **Per Serving**: Kcal 453; Carbs 25g; Fat 26g; Protein 37g

Ingredients

2 tbsp olive oil
1 medium onion, chopped
1 red bell pepper, deseeded and chopped
1 cup sliced cremini mushrooms
2 garlic cloves, minced
1 lb ground beef
2 ½ tbsp tomato paste
Salt and black pepper to taste

½ tsp cumin powder
1 tsp onion powder
1 tsp Italian seasoning
¼ tsp chili powder
1 bay leaf
1 cup basmati rice
1 cup chicken broth
2 cups frozen mixed veggies

Directions

Set your Instant Pot to Sauté mode. Heat olive oil and sauté onion, bell pepper, garlic, and mushrooms until softened, 5 minutes. Mix in beef and cook until brown, 5 minutes. Stir in tomato paste, salt, pepper, cumin, onion powder, Italian seasoning, chili powder, and bay leaf. Allow releasing of fragrance for 1 minute and stir in rice. Cook further for 1 minute. Pour in chicken broth and stir.

Seal the lid, select Manual/Pressure Cook mode on High, and set cooking time to 5 minutes. Allow sitting (covered) for 10 minutes and then perform quick pressure release to let out remaining steam. Unlock the lid and select to Sauté mode. Stir in mixed veggies and cook until warmed, 3 minutes. Dish food into serving bowls and serve warm.

Easy Chili Meatloaf

Total time: 50 minutes | **Servings**: 6 | **Per Serving**: Kcal 533; Carbs 34g; Fat 22g; Protein 48g

Ingredients

Meatloaf

2 pounds ground beef
1 ½ cups breadcrumbs
1 tsp fennel seeds
½ tsp chili flakes
2 eggs

1 onion, minced
1 garlic clove, minced
1 tsp allspice
Salt and black pepper to taste
A bunch of fresh parsley, chopped

Sauce

1 cup ketchup
2 tsp Worcestershire sauce

5 tsp brown sugar
1 tbsp Wasabi powder

Directions

Mix together the beef, breadcrumbs, fennel seeds, chili flakes, eggs, onion, garlic, all spices, salt, pepper, and parsley in a bowl. Shape the mixture into a greased round loaf.

Combine the ketchup, Worcestershire sauce, brown sugar, and wasabi powder in another bowl, and mix until the sugar is dissolved. Spread the mixture over the top of the meatloaf.

Pour 1 cup water in your Instant Pot and fit in a trivet. Lower the meatloaf onto the trivet. Seal the lid, select Manual/Pressure Cook on High, and set time to 30 minutes.

When done, perform a quick pressure to let out steam. Unlock the lid and remove the meatloaf. Let rest for 5 minutes before slicing.

Braised Lamb Shanks

Total Time: 75 minutes | **Servings**: 4 | **Per Serving**: Kcal 523; Carbs 7g; Fat 21g; Protein 58g

Ingredients

2 tbsp olive oil
3 lb lamb shanks
Salt and black pepper to taste
6 garlic cloves, minced
¾ cup red wine

1 cup chicken broth
2 cups crushed tomatoes
1 tsp dried oregano
1 tsp dried basil
¼ cup chopped parsley to garnish

Directions

Set your Instant Pot to Sauté mode. Heat olive oil in inner pot, season with lamb with salt and black pepper, and sear in oil until brown outside, 3 minutes per side. Transfer to a plate. Stir in garlic and sauté until fragrant, 30 seconds.

Mix in red wine and cook for 2 minutes while stirring and scraping the bottom of any attached bits. Add tomatoes, oregano, and basil. Stir and cook for 2 minutes. Return lamb to pot and baste with sauce. Seal the lid, select Manual/Pressure Cook mode on High, and set cooking time to 45 minutes.

After cooking, perform natural pressure release for 15 minutes, then a quick pressure release to let out the remaining steam. Unlock the lid, stir in parsley, and adjust taste with salt and black pepper. Divide between plates and serve.

Croatian Lamb in Milk

Total Time: 80 minutes | **Servings**: 4 | **Per Serving**: Kcal 677; Carbs 37g; Fat 40g; Protein 42g

Ingredients

2 pounds boneless lamb shoulder, cubed
6 carrots, cubed
1 pound potatoes, cubed
5 garlic cloves
2 rosemary sprigs

4 cups milk
Salt and black pepper to taste
1 tbsp vegeta seasoning
2 cups water

Directions

To your Instant Pot, add the cubed lamb shoulder, carrots, potatoes, garlic, rosemary springs, vegeta seasoning, milk, water, salt, and pepper. Lock the lid, select Manual/Pressure Cook mode, and set cooking time to 60 minutes.

Once ready, perform natural pressure release for 10 minutes, then a quick pressure release to let out the remaining steam. Unlock the lid, remove and discard the rosemary spring and serve.

Lamb Shorba

Total Time: 55 minutes | **Servings**: 4 | **Per Serving**: Kcal 408; Carbs 12g; Fat 25g; Protein 36g

Ingredients

3 tbsp olive oil
1 medium white onion, chopped
6 garlic cloves, minced
1 cup chopped tomatoes
1 tsp cumin powder
1 tsp coriander powder
Salt to taste

1 tsp red chili powder
¼ tsp turmeric
4 cups chicken broth
1 ½ lb lamb shoulder, cut into 2-inch cubes
1 cup frozen peas
1 cup chopped cilantro

Directions

Set your Instant Pot to Sauté and heat olive oil. Sauté onion and garlic until softened, 3 minutes. Add tomatoes, cumin, coriander, salt, chili powder, and turmeric. Cook until tomatoes soften and sauce reduces by half, 6 minutes. Add chicken broth, allow boiling for 2 minutes, and add lamb. Seal the lid, select Manual/Pressure Cook mode on High, and set cooking time to 20 minutes.

After cooking, perform natural pressure release for 10 minutes, then quick pressure release to let out the remaining steam. Unlock the lid, stir in frozen peas, cilantro, and adjust taste with salt and black pepper. Cook further in Sauté mode until peas heat through, 1 to 2 minutes. Spoon shorba into serving bowls and serve.

Traditional Indian Lamb Curry

Total Time: 75 minutes | **Servings**: 4 | **Per Serving**: Kcal 359; Carbs 16g; Fat 22g; Protein 27g

Ingredients

2 tbsp oil
1 pound lamb meat, cubed
2 garlic cloves, minced
1 onion, chopped
2 tomatoes, chopped
1-inch piece of ginger, grated
½ tsp garam masala
½ tbsp ground turmeric

½ tbsp ground cumin
½ tbsp chili flakes
1 tbsp fish sauce
½ tbsp ground coriander
¼ cup cilantro, chopped
¼ cup rice, rinsed
½ cup coconut milk
½ cup chicken stock

Directions

Set your Instant Pot to Sauté and heat the oil. Place in the meat and brown for 3-5 minutes per side. Set aside. Add in garlic, onion, tomatoes, and ginger. Stir-fry for 5 minutes. Mix in the spices and cook for 10 minutes until they form a paste. Pour in the coconut milk, chicken stock, fish sauce, and rice and return the lamb.

Seal the lid, select Meat/Stew mode, and set cooking time to 35 minutes on High. When done, perform a natural pressure release for 10 minutes. Select Sauté and cook the curry until thickened. Serve in individual bowls.

Spicy Pulled Lamb

Total Time: 95 minutes | **Servings**: 4 | **Per Serving**: Kcal 447; Carbs 5g; Fat 27g; Protein 47g

Ingredients

2 tbsp olive oil
2 lb boneless lamb shoulder, cut into 4 pieces
2 cups chicken stock
6 tinned anchovies, drained and chopped
1 tsp garlic puree
1 sprig rosemary

1 tsp dried basil
1 tsp dried oregano
3 green chilies, minced
Salt to taste
2 tbsp chopped parsley

Directions

Set your Instant Pot to Sauté mode and heat olive oil. Sear lamb on both sides until brown, 5 minutes. Transfer to a plate and set aside. Pour chicken stock into inner pot, scrape the bottom to deglaze, and mix in anchovies and garlic. Return lamb to pot and top with rosemary, basil, oregano, green chilies, and salt. Seal the lid, select Manual/Pressure Cook mode on High, and set cooking time to 60 minutes.

After cooking, do a natural pressure release for 15 minutes, then quick pressure release to let out remaining steam. Unlock the lid, shred lamb using two forks, adjust taste with salt, and stir in parsley. Serve.

Lamb Rogan Josh

Total Time: 60 minutes | **Servings:** 4 | **Per Serving:** Kcal 486; Carbs 16g; Fat 27g; Protein 49g

Ingredients

2 tbsp ghee
1 large onion, chopped
2 pounds boneless lamb shoulder, cubed
10 garlic cloves, minced
2 tsp minced ginger
1 bay leaf
4 tsp chili powder
3 tsp coriander powder
Salt to taste and black pepper to taste

1 tsp garam masala
1 tsp turmeric
¼ tsp cumin powder
¼ tsp ground cloves
½ tsp cinnamon powder
½ tsp cardamom powder
1 (15 oz) can tomato sauce
8 tbsp plain yogurt
3 tbsp chopped cilantro

Directions

Set your Instant Pot to Sauté mode and adjust to medium heat. Melt ghee in inner pot and cook onion and lamb until lamb is no longer pink on the outside, 6 to 7 minutes. Stir in garlic, ginger, bay leaf, chili powder, coriander, salt, garam masala, turmeric, black pepper, cumin, cloves, cinnamon, and cardamom. Cook until fragrant, 3 minutes.

Mix in tomato sauce, cook for 2 to 3 minutes and stir in yogurt one tablespoon at a time. Seal the lid, select Manual/Pressure Cook mode on High, and set cooking time to 20 minutes. After cooking, perform natural pressure release for 10 minutes, then a quick pressure release to let out the remaining steam.

Unlock the lid and set select Sauté mode. Cook further for 3 to 4 minutes to boil off some liquid until the consistency is stew-like. Spoon food into serving bowls, garnish with cilantro, and serve.

Classic Lamb Tagine

Total Time: 60 minutes | **Servings:** 4 | **Per Serving:** Kcal 286; Carbs 14g; Fat 11g; Protein 32g

Ingredients

2 tbsp ghee
1 ½ lb lamb stew meat, cubed
1 large red onion, chopped
4 large carrots, peeled and chopped
6 cloves garlic, minced
1 lemon, zested and juiced
2 bay leaves
Salt and black pepper to taste
2 tsp cumin powder

2 tsp coriander powder
2 tsp ginger powder
½ tsp turmeric
¼ tsp cinnamon powder
¼ tsp clove powder
¼ tsp red chili flakes
2 cups vegetable stock
2 cups green olives, pitted
3 tbsp chopped parsley

Directions

Set your Instant Pot to Sauté mode and adjust to medium heat. Melt ghee in inner pot and cook lamb until brown on the outside, 6 to 7 minutes. Add onion, carrots, and garlic; cook until vegetables soften, 5 minutes.

Stir in lemon zest, bay leaves, salt, black pepper, cumin, coriander, ginger, turmeric, cinnamon, clove powder, and red chili flakes. Cook until fragrant, 1 to 2 minutes. Mix in vegetable stock.

Seal the lid, select Manual/Pressure Cook mode on High, and set cooking time to 20 minutes. After cooking, perform natural pressure release for 10 minutes, then a quick pressure release to let out the remaining steam.

Unlock the lid, taste stew, and adjust taste with salt. Discard the bay leaves and stir in green olives and parsley. Spoon into serving bowls and serve.

Lamb & Raisin Biryani

Total Time: 70 minutes | **Servings**: 4 | **Per Serving**: Kcal 365; Carbs 19g; Fat 23g; Protein 31g

Ingredients

1 lb lamb leg steak, cut into ¾ -inch cubes
1 large brown onion, thinly sliced
1 green bell pepper, deseeded and sliced
½ lime, juiced
½ cup Greek yogurt
4 tbsp ghee, divided
1 tbsp garlic paste
Salt to taste
1 tsp paprika

½ tsp turmeric
3 tsp garam masala
¼ tsp cayenne pepper
½ tsp cardamom powder
1 cup basmati rice, rinsed
½ cup chopped cilantro
1 cup warm water
½ tsp saffron, soaked in 3 tbsp of hot water
2 tbsp red raisins

Directions

In a bowl, add lamb, onion, and bell pepper. In another bowl, mix lime juice, yogurt, 2 tbsp of ghee, ginger, garlic, salt, paprika, turmeric, garam masala, cayenne pepper, and cardamom. Pour mixture over meat and vegetables, mix, and cover with a plastic wrap. Marinate in refrigerator for 30 minutes. Remove meat after and drain marinade.

Set your Instant Pot to Sauté mode and adjust to medium heat. Melt remaining ghee in inner pot and cook lamb until brown on the outside, 6 to 7 minutes. Add basmati rice, cilantro, warm water, and saffron liquid. Do not mix.

Seal the lid, select Manual/Pressure Cook mode on High, and set cooking time to 10 minutes. After cooking, perform natural pressure release for 10 minutes, then a quick pressure release to let out the remaining steam. Unlock the lid, stir in raisins, and adjust taste with salt. Divide between serving bowls and serve.

Minted Lamb Curry

Total Time: 1 hour 40 minutes | **Servings**: 4 | **Per Serving**: Kcal 622; Carbs 14g; Fat 38g; Protein 58g

Ingredients

2 ½ pounds lamb shoulder, cubed
¼ cup olive oil
4 green onions, sliced
2 tomatoes, peeled and chopped
2 tbsp garlic paste
1 tbsp ginger paste
1 cup vegetable stock
1 potato, cubed
1 large carrot, sliced

2 tsp allspice
2 tsp ground coriander
1 tsp ground cumin
½ tsp curry powder
2 tsp salt
½ tsp ground red chili pepper
2 bay leaves
2 tbsp mint leaves, chopped for garnish

Directions

Set your Instant Pot to Sauté mode and heat 2 tbsp of oil. Add in green onions and cook for 3 minutes, until tender, stirring occasionally. Transfer to a food processor, place in the tomatoes, garlic paste, and ginger paste, and blend until smooth. Heat the remaining oil in the pot and add in the lamb. Cook for 6 minutes. Pour in the onion paste, vegetable stock, potato, carrot, allspice, coriander, cumin, curry powder, salt, red chili pepper, and bay leaves and stir.

Seal the lid, select Manual/Pressure Cook mode on High, and set cooking time to 50 minutes. When done cooking, perform natural pressure release for 10 minutes, then a quick pressure release to let out the remaining steam. Unlock the lid and discard the bay leaves. Garnish with mint leaves and serve right away.

Fish & Seafood Recipes

Speedy Cod Paella

Total Time: 35 minutes | **Servings**: 4 | **Per Serving**: Kcal 260; Carbs 21g; Fat 13g; Protein 23g

Ingredients

2 tbsp olive oil
1 yellow onion, chopped
1 red bell pepper, deseeded and chopped
1 cup basmati rice, rinsed
1 cup fish stock

A pinch saffron threads, soaked in 2 tbsp hot water
Salt and black pepper to taste
¼ cup frozen peas
4 cod fillets, cut into 1-inch cubes
2 tbsp chopped parsley

Directions

Set your Instant Pot to Sauté mode and adjust to medium heat. Heat olive oil in inner pot and sauté onion and bell pepper until softened, 3 minutes. Mix in basmati rice, fish stock, saffron liquid, salt, and black pepper.

Seal the lid, select Manual/Pressure Cook mode on High, and set cooking time to 6 minutes. Allow sitting (covered) for 10 minutes and then perform a quick pressure release. Set the pot to Sauté mode. Mix in frozen peas and cod, cook until softened, 5 minutes. Carefully stir in parsley and serve paella.

Cod in Lettuce Wraps

Total Time: 15 minutes | **Servings**: 4 | **Per Serving**: Kcal 312; Carbs 15g; Fat 19g; Protein 22g

Ingredients

1 tbsp olive oil
2 garlic cloves, minced
½ cup tomato salsa
¼ cup chicken broth
Salt and black pepper to taste

½ lime, juiced
4 cod fillets, cut into 1-inch cubes
1 head iceberg lettuce, four big leaves extracted
2 scallions, chopped to garnish

Directions

Set your Instant Pot to Sauté mode and adjust to medium heat. Heat olive oil in inner pot and sauté garlic until fragrant, 30 seconds. Stir in salsa, chicken broth, salt, black pepper, lime juice, and fish.

Seal the lid, select Manual/Pressure Cook mode on High, and set cooking time to 3 minutes. After cooking, perform a quick pressure release to let out steam and unlock the lid. Stir and adjust taste with salt and black pepper. On lettuce leaves, spoon food, and garnish with scallions.

Tilapia Foil Packs

Total Time: 15 minutes | **Servings**: 2 | **Per Serving**: Kcal 277; Carbs 11g; Fat 12g; Protein 23g

Ingredients

2 tilapia fillets
2 tbsp olive oil
2 garlic cloves, minced
2 tomatoes, chopped

1 tsp chopped rosemary
Salt and black pepper to taste
¼ cup white wine

Directions

Cut out 2 heavy-duty foil papers to contain each tilapia. Place each fish on each foil and arrange on top olive oil, garlic, tomatoes, rosemary, salt, black pepper, and drizzle with white wine. Wrap foil tightly to secure fish well.

Pour 1 cup of water in inner pot, fit in a trivet with slings, and lay fish packs on top. Seal the lid, select Manual/Pressure Cook mode on High, and set cooking time to 3 minutes. When done cooking, perform a quick pressure release to let out steam, and carefully remove fish packs using tongs. Place on serving plates and open. Serve warm.

Crispy Cod on Quinoa

Total Time: 25 minutes | **Servings**: 4 | **Per Serving**: Kcal 546; Carbs 54g; Fat 21g; Protein 28g

Ingredients

1 tbsp olive oil
2 cups quinoa
1 yellow bell pepper, chopped
1 red bell pepper, chopped
4 cups vegetable broth
1 cup panko breadcrumbs

4 tbsp melted butter
¼ cup minced fresh cilantro
1 tsp lemon zest
1 lemon, juiced
Salt to taste
4 cod fillets

Directions

Combine olive oil, quinoa, yellow and red bell peppers, and vegetable broth in your Instant Pot.

Seal the lid, select Manual/Pressure Cook on High, and set the time to 6 minutes. In a bowl, whisk the breadcrumbs, half of the butter, cilantro, lemon zest, lemon juice, and salt. Spoon the breadcrumb mixture evenly on the cod fillets.

When cooking is over, perform a quick pressure release, and unlock the lid. Remove the quinoa and clean the inner pot with a paper towel. Press Sauté. Add in the remaining butter and cod fillets and fry them for 2-3 minutes per side or until browned. Share the quinoa into four plates, and top with the cod fillets to serve.

Thyme Tilapia with Tomato-Olive Sauce

Total Time: 30 minutes | **Servings**: 2 | **Per Serving**: Kcal 295; Carbs 21g; Fat 14g; Protein 25g

Ingredients

2 tilapia fillets
Salt and black pepper to taste
4 sprigs fresh thyme
4 lemon slices

2 tbsp butter
2 garlic cloves, thinly sliced
16 cherry tomatoes, halved
2 tsp green olives, sliced

Directions

Rub the fish with salt and pepper on both sides. Transfer to a foil-lined baking dish and top each fillet with 2 sprigs of thyme and 2 slices of lemon.

Set your Instant Pot to Sauté and melt the butter. Cook the garlic for 30 seconds until slightly pale and fragrant. Stir in the tomatoes and green olives and sauté for 3 minutes. Pour the tomato mixture over the fish.

Wipe inner pot clean. Pour in 1 cup of water and fit in a trivet. Place the baking dish on the trivet. Seal the lid, select Manual/Pressure Cook mode on High, and cook for 10 minutes.

When done, perform a quick pressure release to let out the steam. Unlock the lid and remove the fish to a plate. Top with the sauce to serve.

Lemon Caper Salmon

Total Time: 20 minutes | **Servings:** 4 | **Per Serving:** Kcal 457; Carbs 5g; Fat 18g; Protein 66g

Ingredients

Salmon
4 salmon fillets
Salt and black pepper to taste

4 sprigs dill
1 lemon, sliced

Caper sauce
3 tbsp buttermilk
3 tbsp mayo
1 lemon, juiced and zested

1 tbsp dill, chopped
2 tbsp capers, drained

Directions

In the Instant Pot, pour 1 cup of water and fit in a trivet. Season the salmon with salt and pepper and lay it on the trivet. Top with dill sprigs and lemon slices. Seal the lid, select Steam, and set the cooking time for 5 minutes.

Meanwhile, in a bowl, whisk all the sauce ingredients. When done, perform a quick pressure release to let out the steam. Unlock the lid and remove the salmon. Discard the lemon and dill sprigs. Drizzle with caper sauce and serve.

Spicy Salmon with Avocado Salsa

Total Time: 20 minutes | **Servings:** 4 | **Per Serving:** Kcal 527; Carbs 9g; Fat 24g; Protein 59g

Ingredients

2 tsp olive oil
1 tsp chili powder
1 tsp smoked paprika
½ tsp cumin powder
½ tsp garlic powder
Salt and black pepper to taste

4 salmon fillets
1 avocado, halved, pitted, and chopped
1 tomato, deseeded and chopped
1 small red onion, chopped
½ lime, juiced
2 tbsp chopped cilantro

Directions

Set your Instant Pot to Sauté mode and adjust to medium heat. Heat olive oil in inner pot. Meanwhile, in a small bowl, mix chili powder, paprika, cumin powder, garlic powder, salt, and black pepper. Season salmon on both sides with the spices mixture, and fry in oil on both sides until brown and flaky within, 4 to 5 minutes per side.

Meanwhile, in another bowl, mix avocado, tomato, onion, lime juice, and cilantro. Plate salmon when ready and top with avocado salsa. Serve warm.

Vietnamese Salmon

Total Time: 25 minutes | **Servings:** 4 | **Per Serving:** Kcal 502; Carbs 14g; Fat 19g; Protein 67g

Ingredients

1 tbsp olive oil
¼ cup brown sugar
1 lime, zested and juiced
1 ½ tbsp soy sauce
3 tbsp fish sauce
1 grated ginger

½ cup vegetable broth
Black pepper to taste
4 salmon fillets, cut into 2-inch cubes
2 scallions, sliced diagonally
2 tbsp chopped cilantro leaves
1 lime, cut into wedges for serving

Directions

Set your Instant Pot to Sauté mode and adjust to medium heat. Combine olive oil, brown sugar, lime zest, lime juice, soy sauce, fish sauce, ginger, vegetable broth, and black pepper. Allow simmering for 2 to 3 minutes. Place the salmon inside, Seal the lid, select Manual/Pressure Cook on High, and set cooking time to 5 minutes.

After cooking, do a quick pressure release to let out remaining steam, and unlock the lid. Carefully remove salmon onto serving plates and continue cooking sauce until reduced and syrupy on Sauté. Drizzle sauce over salmon and garnish with scallions, cilantro, and serve with lime wedges.

Red Wine Poached Salmon

Total Time: 15 minutes | **Servings**: 4 | **Per Serving**: Kcal 432; Carbs 4g; Fat 14g; Protein 66g

Ingredients

1 cup dry red wine
2 tbsp red wine vinegar
1 cup water
5 thyme sprigs
2 celery stalks, chopped

1 tbsp sugar
Salt and black pepper to taste
4 salmon fillets
2 tbsp chopped parsley to garnish

Directions

In inner pot, combine red wine, vinegar, water, thyme sprigs, celery, sugar, salt, and black pepper and stir to combine. Place fish in the liquid. Seal the lid, select Steam on High, and the time to 5 minutes.

After cooking, perform a quick pressure release. Remove salmon to serving plates. Set the pot to Sauté, cook sauce further until reduced and syrupy, 3 to 4 minutes. Spoon sauce all over salmon, sprinkle with parsley, and serve.

Spicy Tangy Salmon with Wild Rice

Total Time: 25 minutes | **Servings**: 4 | **Per Serving**: Kcal 373; Carbs 49g; Fat 25g; Protein 43g

Ingredients

1 cup wild rice
2 cups vegetable stock
4 skinless salmon fillets
A bunch of asparagus, trimmed and cut diagonally
3 tbsp olive oil, divided
Salt and black pepper to taste

2 limes, juiced
2 tbsp honey
1 tsp sweet paprika
2 jalapeño peppers, seeded and chopped
4 garlic cloves, minced
2 tbsp chopped fresh parsley

Directions

Pour wild rice and vegetable stock in your Instant Pot and stir to combine. Seal the lid, select Manual/Pressure Cook on High, and set the cooking time to 20 minutes.

Meanwhile, in a bowl, toss the asparagus with 1 tbsp of olive oil and season with salt and black pepper. In another bowl, evenly combine the remaining oil, lime juice, honey, paprika, jalapeño, garlic, and parsley.

When done cooking, do a quick pressure release and unlock the lid. Fit in a trivet. Lay the salmon fillets into a baking pan and brush it with the honey sauce; reserve a little of the sauce for garnish. Arrange the asparagus around the salmon. Place the pan on top of trivet, seal the lid, select Manual/Pressure Cook on High, and set the cooking time to 6 minutes.

When ready, do natural pressure release for 5 minutes, then quick release to let out the remaining steam. Dish salmon with asparagus and rice, top with parsley and reserved sauce and serve.

Salmon Fillets with Parsley Pesto

Total Time: 20 minutes | **Servings**: 4 | **Per Serving**: Kcal 561; Carbs 5g; Fat 29g; Protein 68g

Ingredients

4 salmon fillets
Salt and black pepper to taste
1 lemon, juiced
½ cup chicken broth
2 cups parsley leaves

2 garlic cloves, minced
2 tbsp toasted pine nuts
3 tbsp grated Parmesan cheese
Salt to taste
¼ cup olive oil

Directions

Season salmon with salt and black pepper. In inner pot, pour lemon juice and chicken broth. Fit in a trivet and place the salmon on top of the trivet. Seal the lid, select Steam mode, and set cooking time to 5 minutes.

After cooking, do a quick pressure release and unlock lid. In a food processor, add parsley, garlic, pine nuts, Parmesan cheese, salt, and olive oil. Blend until smooth. Transfer salmon to serving plates. Drizzle with the parsley pesto sauce and serve.

Steamed Salmon with Sweet Chili Sauce

Total Time: 15 minutes | **Servings**: 2 | **Per Serving**: Kcal 587; Carbs 15g; Fat 26g; Protein 56g

Ingredients

For salmon
2 salmon fillets
1 cup water

Salt and black pepper to taste

For sauce
1 tbsp chili garlic sauce
½ lemon, juiced
2 cloves garlic, minced
1 tbsp honey

1 tbsp olive oil
1 tbsp hot water
1 tbsp chopped cilantro
½ tsp cumin

Directions

In a bowl, combine all sauce ingredients. Set aside. Pour 1 cup of water into the pot and fit in a trivet. Place salmon on the trivet and sprinkle with salt and pepper.

Seal the lid, select Steam on High, and set cooking time to 5 minutes. When done, perform a quick pressure release to let out all the steam. Unlock the lid and transfer the salmon to a plate. Drizzle with the sweet chili sauce and serve.

Smoked Salmon Pilaf with Walnuts

Total Time: 20 minutes | **Servings**: 4 | **Per Serving**: Kcal 357; Carbs 31g; Fat 20g; Protein 23g

Ingredients

½ cup walnut pieces
1 tbsp canola oil
1 cup basmati rice
1 cup frozen corn, thawed
Salt to taste
1 smoked salmon fillet, flaked

2 tsp prepared horseradish
1 medium tomato, seeded and chopped
4 green onions, chopped (white part separated from the green part)

Directions

On your Instant Pot, select Sauté. Heat the canola oil and sauté the white part of the green onions for a minute, until starting to soften. Stir in the rice and corn, stirring occasionally for 2-3 minutes or until fragrant. Add in 2 cups of water and salt. Seal the lid, select Manual/Pressure Cook on High, and set the cooking time to 3 minutes.

After cooking, perform a natural pressure release for 5 minutes, then a quick pressure and unlock the lid. Fluff the rice gently with a fork. Stir in the flaked salmon, green parts of the green onions, and the horseradish. Add the tomato and allow sitting a few minutes to warm through. Top the pilaf with walnuts and serve.

Tomato Steamed Trout with Olives

Total Time: 25 minutes | **Servings**: 4 | **Per Serving**: Kcal 289; Carbs 6g; Fat 14g; Protein 34g

Ingredients

2 tbsp olive oil
1 small red onion, chopped
2 garlic cloves, minced
1 ½ cups chopped tomatoes
1 tsp tomato paste
½ cup fish broth

Salt and black pepper to taste
¼ tsp red chili flakes + more to garnish
¼ tsp dried dill
¼ tsp dried basil
4 trout fillets
¼ cup Kalamata olives, pitted

Directions

Set your Instant Pot to Sauté mode. Heat olive oil in inner pot and sauté onion until softened, 3 minutes. Stir in garlic and cook until fragrant, 30 seconds. Add tomatoes, tomato paste, fish broth, salt, black pepper, one-fourth tsp red chili flakes, dill, and basil. Allow boiling for 3 to 4 minutes. Lay trout in tomato sauce and cover well with sauce.

Seal the lid, select Manual/Pressure Cook on High, and set time to 2 minutes. After cooking, perform a quick pressure release. Remove fish onto plates and stir Kalamata olives into sauce. Cook until sauce reduces, 3 to 4 minutes. Adjust taste with salt and black pepper. Spoon sauce over fish and serve warm. Garnish with remaining chili flakes.

Catalan Haddock with Samfaina

Total Time: 25 minutes | **Servings**: 4 | **Per Serving**: Kcal 307; Carbs 17g; Fat 12g; Protein 35g

Ingredients

4 haddock fillets
Salt to taste
3 tbsp olive oil
½ small onion, sliced
1 jalapeño pepper, seeded and minced
2 large garlic cloves, minced
1 eggplant, cubed

1 bell pepper, chopped
1 (14.5-oz) can chopped tomatoes
1 bay leaf
½ tsp dried basil
¼ cup sliced green olives
¼ cup chopped fresh chervil
3 tbsp capers

Directions

Season the fish on both sides with salt and place in the refrigerator.

Press Sauté and heat the olive oil. Cook the onion, eggplant, bell pepper, jalapeño, and garlic for 5 minutes. Stir in tomatoes, bay leaf, basil, and olives. Remove the fish from the refrigerator and lay on top of vegetables in the pot. Add half cup water, seal the lid, select Manual/Pressure Cook on High, and set the cooking time to 5 minutes.

After cooking, do a quick pressure release. Remove and discard the bay leaf. Transfer the fish to a serving platter and spoon the sauce over. Sprinkle with the chervil and capers to serve.

Italian-Style Flounder

Total Time: 30 minutes | **Servings**: 4 | **Per Serving**: Kcal 275; Carbs 3g; Fat 16g; Protein 30g

Ingredients

3 slices prosciutto, chopped
½ small red onion, chopped
Salt and black pepper to taste
2 cups baby kale

½ cup whipping cream
4 flounder fillets
3 tbsp butter, melted
2 tbsp chopped fresh parsley

Directions

Select Sauté, add half of the butter and prosciutto, and cook until crispy, about 3 minutes. Stir in red onion and cook for about 2 minutes. Fetch the kale into the pot and cook, stirring frequently, about 4-5 minutes. Mix in whipping cream. Transfer to a baking dish. Lay the flounder fillets over the kale. Brush the fillets with the remaining butter and sprinkle with salt and pepper.

Wipe clean the pot and add 1 cup of water, fit in a trivet, and place the baking dish on top. Seal the lid, select Manual/Pressure Cook on High, and set the time to 5 minutes. After cooking, perform natural pressure release for 10 minutes, then a quick pressure release to let out the remaining steam. Serve sprinkled with parsley.

Lemon Steamed Catfish

Total Time: 15 minutes | **Servings**: 4 | **Per Serving**: Kcal 253; Carbs 15g; Fat 8g; Protein 32g

Ingredients

5 lemongrass stalks, bottom half chopped
1 cup chicken stock
2 tbsp brown sugar
2 lemons, juiced

6 tbsp fish sauce
2 heads garlic, peeled and chopped
1 cup chopped cilantro
4 catfish fillets

Directions

Pour lemongrass, chicken stock, brown sugar, lemon juice, fish sauce, garlic, and two-thirds of cilantro into inner pot. Set the pot to Sauté mode and allow boiling for 2 minutes. Place catfish in pot and baste with sauce. Seal the lid, select Manual/Pressure Cook on High, and set cooking time to 2 minutes.

After cooking, perform a quick pressure release to let out steam. Unlock the lid and carefully place fish on a serving platter. Spoon sauce all over and garnish with remaining cilantro. Serve warm.

Autumn Succotash with Basil-Crusted Fish

Total Time: 25 minutes | **Servings**: 4 | **Per Serving**: Kcal 520; Carbs 49g; Fat 22g; Protein 30g

Ingredients

1 tbsp olive oil
½ small onion, chopped
1 garlic clove, minced
1 red chili, seeded and chopped
1 cup frozen corn
1 cup frozen mixed green beans
1 cup butternut squash, cubed
1 bay leaf
¼ tsp cayenne pepper

½ cup chicken stock
½ tsp Worcestershire sauce
Salt to taste
4 firm white fish fillets
¼ cup mayonnaise
1 tbsp Dijon mustard
1 ½ cups breadcrumbs
1 tomato, seeded and chopped
¼ cup chopped fresh basil

Directions

Season the fish fillets with salt. In a small bowl, mix the mayonnaise and mustard. Pour the breadcrumbs and basil into another bowl. Spread the mayonnaise mixture on all sides of the fish and dredge each piece in the basil breadcrumbs. Warm the olive oil in the pot and fry the fish for 6-7 minutes in total on Sauté mode. Set aside.

Add in onion, garlic, and red chili pepper and sauté for 4 minutes or until the vegetables are soft. Stir in the corn, butternut squash, mixed beans, bay leaf, cayenne, chicken stock, Worcestershire sauce, and salt. Seal the lid, select Manual/Pressure Cook on High, and set the cooking time to 5 minutes.

Once the succotash is ready, perform a quick pressure release and unlock the lid. Stir in the tomato and remove the bay leaf. Serve the fillets with the succotash.

Tuna Salad with Asparagus & Potatoes

Total Time: 25 minutes | **Servings:** 4 | **Per Serving:** Kcal 314; Carbs 34g; Fat 11g; Protein 21g

Ingredients

1 ½ pounds potatoes, quartered
3 tbsp olive oil
Salt and black pepper to taste
8 oz asparagus, cut into three
2 tbsp red wine vinegar

½ cup pimento-stuffed green olives
½ cup chopped roasted red peppers
2 tbsp chopped fresh parsley
2 cans tuna, drained

Directions

Pour 1 cup water into the inner pot and set a trivet. Place the potatoes on top. Seal the lid, select Manual/Pressure Cook on High, and set the cooking time to 4 minutes. When ready, do a quick pressure release and unlock the lid. Drain the potatoes. Wipe the pot dry with a clean napkin and press Sauté.

Heat half of the olive oil and fry the potatoes and asparagus for 4-5 minutes. Season with salt. Pour the asparagus and potatoes into a salad bowl. Sprinkle with 1 tbsp of red wine vinegar and mix to coat.

In a bowl, pour the remaining oil, vinegar, salt, and pepper. Whisk to combine. To the potatoes and asparagus, add the roasted red peppers, olives, parsley, and tuna and toss. Drizzle the dressing over the salad and serve.

Tuna in Mango Sauce

Total Time: 20 minutes | **Servings:** 4 | **Per Serving:** Kcal 577; Carbs 17g; Fat 31g; Protein 58g

Ingredients

5 tbsp olive oil
4 tuna fillets
Salt and black pepper to taste
1 cup chopped ripe mangoes
1 cup fresh mango juice
1 tbsp apple cider vinegar

1 tsp fresh ginger paste
1 medium red onion, finely chopped
¼ tsp red chili flakes
2 tsp chopped basil
2 tsp chopped parsley

Directions

Set your Instant Pot to Sauté mode and adjust to medium heat. Heat olive oil in inner pot, season tuna with salt and black pepper, and sear on both sides until golden on the outside and flaky within. Set aside.

To the pot, add ginger and red onion and cook for 5 minutes, stirring frequently. Pour in mango juice, mangoes, apple cider vinegar, and chili flakes. Seal the lid, select Manual/Pressure Cook on High, and set time to 5 minutes.

After cooking, do a quick pressure release. Stir in basil and parsley. Pour mango sauce over tuna and serve immediately.

Farfalle Tuna Casserole with Cheese

Total Time: 25 minutes | **Servings**: 4 | **Per Serving**: Kcal 526; Carbs 22g; Fat 33g; Protein 38g

Ingredients

2 tbsp olive oil
1 onion, chopped
1 large carrot, chopped
6 oz farfalle
1 (12-oz) can full cream milk
1 cup vegetable broth

Salt to taste
2 cups shredded Monterey Jack cheese
2 tsp cornstarch
2 (5-oz) cans tuna, drained
1 cup chopped green beans

Directions

Select Sauté to preheat your Instant Pot. Warm the oil and sauté the onion and carrots for 3 minutes, until softened. Add in the farfalle, three-fourths of cream milk, broth, and salt to the pot. Stir to combine.

Seal the lid, select Manual/Pressure Cook on High, and set the cooking time to 5 minutes. After cooking, do a quick pressure release and unlock the lid. Select Sauté and pour in the remaining cream milk.

In a bowl, mix cheese and cornstarch evenly and add the cheese mixture to the sauce while stirring, until the cheese melts and the sauce thickens. Add in tuna and green beans, and stir. Heat for 2 minutes. Serve right away.

Spicy Tuna Cakes

Total Time: 35 minutes | **Servings**: 6 | **Per Serving**: Kcal 443; Carbs 27g; Fat 21g; Protein 36g

Ingredients

2 potatoes, peeled and chopped
4 (7 oz) cans tuna in oil, drained
1 tsp cayenne pepper
1 green onion, chopped
4 tbsp plain flour

1 egg, beaten
Salt and black pepper to taste
¼ tsp dried dill
4 tbsp olive oil

Directions

Pour potatoes and 1 cup of water in inner pot. Seal the lid, select Manual/Pressure Cook mode on High, and set cooking time to 6 minutes.

After cooking, perform a quick pressure release to let out the remaining steam. Drain potatoes and transfer to a large bowl. Mash with a grinder until thoroughly broken. Mix in tuna, cayenne pepper, onion, flour, egg, salt, black pepper, and dill until well combined. Form 6 patties out of the mixture.

Wipe inner pot clean with paper towel, set the pot to Sauté mode and heat olive oil. Fry patties 3 pieces at a time on both sides until golden on the outside, 6 to 8 minutes. Transfer to a wire rack to drain grease and serve.

Tuna Steaks with Capers & Lemon

Total Time: 10 minutes | **Servings**: 2 | **Per Serving**: Kcal 437; Carbs 8g; Fat 23g; Protein 48g

Ingredients

4 tbsp olive oil
2 tuna steaks
Salt and black pepper to taste

1 lemon, zested and lemon juice
2 tbsp chopped thyme + extra for garnishing
3 tbsp drained capers

Directions

Pour 1 cup of water in inner pot and fit in trivet. Season tuna with 1 tbsp of olive oil, salt, black pepper, and arrange on trivet. Seal the lid, select Manual/Pressure Cook mode on High, and set cooking time to 6 minutes.

After cooking, do a quick pressure release. Remove fish to a serving platter. Empty and clean inner pot. Set the pot to Sauté and heat remaining olive oil. Sauté lemon zest, lemon juice, thyme, capers, and 2 tbsp of water. Cook for 3 minutes. Pour sauce over tuna and garnish with thyme.

Tuna Noodle One-Pot

Total Time: 25 minutes | **Servings**: 4 | **Per Serving**: Kcal 854; Carbs 46g; Fat 61g; Protein 31g

Ingredients

16 oz egg noodles
Salt and black pepper to taste
3 tbsp unsalted butter
3 tbsp plain flour
1 ½ cups chicken broth

1 cup milk
2 (3 oz) can tuna packed in oil, drained
5 oz frozen green peas
½ cup panko breadcrumbs
½ cup shredded Monterey Jack cheese

Directions

In inner pot, add noodles, 3 cups of water, and salt. Seal the lid, select Manual/Pressure Cook on High, and set cooking time to 3 minutes. After cooking, perform a quick pressure release, drain noodles and set aside.

Clean inner pot and select Sauté mode. Melt butter pot and stir in flour until lightly golden in color. Mix in chicken broth gradually until a smooth liquid forms. Add milk and cook until thickened, 10 minutes. Season with salt and pepper. Mix in tuna and green peas. Seal the lid, select Manual/Pressure Cook on High, and set time to 1 minute.

After cooking, perform a quick pressure release to let out steam, and unlock the lid. Stir in breadcrumbs, cheese, and cook further in Sauté mode until cheese melts. Dish food into serving plates and serve warm.

Halibut & Butternut Squash Soup

Total Time: 30 minutes | **Servings**: 4 | **Per Serving**: Kcal 544; Carbs 37g; Fat 32g; Protein 29g

Ingredients

3 tbsp butter
1 medium butternut squash, peeled and diced
1 medium Yukon gold potato, peeled and diced
1 medium yellow onion, chopped
2 garlic cloves, minced
1 tsp pureed ginger
1 tsp cumin powder
2 tsp turmeric powder

1 tsp chili powder or to taste
4 cups chicken broth
Salt and black pepper to taste
4 halibut fillets, cut into 1-inch cubes
4 tbsp heavy cream
1 lime, juiced
2 tbsp chopped cilantro to garnish

Directions

Set your Instant Pot to Sauté and melt butter. Sauté squash, potato, and onion until sweaty, 5 minutes. Add garlic, ginger, cumin powder, turmeric, and chili powder. Stir-fry for 1 minute. Pour in chicken broth, salt, pepper, and fish.

Seal the lid, select Manual/Pressure Cook on High, and set cooking time to 12 minutes. After cooking, perform a quick pressure release to let out steam, and unlock the lid. Spoon out fish into a bowl and set aside.

Using an immersion blender, process ingredients until smooth and stir in heavy cream and lime juice. Return fish to the soup, stir, and dish into serving bowls. Garnish with cilantro and serve warm.

Fried Snapper in Orange-Ginger Sauce

Total Time: 25 minutes | **Servings**: 4 | **Per Serving**: Kcal 417; Carbs 25g; Fat 13g; Protein 47g

Ingredients

½ cup plain flour
4 red snapper fillets
Salt and black pepper to taste
3 tbsp olive oil, divided
2 green onions, chopped
3 sprigs thyme, leaves extracted
1 ½ tsp pureed ginger

1 garlic clove, minced
½ red scotch bonnet pepper, deseeded and minced
½ cup chicken broth
1 orange, zested and juiced
1 tbsp honey
4 orange slices to garnish
1 tbsp chopped parsley to garnish

Directions

Pour flour onto a flat plate. Season fish with salt, black pepper, and dredge lightly in flour. Set your Instant Pot to Sauté and adjust to medium heat. Heat 2 tbsp of olive oil in inner pot and fry fish on both sides until golden, 1 minute. Transfer to a plate and set aside. Empty, clean inner pot, and return to base.

Heat remaining oil in the pot and sauté green onions, thyme, ginger, garlic, and scotch bonnet pepper. Cook for 1 minute. Mix in chicken broth, orange zest, orange juice, honey, allow heating for 1 minute and lay fish in sauce.

Seal the lid, select Manual/Pressure Cook on High, and set cooking time to 1 minute. After cooking, perform a quick pressure release to let out remaining steam, and unlock the lid. Remove fish onto serving plates and top with orange sauce. Garnish with orange slices, parsley, and serve warm.

Tangy Shrimp Asparagus

Total Time: 20 minutes | **Servings**: 4 | **Per Serving**: Kcal 213; Carbs 8g; Fat 10g; Protein 19g

Ingredients

3 tbsp butter
1 lb asparagus, trimmed, cut into 2-inch pieces
4 garlic cloves, minced
¼ tsp dried dill
½ cup chicken broth

Salt and black pepper to taste
1 lb shrimp, peeled and deveined
¼ cup lemon juice
¼ tsp red chili flakes to garnish

Directions

Set your Instant Pot to Sauté mode. Melt butter in inner pot and sauté asparagus until slightly softened, 5 minutes. Add garlic, and dill, and keep sautéing until fragrant, 30 seconds. Pour in chicken broth, salt, pepper, and shrimp.

Seal the lid, select Manual/Pressure Cook on High, and set cooking time to 3 minutes. After cooking, perform a quick pressure release to let out steam, and unlock the lid. Stir in lemon juice, adjust taste with salt, black pepper, and spoon food into serving bowls. Garnish with chili flakes and serve warm.

Garlic Lemon Shrimp

Total Time: 20 minutes | **Servings**: 6 | **Per Serving**: Kcal 172; Carbs 2g; Fat 11g; Protein 16g

Ingredients

½ cup butter, divided
4 garlic cloves, minced
1 lb jumbo shrimp, peeled and deveined

Salt and black pepper to taste
½ lemon, juiced
2 tbsp chopped parsley, to garnish

Directions

Set your Instant Pot to Sauté and adjust to medium heat. Melt 2 tbsp of butter in inner pot and sauté garlic until fragrant, 30 seconds. Add shrimp, salt and black pepper, lemon juice, and 2 tbsp water. Seal the lid, select Manual/Pressure Cook mode on High, and set cooking time to 2 minutes.

After cooking, do a quick pressure release to let out steam, and unlock the lid. Stir in remaining butter until melted. Spoon into serving plates and garnish with parsley.

Stewed Paprika Shrimp

Total Time: 10 minutes | **Servings**: 4 | **Per Serving**: Kcal 185; Carbs 19g; Fat 2g; Protein 24g

Ingredients

1 lb jumbo shrimp, peeled and deveined
2 tbsp smoked paprika
3 tbsp honey
1 tsp garlic powder
¼ tsp cayenne pepper
½ lemon, juiced
Salt and black pepper to taste
1 cup chicken broth
1 lemon, cut into wedges

Directions

In inner pot, add shrimp, paprika, honey, garlic, cayenne powder, lemon juice, salt, black pepper, and chicken broth. Seal the lid, select Manual/Pressure Cook on High, and set cooking time to 4 minutes.

After cooking, do a quick pressure release to let out steam, and unlock the lid. Stir food and adjust taste with salt and black pepper. Spoon dish into serving plates and serve with lemon wedges.

Sausage & Shrimp Paella

Total Time: 35 minutes | **Servings**: 4 | **Per Serving**: Kcal 526; Carbs 34g; Fat 26g; Protein 48g

Ingredients

1 tbsp melted butter
1 pound andouille sausage, sliced
1 white onion, chopped
4 garlic cloves, minced
½ cup dry white wine
2 cups Spanish rice
4 cups chicken stock
1 ½ tsp sweet paprika
1 tsp turmeric powder
Salt and black pepper to taste
1 pound baby squid, cut into rings
1 pound jumbo shrimp, peeled and deveined
1 red bell pepper, chopped

Directions

Select Sauté to preheat your Instant Pot. Melt the butter and add the sausage. Cook until browned on both sides, about 3 minutes while stirring frequently. Remove the sausage to a plate and set aside.

Sauté the onion, garlic, and squid in the same fat for 5 minutes or until fragrant. Pour in the wine. Use a wooden spoon to scrape up any browned bits from the bottom of the pot and cook for 2 minutes or until the wine reduces by half. Stir in the rice and water. Season with the paprika, turmeric, black pepper, and salt.

Seal the lid, select Manual/Pressure Cook on High, and set the cooking time to 5 minutes. When done cooking, do a quick pressure release and unlock the lid.

Select Sauté and add the shrimp to the pot and stir gently without mashing the rice. Cook for 6 minutes, until the shrimp are pink and opaque. Return the sausage to the pot and mix in the bell pepper. Warm through for 2 minutes. Dish the paella and serve immediately.

Potato Chowder with Peppery Prawns

Total Time: 25 minutes | **Servings**: 4 | **Per Serving**: Kcal 499; Carbs 71g; Fat 18g; Protein 16g

Ingredients

4 slices serrano ham, chopped

4 tbsp minced garlic

1 onion, chopped

2 Yukon Gold potatoes, chopped

16 oz frozen corn

2 cups vegetable broth

1 tsp dried rosemary

Salt and black pepper to taste

16 prawns, peeled and deveined

2 tbsp olive oil

½ tsp red chili flakes

¾ cup heavy cream

Directions

In a bowl, toss the prawns in the garlic, salt, black pepper, and red chili flakes. Select Sauté to preheat your Instant Pot and warm the olive oil. Cook the prawns for 5-6 minutes and set aside.

Add in the serrano ham and onion, and cook for 3 minutes, stirring occasionally. Fetch out one-third of the ham into a bowl for garnish. Add the potatoes, corn, vegetable broth, rosemary, salt, and black pepper to the pot.

Seal lid, select Manual/Pressure Cook on High, and set time to 10 minutes. When done, do a quick pressure release. Stir in heavy cream. Ladle the chowder into bowls and top with the prawns. Garnish with the reserved ham to serve.

Dill Crab Cake

Total Time: 25 minutes | **Servings**: 4 | **Per Serving**: Kcal 461; Carbs 28g; Fat 26g; Protein 27g

Ingredients

1 lb jumbo lump crabmeat

¼ cup mayonnaise

1 tsp hot sauce

1 green onion, chopped

2 tbsp Dijon mustard

2 tsp Worcestershire sauce

¾ cup panko breadcrumbs

1 egg, beaten

Salt and black pepper to taste

¼ tsp dried dill

Directions

Pour 1 cup of water in inner pot and fit in a trivet. Lightly grease a springform pan with cooking spray and set aside.

In a large mixing bowl, combine crabmeat, mayonnaise, hot sauce, green onion, Dijon mustard, Worcestershire sauce, panko breadcrumbs, egg, salt, black pepper, and dill. Pour the crabmeat mixture into the pan, cover with foil, and place on the trivet. Seal the lid, select Manual/Pressure Cook on High, and set cooking time to 10 minutes.

After cooking, do a quick pressure release to let out steam, and unlock the lid. Carefully remove the pan, take off the foil, and allow cooling to firm up the cake. Release the pan, slice the cake, and serve warm.

Crabmeat & Broccoli Risotto

Total Time: 25 minutes | **Servings**: 4 | **Per Serving**: Kcal 350; Carbs 51g; Fat 8g; Protein 21g

Ingredients

1 pound broccoli, chopped

3 tbsp olive oil

Salt to taste

1 small onion, chopped

1 cup rice

¼ cup white wine

2 cups vegetable stock

8 oz lump crabmeat

¼ cup grated Pecorino Romano cheese

Directions

Select Sauté and heat the olive oil. Add and cook the onion for 3 minutes. Stir in the rice and wine and cook for 3 minutes, stirring frequently. Pour in vegetable stock and broccoli. Seal the lid, select Manual/Pressure Cook on High, and set the cooking time to 8 minutes.

After cooking, perform a quick pressure release and unlock the lid. Gently stir in the crabmeat and cheese and allow it to heat for 1-2 minutes. Serve right away.

Crab Bisque

Total Time: 25 minutes | **Servings**: 4 | **Per Serving**: Kcal 225; Carbs 12g; Fat 15g; Protein 8g

Ingredients

1 tbsp butter
1 small red onion, chopped
2 medium carrots, peeled and chopped
2 celery stalks, chopped
2 garlic cloves, minced
½ cup diced tomatoes
2 ½ cups chicken broth

1 tsp dried dill
1 tsp Old Bay seasoning
Salt and black pepper to taste
5 tsp paprika
2 cups chopped crab meat
1 cup heavy cream
1 tbsp chopped parsley

Directions

Set your Instant Pot to Sauté mode. Melt butter in inner pot and sauté onion, carrots, and celery until softened, 5 minutes. Mix in garlic and cook until fragrant, 30 seconds. Add tomatoes, chicken broth, dill, Old Bay seasoning, salt, pepper, paprika, and crab meat. Seal the lid, select Manual/Pressure Cook on High, and set time to 4 minutes.

After cooking, do a natural pressure release for 10 minutes, then quick pressure release to let out remaining steam. Unlock the lid and fetch out crab meat onto a plate. Set aside. Using an immersion blender, puree soup until smooth and stir in heavy cream. Spoon soup into serving bowls, top with crabmeat, and garnish with parsley. Serve warm.

Creamy Mussels with Pancetta

Total Time: 30 minutes **Servings**: 4 | **Per Serving**: Kcal 343; Carbs 18g; Fat 21g; Protein 20g

Ingredients

Salt to taste
2 thick pancetta slices, cubed
2 celery stalks, chopped
1 onion, chopped
1 tbsp flour
¼ cup white wine

18 oz canned chopped mussels, drained, liquid reserved
1 parsnip, cut into chunks
1 tsp dried rosemary
1 bay leaf
1 ½ cups heavy cream
2 tbsp chopped fresh chervil

Directions

Select Sauté to preheat your Instant Pot, add the pancetta, and cook for 5 minutes, until crispy. Remove to a paper towel-lined plate to drain fat; set aside.

In the same fat, sauté the celery and onion for 1 minute or until softened. Mix in the flour and pour wine over veggies — cook for 1 minute or until reduced by about one-third. Pour in 1 cup of water, reserved mussel liquid, parsnip chunks, salt, rosemary, and bay leaf.

Seal the lid, select Manual/Pressure Cook on High, and set the cooking time to 4 minutes. After cooking, perform a natural pressure release for 5 minutes. Stir in the mussels and heavy cream, and cook for 2 minutes on Sauté. Remove the bay leaf. Scatter the pancetta over the top and garnish with the chervil to serve.

Spaghetti with Arugula & Scallops

Total Time: 20 minutes | **Servings:** 4 | **Per Serving:** Kcal 232; Carbs 27g; Fat 4g; Protein 22g

Ingredients

1 ¼ pounds scallops, peeled and deveined
Salt to taste
1 tbsp butter
2 large garlic cloves, minced
¼ cup white wine
10 oz spaghetti

½ cup tomato puree
½ tsp red chili flakes
1 tsp grated lemon zest
1 tbsp lemon juice
6 cups arugula

Directions

Select Sauté to preheat your Instant Pot. Melt the butter and add the scallops. Season with salt and garlic. Cook for 6 minutes. Pour in the wine and simmer for 2 minutes until reduced by half. Add the spaghetti, 2 ½ cups of water, tomato puree, and chili flakes. Stir to combine.

Seal the lid, select Manual/Pressure Cook on High, and set the cooking time to 5 minutes. Once done, perform a quick pressure release. Stir in the lemon zest, juice, and arugula until wilted and soft. Serve immediately.

Scallops in Cilantro Sauce

Total Time: 15 minutes | **Servings:** 4 | **Per Serving:** Kcal 226; Carbs 7g; Fat 16g; Protein 15g

Ingredients

2 tbsp unsalted butter
1 lb scallops, tendons removed
Salt and black pepper to taste
2 tbsp olive oil
4 garlic cloves, minced

1 lemon, zested and juiced
3 tbsp heavy cream
1 tbsp Dijon mustard
3 tbsp chopped cilantro

Directions

Set your Instant Pot to Sauté mode and adjust to medium heat. Melt butter in inner pot, season scallops with salt and black pepper, and sear on both sides until golden brown, 1 minute on each side. Transfer to a plate and set aside.

Add olive oil to pot and sauté garlic for 30 seconds. Stir in lemon zest, lemon juice, heavy cream, mustard, cilantro, and half cup water. Return the scallops. Seal the lid, select Manual/Pressure Cook on High, and set time to 2 minutes. After cooking, do a quick pressure release, and unlock the lid. Divide between serving plates and serve.

Tuscan Seafood Stew

Total Time: 20 minutes | **Servings:** 4 | **Per Serving:** Kcal 313; Carbs 25g; Fat 7g; Protein 37g

Ingredients

1 medium white onion, roughly chopped
¼ cup parsley leaves + extra for garnishing
½ tsp red pepper flakes
5 garlic cloves, whole
1 tbsp olive oil
1 tbsp tomato paste
1 ½ cups white wine
1 cup diced tomatoes

2 cups chicken broth
Salt and black pepper to taste
1 lb clams, scrubbed
1 lb white fish, cut into 2-inch pieces
½ lb shrimp, peeled and deveined
¼ lb scallops
1 lemon, juiced
Parsley to garnish

Directions

In a blender, add onion, parsley, red pepper flakes, garlic, and process until smooth. Set your Instant Pot to Sauté mode. Heat olive oil, pour in parsley mixture and stir-fry until fragrant, 4 minutes. Stir in tomato paste and cook for 1 minute. Pour in white wine, tomatoes, chicken broth, and season with salt and pepper. Cook for 2 minutes.

Stir in clams, fish, shrimp, scallops and lemon juice. Seal the lid, select Manual/Pressure Cook on High, and set time to 3 minutes. After cooking, do a quick pressure release to let out steam, and unlock the lid. Stir and remove any closed clams. Season stew with salt and black pepper. Spoon into serving bowls, garnish with parsley, and serve.

Wine-Steamed Mussels with Garlic

Total Time: 20 minutes | **Servings**: 4 | **Per Serving**: Kcal 263; Carbs 16g; Fat 11g; Protein 25g

Ingredients

2 tbsp unsalted butter
3 shallots, chopped
4 garlic cloves, minced
2 Roma tomatoes, diced
1 lemon, zested and 2 tbsp juice
½ cup dry white wine

½ cup fish stock
Salt and black pepper to taste
1 ½ lb fresh mussels, debearded and washed
2 tbsp chopped parsley
4 wedges lemon

Directions

Set your Instant Pot to Sauté and adjust to medium heat. Melt butter in inner pot and sauté shallots and garlic until softened, 3 minutes. Stir in tomatoes, lemon zest, lemon juice, white wine, fish stock, salt, and black pepper. Cook for 2 to 3 minutes. Mix in mussels.

Seal the lid, select Manual/Pressure Cook mode on High, and set cooking time for 4 minutes. Once done cooking, perform a quick pressure release to let out all the steam, and unlock the lid. Fetch mussels into serving bowls, discard any closed mussel, and spoon sauce all over. Garnish with parsley and serve with lemon wedges.

Penne all' Arrabbiata with Seafood & Chorizo

Total Time: 50 minutes | **Servings**: 4 | **Per Serving**: Kcal 468; Carbs 40g; Fat 16g; Protein 42g

Ingredients

1 tbsp olive oil
1 onion, chopped
1 garlic, chopped
16 oz penne
1 (24-oz) jar Arrabbiata sauce
3 cups fish broth

1 chorizo, sliced
Salt and black pepper to taste
8 oz shrimp, peeled and deveined
8 oz scallops
12 clams, cleaned and debearded

Directions

Select Sauté to preheat your Instant Pot. Warm the oil and add the chorizo, onion, and garlic; sauté for about 5 minutes. Stir in the penne, Arrabbiata sauce, and fish broth. Season with the pepper and salt and mix.

Seal the lid, select Manual/Pressure Cook on High, and set the cooking time to 2 minutes. When the time is over, do a quick pressure release and take out the lid. Select Sauté.

Stir in the shrimp, scallops, and clams. Cook for 5 minutes, until the clams have opened and the shrimp and scallops are opaque. Discard any unopened clams. Spoon the seafood and chorizo pasta into bowls and serve.

Ginger Squid with Oyster Mushrooms

Total Time: 20 minutes | **Servings**: 4 | **Per Serving**: Kcal 241; Carbs 9g; Fat 14g; Protein 20g

Ingredients

3 tbsp olive oil
1 red bell pepper, deseeded and sliced
1 cup chopped oyster mushrooms
2 garlic cloves, minced
1 lb squid rings

2 tsp ginger paste
½ cup chicken stock
1 tbsp soy sauce
1 tsp cornflour
2 tsp toasted sesame seed to garnish

Directions

Set your Instant Pot to Sauté and heat oil. Sauté bell pepper and mushrooms until sweaty, 3 minutes. Stir in garlic and cook until fragrant, 30 seconds. Mix in squid, ginger, chicken stock, and soy sauce.

Seal the lid, select Manual/Pressure Cook on High, and set time to 12 minutes. After cooking, do a quick pressure release. Stir in cornflour and cook on Sauté until food is syrupy, 1 minute. Garnish with sesame seeds. Serve warm.

Calamari with Broad Beans & Kale

Total Time: 45 minutes | **Servings**: 4 | **Per Serving**: Kcal 274; Carbs 11g; Fat 15g; Protein 25g

Ingredients

2 tbsp olive oil
4 green onions, chopped
2 garlic cloves, minced
1 lb prepared squid rings
1 cup dry white wine

½ cup canned broad beans, drained
Salt and black pepper to taste
½ cup chopped kale
2 tbsp chopped parsley

Directions

Set your Instant Pot to Sauté and heat olive oil. Sauté onion and garlic until softened, 4 minutes. Mix in squid rings, wine, broad beans, salt, and pepper. Cook until squid is opaque and beans warmed, 3 minutes. Pour in ½ cup water and stir. Seal the lid; select Manual/Pressure Cook mode on High, and set cooking time to 15 minutes.

After cooking, perform a quick pressure release to let out steam. Unlock the lid and add kale, stir, and allow wilting for 2 to 3 minutes. Stir in parsley and plate. Serve warm.

Scallops in Chili Sauce

Total Time: 15 minutes | **Servings**: 4 | **Per Serving**: Kcal 310; Carbs 10g; Fat 23g; Protein 16g

Ingredients

3 tbsp butter
4 garlic cloves, minced
¼ cup Thai basil, chopped
1 tsp red chili paste

1 cup coconut milk
1 lb scallops, tendons removed and patted dry
Salt and black pepper to taste
1 lemon, cut into wedges

Directions

Set your Instant Pot to Sauté mode. Melt butter in inner pot and sauté garlic, basil, and chili paste until golden, 30 seconds. Season scallops with salt and black pepper, and add them, along with coconut milk, to the pot. Seal the lid, select Manual/Pressure Cook on High, and set cooking time to 1 minute. After cooking, perform a quick pressure release. Serve with lemon wedges.

Rustic Seafood One-Pot

Total Time: 15 minutes | **Servings**: 4 | **Per Serving**: Kcal 355; Carbs 20g; Fat 14g; Protein 37g

Ingredients

½ lb clams, scrubbed

2 tbsp olive oil

1 white onion, chopped

2 celery stalks, chopped

2 garlic cloves, minced

4 white fish fillets, cut into 1-inch cubes

½ lb prepared squid rings

½ cup white wine

6 tomatoes, chopped

Salt and black pepper to taste

Directions

Discard any clams with broken shells or that refuse to open when tapped. Set your Instant Pot to Sauté and heat olive oil. Sauté onion, garlic, and celery until softened, 3 minutes. Mix in fish, squid, wine, 1 cup of water, tomatoes, salt, pepper, and clams. Seal the lid, select Manual/Pressure Cook on High, and set time to 2 minutes. After cooking, perform a quick pressure release. Stir and adjust taste with salt and pepper. Divide between into plates and serve.

Seafood Spaghetti

Total Time: 20 minutes | **Servings**: 4 | **Per Serving**: Kcal 418; Carbs 38g; Fat 20g; Protein 21g

Ingredients

1 tbsp butter

1 medium white onion, chopped

4 garlic cloves, minced

½ tsp red chili flakes

2 cups crushed tomatoes

3 cups chicken broth

Salt and black pepper to taste

½ cup red wine

16 oz dried penne pasta

20 frozen jumbo shrimp

½ cup heavy cream

1 cup grated Parmesan cheese

Directions

Set your Instant Pot to Sauté mode and melt butter. Stir-fry onion and garlic for 3 minutes. Add red chili flakes, tomatoes, chicken broth, salt, pepper, and red wine. Pour in penne and shrimp. Seal the lid, select Manual/Pressure Cook on High, and set time to 4 minutes. After cooking, perform a quick pressure release. Select Sauté. Stir in heavy cream and half of Parmesan cheese. Allow melting for 1 minute. Garnish with remaining cheese, parsley, and serve.

Easy Seafood Jambalaya

Total Time: 30 minutes | **Servings**: 4 | **Per Serving**: Kcal 435; Carbs 44g; Fat 21g; Protein 28g

Ingredients

2 tbsp olive oil

1 onion, chopped

2 garlic cloves, minced

2 cups chicken broth

1 cup white rice, long-grain

½ pound shrimp, peeled and deveined

2 andouille sausages, sliced

Salt and black pepper to taste

Directions

Select Sauté on your Instant Pot and heat olive oil. Cook sausage, onion, and garlic for 5 minutes. Pour in broth and rice. Season with salt and pepper and stir well.

Seal the lid, select Manual/Pressure Cook on High, and set time to 8 minutes. After cooking, perform a natural pressure for 10 minutes. Stir in the shrimp for 3 minutes on Sauté. Serve.

Soups & Stews

Chicken & Spinach Soup

Total Time: 30 minutes | **Servings**: 5 | **Per Serving**: Kcal 163; Carbs 21g; Fat 4g; Protein 10g

Ingredients

1 onion, chopped
1 carrot, chopped
½ cup celery, chopped
1 garlic clove, minced
Salt and black pepper to taste

½ lb boneless, skinless chicken breasts, cubed
5 cups chicken broth
¼ cup vermicelli
1 cup spinach, chopped
¼ cup parsley, chopped

Directions

Place the onion, carrot, celery, garlic, salt, pepper, chicken, and broth into inner pot of your Instant Pot. Seal the lid, select Manual/Pressure Cook mode, and cook for 15 minutes on High.

When done, perform a quick pressure release. Unlock the lid and press Sauté. Stir in vermicelli and cook 5 minutes. Add in the spinach and cook for another 5 minutes until wilted. Adjust the seasoning and serve topped with parsley.

Chicken Lime Soup

Total Time: 30 minutes | **Servings**: 4 | **Per Serving**: Kcal 484; Carbs 24g; Fat 29g; Protein 38g

Ingredients

1 tbsp olive oil
1 cup green onions, chopped
2 green chilies, sliced
2 garlic cloves, minced
2 chicken breasts, cut into 1-inch cubes
4 cups chicken broth

2 tomatoes, chopped
Salt and black pepper to taste
¼ cup chopped cilantro
2 limes, juiced
2 avocados, halved, pitted, and sliced
1 cup sour cream for topping

Directions

Set your Instant Pot to Sauté and heat olive oil. Sauté green onions, green chilies, and garlic until fragrant, 1 minute. Add chicken, chicken broth, tomatoes, salt, and black pepper.

Seal the lid, select Manual/Pressure Cook mode on High, and set cooking time to 7 minutes. After cooking, perform a natural pressure release for 10 minutes. Stir in cilantro and lime juice. Top with avocados and sour cream to serve.

Herby Tomato Soup

Total Time: 30 minutes | **Servings**: 5 | **Per Serving**: Kcal 172; Carbs 20g; Fat 10g; Protein 3g

Ingredients

1 onion, chopped
2 tbsp olive oil
2 garlic cloves, minced
2 (14-oz each) cans pureed tomatoes
4 cups chicken broth

1 tsp herbs de Provence
1 tsp Worcestershire sauce
½ cup heavy cream

Directions

Set your Instant Pot to Sauté mode and heat the olive oil. Sauté the onion and garlic for 5 minutes, until browned and caramelized. Pour in the tomatoes, broth, herbs de Provence, and Worcestershire sauce. Seal the lid, select Manual/Pressure Cook mode on High, and set time to 6 minutes.

When done, perform a natural pressure release for 10 minutes, then a quick pressure release to let out the remaining steam. Unlock the lid, pour in the heavy cream, and stir. Allow to rest for a few minutes and serve.

Chicken Soup with Tortilla Chips

Total Time: 40 minutes | **Servings**: 4 | **Per Serving**: Kcal 257; Carbs 14g; Fat 15g; Protein 17g

Ingredients

2 tbsp olive oil
4 cups water
3 ounces tomato paste
2 tsp taco seasoning
1 tsp chili powder
½ tbsp ground cumin
Salt and black pepper to taste
1 garlic clove, minced

1 onion, chopped
2 celery stalks, chopped
1 chicken breast, cubed
2 tsp fresh lime juice
Broken tortilla chips for garnish
4 radishes, julienned
½ bunch cilantro, chopped

Directions

Set your Instant Pot to Sauté and heat the oil. Add in onion, garlic, chicken, celery, salt, and pepper and cook for 5-6 minutes, until the chicken is no longer pink, stirring occasionally. Stir in taco seasoning, chili powder, ground cumin, tomato paste, then pour in the water.

Seal the lid, select Manual/Pressure Cook on High, and cook for 15 minutes. When done, perform a quick pressure release. Unlock the lid and stir in the lime juice. Top with radishes, cilantro, and tortilla chips to serve.

Italian Gremolata Prawn Soup

Total Time: 25 minutes | **Servings**: 4 | **Per Serving**: Kcal 297; Carbs 35g; Fat 5g; Protein 31g

Ingredients

1 tbsp olive oil
1 small fennel bulb, chopped and fronds reserved
1 medium red onion, chopped
1 large carrot, chopped
1 celery stick, chopped
1 red chili, minced
6 garlic cloves, minced
¾ cup white wine

4 cups chicken stock
2 cups chopped tomatoes
1 lb prawns, peeled and tails intact
½ cup canned pinto beans, rinsed and drained
Salt and black pepper to taste
1 lemon, zested and juiced
¼ cup chopped parsley
1 cup chopped spinach

Directions

Set your Instant Pot to Sauté mode. Heat olive oil and sauté fennel, onion, carrot, and celery until softened, 5 minutes. Stir in red chili and half of garlic until fragrant, 30 seconds. Mix in white wine, chicken stock, tomatoes, prawns, and pinto beans. Season with salt and black pepper. Seal the lid, select Soup mode on High and set time to 5 minutes.

After cooking, do a quick pressure release to let out the steam. Unlock the lid, stir in lemon juice, and adjust taste with salt and black pepper. In a medium bowl, mix remaining garlic, lemon zest, parsley, and spinach to make gremolata. Ladle the soup into four serving bowls and top with gremolata. Serve warm.

Spring Minestrone Soup

Total Time: 25 minutes | **Servings**: 4 | **Per Serving**: Kcal 432; Carbs 24g; Fat 23g; Protein 17g

Ingredients

1 tbsp olive oil

3 garlic cloves, minced

4 cups chicken stock

1 cup ditalini pasta

2 zucchinis, chopped

1 cup asparagus, trimmed, sliced diagonally

1 leek, trimmed and thinly sliced

¾ cup frozen peas

½ cup canned pinto beans, drained and rinsed

1 cup chopped kale

½ lemon, juiced

Salt and black pepper to taste

¼ cup chopped parsley

1 cup crumbled goat cheese, for topping

Directions

Set your Instant Pot to Sauté mode and adjust to medium heat. Heat olive oil in inner pot and sauté garlic until fragrant, 30 seconds. Pour in chicken stock and pasta. Stir in zucchinis, asparagus, leek, peas, and pinto beans. Seal the lid, select Manual/Pressure Cook mode on High, and set cooking time to 5 minutes.

After cooking, perform a quick pressure release to let out steam. Unlock the lid, set to Sauté mode, and stir in kale and lemon juice. Allow wilting for 2 to 3 minutes. Adjust taste with salt and black pepper. Mix in parsley and ladle soup into serving bowls. Top with goat cheese and serve.

Mexican Sweetcorn Soup

Total Time: 35 minutes | **Servings**: 4 | **Per Serving**: Kcal 350; Carbs 36g; Fat 23g; Protein 5g

Ingredients

3 tbsp olive oil

1 garlic clove, minced

2 cups sweet corn kernels

1 red bell pepper, deseeded and cut into chunks

1 small potato, peeled and chopped

Salt and black pepper to taste

1 tsp Mexican spice mix

4 cups vegetable broth

¼ tsp dried thyme

1 cup heavy cream

2 tbsp chopped parsley

Directions

Set your Instant Pot to Sauté mode and adjust to medium heat. Heat olive oil in inner pot and saute garlic until fragrant, 30 seconds. Stir in sweet corn, bell pepper, potato, salt, black pepper, Mexican spice mix, vegetable broth, and thyme. Seal the lid, select Manual/Pressure Cook mode on High, and set cooking time to 10 minutes.

After cooking, do a natural pressure release for 10 minutes. Using an immersion blender, puree ingredients until smooth. Stir in heavy cream. Divide the soup between serving bowls, garnish with parsley and serve.

Miso & Sweet Potato Soup

Total Time: 35 minutes | **Servings**: 4 | **Per Serving**: Kcal 213; Carbs 28g; Fat 9g; Protein 4g

Ingredients

2 tsp olive oil

2 tbsp butter

1 medium white onion, chopped

3 garlic cloves, minced

4 cups chicken stock

2 tbsp white miso paste

2 large sweet potatoes, peeled and diced

Salt and black pepper to taste

4 chives, chopped

Directions

Set your Instant Pot to Sauté. Heat olive oil and butter and sauté onion and garlic until softened, 3 minutes. Add in ½ cup of chicken stock, and when hot, stir in miso paste for 30 seconds. Pour in sweet potatoes and the remaining chicken stock. Seal the lid, select Manual/Pressure Cook mode on High, and set cooking time to 15 minutes.

After cooking, perform natural pressure release for 10 minutes, and then quick pressure release to let out remaining steam. Unlock the lid and using an immersion blender, puree ingredients until smooth. Adjust taste with salt and black pepper. Mix in chives and spoon into bowls. Serve warm.

Ginger Broccoli Soup with Almonds

Total Time: 25 minutes | **Servings**: 4 | **Per Serving**: Kcal 312; Carbs 18g; Fat 27g; Protein 6g

Ingredients

1 tbsp butter
3 garlic cloves, minced
1 tbsp fresh ginger paste
1 tsp turmeric
1 tsp cumin powder
1 medium head broccoli, cut into florets

4 cups chicken broth
Salt and black pepper to taste
1 avocado, halved, pitted, and peeled
1 cup coconut milk
¼ cup sliced almonds

Directions

Set your Instant Pot to Sauté mode and adjust to medium heat. Melt butter and sauté garlic, ginger, turmeric, and cumin until fragrant, 1 minute. Pour in broccoli, chicken broth, and season with salt and black pepper. Seal the lid, select Manual/Pressure Cook mode on High, and set cooking time to 2 minutes.

After cooking, perform natural pressure release for 10 minutes, then quick pressure release to let out the remaining steam. Unlock the lid, add avocado, and using an immersion blender, puree ingredients until smooth. Stir in coconut milk, adjust taste with salt and black pepper, and ladle into individual bowls. Top with almonds and serve.

Beer & Cheddar Cheese Soup

Total Time: 30 minutes | **Servings**: 4 | **Per Serving**: Kcal 338; Carbs 37g; Fat 16g; Protein 9g

Ingredients

4 tbsp butter
1 medium white onion, chopped
2 medium celery, chopped
2 medium carrots, peeled and chopped
4 garlic cloves, minced
Salt and black pepper to taste
¾ cup all-purpose flour

4 cups chicken broth
1 cup whole milk
12 oz wheat beer
2 ½ cups shredded cheddar cheese + extra for garnishing
2 tbsp Dijon mustard
½ tsp Worcestershire sauce

Directions

Set your Instant Pot to Sauté mode and adjust to medium heat. Melt butter in inner pot and sauté onion, celery, and carrots until softened, 5 minutes. Stir in garlic until fragrant, 30 seconds. Season with salt and black pepper.

Stir in flour until roux forms and then mix in a few tablespoons of chicken broth until smooth. Pour in remaining chicken broth and milk. Seal the lid, select Manual/Pressure Cook mode on High, and set cooking time to 1 minute.

After cooking, do a natural pressure release for 10 minutes. Unlock the lid and puree ingredients until smooth using an immersion blender. Select Sauté mode and stir in beer, cheddar cheese, Dijon mustard, and Worcestershire sauce until cheese melts, 3 minutes. Spoon soup into serving bowls and top with remaining cheddar cheese. Serve warm.

Potato Peanut Soup

Total Time: 20 minutes | **Servings**: 4 | **Per Serving**: Kcal 508; Carbs 52g; Fat 29g; Protein 16g

Ingredients

2 tbsp olive oil

1 large brown onion, chopped

4 garlic cloves, minced

2 tbsp ginger puree

Salt and black pepper to taste

2 tsp cumin powder

¼ tsp cayenne powder

1 ½ lb russet potatoes, peeled and diced

1 cup crushed tomatoes

½ cup creamy peanut butter

4 cups chicken broth

2 tbsp chopped cilantro

3 tbsp toasted peanuts, chopped

Directions

Set your Instant Pot to Sauté mode. Heat olive oil and sauté onion until softened, 3 minutes. Stir in garlic, ginger, salt, black pepper, cumin powder, cayenne powder, and cook until fragrant, 1 minute. Pour in potatoes, tomatoes, peanut butter, and chicken broth; mix well. Seal the lid, select Manual/Pressure Cook on High, and set time to 8 minutes.

After cooking, perform a quick pressure release to let out steam. Unlock the lid and using an immersion blender, puree ingredients until smooth. Adjust taste with salt and black pepper. Ladle the soup into individual bowls soup and top with cilantro and peanuts.

Red Lentil & Carrot Soup

Total Time: 15 minutes | **Servings**: 4 | **Per Serving**: Kcal 231; Carbs 27g; Fat 12g; Protein 8g

Ingredients

1 tbsp olive oil

1 small yellow onion, chopped

2 garlic cloves, minced

Salt and black pepper to taste

½ tsp curry powder

2 ½ cups vegetable stock

3 carrots, cut into 1-inch slices

½ cup red lentils, rinsed

1 ½ cups coconut milk

4 tbsp coconut cream for topping

3 tbsp chopped parsley for topping

Directions

Set your Instant Pot to Sauté mode. Heat olive oil in inner pot and sauté onion until softened, 3 minutes. Stir in garlic, salt, black pepper, curry powder, and allow releasing of fragrance for 1 minute. Stir in vegetable stock, carrots, red lentils, and coconut milk. Seal the lid, select Manual/Pressure Cook mode on High, and set time to 2 minutes.

After cooking, perform a quick pressure release to let out steam. Unlock the lid and using an immersion blender, puree ingredients until smooth. Adjust taste with salt and black pepper. Ladle into individual soup bowls, top with coconut cream and garnish with parsley.

Vietnamese Green Soup

Total Time: 15 minutes | **Servings**: 4 | **Per Serving**: Kcal 118; Carbs 7g; Fat 6g; Protein 10g

Ingredients

1 tbsp coconut oil

1 opo squash, halved, deseeded, and thinly julienned

1 small yellow onion, thinly sliced

1 tsp fish sauce

6 cups vegetable stock

Salt and white pepper to taste

½ cup frozen peas

¼ cup chopped cilantro

Directions

Set your Instant Pot to Sauté mode and adjust to medium heat. Heat coconut oil in inner pot and sauté squash and onion until slightly softened, 3 minutes. Stir in vegetable stock, fish sauce, salt, white pepper, and frozen peas. Seal the lid, select Manual/Pressure Cook mode on High, and set cooking time to 1 minute.

After cooking, perform a quick pressure release to let out all the steam. Unlock the lid and stir in cilantro. Ladle into individual soup bowls and serve warm.

Mushroom Sour Soup with Tofu

Total Time: 25 minutes | **Servings**: 4 | **Per Serving**: Kcal 292; Carbs 15g; Fat 16g; Protein 24g

Ingredients

6 cups chicken stock
2 cups mixed mushrooms, sliced
¼ cup white wine vinegar
¼ cup soy sauce
2 tsp ginger paste
2 tsp garlic paste
1 tsp chili paste

¼ cup cornstarch
2 large eggs, beaten
8 ounces firm tofu, cut into ½ -inch cubes
4 scallions, thinly sliced
1 tsp sesame oil
Salt and black pepper to taste

Directions

In inner pot, combine chicken stock (reserve ¼ cup), mushrooms, vinegar, soy sauce, ginger, garlic, and chili paste. Seal the lid, select Manual/Pressure Cook on High, and set time to 2 minutes. After cooking, perform a natural pressure release for 10 minutes, then a quick pressure release to let out steam. Unlock the lid and select Sauté.

In a medium bowl, combine reserved chicken stock with cornstarch, and stir into soup. Pour in eggs in a thin stream while mixing soup to form thin egg ribbons. Mix in tofu, half of scallions, sesame oil, salt, and black pepper. Cook further for 2 to 3 minutes. Turn Instant Pot off. Spoon soup into serving bowls and garnish with remaining scallions.

Beef & Cannellini Bean Soup

Total Time: 40 minutes | **Servings**: 4 | **Per Serving**: Kcal 264; Carbs 13g; Fat 16g; Protein 17g

Ingredients

2 tbsp olive oil
1 cup kale, chopped
½ pound ground beef
1 carrot, chopped
1 celery stalk, chopped
1 red onion, chopped
1 garlic clove, minced
1 can (14 ounces) crushed tomatoes

1 ½ cups beef broth
1 bay leaf
½ tsp dried oregano
½ tsp dried basil
¼ tsp dried thyme
1 can (8 ounces) cannellini beans, drained
½ cup penne pasta
Salt and black pepper to taste

Directions

Set your Instant Pot to Sauté and warm olive oil. Add in ground beef, carrot, celery, onion, garlic, salt, and pepper and cook for 8 minutes until the meat is browned. Pour in the remaining ingredients, except for the beans, kale, and pasta. Seal the lid, select Manual/Pressure Cook mode, and set cooking time to 15 minutes on High.

After cooking, perform a quick pressure release to let out remaining steam. Unlock the lid. Stir in the pasta, kale and beans. Seal the lid again and cook for 4 minutes on Manual/Pressure Cook mode. Perform a quick pressure release. Discard the bay leaves and serve in bowls.

Spiced Turnip Soup

Total Time: 35 minutes | **Servings**: 4 | **Per Serving**: Kcal 225; Carbs 20g; Fat 13g; Protein 9g

Ingredients

1 tbsp avocado oil
2 tbsp butter
1 large white onion, chopped
2 garlic cloves, minced
1 tbsp turmeric
1 tsp cumin powder

1 tsp coriander powder
3 large turnips, peeled and diced
3 cups vegetable stock
1 cup whole milk
2 tbsp toasted pine nuts
2 tsp chopped cilantro

Directions

Set your Instant Pot to Sauté mode and adjust to medium heat. Heat avocado oil and butter and sauté onion until softened, 3 minutes. Stir in garlic, turmeric, cumin, coriander, and cook until fragrant, 1 minute. Add turnips and vegetable stock. Seal the lid, select Manual/Pressure Cook mode on High, and set cooking time to 15 minutes.

After cooking, perform a natural pressure release for 10 minutes and then a quick pressure release to let out the steam. Unlock the lid. Using an immersion blender, puree ingredients until smooth. Adjust taste with salt and black pepper, and mix in milk. Ladle into individual soup bowls and garnish with pine nuts and cilantro.

Creamy Pomodoro Soup

Total Time: 30 minutes | **Servings**: 4 | **Per Serving**: Kcal 211; Carbs 10g; Fat 16g; Protein 6g

Ingredients

¼ cup unsalted butter
1 medium onion, thinly sliced
2 garlic cloves, minced
2 cups canned whole tomatoes
2 cups chicken stock

10 sprigs rosemary, tied together
2 tsp granulated sugar, divided
½ cup heavy cream
Salt and black pepper to taste
1 cup croutons for topping

Directions

Set your Instant Pot to Sauté mode and adjust to medium heat. Melt butter in inner pot and sauté onion until softened, 3 minutes. Stir in garlic until fragrant, 30 seconds. Add tomatoes, chicken stock, rosemary, and sugar. Seal the lid, select Manual/Pressure Cook mode on High, and set cooking time to 3 minutes.

After cooking, do a natural pressure release for 10 minutes, then quick pressure release to let out remaining steam. Unlock the lid, discard rosemary bundle, and using an immersion blender, puree ingredients until smooth. Mix in heavy cream, ladle the soup into four individual bowls, top with croutons, and serve warm.

Spicy Chicken Coconut Soup

Total Time: 30 minutes | **Servings**: 4 | **Per Serving**: Kcal 351; Carbs 12g; Fat 18g; Protein 35g

Ingredients

2 cups coconut milk
3 cups chicken broth
2 tsp fresh ginger puree
1 stalk lemongrass, cut in 1-inch pieces
1 cup sliced cremini mushrooms
2 chicken breasts, cut into 1-inch cubes

1 lime, juiced
1 tsp coconut sugar
1 tsp Thai chili paste
1 tbsp fish sauce
¼ cup chopped cilantro
¼ cup fresh basil leaves

Directions

In inner pot, combine coconut milk, chicken broth, ginger, and lemongrass. Set your Instant Pot to Sauté mode and allow boiling, 3 to 5 minutes. Add mushrooms, chicken, lime juice, coconut sugar, chili paste, and fish sauce. Seal the lid, select Manual/Pressure Cook mode on High, and set cooking time to 7 minutes.

After cooking, perform a natural pressure release for 10 minutes, then a quick pressure release to let out remaining steam. Unlock the lid and stir in cilantro and basil. Ladle the soup into individual bowls and serve warm.

Jalapeño Corn Soup with Cheesy Topping

Total Time: 30 minutes | **Servings**: 4 | **Per Serving**: Kcal 306; Carbs 35g; Fat 16g; Protein 11g

Ingredients

2 tbsp olive oil
1 red onion, chopped
1 jalapeño pepper, seeded, chopped
½ cup cilantro stems, chopped
1 tsp paprika

1 lime, zested
2 cups corn kernels
4 cups chicken broth
½ cup celery stick, chopped
Salt and black pepper to taste

Topping

1 cup corn kernels
1 lime, juiced
1 ½ tbsp cilantro, chopped
1 jalapeño pepper, seeded and chopped

1 cup cotija cheese, crumbled
½ tbsp olive oil
Salt and black pepper to taste

Directions

Set your Instant Pot to Sauté and heat the olive oil. Sweat the onion for 8 minutes, stirring occasionally. Mix in jalapeño pepper, cilantro, celery, paprika, and lime zest. Pour in the corn kernels, chicken broth, salt, and pepper. Seal the lid, select Manual/Pressure Cook mode on High, and set the cooking time to 5 minutes.

When done, perform a quick pressure release to let out the remaining steam. Puree the soup using an immersion blender until smooth. In a bowl, toss to coat all the topping ingredients, except for the cotija cheese. Ladle the soup into bowls, spoon the topping over, and sprinkle with cotija cheese to serve.

Mushroom & Brown Onion Soup

Total Time: 30 minutes | **Servings**: 4 | **Per Serving**: Kcal 184; Carbs 14g; Fat 12g; Protein 7g

Ingredients

3 tbsp butter
2 medium brown onions, chopped
2 cups sliced white button mushrooms
2 tbsp all-purpose flour
4 cups chicken broth

¼ cup basmati rice, rinsed
1 bay leaf
Salt and black pepper to taste
2 tbsp chopped parsley

Directions

Set your Instant Pot to Sauté mode. Melt butter in inner pot and sauté onions and mushrooms until softened, 5 minutes. Stir in flour until roux forms and then gradually mix in chicken broth a few tablespoons at a time, until smooth. Stir in basmati rice, bay leaf, salt, and black pepper. Seal the lid, select Soup and cook for 6 minutes on High.

After cooking, do a natural pressure release for 10 minutes, then a quick pressure release to let out remaining steam. Unlock the lid, adjust taste with salt and black pepper. Spoon into bowls, garnish with parsley, and serve warm.

Caribbean Fish Soup

Total Time: 30 minutes | **Servings**: 4 | **Per Serving**: Kcal 347; Carbs 38g; Fat 12g; Protein 22g

Ingredients

4 tbsp butter
3 stalks celery, chopped
2 medium onions, chopped
Salt and black pepper to taste
4 cups chicken broth
4 Yukon gold potatoes, peeled and diced

4 bay leaves
1 Scotch bonnet pepper, minced
4 cod fillets, cut into 1-inch cubes
3 green onions, thinly sliced
1 tbsp chopped parsley to garnish

Directions

Set your Instant Pot to Sauté mode and adjust to medium heat. Melt butter in inner pot and sauté celery and onions until softened, 5 minutes. Season with salt and black pepper. Pour in chicken broth. Stir in potatoes, bay leaves, Scotch bonnet pepper, and allow boiling.

Add fish, seal the lid, select Manual/Pressure Cook mode on High, and set time to 10 minutes. After cooking, perform a quick pressure. Unlock the lid, carefully stir in the green onions to not break fish fillets, and adjust taste with salt and black pepper. Ladle into individual soup bowls, garnish with parsley and serve warm.

Brown Rice & Chorizo Soup

Total Time: 35 minutes | **Servings**: 4 | **Per Serving**: Kcal 261; Carbs 30g; Fat 13g; Protein 7g

Ingredients

2 tbsp olive oil
1 cup diced chorizo
1 medium onion, chopped
1 medium leek, chopped
1 red bell pepper, deseeded and chopped

4 cups chicken stock
½ cup brown rice
Salt and black pepper to taste
1 tsp red chili flakes to garnish

Directions

Set your Instant Pot to Sauté mode and adjust to medium heat. Heat olive oil, add chorizo and cook until brown, 5 minutes. Add and sauté onion, leek, and bell pepper, in inner pot until softened, 5 minutes. Pour in chicken stock and brown rice, season with salt and black pepper, and stir. Seal the lid, select Soup on High, and set time to 10 minutes.

After cooking, do a natural pressure release for 10 minutes, then a quick pressure release to let out the steam. Unlock the lid; stir soup and ladle into individual bowls. Garnish with red chili flakes and serve warm.

Beef Farfalle Soup

Total Time: 25 minutes | **Servings**: 6 | **Per Serving**: Kcal 412; Carbs 21g; Fat 21g; Protein 36g

Ingredients

2 tbsp olive oil
1 yellow onion, chopped
2 garlic cloves, minced
1 green bell pepper, seeded and chopped
1 pound ground beef
2 (14.5 oz) cans crushed tomatoes
5 cups beef broth

½ tsp dried basil
¼ tsp dried oregano
½ tsp dried thyme
Salt and black pepper, to taste
8 oz farfalle pasta
1 cup ricotta cheese, for serving
1 cup shredded mozzarella cheese, for serving

Directions

Set your Instant Pot to Sauté mode and warm the olive oil. Cook the onion, garlic, bell pepper, and ground beef for 5 minutes. Stir in tomatoes, broth, basil, oregano, thyme, salt, and black pepper. Put in the farfalle and stir. Seal the lid, select Manual/Pressure Cook on High, and set time to 4 minutes.

When done, perform a natural pressure release for 10 minutes, then a quick pressure release to let out the remaining steam. Unlock the lid and serve into bowls, topped with the ricotta and mozzarella cheese.

Thai Shrimp Soup

Total Time: 25 minutes | **Servings**: 4 | **Per Serving**: Kcal 210; Carbs 11g; Fat 8g; Protein 23g

Ingredients

1 tbsp coconut oil
1 medium white onion, finely sliced
1 carrot, peeled and julienned
1 red bell pepper, deseeded, finely sliced
1 tsp grated ginger
2 garlic cloves, minced
1 long red chili, minced
1 tbsp Thai green curry paste

4 cups chicken broth
1 cup coconut milk
1 tbsp fish sauce
1 lb shrimp, peeled and deveined
3 green onions, diagonally sliced
2 tbsp chopped cilantro
2 limes, juiced

Directions

Set your Instant Pot to Sauté mode. Heat coconut oil and sauté onion, carrot, and bell pepper until softened, 5 minutes. Stir in ginger, garlic, red chili, and curry paste. Cook for 1 minute or until fragrant. Mix in chicken broth, coconut milk, fish sauce, and add shrimp. Seal lid, select Manual/Pressure Cook on High, and set time to 3 minutes.

After cooking, perform a quick pressure release to let out steam. Unlock the lid, stir in green onions, and cilantro. Spoon soup into serving bowls and drizzle lime juice on top.

Chicken Bean Soup

Total Time: 30 minutes | **Servings**: 4 | **Per Serving**: Kcal 395; Carbs 47g; Fat 11g; Protein 31g

Ingredients

15 oz canned black beans, rinsed and drained
½ lb chicken breasts, skinless and boneless
14 oz canned diced tomatoes, drained
1 cup frozen corn kernels
2 green onions chopped
1 green bell pepper, seeded and chopped
1 jalapeño pepper, seeded and diced

1 (10-oz) can enchilada sauce
½ cup chicken broth
1 ½ cups milk
3 tbsp cornstarch
3 tbsp cold water
1 cup mozzarella cheese shredded, for garnish

Directions

In your Instant Pot, mix the chicken, beans, tomatoes, corn, green onions, bell pepper, jalapeño, enchilada sauce, and broth. Stir to combine. Seal the lid, select Manual/Pressure Cook mode on High, and set time to 15 minutes.

When done, perform a natural pressure release for 10 minutes, then a quick pressure release to let out the remaining steam. Unlock the lid and remove the chicken to a cutting board. Using two forks, shred chicken into small strands and place it back to the pot. Stir in the milk.

In a bowl, combine the cornstarch and cold water; whisk until smooth. Set the pot to Sauté and pour in the mixture; stir until the soup slightly thickens, 2 to 3 minutes. Serve topped with mozzarella cheese.

Lemongrass & Carrot Soup

Total Time: 25 minutes | **Servings**: 2 | **Per Serving**: Kcal 338; Carbs 19g; Fat 28g; Protein 7g

Ingredients

2 tbsp butter
1 large red onion, diced
6 large carrots, peeled and chopped
2-inch long lemongrass, pounded
2 tsp ginger puree

3 cups chicken broth
1 cup coconut cream
Salt to taste
4 basil leaves, chopped for garnishing

Directions

Set your Instant Pot to Sauté mode and adjust to medium heat. Melt butter in inner pot and sauté onion, carrots, and lemongrass until softened, 5 minutes. Stir in ginger until fragrant, 1 minute, and pour in chicken broth. Seal the lid, select Manual/Pressure Cook on High, and set cooking time to 1 minute.

After cooking, do a natural pressure release for 10 minutes, then a quick pressure release to let out remaining steam. Unlock the lid, add coconut cream, and using an immersion blender, puree ingredients until smooth. Season with salt. Spoon soup into serving bowls and garnish with basil. Serve warm.

Squash Soup with Yogurt

Total Time: 40 minutes | **Servings**: 4 | **Per Serving**: Kcal 240; Carbs 20g; Fat 16g; Protein 8g

Ingredients

1 tbsp olive oil
2 garlic cloves, minced
1 medium white onion, chopped
1 large butternut squash, deseeded and diced
1 cup vegetable stock
2 cups Greek yogurt

1 small avocado, halved, pitted, and peeled
1 lemon, juiced
¼ cup chopped dill
¼ cup chopped parsley + more for garnishing
Salt and white pepper to taste
1 small red onion, chopped for garnishing

Directions

Set your Instant Pot to Sauté mode and adjust to medium heat. Heat olive oil in inner pot and sauté the garlic and onion until softened, 5 minutes. Stir in squash and vegetable stock. Seal the lid, select Manual/Pressure Cook mode on High, and set cooking time to 10 minutes.

After cooking, perform a quick pressure release to let out the steam. Unlock the lid and stir in Greek yogurt, avocado, lemon juice, dill, parsley, salt, white pepper. Puree ingredients using an immersion blender until smooth. Spoon soup into serving bowls, garnish with parsley, and red onion and serve.

Zucchini Leek Soup with Goat Cheese

Total Time: 25 minutes | **Servings**: 4 | **Per Serving**: Kcal 397; Carbs 15g; Fat 34g; Protein 12g

Ingredients

1 tbsp olive oil
1 medium white onion, chopped
1 leek stalk, chopped
3 large zucchinis, chopped
2 garlic cloves, minced
1 tsp dried basil

½ tsp dried rosemary
1 tsp dried thyme
4 cups vegetable stock
1 cup coconut cream
Salt and black pepper to taste
1 cup crumbled goat cheese

Directions

Set your Instant Pot to Sauté mode and adjust to medium heat. Heat olive oil in inner pot and sauté onion, leek, and zucchinis until softened, 5 minutes. Stir in garlic, basil, rosemary, and thyme. Cook until fragrant, 30 seconds. Add vegetable stock and coconut cream. Seal the lid, select Manual/Pressure Cook on High, and set time to 1 minute.

After cooking, perform a natural pressure release for 10 minutes, then a quick pressure release to let out remaining steam. Unlock the lid and using an immersion blender, puree ingredients until smooth. Season with salt and black pepper. Spoon soup into serving bowls and top with goat cheese. Serve warm.

Spicy Red Pepper Soup

Total Time: 30 minutes | **Servings**: 4 | **Per Serving**: Kcal 258; Carbs 14g; Fat 17g; Protein 13g

Ingredients

2 tbsp butter
8 red bell peppers, deseeded, diced
½ red onion, diced
5 garlic cloves
1 tsp dried basil
¼ tsp smoked paprika

4 cups chicken stock
2 tsp Sriracha sauce
Salt and black pepper to taste
¼ cup heavy cream
1 cup grated Parmesan cheese

Directions

Set your Instant Pot to Sauté mode. Melt butter in inner pot and sauté bell peppers and onion until softened, 5 minutes. Stir in garlic, basil, and paprika. Cook until fragrant, 30 seconds. Add chicken stock, Sriracha sauce, salt, and black pepper. Seal the lid, select Manual/Pressure Cook mode on High, and set cooking time to 3 minutes.

After cooking, perform a natural pressure release for 10 minutes, then a quick pressure release to let out remaining steam. Unlock the lid and using an immersion blender, puree ingredients until smooth. Stir in heavy cream until well-mixed. Serve warm and top with Parmesan cheese.

Seafood Gumbo

Total Time: 35 minutes | **Servings**: 4 | **Per Serving**: Kcal 460; Carbs 33g; Fat 22g; Protein 40g

Ingredients

1 pound jumbo shrimp
8 oz lump crabmeat
Salt to taste
¼ cup olive oil + 2 tsp
¼ cup all-purpose flour
1 ½ tsp Cajun Seasoning
1 medium onion, chopped

1 small red bell pepper, chopped
2 celery stalks, chopped
2 garlic cloves, minced
1 small banana pepper, minced
3 cups chicken broth
1 cup jasmine rice
2 green onions, finely sliced

Directions

Select Sauté to preheat your Instant Pot. Season the shrimp with salt and 2 tsp of olive oil; toss to coat. Add to the pot and cook for 5 minutes, until opaque and pink. Set aside.

Heat the remaining ¼ cup of olive oil. Whisk in the flour and cook until roux forms, for 3-4 minutes, stirring constantly. Turn the pot off. Stir in the Cajun seasoning, onion, bell pepper, celery, garlic, and banana pepper for about 5 minutes until the mixture cools slightly. Add the chicken broth, rice, and crabmeat.

Seal the lid, select Manual/Pressure Cook on High, and set time to 8 minutes. After cooking, perform a natural pressure for 8 minutes. Stir in the shrimp and cook for 3 minutes on Sauté. Garnish with the green onions to serve.

Homemade German Soup

Total Time: 30 minutes | **Servings**: 6 | **Per Serving**: Kcal 473; Carbs 28g; Fat 32g; Protein 19g

Ingredients

4 tbsp butter
2 Yukon gold potatoes, cubed
4 shallots, chopped
1 celery stalk, chopped
2 carrots, chopped
¼ cup flour
6 cups chicken broth

1 tbsp Dijon mustard
½ small head cabbage, shredded
1 pound cooked bratwurst, sliced
2 cups buttermilk
Black pepper to taste
3 cups shredded cheddar cheese

Directions

Set your Instant Pot to Sauté mode and melt the butter. Cook the potatoes, shallots, celery and carrots for 5 minutes, until tender. Stir in the flour and broth. Add in the mustard and stir until there are no lumps. Put the cabbage and bratwurst. Seal the lid, select Manual/Pressure Cook mode on High, and set time to 5 minutes.

When done, perform a natural pressure release for 10 minutes, then a quick pressure release to let out the remaining steam. Unlock the lid and pour in buttermilk and black pepper. Stir in the cheese until it is completely melted. Serve.

Pumpkin-Ginger Soup

Total Time: 20 minutes | **Servings**: 4 | **Per Serving**: Kcal 330; Carbs 11g; Fat 28g; Protein 14g

Ingredients

3 tbsp olive oil
1 medium pumpkin, peeled and chopped
1 small red onion, finely chopped
1 tbsp ginger paste
3 tbsp chopped mint + parsley + sage leaves
3 cups vegetable stock

1 cup almond milk
½ tbsp chili powder
Salt and black pepper to taste
1 lime, juiced
1 tbsp chopped cilantro

Directions

Set your Instant Pot to Sauté mode and adjust to medium heat. Heat olive oil and sauté pumpkin, onion, and ginger paste until vegetables soften, 5 minutes. Mix in fresh herbs, allow releasing of fragrance, and pour in vegetable stock, almond milk, chili powder, salt, and black pepper.

Seal the lid, select Manual/Pressure Cook mode on High, and set cooking time to 3 minutes. After cooking, perform a quick pressure release to let out steam. Unlock the lid, stir in lime juice, and ladle into individual bowls. Garnish with cilantro and serve.

Effortless Lentil Soup

Total Time: 35 minutes | **Servings**: 4 | **Per Serving**: Kcal 147; Carbs 19g; Fat 8g; Protein 4g

Ingredients

2 tbsp olive oil
1 onion, chopped
1 cup dried lentils, rinsed
1 (28-oz) can diced tomatoes, drained
2 cloves garlic, chopped

2 carrots, chopped
1 tbsp parsley
1 tsp paprika
Salt and black pepper to taste
Chopped scallions, for garnish

Directions

Set your Instant Pot to Sauté mode and heat the olive oil. Cook the onion, garlic, and carrots for 5 minutes, until tender, and stir in paprika. Pour in 6 cups of water, lentils, tomatoes, salt, and pepper. Seal the lid, select Manual/Pressure Cook mode on High, and set time to 10 minutes.

When done, perform a natural pressure release for 10 minutes, then a quick release to let out the remaining steam. Unlock lid and add in the scallions. Give it a good stir, taste, and adjust the seasoning. Sprinkle with parsley and serve.

Amazing Florentine Soup

Total Time: 35 minutes | **Servings**: 4 | **Per Serving**: Kcal 619; Carbs 43g; Fat 35g; Protein 40g

Ingredients

1 pound Italian sausages, casings removed
1 tbsp olive oil
1 onion, chopped
2 garlic cloves, minced
1 zucchini, chopped
1 cup canned Cannellini beans, rinsed
1 cup canned tomatoes, chopped
½ tsp red chili pepper flakes

4 cups chicken broth
2 russet potatoes, sliced
2 cups kale, chopped
Salt and black pepper to taste
1 cup half and half
3 oz pancetta, cooked and chopped
Shredded Parmesan cheese, for serving

Directions

Set your Instant Pot to Sauté mode and heat olive oil. Cook pancetta for 5 minutes and set aside. Add in onion, garlic, and sausages, and sauté for 5 minutes. Stir in zucchini, beans, tomatoes, and red pepper flakes. Pour in chicken broth and stir. Add in potatoes and season with salt and pepper.

Seal the lid, select Manual/Pressure Cook on High, and set time to 15 minutes. When done, perform a quick pressure to let out steam. Unlock the lid and add in the kale. Select Sauté and cook until it is wilted, about 3 minutes. Pour in the half and half and stir. Add in the pancetta and divide between bowls. Serve sprinkled with Parmesan cheese.

Chicken & Rice Soup

Total Time: 35 minutes | **Servings**: 4 | **Per Serving**: Kcal 435; Carbs 20g; Fat 25g; Protein 38g

Ingredients

2 tbsp olive oil
1 leek, chopped
2 cloves garlic, minced
2 chicken breasts, cubed
1 carrot, chopped
3 stalks celery, chopped

½ cup rice
5 cups chicken broth
1 cup frozen peas
Salt and black pepper to taste
Chopped parsley for garnish

Directions

Set your Instant Pot to Sauté mode and warm the olive oil. Add in leek, garlic, carrot, and celery. Stir-fry for 5 minutes, until softened. Stir in the chicken and brown it for 6 minutes on all sides. Pour in the chicken broth, rice, salt, and pepper. Seal the lid, select Manual/Pressure Cook mode on High, and set cooking time to 15 minutes.

When done, perform a quick pressure to let out steam. Unlock the lid and add in the frozen peas. Serve immediately in individual bowls sprinkled with parsley.

Tapioca Cold Fruit Soup

Total Time: 20 minutes + chilling time | **Servings**: 4 | **Per Serving**: Kcal 243; Carbs 61g; Fat 1g; Protein 2g

Ingredients

½ cup granulated sugar
4 tbsp tapioca
1 cup peach juice
2 apricots, cored and chopped

1 ½ cups raspberry juice
2 cups raspberries
1 cup strawberries, halved
1 cup blueberries

Directions

In inner pot, combine sugar, 1 cup water, tapioca, peach juice, and apricots. Seal the lid, select Manual/Pressure Cook on High, and set time to 3 minutes. After cooking, perform a natural pressure release for 10 minutes. Unlock the lid.

Stir in raspberry juice, raspberries, strawberries, and blueberries. Spoon soup into serving bowls, allow cooling. Then chill in refrigerator for 45 minutes to 1 hour. Serve chilled.

Cheesy Asparagus Soup

Total Time: 30 minutes | **Servings**: 4 | **Per Serving**: Kcal 202; Carbs 23g; Fat 10g; Protein 9g

Ingredients

1 onion, chopped
2 tbsp butter
1 carrot, sliced
4 cups chicken broth
1 cup milk

1 ½ pounds asparagus, chopped
1 cup half-and-half
2 cups shredded Cheddar cheese
Salt and black pepper to taste

Directions

Set your Instant Pot to Sauté mode and melt the butter. Cook the onion, asparagus, and carrot for 3 minutes, until tender. Pour in the chicken broth. Seal the lid, select Manual/Pressure Cook mode on High, and set time to 8 minutes.

When done, perform a natural pressure release for 10 minutes, then a quick pressure release to let out the remaining steam. Stir in milk, half-and-half, and cheddar cheese until the cheese has melted. Season with salt and pepper. Serve.

Chili & Basil Tomato Soup

Total Time: 20 minutes | **Servings**: 4 | **Per Serving**: Kcal 287; Carbs 22g; Fat 14g; Protein 17g

Ingredients

3 lb tomatoes, peeled, chopped, with juice
1 onion, chopped
½ tsp chili flakes
1 cup chicken broth
Salt to taste

1 ½ cups milk
½ cup crème fraîche
2 tbsp basil, chopped
Salt and black pepper to taste

Directions

In your Instant Pot, add tomatoes, chicken broth, and salt. Seal the lid, select Manual/Pressure Cook on High, and set cooking time to 5 minutes. When done, perform a quick pressure to let out steam.

Add in milk and crème fraîche and stir. Transfer to a food processor and puree the soup until smooth. Return to the pot, press Sauté and stir until heated through, about 5 minutes. Sprinkle with chili flakes and basil to serve.

Delicious Bacon & Bean Soup

Total Time: 50 minutes | **Servings**: 4 | **Per Serving**: Kcal 229; Carbs 20g; Fat 15g; Protein 9g

Ingredients

3 tbsp butter
1 onion, finely chopped
1 cup finely chopped fennel bulb
2 carrots, finely chopped
2 garlic cloves, minced

1 pound dried beans, soaked overnight
4 cups chicken broth
2 slices smoked bacon, chopped
2 tsp ground cumin
Salt and black pepper to taste

Directions

Set your Instant Pot to Sauté and melt the butter. Cook bacon for 5 minutes, until crispy. Set aside. Add in onion, fennel, carrots, and garlic, and sauté for 5 minutes. Pour in broth, beans, cumin, and salt. Stir to combine.

Seal the lid, select Manual/Pressure Cook on High, and set time to 25 minutes. When done, perform a natural pressure release for 10 minutes. Unlock the lid and ladle soup in individual bowls. Top with reserved bacon to serve.

Cream of Butternut Squash

Total Time: 25 minutes | **Servings**: 4 | **Per Serving**: Kcal 276; Carbs 25g; Fat 18g; Protein 9g

Ingredients

2 pounds butternut squash, peeled and cubed
2 sprigs parsley, chopped
1 onion, chopped
¼ tsp cumin
½ inch piece ginger, peeled and sliced

4 cups vegetable stock
½ cup sour cream
½ cup pumpkin seeds toasted, for garnish
Salt and black pepper to taste
2 tbsp olive oil + some for drizzling

Directions

Set your Instant Pot to Sauté and warm olive oil. Add in onion, parsley, salt, and pepper, and sauté until the onion is soft. Place in squash and brown for 5 minutes, stirring often. Put in ginger, cumin, and vegetable stock, and stir.

Seal the lid, select Manual/Pressure Cook, cook f 10 minutes on High. When done, perform a quick pressure release. Pour mixture in a blender and puree until smooth. Stir in sour cream. Serve garnished with pumpkin seeds, and a drizzle of olive oil.

Squid Potato Stew

Total Time: 20 minutes | **Servings**: 4 | **Per Serving**: Kcal 415; Carbs 63g; Fat 9g; Protein 15g

Ingredients

2 tbsp olive oil
1 medium white onion, chopped
4 potatoes, peeled and diced
2 garlic cloves, minced
¼ tsp smoked paprika

¼ tsp curry powder
1 ¼ cups frozen squid rings, defrosted
1 cup chicken broth
Salt and black pepper to taste
¼ cup parsley leaves, chopped

Directions

Set your Instant Pot to Sauté and heat olive oil. Cook onion, garlic, paprika, curry powder, and potatoes for 3 minutes. Pour in squid rings, chicken broth, salt, and pepper. Seal the lid, select Manual/Pressure Cook on High, and set time to 10 minutes. After cooking, do a quick pressure release. Spoon stew into bowls and garnish with parsley. Serve.

Trout Radish Stew

Total Time: 20 minutes | **Servings:** 4 | **Per Serving:** Kcal 488; Carbs 25g; Fat 33g; Protein 26g

Ingredients

4 tbsp olive oil, divided
1 red onion, thinly sliced
4 garlic cloves, minced
½ cup dry white wine
8 oz bottle clam juice
2 ½ cups chicken broth

½ lb radishes, diced
1 (15 oz) can diced tomatoes with juice
Salt and black pepper to taste
¼ tsp red chili flakes
4 trout fillets, cut into 2-inch cubes
1 lemon, juiced

Directions

Set your Instant Pot to Sauté mode. Heat olive and sauté onion and garlic until softened, 3 minutes. Pour in white wine, cook until reduced by one-third, and add clam juice, chicken broth, radishes, tomatoes, salt, pepper, and red chili flakes; stir and add in the fish. Seal the lid, select Manual/Pressure Cook on High, and set time to 3 minutes.

After cooking, do a quick pressure release to let out steam, and unlock the lid. Stir and adjust taste with salt and black pepper. Mix in lemon juice. Spoon into serving bowls and serve warm.

Lamb & Mushroom Stew

Total Time: 50 minutes | **Servings:** 4 | **Per Serving:** Kcal 345; Carbs 12g; Fat 18g; Protein 36g

Ingredients

1 tbsp olive oil
1 ½ lb lamb shoulder, cut into 1-inch cubes
Salt and black pepper to taste
1 small onion, chopped
½ lb baby Bella mushrooms, chopped

1 garlic cloves minced
½ tbsp tomato paste
1 cup cherry tomatoes, halved
1 cup chicken broth
½ cup chopped parsley

Directions

Set your Instant Pot to Sauté mode. Heat olive oil, season lamb with salt and pepper, and sear meat in oil until brown on the outside, 6 to 7 minutes. Stir in onion and mushrooms, and cook until softened, 5 minutes. Add garlic and cook until fragrant, 30 seconds. Mix in tomato paste, cherry tomatoes, chicken broth, and season with salt and pepper.

Seal the lid, select Manual/Pressure Cook mode on High, and set cooking time to 15 minutes. After cooking, perform natural pressure release for 10 minutes, then a quick pressure release. Sprinkle with parsley and serve.

Tunisian Lamb Stew

Total Time: 55 minutes | **Servings:** 4 | **Per Serving:** Kcal 450; Carbs 44g; Fat 18g; Protein 31g

Ingredients

2 tbsp olive oil
1 pound lamb shoulder, cubed
1 medium red onion, thinly sliced
8 cloves garlic, thickly sliced
2-3 tsp ras-el-hanout
1 tsp turmeric
1 tsp red chili flakes
1 tbsp rosemary leaves

¼ cup thyme leaves
1 cup chopped parsley + a little extra for garnishing
2 tomatoes, roughly chopped
2 red bell peppers, peeled and cut into thick strips
2 russet potatoes, peeled and cut into 8 wedges each
2 cups vegetable stock
Salt to taste

Directions

Set your Instant Pot to Sauté mode. Heat olive oil and cook lamb until brown on the outside, 6 to 7 minutes. Add onion and garlic; cook until onion softens, 3 minutes. Stir in ras el hanout, turmeric, red chili flakes, rosemary, thyme, and parsley. Cook until fragrant, 3 minutes. Mix in tomatoes, bell peppers, potatoes, vegetable stock, and salt.

Seal the lid, select Manual/Pressure Cook mode on High, and set cooking time to 20 minutes. After cooking, perform natural pressure release for 10 minutes. Spoon into serving bowls, garnish with parsley, and serve.

Easy Beef Stew

Total Time: 50 minutes | **Servings**: 4 | **Per Serving**: Kcal 429; Carbs 49g; Fat 22g; Protein 11g

Ingredients

1 ½ pounds beef stew meat
¼ cup flour
2 tbsp olive oil
6 cups beef broth
1 onion, cut into wedges
2 carrots, chopped
2 tomatoes, chopped

5 cloves garlic, minced
1 tbsp oregano
4 potatoes, cubed
3 celery stalks, chopped
Salt and black pepper to taste
2 tbsp parsley, chopped for garnish

Directions

Coat the beef with the flour in a bowl. Set your Instant Pot to Sauté mode and heat olive oil. Cook the meat for 5 minutes, until browned. Add in the onion and cook for 3 minutes. Pour in the broth.

Seal the lid, select Manual/Pressure Cook mode on High, and set time to 30 minutes. When done, perform a quick pressure release, unlock the lid, and put in the carrots, tomatoes, garlic, oregano, potatoes, celery, salt, and pepper.

Seal the lid again, select Manual/Pressure Cook mode on High, and set time to 5 minutes. When done, perform a quick pressure to let out steam. Sprinkle with parsley to serve.

Beef Stew with Potatoes & Mushrooms

Total Time: 65 minutes | **Servings**: 4 | **Per Serving**: Kcal 377; Carbs 37g; Fat 12g; Protein 31g

Ingredients

2 tbsp olive oil
1 pound beef stew meat, cubed
2 tbsp flour
Salt and black pepper to taste
½ tbsp paprika
1 onion, chopped
1 carrot, chopped
1 celery stalk, chopped

1 garlic clove, minced
¼ cup red wine
1 bay leaf
1 tbsp dry thyme
4 potatoes, cubed
1 cup canned tomatoes
1 cup mushrooms, sliced
2 cups beef stock

Directions

Set your Instant Pot to Sauté and heat olive oil. Toss the beef with flour, salt, and pepper until coated. Place into the pot and brown for 5-7 minutes per side until golden; set aside. Add in the onion, carrot, celery, garlic, mushrooms, salt, and pepper and cook for 5 minutes, until tender. Pour in the remaining ingredients and stir to combine.

Seal the lid, select Meat/Stew mode, and set the cooking time to 35 minutes on High. When done, perform a natural pressure release for 10 minutes, then a quick pressure release to let out the remaining steam. Unlock the lid and adjust the seasoning. Remove and discard the bay leaf. Ladle the stew into individual bowls to serve.

Beef & Butternut Squash Stew

Total Time: 40 minutes | **Servings**: 4 | **Per Serving**: Kcal 315; Carbs 17g; Fat 12g; Protein 26g

Ingredients

2 tbsp olive oil
1 lb beef stew meat, cubed
Salt and black pepper to taste
1 cup beef broth
1 tsp onion powder

1 tsp garlic powder
1 medium butternut squash, chopped
2 thyme sprigs, chopped
1 tsp cumin powder
1 tsp cornstarch

Directions

Set your Instant Pot to Sauté mode. Heat olive oil in inner pot, season beef with salt and pepper and fry in oil until brown on all sides, 4 minutes. Pour in beef broth; add onion powder, garlic powder, butternut squash, thyme, and cumin powder. Seal the lid, select Manual/Pressure Cook on High, and set cooking time to 15 minutes.

After cooking, perform natural pressure release for 10 minutes. Unlock the lid and stir in cornstarch, adjust taste with salt and black pepper, and cook further for 1 minute on Sauté mode. Serve with freshly baked bread.

Sausage & Red Kidney Stew

Total Time: 35 minutes | **Servings**: 4 | **Per Serving**: Kcal 498; Carbs 47g; Fat 28g; Protein 26g

Ingredients

6 bacon slices, chopped
½ lb kielbasa sausage, chopped
1 cup chopped tomatoes
2 red bell peppers, deseeded and diced
1 red onion, chopped
1 cup dried red kidney beans, soaked overnight

3 cups chicken broth
¼ cup honey
1 cup ketchup
1 tbsp Worcestershire sauce
1 tsp mustard powder

Directions

Set your Instant Pot to Sauté and fry bacon until brown and crispy, 5 minutes. Remove to a plate. Add sausages to inner pot and cook until brown on both sides, 5 minutes. Set aside next to bacon.

Wipe inner pot clean and combine bell peppers, onion, kidney beans, chicken broth, honey, ketchup, Worcestershire sauce, and mustard powder. Seal the lid, select Manual/Pressure Cook on High, and set time to 10 minutes. After cooking, perform a quick pressure release. Stir in bacon and sausage, and simmer on Sauté mode for 5 minutes. Serve stew with bread or cooked white rice.

Classic Beef Stew

Total Time: 40 minutes | **Servings**: 4 | **Per Serving**: Kcal 355; Carbs 8g; Fat 12g; Protein 27g

Ingredients

2 tbsp olive oil
1 lb beef stew meat, cubed
Salt and black pepper to taste
2 shallots, chopped
2 garlic cloves, minced
1 carrot, peeled and chopped
2 red bell peppers, chopped

2 tomatoes, chopped
2 bay leaves
1 tsp dried mixed herbs
1 ½ cups beef broth
1 tsp cornstarch

Directions

Set your Instant Pot to Sauté mode and adjust to medium heat. Heat olive oil in inner pot, season beef with salt and black pepper, and brown on both sides, 5 minutes. Set aside. To the pot, add shallots, garlic, carrot, bell peppers, and cook for 5 minutes. Stir in tomatoes, mixed herbs, bay leaves, and beef broth, and return the beef.

Seal the lid, select Manual/Pressure Cook mode on High, and set cooking time to 20 minutes. Do a natural pressure release for 10 minutes, then a quick pressure release, and unlock the lid. Discard bay leaves. Stir in cornstarch and thicken sauce on Sauté mode for 1 to 2 minutes. Adjust taste with salt, black pepper, and serve.

Moroccan Beef Stew with Couscous

Total Time: 45 minutes | **Servings**: 4 | **Per Serving**: Kcal 288; Carbs 39g; Fat 13g; Protein 6g

Ingredients

1 ¼ lb beef stew meat, cut into bite-size pieces
1 tbsp ras el hanout
Salt and black pepper to taste
3 carrots, peeled and julienned
1 celery root, cut into 1-inch chunks
¾ cup pitted prunes, chopped

2 cups chicken broth
2 tbsp tomato paste
1 cup couscous
2 tsp harissa paste, plus more for serving
¼ cup chopped cilantro for garnishing

Directions

Season beef with ras el hanout, salt, and pepper, and add to inner pot. Pour in carrots, celery, prunes, chicken broth, tomatoes, and stir. Seal the lid, select Manual/Pressure Cook mode on High, and set cooking time to 30 minutes.

Meanwhile, pour couscous into a medium bowl, season with salt, and pour in 1 cup of boiling water. Cover the bowl with a napkin and allow water to absorb.

Once Instant Pot beeps, perform a natural pressure release. Unlock the lid. Stir in harissa paste, adjust taste with salt, black pepper, and dish stew into serving bowls. Garnish with cilantro and serve beef stew with couscous.

Red Wine Beef Stew

Total Time: 50 minutes | **Servings**: 4 | **Per Serving**: Kcal 576; Carbs 42g; Fat 21g; Protein 56g

Ingredients

2 lb stewing beef, fat trimmed, cubed
½ cup white flour
Salt and pepper to taste
2 bay leaves
2 garlic cloves, minced
1 lb red potatoes, cut into ½-inch pieces
1 tbs tomato paste

3 carrots, peeled and chopped
½ cup red wine
½ fennel bulb, sliced
1 onion, chopped
2 ½ cups beef stock
3 tbs olive oil
¼ cup chopped parsley

Directions

Season the beef with salt and pepper, then roll in the flour until well coated. Set your Instant Pot to Sauté and heat olive oil. Cook beef for 8 minutes in total. Transfer to a bowl. Stir in red wine and cook until reduced by half, scraping off any bits at the bottom. Return the meat and add in onion, garlic, bay leaves, carrots, fennel, potatoes, tomato paste, beef stock, salt, and pepper.

Seal the lid, select Manual/Pressure Cook mode on High, and set cooking time to 20 minutes. When done, perform a natural pressure release for 10 minutes, then a quick pressure release to let out the remaining steam. Unlock the lid and stir the parsley. Serve warm.

Sweet & Sour Pork Stew

Total Time: 55 minutes | **Servings**: 4 | **Per Serving**: Kcal 591; Carbs 30g; Fat 36g; Protein 36g

Ingredients

¼ cup cornstarch
1 lb pork shoulder, cut into bite-size pieces
Salt and black pepper to taste
3 tbsp olive oil
1 red bell pepper, deseeded, cut into strips
1 white onion, thinly sliced

¼ cup white vinegar
¼ cup granulated sugar
¼ cup ketchup
1 tsp freshly grated ginger
1 cup chopped pineapples
½ cup chicken broth

Directions

Reserve 1 tbsp of cornstarch and pour remaining onto a plate. Season pork with salt, pepper, and dredge lightly in cornstarch. Set your Instant Pot to Sauté and heat olive oil. Fry pork until golden brown on the outside, 8 minutes. Remove onto a plate and set aside. Add and sauté bell pepper and onion until softened, 5 minutes.

In a bowl, mix vinegar, sugar, ketchup, and ginger. Pour mixture onto vegetables and cook for 2 minutes. Return pork to inner pot and top with pineapples and chicken broth. Seal the lid, set on Manual/Pressure Cook mode on High, and set time to 15 minutes. After cooking, perform a natural pressure release for 10 minutes. Serve.

Spinach & Pumpkin Stew

Total Time: 20 minutes | **Servings**: 6 | **Per Serving**: Kcal 355; Carbs 54g; Fat 8g; Protein 15g

Ingredients

1 tbsp butter
1 white onion, chopped
4 garlic cloves, minced
2 lb pumpkin, cubed
4 cups vegetable broth
1 (15-oz) can sundried tomatoes, undrained

2 (15-oz) cans chickpeas, drained
1 ½ tsp cumin powder
½ tsp smoked paprika
1 tsp coriander powder
Salt and black pepper to taste
4 cups baby spinach

Directions

Select Sauté on your Instant Pot. Combine butter, onion, and garlic in the pot. Cook for 5 minutes. Add in pumpkin, broth, tomatoes, chickpeas, cumin, paprika, coriander, salt, and pepper. Seal the lid, select Manual/Pressure Cook on High, and cook for 8 minutes. Perform a quick pressure release. Stir in spinach to wilt, 5 minutes on Sauté. Serve.

Easy Zucchini Stew with Gruyère Cheese

Total Time: 15 minutes | **Servings**: 4 | **Per Serving**: Kcal 324; Carbs 28g; Fat 16g; Protein 18g

Ingredients

4 zucchinis, sliced
Salt to taste
3 tbsp melted butter

½ cup grated Gruyere cheese
2 cups tomato sauce
1 cup shredded mozzarella cheese

Directions

Arrange zucchini in the pot, pour the tomato sauce, and 1 cup water over the slices. Sprinkle with the mozzarella cheese. Seal the lid, select Manual/Pressure Cook on High, and set time to 5 minutes. Perform a quick pressure release. Open the lid and sprinkle with Gruyere cheese and melted butter and serve.

Swiss Cheese & Mushroom Stew with Pasta

Total Time: 25 minutes | **Servings**: 4 | **Per Serving**: Kcal 415; Carbs 25g; Fat 24g; Protein 25g

Ingredients

8 oz garganelli pasta
1 (12–oz) can evaporated milk
Salt to taste
1 large egg
1 ½ tsp arrowroot starch

8 oz Swiss cheese, shredded
1 cup mushrooms, stems removed
3 tbsp sour cream
3 tbsp grated cheddar cheese
2 tbsp olive oil

Directions

Select Sauté on your Instant Pot. Heat olive oil and sauté mushrooms for 5 minutes. Remove to a plate. Pour the garganelli pasta into the pot, add half of the evaporated milk, 3 cups of water, and salt. Seal the lid, select Manual/Pressure Cook on High, and set time to 4 minutes. When done, perform a natural pressure release for 10 minutes.

In a bowl, whisk the remaining milk with egg. In another bowl, combine arrowroot starch with Swiss cheese. Pour the milk-egg and starch mixtures in the pot. Mix in mushrooms and sour cream. Serve sprinkled with cheddar cheese.

Easy Spanish Stew with Chorizo

Total Time: 30 minutes | **Servings**: 4 | **Per Serving**: Kcal 455; Carbs 36g; Fat 21g; Protein 17g

Ingredients

3 tbsp olive oil
1 onion, chopped
2 garlic cloves, minced
1 banana pepper, chopped
1 cup Spanish rice
¼ cup red salsa

1 cup canned tomatoes
2 cups vegetable stock
1 (16-oz) can pinto beans, drained
Salt to taste
1 tbsp chopped fresh parsley
2 small Spanish chorizo sausages, sliced

Directions

Select Sauté on your Instant Pot. Heat olive oil and cook chorizo, onion, garlic, and banana pepper for 3 minutes. Stir in rice, salsa, tomatoes, stock, beans, and salt. Seal the lid, select Manual/Pressure Cook, and set time to 8 minutes.

After cooking, do a natural pressure release for 10 minutes. Stir in the parsley, dish the rice, and serve.

Garlic Quinoa & Vegetable Stew

Total time: 25 minutes | **Servings**: 4 | **Per Serving**: Kcal 412; Carbs 47g; Fat 19g; Protein 11g

Ingredients

3 tbsp sesame oil
1 onion, chopped
2 cups vegetable broth
2 garlic cloves, minced

1 cup quinoa
¼ cup peanut butter
1 cup frozen vegetables, thawed
Salt and black pepper to taste

Directions

Set your Instant Pot to Sauté and warm sesame oil. Cook onion and garlic for 3 minutes, until tender. Stir in the broth, quinoa, salt, and pepper. Seal the lid, select Manual/Pressure Cook mode on High, and set time to 8 minutes. When done, perform a quick pressure. Set the pot to Sauté. Put in peanut butter and vegetables and cook for 3 minutes. Divide between plates and serve.

Pasta & Side Dishes

Pappardelle with Tomatoes, Mozzarella & Arugula

Total Time: 20 minutes | **Servings**: 4 | **Per Serving**: Kcal 259; Carbs 37g; Fat 9g; Protein 12g

Ingredients

2 cups dried pappardelle
Salt and black pepper to taste
2 tbsp olive oil
2 garlic cloves, minced

1 cup cherry tomatoes, halved
A handful of baby arugula
1 cup grated mozzarella cheese
¼ cup grated Parmesan cheese

Directions

Add pappardelle, 4 cups of water, and salt to your Instant Pot. Seal the lid, select Manual/Pressure Cook on High, and set time to 3 minutes. After cooking, do a quick pressure release. Drain pasta through a colander. Set aside.

Wipe inner pot clean with a napkin and set to Sauté mode. Heat olive oil and stir-fry garlic until fragrant, 30 seconds. Add tomatoes and cook until softened, 2 to 3 minutes. Stir in pasta, arugula, and mozzarella cheese. Season with salt and black pepper. Allow arugula to wilt for 1 to 2 minutes. Garnish with Parmesan cheese and serve.

Tagliatelle with Hazelnut Pesto

Total Time: 15 minutes | **Servings**: 4 | **Per Serving**: Kcal 213; Carbs 14g; Fat 11g; Protein 8g

Ingredients

1 ½ cups tagliatelle
Salt and black pepper to taste
1 cup spinach
3 tbsp hazelnuts

1 garlic clove, minced
4 tsp olive oil
¼ cup grated Parmesan cheese

Directions

Add pasta, 3 ½ cups of water, and salt to inner pot. Seal the lid, select Manual/Pressure Cook/Pressure Cook mode on High, and set cooking time to 4 minutes. After cooking, do a quick pressure release to let out steam, and unlock the lid. Drain pasta through a colander and pour into a large bowl.

Meanwhile, in a food processor, combine spinach, hazelnuts, garlic, olive oil, salt, and black pepper. Blend until smooth. Pour pesto over pasta and toss until well mixed. Divide between plates and garnish with Parmesan cheese.

Cavatelli in Tomato, Bacon & Mushroom Sauce

Total Time: 30 minutes | **Servings**: 4 | **Per Serving**: Kcal 265; Carbs 21g; Fat 18g; Protein 6g

Ingredients

2 cups dried cavatelli
2 tbsp olive oil
4 bacon slices, chopped
1 small white onion, finely chopped
½ cup white button mushrooms, sliced
2 garlic cloves, minced

2 cups chopped tomatoes
2 tsp tomato paste
4 cups of water + ½ cup water
Salt and black pepper to taste
1 tbsp chopped parsley + more to garnish
2 tbsp sour cream

Directions

Add cavatelli, 4 cups of water, and salt to inner pot of your Instant Pot. Seal the lid, select Manual/Pressure Cook on High, and set cooking time to 3 minutes. After cooking, do a quick pressure release to let out steam, and unlock the lid. Drain pasta through a colander. Set aside.

Wipe inner pot clean with paper towel and set your Instant Pot to Sauté mode. Heat 1 tbsp of olive oil and cook bacon until crispy and brown, 5 minutes. Transfer to a paper towel-lined plate and set aside.

Add remaining olive oil to inner pot and sauté onion and mushrooms until softened, 5 minutes. Stir in garlic until fragrant, 30 seconds. Add tomatoes, tomato paste, half cup of water, salt, and black pepper. Seal the lid, select a Manual/Pressure Cook mode on High, and set cooking time to 2 minutes.

After cooking, perform natural pressure release for 10 minutes, and then quick pressure release to let out remaining steam. Unlock the lid and stir in parsley, bacon, and sour cream until well mixed. Adjust taste with salt and black pepper. Mix in pasta until well coated in sauce, then plate and serve.

Minty Buttered Pea Spaghetti

Total Time: 15 minutes | **Servings**: 4 | **Per Serving**: Kcal 364; Carbs 38g; Fat 21g; Protein 11g

Ingredients

16 oz green spaghetti
2 tbsp butter
1 cup frozen green peas
1 cup cooking cream

A pinch nutmeg powder
Salt and black pepper to taste
¼ cup shaved Parmesan cheese
2 tbsp mint, chopped

Directions

Add green spaghetti, 4 cups of water, and salt to inner pot. Seal the lid, select Manual/Pressure Cook mode on High, and set cooking time to 3 minutes. After cooking, do a quick pressure release to let out steam, and unlock the lid. Drain pasta through a colander and pour in a large bowl.

Wipe inner pot clean with a paper towel and set the pot to Sauté mode. Melt butter in inner pot and sauté frozen peas until softened and warmed through. Mix in cooking cream, nutmeg, salt, and black pepper. Cook for 1 minute and toss pasta in sauce. Top with Parmesan cheese and mint. Serve warm.

Mediterranean Fettuccine

Total Time: 15 minutes | **Servings**: 4 | **Per Serving**: Kcal 376; Carbs 36g; Fat 20g; Protein 15g

Ingredients

1 cup heavy cream
16 oz dried fettuccine
2 tbsp olive oil
1 ¼ cups grated Parmesan cheese

A pinch of mustard powder
Salt and black pepper to taste
2 tbsp capers, drained
1 tbsp dried oregano

Directions

Add fettuccine, 4 cups of water, and salt to inner pot. Seal the lid, select Manual/Pressure Cook on High, and set cooking time to 4 minutes. After cooking, do a quick pressure release to let out steam, and Unlock the lid. Drain pasta through a colander. Set aside.

Wipe inner pot clean and set the pot to Sauté. Heat olive oil and mix in heavy cream, oregano, mustard powder, and 1 cup of Parmesan cheese until the cheese melts, 2 minutes. Season with salt and pepper. Toss fettuccine in sauce until well coated and transfer to serving plates. Garnish with remaining Parmesan cheese and capers. Serve.

Tagliatelle in Saffron Sauce

Total Time: 20 minutes | **Servings**: 4 | **Per Serving**: Kcal 468; Carbs 33g; Fat 35g; Protein 8g

Ingredients

16 oz tagliatelle
1 tbsp olive oil
2 tbsp butter
1 medium brown onion, chopped
2 garlic cloves, minced
2 tsp cornflour

2 cups heavy cream
A pinch saffron powder
1 egg yolk
½ lemon, juiced
Salt and black pepper to taste

Directions

Add tagliatelle, 4 cups of water, and salt to inner pot of your Instant Pot. Seal the lid, select Manual/Pressure Cook mode on High, and set cooking time to 3 minutes. After cooking, do a quick pressure release to let out steam, and unlock the lid. Drain pasta through a colander. Set aside.

Wipe inner pot clean with paper towel and set your Instant Pot to Sauté mode. Heat olive oil and butter in inner pot and sauté onion until softened, 3 minutes. Stir in garlic until fragrant, 30 seconds.

Whisk in cornflour and cook for 1 minute. Gradually stir in heavy cream until smoothly combined and whisk in saffron and egg yolk. Make sure to mix fast to prevent the egg from cooking. Stir in lemon juice, salt, black pepper, and then pasta until well combined. Serve warm.

Creamy Penne with Chicken

Total Time: 25 minutes | **Servings**: 4 | **Per Serving**: Kcal 585; Carbs 23g; Fat 15g; Protein 67g

Ingredients

1 ½ cups dried penne
1 tbsp olive oil
4 chicken breasts, cut into 1-inch cubes
Salt and black pepper to taste

4 tbsp white wine
¼ cup heavy cream
¼ cup frozen peas
2 tbsp chopped parsley to garnish

Directions

Add penne, 3 cups of water, and salt to inner pot. Seal the lid, select Manual/Pressure Cook mode on High, and set cooking time to 3 minutes. After cooking, do a quick pressure release to let out steam, and unlock the lid. Drain pasta through a colander. Set aside.

Wipe inner pot clean with paper towel and set to Sauté. Heat olive oil in inner pot, season chicken with salt and black pepper, and cook until golden brown on the outside and cooked within, 6 to 8 minutes.

Pour in wine, cook further for 1 minute, and stir in heavy cream. Heat for 1 minute. Stir in peas and penne until well coated. Season with salt and black pepper. Spoon food into serving plates and garnish with parsley. Serve warm.

Watercress Rigatoni with Smoked Salmon

Total Time: 20 minutes | **Servings**: 4 | **Per Serving**: Kcal 288; Carbs 34g; Fat 5g; Protein 12g

Ingredients

1 ½ cups rigatoni
1 tbsp olive oil
2 garlic cloves, minced

2 oz smoked salmon, cut into thin strips
1 cup watercress leaves + more to garnish
Salt and black pepper to taste

Directions

Add pasta, 3 cups of water, and salt to inner pot. Seal the lid, select Manual/Pressure Cook mode on High, and set cooking time to 3 minutes. After cooking, do a quick pressure release to let out steam, and unlock the lid. Drain rigatoni through a colander. Set aside.

Wipe inner pot clean with paper towel and set to Sauté. Heat olive oil in inner pot and stir-fry garlic until fragrant, 30 seconds. Stir in salmon and watercress; cook for 2 minutes. Toss in rigatoni, season with salt and black pepper, and plate. Garnish with some watercress leaves and serve warm.

Beef Bucatini with Yellow Pepper Sauce

Total Time: 40 minutes | **Servings**: 4 | **Per Serving**: Kcal 502; Carbs 33g; Fat 23g; Protein 32g

Ingredients

2 cups bucatini
4 tbsp olive oil
1 lb ground beef
Salt and black pepper to taste
1 garlic clove, minced

1 bay leaf
¼ cup dry white wine
2 yellow bell peppers, deseeded and chopped
4 tomatoes, chopped

Directions

Add bucatini, 4 cups of water, and salt to inner pot. Seal the lid, select Manual/Pressure Cook mode on High, and set cooking time to 3 minutes. After cooking, do a quick pressure release to let out steam, and unlock the lid. Drain pasta through a colander. Set aside for serving.

Wipe inner pot clean with paper towel and set your Instant Pot to Sauté. Heat olive oil in inner pot and cook beef until brown, 5 minutes. Season with salt and black pepper. Add garlic and bay leaf, cook further for 3 minutes. Pour in wine and half cup of water, and cook further for 3 minutes. Top with bell peppers and tomatoes.

Seal the lid, select a Manual/Pressure Cook mode on High, and set cooking time to 2 minutes. After cooking, perform a natural pressure release for 10 minutes, and then a quick pressure release to let out remaining steam. Unlock the lid and stir sauce and adjust taste with salt and black pepper. Plate bucatini and top with beef sauce. Serve warm.

Smoked Sausage & Cabbage Noodles

Total Time: 20 minutes | **Servings**: 4 | **Per Serving**: Kcal 448; Carbs 23g; Fat 23g; Protein 39g

Ingredients

3 oz pancetta, chopped
1 tbsp olive oil
1 onion, sliced
¼ cup dry white wine
1 cup chicken stock

Salt and black pepper to taste
5 oz wide egg noodles
4 cups shredded green cabbage
1 ½ pounds smoked sausage, sliced

Directions

Set on Sauté and heat the olive oil. Cook the pancetta for 6 minutes until crisp. Using a slotted spoon, transfer to a paper towel-lined plate to drain. Sauté onion for 2 minutes, until softened. Pour in wine and simmer until the wine reduces while scraping the bottom of the pot with a wooden spoon. Pour in chicken stock, salt, pepper, and noodles and stir. Top with cabbage and sausages.

Seal the lid, select Manual/Pressure Cook on High, and set the cooking time to 3 minutes. When the cooking time is over, do a quick pressure release and unlock the lid. Serve topped with pancetta.

Green Vegetable Pasta

Total Time: 20 minutes | **Servings**: 4 | **Per Serving**: Kcal 403; Carbs 44g; Fat 24g; Protein 11g

Ingredients

16 oz gemelli pasta

1 head broccoli, cut into florets

¼ lb asparagus, spears only

2 zucchinis, chopped

¼ cup snap peas

3 tbsp butter

3 tbsp vegetable stock

¼ cup heavy cream

2 tbsp chopped parsley

A pinch nutmeg powder

Salt and black pepper to taste

2 tbsp shaved Parmesan cheese

Directions

Add gemelli pasta, 4 cups of water, and salt to inner pot. Fit a steamer basket over pasta and add broccoli, asparagus, zucchinis, and snap peas. Seal the lid, select Steam on High, and set time to 3 minutes. After cooking, do a quick pressure release to let out steam. Remove steamer basket with vegetables. Drain pasta through a colander. Set aside.

Wipe inner pot clean with paper towels and set to Sauté. Melt butter and sauté steamed vegetables for 2 minutes. Add vegetable stock and mix in heavy cream until heated. Mix in parsley, nutmeg, salt, and pepper. Allow flavors to incorporate for 1 minute. Add in the pasta and toss to coat well. Top with Parmesan cheese and serve.

Italian Turkey Drunken Noodles

Total Time: 25 minutes | **Servings**: 4 | **Per Serving**: Kcal 447; Carbs 43g; Fat 16g; Protein 31g

Ingredients

2 tbsp olive oil

1 lb ground turkey

1 red onion, thinly sliced

2 cups sliced mixed bell peppers

4 garlic cloves, minced

Salt and black pepper to taste

1 tsp Italian seasoning

½ cup white wine

1 (28 oz) can diced tomatoes with juice

1 cup chicken broth

16 oz Pappardelle noodles

2 tbsp chopped parsley

¼ cup basil chiffonade

Directions

Set your Instant Pot to Sauté mode. Heat olive oil in inner pot and cook turkey until brown, while occasionally stirring and breaking any lumps that form, 5 minutes. Add red onion, bell peppers, and cook until softened, 3 minutes. Top with garlic and cook until fragrant, 30 seconds. Season with salt, black pepper, and Italian seasoning.

Stir and cook for 1 minute. Pour in white wine and allow reduction by two-thirds. Stir in tomatoes, chicken broth, and noodles. Seal the lid, select Manual/Pressure Cook on High, and set time to 3 minutes. After cooking, perform a quick pressure release. Stir in parsley, basil, and adjust taste with salt and black pepper. Dish food and serve warm.

Herbed Spaghetti with Garlic

Total Time: 15 minutes | **Servings**: 4 | **Per Serving**: Kcal 269; Carbs 32g; Fat 14g; Protein 7g

Ingredients

16 oz spaghetti

4 tbsp olive oil

3 garlic cloves, minced

3 tbsp chopped basil

2 tbsp chopped oregano

2 tbsp chopped parsley

Salt and black pepper to taste

½ cup grated Parmesan cheese

Directions

Add spaghetti, 4 cups of water, and salt to inner pot. Seal the lid, select Manual/Pressure Cook mode on High, and set cooking time to 2 minutes. After cooking, do a quick pressure release to let out steam, and unlock the lid. Drain pasta through a colander. Set aside.

Wipe inner pot clean with paper towel and set the pot to Sauté. Heat half of olive oil in inner pot and stir-fry garlic, basil, oregano, and parsley. Cook for 1 minute and toss spaghetti in sauce. Season with salt and pepper, drizzle with remaining olive oil, plate and serve topped with Parmesan cheese.

Chicken & Cherry Tomatoes Spaghetti

Total Time: 25 minutes | **Servings**: 4 | **Per Serving**: Kcal 511; Carbs 43g; Fat 39g; Protein 27g

Ingredients

2 tbsp olive oil
2 chicken breasts, cut into 1-inch cubes
Salt and black pepper to taste
16 oz spaghetti, broken into 1-inch pieces
½ tsp paprika
2 garlic cloves, minced

1 cup dry white wine
2 cups cherry tomatoes, halved
3 tbsp unsalted butter, cut into ½-in cubes
¼ cup heavy cream
1 lemon, zested and juiced
1 cup packed basil leaves

Directions

Set your Instant Pot to Sauté and adjust to medium heat. Heat olive oil in inner pot, season chicken with salt and black pepper, and cook until golden brown. Add paprika and garlic to stir-fry for 1 minute. Pour in white wine, 3 cups of water, spaghetti, and salt. Seal the lid, select Manual/Pressure Cook mode on High, and set time to 4 minutes.

After cooking, do a quick pressure release to let out steam, and unlock the lid. Set the pot to Sauté and adjust to medium heat. Stir in tomatoes, butter, heavy cream, lemon zest, and lemon juice. Cook for 1 to 2 minutes and dish food onto serving plates. Garnish with basil and serve warm.

Arugula & Marinated Feta Rigatoni

Total Time: 25 minutes | **Servings**: 4 | **Per Serving**: Kcal 403; Carbs 57g; Fat 16g; Protein 13g

Ingredients

1 lemon, zested and juiced
½ tsp red pepper flakes
3 tbsp olive oil, divided
½ cup crumbled feta cheese
½ cup Greek yogurt

Salt and black pepper to taste
1 garlic clove, minced
16 oz whole-wheat rigatoni
2 cups baby arugula
2 tbsp chopped chives

Directions

In a medium bowl, mix lemon zest, lemon juice, red pepper flakes, and 1 tablespoon of olive oil. Add feta cheese and combine well. Set aside to marinate for 5 minutes. In a large bowl, combine Greek yogurt, salt, black pepper, garlic, and remaining olive oil until adequately mixed. Set aside.

In inner pot, add rigatoni, 3 cups of water, and salt. Seal the lid, select Manual/Pressure Cook mode on High, and set cooking time to 4 minutes. After cooking, do a quick pressure release, and unlock the lid.

Drain pasta through a colander and pour hot pasta into yogurt mixture. Toss with two spoons until well coated in the sauce. Top with marinated feta, arugula, and mix again. Garnish with chives and serve.

Parsley Shrimp Fra Diavolo

Total Time: 20 minutes | **Servings:** 4 | **Per Serving:** Kcal 360; Carbs 41g; Fat 13g; Protein 22g

Ingredients

2 tbsp olive oil

3 garlic cloves, minced

2 green onions, chopped

½ tsp red pepper flakes

Salt and black pepper to taste

16 oz linguine

2 tbsp unsalted butter

1 lb shrimp, peeled and deveined

1 bunch asparagus, trimmed and cut into 2-inch pieces

1 lemon, zested and juiced

¼ cup parsley leaves

Directions

Set your Instant Pot to Sauté mode. Heat olive oil and sauté garlic and green onions until fragrant and softened, 1 minute. Season with red pepper flakes, salt, black pepper, and cook further for 1 minute. Pour in 2 cups of water, linguine, and butter, and stir. Seal the lid, select Manual/Pressure Cook on High, and set cooking time to 4 minutes.

After cooking, do a quick pressure release. Arrange shrimp and asparagus on top. Seal the lid, select Manual/Pressure Cook on High, and set time to 2 minutes. After cooking, do a quick pressure release, and unlock the lid. Add lemon zest, lemon juice, parsley, and stir food. Adjust taste with salt and black pepper. Dish and serve warm.

Cheesy Smoked Sausage Farfalle

Total Time: 20 minutes | **Servings:** 4 | **Per Serving:** Kcal 690; Carbs 35g; Fat 47g; Protein 41g

Ingredients

1 tbsp olive oil

1 lb smoked Italian sausages, sliced

1 medium onion, chopped

3 garlic cloves, minced

2 cups chicken broth

1 (10 oz) can diced tomatoes

½ cup heavy cream

16 oz farfalle

Salt and black pepper to taste

1 ¼ cups shredded pepper jack cheese

4 scallions, chopped to garnish

Directions

Set your Instant Pot to Sauté mode. Heat olive oil in inner pot and cook sausages and onion until lightly brown, 4 minutes. Add garlic and cook until fragrant, 30 seconds. Pour in chicken broth, tomatoes, heavy cream, farfalle, salt, and black pepper. Seal the lid, select Manual/Pressure Cook mode on High, and set cooking time to 4 minutes.

After cooking, perform a quick pressure release to let out steam, and unlock the lid. Set the pot to Sauté mode and adjust taste with salt and black pepper. Add cheese to pasta and mix until melted. Spoon food into serving bowls, garnish with scallions, and serve warm.

Bacon & Broccoli Carbonara

Total Time: 25 minutes | **Servings:** 4 | **Per Serving:** Kcal 536; Carbs 36g; Fat 24g; Protein 26g

Ingredients

1 pound spaghetti

1 head broccoli, cut into florets

1 garlic clove, crushed

4 cups water

Salt and black pepper to taste

4 eggs

8 ounces bacon

1 cup Pecorino cheese, grated

1 tbsp butter

Directions

Place spaghetti, water, and salt into inner pot. Seal the lid, select Manual/Pressure Cook on High, and set time to 5 minutes. When done, perform a quick pressure release. Remove pasta with a perforated spoon to a bowl. Place a steamer basket inside, and add in broccoli. Seal the lid and cook for 4 minutes on High. When ready, do a quick pressure release, and set aside.

In a bowl, whisk the eggs with cheese and pepper. Wipe clean the pot with a paper towel. Set to Sauté and add in bacon and garlic. Cook for 5 minutes, until crispy. Discard the garlic and set aside. Add in butter. Return pasta in the pot and reheat it for 30 seconds. Press Cancel. Add in the egg mixture and stir until the eggs thicken into a sauce. Top with broccoli and serve right away.

Chili Spaghetti with Red Wine & Tomatoes

Total Time: 45 minutes | **Servings**: 4 | **Per Serving**: Kcal 571; Carbs 43g; Fat 28g; Protein 38g

Ingredients

16 oz spaghetti
1 tbsp olive oil
1 medium onion, chopped
2 garlic cloves, minced
1 lb ground pork
1 tbsp tomato puree
1 tsp granulated sugar
1 tbsp dried oregano

1 tsp red chili flakes
1 red bell pepper
2 red chilies, chopped
½ cup red wine
½ cup chicken broth
1 (28 oz) can chopped tomatoes
Salt and black pepper to taste
2 tbsp chopped parsley

Directions

In inner pot, add spaghetti, 3 cups of water, and salt. Seal the lid, select Manual/Pressure Cook on High, and set time to 3 minutes. After cooking, perform a quick pressure release. Drain pasta and set aside.

Clean inner pot and select Sauté mode. Heat olive oil and sauté onion until softened, 3 minutes. Mix in garlic and cook until fragrant, 30 seconds. Add pork, cook until brown, 5 minutes, and stir in tomato puree, sugar, oregano, red chili flakes, red bell pepper, and red chilies. Cook until peppers soften, 3 minutes.

Stir in red wine, chicken broth, tomatoes, and season with salt and black pepper. Seal the lid, select Manual/Pressure Cook mode on High, and set cooking time to 10 minutes. After cooking, perform a natural pressure release for 10 minutes. Stir in parsley. Divide pasta onto serving plates and top with pork sauce.

Sriracha Mac n' Cheese

Total Time: 20 minutes | **Servings**: 4 | **Per Serving**: Kcal 670; Carbs 57g; Fat 18g; Protein 31g

Ingredients

1 ½ cups Gruyere cheese, grated
4 cups water
A pinch of salt
1 lb elbow macaroni

2 large eggs
1 tsp ground mustard
1 tsp sriracha sauce
1 ½ cups half and half

Directions

Place the macaroni, water, and salt into inner pot. Seal the lid, select Manual/Pressure Cook mode on High, and set cooking time to 4 minutes. In a bowl, whisk the eggs with ground mustard, sriracha sauce, and half and half. Set aside. When the pot beeps, perform a quick pressure release and unlock the lid. Set the pot to Sauté. Toss in the egg mixture, stir in Gruyere cheese until melted, and serve warm.

Tri-Color Rotini Pasta with Spinach & Pine Nuts

Total Time: 30 minutes | **Servings**: 4 | **Per Serving**: Kcal 390; Carbs 52g; Fat 17g; Protein 11g

Ingredients

1 lb tri-color rotini pasta
1 onion, chopped
3 cloves garlic, minced
12 white mushrooms, sliced
1 zucchini, sliced
1 tsp dried oregano
1 tsp dried basil
Salt and black pepper to taste

2 tbsp olive oil
Freshly grated Parmesan cheese
¼ cup pine nuts
6 cups baby spinach
1 cup vegetable stock
2 cups water
½ cup tomato paste
3 tbsp light soy sauce

Directions

Set your Instant Pot to Sauté and heat olive oil. Place in the onion and garlic and sauté until fragrant, about 3 minutes, stirring occasionally. Season with salt and pepper.

Put in the mushrooms, zucchini, oregano, and basil and cook for 3 more minutes, until tender. Pour in the stock, rotini pasta, spinach, tomato paste, water, and soy sauce and stir to combine.

Seal the lid, select Manual/Pressure Cook on High, and set time to 4 minutes. When done cooking, perform natural pressure release for 10 minutes. Top with Parmesan cheese and pine nuts and serve immediately.

Quick & Easy Basil Spaghetti

Total Time: 15 minutes | **Servings**: 4 | **Per Serving**: Kcal 394; Carbs 34g; Fat 22g; Protein 10g

Ingredients

1 ½ cups water
3 cups dry red wine
16 oz spaghetti
Salt to taste

¼ cup olive oil
8 garlic cloves, minced
½ cup grated Parmesan cheese
4 basil leaves, cut into long, thin strips

Directions

In inner pot, add water, red wine, spaghetti, and salt. Seal the lid, select Manual/Pressure Cook mode on High, and set cooking time to 3 minutes. After cooking, perform a quick pressure release. Drain pasta and set aside.

Clean inner pot and select Sauté mode. Heat olive oil in inner pot and sauté garlic until fragrant, 30 seconds. Return pasta to inner pot and stir to coat thoroughly. Top with Parmesan cheese and mix until cheese melts. Spoon pasta into serving plates and garnish with basil.

Sage Butternut Squash Pasta

Total Time: 25 minutes | **Servings**: 4 | **Per Serving**: Kcal 241; Carbs 4g; Fat 18g; Protein 18g

Ingredients

1 (4-pound) butternut squash
2 tbsp fresh sage, chopped
4 oz pancetta, cooked and crumbled
5 cloves garlic sliced

2 tbsp olive oil
Salt to taste
¼ tsp nutmeg
1 cup Gruyere cheese, grated

Directions

Set your Instant Pot to Sauté mode and heat olive oil. Place in the sage and garlic, and cook until the sage is crispy, about 2-3 minutes. Set aside. Cut the butternut squash in half, lengthwise, and deseed.

Wipe inner pot clean. Pour in 1 cup of water and fit in a trivet. Put the butternut squash on the trivet. Seal the lid, select Manual/Pressure Cook mode on High, and set cooking time to 3 minutes.

When done, perform a quick pressure release to let out all the steam. Unlock the lid and remove the squash. Take a fork and make spaghetti by scraping the butternut squash lengthwise; season with salt. Pour the sage mixture over and sprinkle with nutmeg. Top with Gruyere cheese and pancetta to serve.

Short Ribs with Egg Noodles

Total Time: 55 minutes | **Servings**: 4 | **Per Serving**: Kcal 887; Carbs 33g; Fat 39g; Protein 63g

Ingredients

4 pounds beef bone-in short ribs
2 cups beef broth
6 oz egg noodles
2 tbsp prepared horseradish
6 tbsp Dijon mustard

1 garlic clove, minced
Salt and black pepper to taste
3 tbsp melted butter
1 ½ cups breadcrumbs

Directions

Season the short ribs on all sides with salt. Pour 1 cup of broth into the inner pot. Put in a trivet and place the short ribs on top. Seal the lid, choose Manual/Pressure Cook, on High and the time to 25 minutes. After cooking, perform a natural pressure release for 5 minutes, then a quick pressure release, and unlock the lid. Remove the trivet and short ribs. Add the egg noodles.

Seal the lid, select Manual/Pressure Cook on High, and set the cooking time to 4 minutes. After cooking, perform a quick pressure release. In a bowl, combine the horseradish, Dijon mustard, garlic, and black pepper. Brush the sauce on all sides of the short ribs and reserve any extra sauce.

In another bowl, mix the butter and breadcrumbs. Coat the ribs with the crumbs. Place the ribs in a foil-lined roasting pan. Preheat your oven to 420°F and bake for 15 minutes, turning once. Serve the beef and noodles, with the extra sauce on the side.

Roasted Pepper Pasta Salad

Total Time: 15 minutes | **Servings**: 4 | **Per Serving**: Kcal 277; Carbs 23g; Fat 17g; Protein 3g

Ingredients

1 cup dried conchiglie
5 tbsp olive oil
2 garlic cloves, minced
2 roasted red bell peppers, chopped

2 tbsp freshly squeezed lemon juice
2 tbsp basil pesto
Salt and black pepper to taste
3 tbsp chopped basil

Directions

Add conchiglie, 3 cups of water, and salt to inner pot of your Instant Pot. Seal the lid, select Manual/Pressure Cook mode on High, and set cooking time to 3 minutes. After cooking, do a quick pressure release to let out steam, and unlock the lid. Drain pasta through a colander.

In a large bowl, whisk olive oil with garlic, bell peppers, lemon juice, pesto, salt, and black pepper. Toss pasta in dressing and mix in fresh basil. Adjust taste with salt and black pepper, and serve.

Sicilian-Style Cavatappi Pasta

Total Time: 30 minutes | **Servings**: 4 | **Per Serving**: Kcal 486; Carbs 42g; Fat 17g; Protein 42g

Ingredients

1 tbsp olive oil
4 shallots, chopped
2 cloves minced garlic
3 cups mushrooms, sliced
½ tsp dried parsley
½ tsp dried basil
¼ tsp dried oregano
¼ tsp red pepper flakes

3 cups water
2 cups milk
¼ cup flour
16 oz cavatappi pasta
2 cups frozen peas, thawed
1 cup canned pinto beans
½ cup Parmigiano Reggiano shavings

Directions

Set your Instant Pot to Sauté mode and warm olive oil. Place in the mushrooms, garlic, parsley, basil, oregano, red pepper flakes, and shallots; cook until tender, about 5 minutes. Stir in water, milk, and flour. Place in the remaining ingredients, except Parmigiano Reggiano shavings and pinto beans.

Seal the lid, select Manual/Pressure Cook mode on High, and set cooking time to 8 minutes. When done, perform natural pressure release for 10 minutes, then a quick pressure release. Stir in pinto beans and cook until everything is heated through on Sauté mode. Scatter with Parmigiano Reggiano shavings and serve.

Pizza-Pasta Salad

Total Time: 15 minutes | **Servings**: 4 | **Per Serving**: Kcal 720; Carbs 26g; Fat 54g; Protein 33g

Ingredients

1 ½ cups bow tie pasta
6 sprigs oregano
¼ cup chopped basil
3 garlic cloves, minced
1 cup cubed mozzarella cheese
1 ½ cups Parmesan cheese, shaved

1 cup black olives, pitted and sliced
7 oz pepperoni, thinly sliced
¼ cup olive oil
¼ cup red wine vinegar
Salt and black pepper to taste

Directions

In inner pot, add pasta, 3 cups of water, and salt. Seal the lid, select Manual/Pressure Cook mode on High, and set cooking time to 3 minutes. After cooking, perform a quick pressure release. Drain pasta and pour it into a salad bowl.

Add oregano, basil, garlic, mozzarella, Parmesan cheese, black olives, pepperoni, olive oil, red wine vinegar, salt, and black pepper. Toss until well mixed. Serve salad immediately.

Linguine with Bacon & Tomatoes

Total Time: 30 minutes | **Servings**: 4 | **Per Serving**: Kcal 438; Carbs 41g; Fat 24g; Protein 18g

Ingredients

16 oz linguine
4 bacon slices, chopped
2 tbsp olive oil
1 white onion, chopped
2 garlic cloves, minced

Salt and black pepper to taste
A pinch red chili flakes
1 (14-oz) can tomato sauce
½ cup chicken broth
½ cup grated Parmesan cheese

Directions

In inner pot, add pasta, 3 cups of water, and salt. Seal the lid, set on Manual/Pressure Cook on High, and set cooking time to 3 minutes. After cooking, perform a quick pressure release to let out steam, and unlock the lid. Drain pasta through a colander and set aside.

Clean inner pot and select Sauté mode. Add bacon to inner pot and fry until brown and crispy, 5 minutes. Transfer to a paper towel-lined plate to drain grease and set aside. Heat olive oil in inner pot with bacon fat and sauté onion until softened, 3 minutes. Add garlic and stir-fry until fragrant, 30 seconds. Season with salt, black pepper, and red chili flakes. Stir in tomato sauce and chicken broth.

Seal the lid, set on Manual/Pressure Cook on High, and cook for 3 minutes. After cooking, perform a quick pressure release to let out remaining steam, and unlock the lid. Adjust taste with salt, black pepper, and stir in pasta until well coated in sauce. Dish food, sprinkle Parmesan cheese on top and serve warm.

Cheesy Pumpkin Pasta with Walnuts

Total Time: 20 minutes | **Servings**: 4 | **Per Serving**: Kcal 687; Carbs 46g; Fat 49g; Protein 29g

Ingredients

16 oz pasta noodles
1 medium yellow onion, diced
2 garlic cloves, minced
2 cups pumpkin puree
4 cups vegetable broth
Salt and black pepper to taste

2 tbsp butter
4 oz cream cheese, room temperature
¼ cup walnuts, chopped
¼ tsp red chili flakes
½ tsp nutmeg powder
3 tbsp chopped parsley

Directions

In inner pot, add noodles, onion, garlic, pumpkin puree, vegetable broth, salt, and black pepper. Seal the lid, select Manual/Pressure Cook on High, and set cooking time to 5 minutes. After cooking, perform a quick pressure release to let out remaining steam, and unlock the lid.

Set the pot to Sauté mode and stir in butter, cream cheese, and half of walnuts. Cook until cream cheese melts. Adjust taste with salt, black pepper, red chili flakes, and nutmeg powder. Dish food and garnish with parsley.

Cauliflower & Broccoli Gruyere Side

Total Time: 25 minutes | **Servings**: 4 | **Per Serving**: Kcal 312; Carbs 12g; Fat 17g; Protein 22g

Ingredients

1 medium cauliflower, cut into small florets
1 medium broccoli, cut into small florets
½ tsp garlic powder
½ tsp onion powder
½ cup chicken broth

Salt and black pepper to taste
1 cup evaporated milk
¼ cup grated Gruyere cheese
1 cup grated cheddar cheese
1 tbsp chopped parsley

Directions

In inner pot, add cauliflower, broccoli, garlic powder, onion powder, chicken broth, salt, and black pepper. Seal the lid, select Manual/Pressure Cook mode on High, and set cooking time to 3 minutes.

After cooking, do a natural pressure release for 10 minutes, then a quick pressure release to let out remaining steam, and unlock the lid. Set the cooker to Sauté mode. Add evaporated milk, cheeses and stir until they melt. Spoon food into serving bowls, garnish with parsley, and serve warm.

Parsley Rice & Beans with Avocado

Total Time: 25 minutes | **Servings**: 6 | **Per Serving**: Kcal 291; Carbs 52g; Fat 7g; Protein 8g

Ingredients

1 ½ cups brown rice
1 ¼ cups canned red kidney beans
1 cup salsa
½ bunch parsley, leaves and stems separated
3 cups vegetable broth

2 cups water
Salt and black pepper to taste
1 avocado, halved, pitted, and sliced
1 large lime, cut into wedges

Directions

In inner pot, add brown rice, kidney beans, salsa, parsley stems, vegetable broth, and water. Season with salt and black pepper. Seal the lid, select Manual/Pressure Cook on High, and time to 8 minutes.

After cooking, perform a quick pressure release to let out steam. Unlock the lid, fluff rice and beans, and spoon into serving bowls. Garnish with parsley leaves and top with avocado and lime wedges. Serve warm.

Bacon Snap Peas

Total Time: 15 minutes | **Servings**: 4 | **Per Serving**: Kcal 145; Carbs 8g; Fat 8g; Protein 4g

Ingredients

3 bacon slices, chopped
2 garlic cloves, minced
1 ½ cups snap peas
½ cup vegetable broth

Salt and black pepper to taste
¼ tsp red chili flakes
2 tsp lemon juice

Directions

Set your Instant Pot to Sauté mode and adjust to medium heat. Add bacon to inner pot and cook until brown and crispy, 5 minutes. Transfer to a paper towel-lined plate to drain grease. Sauté garlic until fragrant, 30 seconds, and top with snap peas, vegetable broth, salt, black pepper, and red chili flakes.

Seal the lid, select Manual/Pressure Cook on High, and set time to 1 minute. After cooking, do a quick pressure release to let out steam, and unlock the lid. Stir in bacon and lemon juice. Spoon into serving plates and serve.

Tomato & Hummus Macaroni

Total Time: 15 minutes | **Servings**: 4 | **Per Serving**: Kcal 250; Carbs 42g; Fat 6g; Protein 8g

Ingredients

1 ½ cups macaroni
¾ cup hummus
1 tsp garlic paste
½ cup cherry tomatoes, halved

¼ cup chopped basil
Salt and black pepper to taste
¼ cup black olives, pitted

Directions

Add 3 cups of water, salt, and macaroni to inner pot. Seal the lid, select Manual/Pressure Cook on High, and set cooking time to 4 minutes. After cooking, do a quick pressure release to let out steam, and unlock the lid. Drain pasta through a colander and transfer to a bowl.

In a bowl, add hummus, garlic, tomatoes, basil, salt, pepper, and black olives. Stir well, and top the pasta to serve.

Hot Potatoes with Feta & Bell Peppers

Total Time: 20 minutes | **Servings**: 4 | **Per Serving**: Kcal 213; Carbs 16g; Fat 13g; Protein 7g

Ingredients

2 tbsp olive oil
1 cup vegetable broth
1 ½ cups russet potatoes, cubed
Salt and black pepper to taste

½ cup roasted red bell peppers, diced
4 oz crumbled feta cheese
½ jar of hot sauce

Directions

Set your Instant Pot to Sauté mode and adjust to medium heat. Heat olive oil, pour potatoes and season with salt and black pepper. Stir-fry until the backs of potatoes begin to crisp. Pour in vegetable broth, seal the lid, select Manual/Pressure Cook mode on High, and set cooking time to 6 minutes.

After cooking, do a quick pressure release to let out steam, and unlock the lid. Drain potatoes through a colander and transfer to a large bowl. Add bell peppers, feta cheese, and hot sauce. Mix until well combined. Dish and serve.

Cayenne Corn with Cream Cheese & Scallions

Total Time: 25 minutes | **Servings**: 4 | **Per Serving**: Kcal 389; Carbs 20g; Fat 33g; Protein 7g

Ingredients

2 cups canned sweet corn kernels, drained
½ cup whole milk
8 oz cream cheese
3 tbsp butter
½ cup heavy cream

1 tsp cayenne pepper
1 tsp sugar
Salt and black pepper to taste
2 tbsp scallions to garnish, chopped

Directions

In inner pot, add sweet corn, milk, cream cheese, butter, heavy cream, cayenne pepper, sugar, salt, and black pepper. Seal the lid, select Manual/Pressure Cook on High, and set cooking time to 15 minutes.

After cooking, perform a quick pressure release to let out steam, and unlock the lid. Stir food vigorously until creamy. Ladle into serving bowls, garnish with scallions, and serve.

Swedish Cabbage Slaw

Total Time: 10 minutes | **Servings**: 4 | **Per Serving**: Kcal 109; Carbs 3g; Fat 10g; Protein 1g

Ingredients

1 large cabbage, shredded
3 tbsp olive oil
Salt and black pepper to taste
1 roasted bell peppers (in jar), chopped

1 tsp dried oregano
1 tsp white vinegar
1 tsp poppy seeds

Directions

Pour 1 cup of water in inner pot, fit in a steamer basket, and add cabbage to basket. Seal the lid, select Manual/Pressure Cook on High, and set cooking time to 1 minute.

After cooking, do a quick pressure release to let out steam, and unlock the lid. Transfer cabbage to a large bowl and add olive oil, salt, black pepper, bell pepper, oregano, vinegar, and poppy seeds. Toss well. Plate and serve.

Tangy Steamed Veggies

Total Time: 15 minutes | **Servings**: 4 | **Per Serving**: Kcal 235; Carbs 47g; Fat 5g; Protein 9g

Ingredients

1 cup vegetable broth
½ lb carrots, peeled and cut into large chunks
1 lb green beans, trimmed
1 lb asparagus, trimmed and cut into thirds

1 ½ lb russet potatoes, halved
1 lemon, juiced
1 tbsp olive oil

Directions

Pour vegetable broth in inner pot, fit in a trivet, and pour carrots, green beans, asparagus, and potatoes on top. Seal the lid, select Manual/Pressure Cook mode on High, and set cooking time to 2 minutes.

After cooking, do a quick pressure release to let out steam, and unlock the lid. Using tongs, remove vegetables into a large bowl and drizzle with lemon juice and olive oil. Serve warm.

Honey-Glazed Carrots

Total Time: 10 minutes | **Servings**: 4 | **Per Serving**: Kcal 166; Carbs 14g; Fat 12g; Protein 2g

Ingredients

3 large carrots, cut into chunks
1 cup vegetable stock
¼ cup butter, melted

2 tbsp honey
1 tbsp chopped parsley
Salt and black pepper to taste

Directions

Add carrots, vegetable stock, salt, and pepper to inner pot. Seal the lid, select Manual/Pressure Cook on High, and set time to 2 minutes. After cooking, do a quick pressure release. Using a slotted spoon, fetch out carrots into a baking sheet. Brush with butter and honey and cook under the broiler for 4 minutes. Top with parsley and serve.

Traditional Lebanese Hummus

Total Time: 65 minutes | **Servings**: 4 | **Per Serving**: Kcal 576; Carbs 62g; Fat 29g; Protein 28g

Ingredients

__Chickpeas:__
1 pound dried chickpeas, soaked

8 cups water

__Hummus:__
¼ cup tahini
2 medium cloves garlic
Juice from 1 lemon
1 tsp salt

½ tsp ground cumin
¼ tsp sumac
¼ cup olive oil
2 tbsp parsley, chopped

Directions

Pour the water and chickpeas into inner pot. Seal the lid, select Manual/Pressure Cook, and set cooking time to 35 minutes. When done cooking, perform natural pressure release for 15 minutes, then a quick pressure release to let out the remaining steam.

Unlock the lid and drain the chickpeas. Reserve the liquid. Place the chickpeas into a food processor, add in 1 cup of reserved liquid and the remaining ingredients. Blend until smooth and creamy. Serve.

Pearl Barley Salad with Avocado & Tomato

Total Time: 60 minutes | **Servings**: 4 | **Per Serving**: Kcal 392; Carbs 45g; Fat 23g; Protein 6g

Ingredients

1 cup pearled barley, rinsed
4 cups water
4 tbsp olive oil
Salt to taste

Dressing

2 tbsp extra-virgin olive oil
1 lime, juiced
1 spring onion, sliced

1 garlic clove, minced
½ cup cherry tomatoes, halved
1 avocado, sliced

2 tbsp parsley, finely chopped
Salt and black pepper, to taste

Directions

Place the barley, water, olive oil, salt, and garlic into inner pot. Seal the lid, select Manual/Pressure Cook, and set cooking time to 30 minutes on High. When done, perform a natural pressure release for 10 minutes, then a quick pressure release to let out the remaining steam.

Unlock the lid and drain the barley. Let cool for 10 minutes. In a bowl, combine all the dressing ingredients. Add in the barley and toss to combine. Top with cherry tomatoes and avocado and serve.

Barbecued Mushrooms

Total Time: 10 minutes | **Servings**: 4 | **Per Serving**: Kcal 55; Carbs 5g; Fat 4g; Protein 1g

Ingredients

1 ½ cups cremini mushrooms, chopped
½ cup water
2 tbsp barbecue sauce

2 garlic cloves, crushed
1 tbsp olive oil
1 tbsp chopped parsley to garnish

Directions

Combine mushrooms, water, barbecue sauce, and garlic in inner pot. Seal the lid, select Manual/Pressure Cook on High, and set cooking time to 1 minute.

After cooking, do a quick pressure release to let out steam, and unlock the lid. Using a slotted spoon, fetch out mushrooms into a medium bowl. Discard garlic. Drizzle with olive oil and toss well. Garnish with parsley and serve.

Easy Steamed Potatoes

Total Time: 15 minutes | **Servings**: 4 | **Per Serving**: Kcal 336; Carbs 65g; Fat 6g; Protein 8g

Ingredients

4 large potatoes
Salt and black pepper to taste

2 tbsp butter, melted
2 tbsp chopped parsley to garnish

Directions

Pierce holes all around potatoes using a fork. Pour 1 cup of water in inner pot, fit in a trivet, and put potatoes on the trivet. Seal the lid, select Manual/Pressure Cook on High, and set cooking time to 6 minutes.

After cooking, perform a quick pressure release to let out steam, and unlock lid. Remove potatoes onto a plate, break or crush the top parts opened, and season with salt and pepper. Drizzle butter on top and garnish with parsley. Serve.

Chili Broccoli with Couscous

Total Time: 20 minutes | **Servings**: 4 | **Per Serving**: Kcal 135; Carbs 15g; Fat 7g; Protein 6g

Ingredients

½ cup couscous
1 head broccoli, cut into florets
2 garlic cloves, minced
1 red chili, seeded and chopped

2 tbsp olive oil
Salt and black pepper to taste
2 tbsp parsley, chopped

Directions

Pour 1 cup of water into the pot and fit in a trivet. Place the broccoli on the trivet. Seal the lid, select Steam, and set cooking time to 1 minute. When done, perform a quick pressure release to let out the remaining steam. Unlock the lid and remove the broccoli to a bowl. Take out the water and the trivet.

In another bowl, cover the couscous with boiled water. Let sit for 2-3 minutes, until all the water is absorbed. Fluff up with a fork and set aside. Press Sauté and warm the olive oil. Add in garlic, red chili, salt, and pepper and cook for 1 minute. Stir in broccoli for 30 more seconds. Serve the couscous topped with broccoli mixture and parsley.

Cheesy Vegetable Rice

Total Time: 25 minutes | **Servings**: 4 | **Per Serving**: Kcal 261; Carbs 19g; Fat 22g; Protein 7g

Ingredients

1 cup jasmine rice, rinsed
¼ cup frozen mixed vegetables
½ tsp garlic powder
½ tsp onion powder

1 ½ cups chicken broth
Salt and black pepper to taste
¼ cup grated Parmesan cheese
1 cup grated cheddar cheese

Directions

In inner pot, add jasmine rice, mixed vegetables, garlic, onion, chicken broth, salt, and black pepper. Seal the lid, select Manual/Pressure Cook mode on High, and set cooking time to 6 minutes.

After cooking, do a natural pressure release for 10 minutes. Set the pot to Sauté. Add cheeses and stir vigorously until melted. Spoon food into serving bowls and serve warm.

Creamy Cardamom Polenta

Total Time: 15 minutes | **Servings**: 4 | **Per Serving**: Kcal 187; Carbs 15g; Fat 10g; Protein 7g

Ingredients

1 cup polenta
4 cups chicken broth
1 tsp cardamom powder
Salt to taste

4 tsp unsalted butter
½ cup shredded cheddar cheese
¼ cup half and half

Directions

Set your Instant Pot to Sauté mode and adjust to medium heat. Combine polenta and chicken broth in inner pot until boiling. Seal the lid, select Manual/Pressure Cook on High, and set cooking time to 7 minutes.

After cooking, perform a natural pressure release until all the steam is out. Unlock the lid and whisk in cardamom, salt, butter, cheddar cheese, and half and half. Spoon into serving bowls and serve.

Venezuelan Black Beans

Total Time: 70 minutes | **Servings**: 4 | **Per Serving**: Kcal 398; Carbs 69g; Fat 5g; Protein 24g

Ingredients

2 cups dry black beans, soaked
1 onion, chopped
1 red bell pepper, chopped
2 tsp olive oil
2 garlic cloves, chopped
1 tbsp chili powder

½ tsp Worcestershire sauce
½ tsp ground cumin
Salt and black pepper to taste
4 cups chicken stock
1 lime, juiced

Directions

Set your Instant Pot to Sauté and warm the olive oil. Add in the onion, garlic, chili powder, red bell pepper, cumin, Worcestershire sauce, salt, and black pepper and cook for 5 minutes, until tender. Add in the beans and chicken stock and stir. Seal the lid, select Manual/Pressure Cook on High, and cook for 40 minutes.

When done, perform a natural pressure release for 15 minutes, then a quick pressure release to let out the remaining steam. Unlock the lid and mix in the lime juice. Select Sauté and cook until the liquid has reduced to half, stirring often. Adjust seasoning and serve.

Turmeric & Cilantro Pilaf

Total Time: 25 minutes | **Servings**: 4 | **Per Serving**: Kcal 164; Carbs 18g; Fat 12g; Protein 7g

Ingredients

1 tbsp olive oil
1 onion, thinly sliced
1 tsp turmeric
1 cup rice, rinsed

½ tsp lemon zest
1 lemon, juiced
1 cup vegetable stock
2 tbsp chopped cilantro

Directions

Set your Instant Pot to Sauté and heat the olive oil. Place in the onion and cook for 3 minutes, stirring occasionally. Stir in the rice to coat. Add in the lemon zest, lemon juice, turmeric, and stock and mix.

Seal the lid, select Manual/Pressure Cook, and set time to 8 minutes on High. When done, perform a quick pressure release. Unlock the lid and fluff the rice using a fork and serve. Stir through the cilantro and serve.

Easy Scallion & Cauliflower Rice

Total Time: 20 minutes | **Servings**: 2 | **Per Serving**: Kcal 154; Carbs 9g; Fat 13g; Protein 3g

Ingredients

1 tbsp oil
2 scallions, sliced
1 garlic clove, minced
2 cups cauliflower rice

1 tbsp butter, sliced
Salt and black pepper to taste
¼ tsp hot sauce

Directions

Set your Instant Pot to Sauté and heat the oil. Place in the scallions and garlic and cook for 2-3 minutes, stirring often. Stir in the cauliflower rice and butter. Cook for 7-8 minutes. Add in the hot sauce and mix well. Season with salt and pepper and serve hot.

Greek-Style Potato Salad

Total Time: 30 minutes | **Servings**: 2 | **Per Serving**: Kcal 164; Carbs 25g; Fat 5g; Protein 4g

Ingredients

3 small potatoes, peeled
1 cup water
2 tbsp Greek yogurt
2 tbsp light mayonnaise
1 garlic clove, minced

1 tsp lemon zest
1 tbsp dill, chopped
½ small red onion, sliced
Salt and black pepper to taste

Directions

Place the potatoes, salt, and water into inner pot. Seal the lid, select Steam, and set the cooking time to 10 minutes on High. When done, perform a natural pressure release for 10 minutes, then a quick pressure release. Drain the potatoes and set aside to cool before slicing them.

For the dressing, mix together the remaining ingredients, except for the dill, and add it to the chopped potatoes, toss to coat. Serve sprinkled with dill.

Quick Almond Quinoa

Total Time: 30 minutes | **Servings**: 4 | **Per Serving**: Kcal 258; Carbs 30g; Fat 12g; Protein 8g

Ingredients

2 tbsp olive oil
1 cup quinoa
1 cup almond milk

1 cup water
3 tbsp toasted flaked almonds, for garnish

Directions

Combine quinoa, almond milk, olive oil, and water into inner pot. Seal the lid, select Manual/Pressure Cook, and set cooking time to 8 minutes on High.

When done, perform a natural pressure release for 10 minutes, then a quick pressure release to let out the remaining steam. Unlock the lid and fluff the quinoa with a fork. Garnish with flaked almonds to serve.

Spring Onion & Sprout Rice

Total Time: 35 minutes | **Servings**: 4 | **Per Serving**: Kcal 224; Carbs 28g; Fat 14g; Protein 9g

Ingredients

1 pound Brussels sprouts, trimmed and sliced
1 cup jasmine rice
4 spring onions, sliced
2 cups water

1 tbsp light soy sauce
2 tbsp sesame oil
1 garlic clove, minced
Salt and black pepper to taste

Directions

Set your Instant Pot to Sauté and warm the sesame oil. Add in the spring onions, garlic, Brussels sprouts, salt, and pepper and cook for 5 minutes, until tender. Mix in the rice and water. Seal the lid, and cook on Manual/Pressure Cook for 10 minutes on High.

When rice is done, perform a natural pressure release for 10 minutes, then a quick pressure release to let out the remaining steam. Unlock the lid and fluff the rice with a fork. Stir in soy sauce and serve.

Mixed Quinoa & Brown Rice with Mushrooms

Total Time: 35 minutes | **Servings:** 2 | **Per Serving:** Kcal 313; Carbs 44g; Fat 12g; Protein 8g

Ingredients

2 tbsp olive oil
1 onion, chopped
2 garlic cloves, minced
1 cup button mushrooms, sliced

1 cup mixed quinoa and brown rice, rinsed
2 cups vegetable stock
1 tbsp butter
½ cup Parmesan shavings

Directions

Set your Instant Pot to Sauté and heat the oil. Place in the onion and mushrooms, and sauté for 5 minutes, until softened. Stir in the quinoa, brown rice and vegetable stock. Seal the lid, select Rice, and set time to 12 minutes.

When done, perform a natural pressure release for 10 minutes, then a quick pressure release to let out the remaining steam. Unlock the lid and stir in the butter to melt. Scatter over the Parmesan shavings and serve.

Roasted Bell Pepper Pilaf

Total Time: 35 minutes | **Servings:** 4 | **Per Serving:** Kcal 191; Carbs 23g; Fat 13g; Protein 6g

Ingredients

2 tbsp olive oil
1 onion, chopped
1 cup rice
4 roasted bell peppers, chopped

1 cup chicken broth
4 garlic cloves, minced
2 tbsp parsley, chopped
Salt to taste

Directions

Set your Instant Pot to Sauté and add in olive oil and onion. Cook for 5 minutes. Stir in the remaining ingredients, except for the bell peppers and parsley. Seal the lid, select Manual/Pressure Cook mode, and set time to 10 minutes.

When done, perform a natural pressure release for 10 minutes, then a quick pressure release to let out the remaining steam. Unlock the lid and fluff the rice with a fork. Stir in the roasted bell peppers, sprinkle with parsley and serve.

Herbed Potatoes with Chives

Total Time: 20 minutes | **Servings:** 4 | **Per Serving:** Kcal 359; Carbs 34g; Fat 14g; Protein 7g

Ingredients

2 pounds baby potatoes, washed
½ tsp dried rosemary
½ tsp dried thyme
½ tsp dried tarragon
½ tsp dried oregano

½ tsp garlic powder
Salt and black pepper to taste
3 tbsp butter
2 cups vegetable stock
Chopped chives for garnish

Directions

In a bowl, mix the rosemary, thyme, tarragon, oregano, garlic powder, salt, and pepper. Set your Instant Pot to Sauté and melt the butter. Place in potatoes and cook for 5-6 minutes until lightly browned, stirring frequently. Pour in the herb mixture and vegetable stock. Seal the lid, select Manual/Pressure Cook, and set time to 7 minutes. When done, perform a quick pressure release. Transfer the potatoes to a serving platter. Serve topped with chives.

Cilantro & Green Pea Rice

Total Time: 30 minutes | **Servings**: 4 | **Per Serving**: Kcal 264; Carbs 45g; Fat 7g; Protein 5g

Ingredients

1 onion, chopped
1 cup frozen green peas
1 cup rice, rinsed
2 cups water
2 tbsp olive oil

1 garlic clove, minced
Salt and black pepper to taste
3 tbsp cilantro, chopped
½ lime, juiced

Directions

Set your Instant Pot to Sauté and heat the oil. Add in onion and garlic; cook for 5 minutes. Mix in the rice, water, black pepper and salt and stir to combine. Seal the lid, select Manual/Pressure Cook, and set time to 7 minutes.

When done, perform a natural pressure release for 10 minutes, then a quick pressure release to let out the remaining steam. Unlock the lid and stir in the peas and lime juice until heated through. Sprinkle with cilantro to serve.

Sweet Buttered Baby Carrots

Total Time: 20 minutes | **Servings**: 4 | **Per Serving**: Kcal 137; Carbs 22g; Fat 6g; Protein 2g

Ingredients

1 pound baby carrots, peeled
2 tbsp butter
¼ tsp salt
2 tbsp honey

1 orange, juiced and zested
A pinch cinnamon
2 tbsp sesame seeds, for garnish

Directions

Pour 1 cup of water into the pot and fit in a trivet. Place the carrots on the trivet. Seal the lid, select Steam, and set cooking time to 2 minutes. When done, perform a quick pressure release to let out the remaining steam. Unlock the lid and remove the carrots.

Clean the inner pot. Press Sauté and melt the butter. Add in salt, honey, orange juice, orange zest, and cinnamon; cook for 5 minutes. Add the mixture to the carrots and toss to coat. Scatter sesame seeds over the top and serve.

Blue Cheese Polenta

Total Time: 17 minutes | **Servings**: 4 | **Per Serving**: Kcal 161; Carbs 8g; Fat 12g; Protein 6g

Ingredients

½ cup polenta
2 cups chicken stock
2 tbsp unsalted butter
¼ cup heavy cream

½ cup blue cheese, crumbled
Salt and black pepper, to taste
2 tbsp parsley, chopped

Directions

Place the polenta and chicken stock into inner pot. Seal the lid, select Manual/Pressure Cook, and set cooking time to 7 minutes on High. When done, perform a quick pressure release. Unlock the lid.

Stir in butter, heavy cream, and blue cheese, until smooth and the cheese fully melted. Adjust the seasoning. Spoon into bowls topped with parsley to serve.

Celeriac & Potato Mash

Total Time: 30 minutes | **Servings**: 4 | **Per Serving**: Kcal 205; Carbs 27g; Fat 10g; Protein 4g

Ingredients

1 cup water
Salt and black pepper to taste
1 pound potatoes, chopped
½ pound celeriac, chopped

½ cup milk
3 tbsp butter, softened
1 garlic clove, minced
¼ handful chives, chopped

Directions

Place the water, salt, celeriac, and potatoes into inner pot. Seal the lid, select Steam on High, and set the cooking time to 10 minutes. When done, perform a natural pressure release for 10 minutes, then a quick pressure release. Unlock the lid and drain the celeriac and potatoes.

Use a potato mash to mash the potatoes and slowly pour in the milk until uniform and smooth. Add in the butter, black pepper, and garlic and whisk until you get the desired texture. Taste and adjust the seasoning. Serve scattered with a handful of chives.

Cheddar-Parmesan Mac & Cheese

Total Time: 15 minutes | **Servings**: 2 | **Per Serving**: Kcal 658; Carbs 61g; Fat 17g; Protein 27g

Ingredients

8 ounces elbow macaroni
½ tsp mustard powder
1 tbsp butter
A pinch of cayenne pepper
2 cups water

1 cup milk
¼ cup Greek yogurt
1 ½ cups cheddar cheese, shredded
¼ cup Parmesan cheese, grated
Salt and black pepper to taste

Directions

Place the macaroni, salt, and water into inner pot. Seal the lid, select Manual/Pressure Cook, and set cooking time to 4 minutes on High. When done, perform a quick pressure release.

Drain the pasta and return to the pot. Mix in the milk, mustard powder, butter, cayenne pepper, Greek yogurt, and the cheeses. Stir for 1 minute until the cheeses melt. Adjust the seasoning with salt and pepper, and serve.

Fall Veggie Mix

Total Time: 10 minutes | **Servings**: 4 | **Per Serving**: Kcal 80; Carbs 6g; Fat 6g; Protein 2g

Ingredients

1 carrot, sliced
1 head cauliflower florets
½ cup celeriac, sliced

2 tbsp butter
Salt and black pepper to taste

Directions

Pour 1 cup of water into the pot and fit in a steamer basket. Place the carrots, cauliflower and celeriac in the basket. Seal the lid, select Steam, and set cooking time to 2 minutes. When done, perform a quick pressure release.

Unlock the lid and transfer the veggies to a bowl. Add in the butter and stir until melted. Adjust the seasoning with salt and pepper and serve.

Kale & Potato Gratin

Total Time: 30 minutes | **Servings**: 4 | **Per Serving**: Kcal 528; Carbs 40g; Fat 37g; Protein 12g

Ingredients

2 pounds potatoes, thinly sliced
1 cup kale, steamed
1 tbsp dill, chopped

1 cup crème fraîche
3 oz of cheddar cheese
Salt to taste

Directions

Put half of the potatoes in a greased baking dish, and season with salt. Spread kale over potatoes, sprinkle with half of the cheese, then top with the remaining potatoes. Pour over crème fraîche and finish with the remaining cheese.

To your pot, add 1 cup water and fit in a trivet. Place the baking dish on the trivet. Seal the lid, select Manual/Pressure Cook, and cook for 15 minutes on High. When done, perform a quick pressure release. Serve garnished with dill.

Savory Custards with Ham & Emmental Cheese

Total Time: 25 minutes | **Servings**: 4 | **Per Serving**: Kcal 156; Carbs 6g; Fat 11g; Protein 8g

Ingredients

2 Serrano ham slices, halved widthwise
1 tbsp olive oil
4 large eggs
1 oz cottage cheese, at room temperature

¼ cup half and half
Salt and black pepper to taste
¼ cup grated Emmental cheese
¼ cup caramelized white onions

Directions

Set the Instant Pot to Sauté. Heat the olive oil and cook the ham for 2 minutes, turning occasionally. Remove the ham to a plate. Rush the inside of four ramekins with the ham fat. Set the cups aside.

Beat eggs with cottage cheese, half and half, salt, and pepper. Stir in Emmental cheese. Lay a piece of ham on the bottom of each custard cup. Share the onions among the cups as well as the egg mixture.

Pour 1 cup water into the inner pot and fit in a trivet. Arrange the ramekins on top. Seal the lid, select Manual/Pressure Cook on High, and set time to 7 minutes. Perform a quick pressure release. Chill before serving.

Sweet Potato Gratin with Peas & Bacon

Total Time: 20 minutes | **Servings**: 4 | **Per Serving**: Kcal 456; Carbs 21g; Fat 27g; Protein 36g

Ingredients

1 ½ lb sweet potatoes, peeled and quartered
Salt and black pepper to taste
½ cup heavy cream, or more to taste
1 cup shredded Provolone cheese

10 oz prosciutto, chopped
¾ cup frozen peas, thawed
½ cup grated Pecorino Romano cheese
3 tbsp chopped fresh chives

Directions

Pour 1 cup of water into your Instant Pot and put in a trivet. Arrange sweet potatoes on top. Seal the lid, select Manual/Pressure Cook on High, and set the time to 4 minutes. After cooking, perform a quick pressure release.

Use a large fork to break the potatoes into pieces. Empty the water of the pot. Put the potatoes back in the pot and season with the salt and pepper. Mix in the heavy cream, Provolone cheese, and prosciutto. Gently stir in the peas. Select Sauté and cook for 3-4 minutes. Sprinkle with Pecorino Romano cheese and chives to serve.

Spinach & Mushroom Risotto

Total time: 25 minutes | **Servings**: 4 | **Per Serving**: Kcal 425; Carbs 66g; Fat 20g; Protein 13g

Ingredients

4 tbsp butter
1 red onion, chopped
3 garlic cloves, minced
2 celery sticks, chopped
8 oz button mushrooms, sliced
Salt and black pepper to taste

¼ tsp dried thyme
1 cup carnaroli rice
2 cups vegetable broth
2 cups baby spinach
¼ cup grated Parmesan cheese

Directions

Set your Instant Pot to Sauté and melt 2 tbsp of butter. Cook onion, garlic, celery, and mushrooms for 5 minutes. Stir in salt, pepper, thyme, rice, and broth. Seal the lid, select Manual/Pressure Cook on High, and set time to 8 minutes.

When done, perform a quick pressure to let out steam. Unlock the lid and set to Sauté. Add in the remaining butter and spinach and cook for 2 minutes, until the spinach wilts. Top with Parmesan cheese and stir. Serve immediately.

Effortless Mac & Cheese

Total time: 15 minutes | **Servings**: 6 | **Per Serving**: Kcal 490; Carbs 61g; Fat 20g; Protein 15g

Ingredients

1 pound elbow macaroni
4 cups water, divided
Salt to taste
1 cup heavy cream

½ cup whole milk
3 tbsp butter
2 ½ cups mozzarella cheese, shredded
½ cup Pecorino Romano cheese shredded

Directions

In your Instant Pot, mix the water, macaroni, and salt. Seal the lid, select Manual/Pressure Cook on High, and set time to 4 minutes. When done, perform a quick pressure to let out steam.

Stir in the heavy cream, milk, and butter. Gradually add mozzarella cheese, stirring often, until melted. Serve sprinkled with Pecorino Romano cheese.

Party Baba Ganoush with Nachos

Total Time: 20 minutes | **Servings**: 2 | **Per Serving**: Kcal 491; Carbs 32g; Fat 40g; Protein 7g

Ingredients

1 pound eggplants, sliced
¼ cup olive oil
2 tbsp tahini
1 garlic clove

1 ¼ tbsp lemon juice
1 tsp parsley. chopped
Salt and black pepper to taste
Nacho Tortilla Chips

Directions

Pour 1 cup of water into your Instant Pot and fit in a trivet. Place the eggplants on the trivet. Seal the lid, select Steam on High, and cook for 6 minutes. When done, do a quick pressure release.

In a food processor, blend the eggplants and the remaining ingredients, except for the parsley, until smooth. Season to taste and sprinkle with parsley. Serve with tortilla chips.

Eggs & Vegetables

Greek-Style Eggs with Feta Cheese

Total Time: 25 minutes | **Servings**: 4 | **Per Serving**: Kcal 235; Carbs 13g; Fat 17g; Protein 11g

Ingredients

3 tbsp ghee
1 small red onion, chopped
½ red bell pepper, chopped
2 garlic cloves, chopped
Salt and black pepper to taste
29 oz canned chopped tomatoes with juice

½ tsp coriander, ground
½ tsp smoked paprika
½ tsp red chili flakes
4 eggs
¼ cup crumbled feta cheese
2 tbsp fresh dill, chopped

Directions

Set Instant Pot to Sauté and melt the ghee. Sauté the onion, bell pepper, and garlic. Season lightly with salt and cook for 2 minutes until the vegetables are fragrant and beginning to soften. Stir in the tomatoes, ground coriander, smoked paprika, red chili flakes, and black pepper.

Seal the lid, select Manual/Pressure Cook on High, and set the cooking time to 4 minutes. When the timer beeps, perform a quick pressure release. Gently crack the eggs onto tomato sauce in different areas. Set on Sauté mode and cook until the eggs are set, 4-5 minutes. Don't stir. Sprinkle the shakshuka with feta cheese and dill. Dish into a serving platter and serve.

Egg Breakfast Burritos

Total Time: 25 minutes | **Servings**: 2 | **Per Serving**: Kcal 512; Carbs 36g; Fat 28g; Protein 31g

Ingredients

4 eggs
½ cup heavy cream
½ tsp garlic powder
Salt and black pepper to taste
1 red bell pepper, deseeded and diced
1 yellow onion, diced

2 tbsp chopped chives
¾ cup chopped turkey ham
2 cups water
2 whole-wheat tortillas
¾ cup grated Monterey Jack cheese

Directions

In a medium bowl, whisk eggs with heavy cream, garlic powder, salt, and black pepper. Mix in bell pepper, onion, chives, and ham. Transfer mixture to a large ramekin and cover with aluminum foil. Pour water into inner pot, fit in trivet, and place ramekin on top.

Seal the lid, select Manual/Pressure Cook on High, and set time to 10 minutes. After cooking, perform natural pressure release for 10 minutes. Unlock the lid, remove ramekin and stir eggs until broken into small pieces.

Lay tortilla wraps on a clean, flat surface, divide eggs on top and sprinkle with cheese. Roll and slice wraps into halves. Serve immediately.

Spicy Garam Masala Eggs

Total Time: 30 minutes | **Servings**: 2 | **Per Serving**: Kcal 421; Carbs 24g; Fat 28g; Protein 22g

Ingredients

2 cups water

4 eggs, whole

Ice bath

3 tsp ghee

¼ tsp fennel seeds

¼ tsp cumin seeds

4 cloves

1 tbsp cinnamon powder

3 long, red chilies, halved

1-star anise

¼ tsp ground black pepper

2 large white onions, finely chopped

2 large tomatoes, finely chopped

¼ tsp garam masala

¼ tsp turmeric powder

½ tsp chili powder

Salt to taste

2 tbsp chopped cilantro leaves

Directions

Pour water in your Instant Pot and place in eggs. Seal the lid, select Manual/Pressure Cook on High, and set time to 5 minutes. After cooking, perform a quick pressure release to let out the steam. Unlock lid and transfer eggs to an ice bath. Discard water in inner pot and wipe clean with paper towels. Peel eggs, cut in halves and set aside.

Select Sauté and adjust to medium heat. Melt half of ghee and stir-fry fennel seeds, cumin, cloves, cinnamon, red chilies, and star anise, for 3 minutes or until fragrant. Add half of onions, all of tomatoes and sauté until softened, 5 minutes. Spoon mixture into a blender and process on low speed until smooth paste forms. Set aside.

Melt remaining ghee in inner pot and sauté remaining onions until softened. Add the tomato paste, garam masala, turmeric powder, chili powder, and salt. Mix and cook for 3 minutes.

Add eggs to coat in sauce, making sure not to break them. Allow heating for 1 to 2 minutes and spoon masala with eggs over bed rice. Garnish with cilantro and serve for lunch.

Tortilla de Patatas (Spanish Omelet)

Total Time: 45 minutes | **Servings**: 2 | **Per Serving**: Kcal 486; Carbs 30g; Fat 33g; Protein 19g

Ingredients

1 tbsp butter, melted

4 oz frozen hash browns, defrosted

6 large eggs

Salt and black pepper to taste

1 tsp tomato paste

¼ cup milk

¼ cup diced yellow onion

1 garlic clove, minced

4 oz grated cheddar cheese

1 ½ cups water

Directions

Grease a ramekin with butter and spread hash browns at the bottom. In a medium bowl, whisk eggs, salt, and black pepper until frothy.

In another bowl, smoothly combine tomato paste with milk and mix into eggs along with onion and garlic. Pour mixture on top of hash browns. Add water to inner pot, fit in a trivet, and place ramekin on top.

Seal the lid, select Manual/Pressure Cook on High, and set cooking time to 15 minutes. After cooking, perform natural pressure release for 10 minutes, then a quick pressure release to let out the remaining steam.

Unlock the lid and remove ramekin. Sprinkle with cheddar cheese and place ramekin back on top of the trivet. Cover with the lid, without locking, to melt the cheese, for a minute or so. Once melted, slice, and serve the omelet.

Menemen (Turkish Baked Eggs)

Total Time: 25 minutes | **Servings**: 2 | **Per Serving**: Kcal 350; Carbs 29g; Fat 23g; Protein 10g

Ingredients

2 tbsp olive oil

1 onion, finely chopped

1 red bell pepper, deseeded and chopped

1 green bell pepper, deseeded and chopped

4 garlic cloves, minced

2 cups chopped tomatoes

2 scallions, chopped

4 large eggs

Salt and black pepper to taste

2 tbsp chopped mint leaves

Directions

Set your Instant Pot to Sauté. Heat olive oil and sauté onion, garlic, and bell peppers for 4 minutes. Mix in tomatoes and scallions; cook for 10 minutes, stirring frequently until the sauce thickens. Transfer to a greased baking dish.

Create 4 holes in the sauce and pour in each, an egg. Season with salt and pepper. Pour 1 cup of water into inner pot, fit in a trivet, and place baking dish on top. Seal the lid, select Manual/Pressure Cook on High, and set time to 3 minutes. After cooking, perform quick pressure. Garnish with mint leaves to serve.

Goat Cheese Shakshuka

Total Time: 15 minutes | **Servings**: 2 | **Per Serving**: Kcal 183; Carbs 9g; Fat 13g; Protein 9g

Ingredients

1 cup tomato passata

¼ tsp coriander powder

½ tsp smoked paprika

¼ tsp cumin powder

¼ tsp red pepper flakes

1 garlic clove, minced

Salt and black pepper to taste

4 large eggs, cracked into a bowl

2 tbsp crumbled goat cheese

2 cups water

Directions

Grease a large ramekin with cooking spray. Set aside. In a medium bowl, mix passata, coriander, paprika, cumin, red pepper flakes, garlic, salt, and black pepper. Spread mixture in ramekin and create a hole for the eggs at the center. Pour eggs onto passata bed, scatter goat cheese on top, and season with salt and black pepper.

Pour water into inner pot, fit in a trivet, and place ramekin on top. Seal the lid, select Manual/Pressure Cook on High, and set time to 2 minutes. After cooking, perform a quick pressure release. Serve eggs for breakfast.

Egg Caprese Breakfast Cups

Total Time: 15 minutes | **Servings**: 2 | **Per Serving**: Kcal 113; Carbs 6g; Fat 6g; Protein 8g

Ingredients

1 ½ cups water

2 thin slices ham

2 tbsp shredded mozzarella cheese

2 cherry tomatoes, halved

1 tsp dried basil

Salt and black pepper to taste

Directions

Pour water into inner pot and fit in a trivet. Line 2 medium ramekins with a slice of ham each, crack in an egg into each and divide mozzarella, basil, and tomatoes on top. Season with salt, black pepper, and cover with foil. Place ramekins on trivet. Seal the lid, select Manual/Pressure Cook on High, and set cooking time to 3 minutes. After cooking, perform a quick pressure release to let out steam. Unlock the lid, remove bowls, and serve immediately.

Kielbasa Baked Eggs

Total Time: 15 minutes | **Servings**: 2 | **Per Serving**: Kcal 248; Carbs 11g; Fat 16g; Protein 15g

Ingredients

½ cup diced smoked kielbasa sausages
½ cup frozen hash brown potatoes
¼ cup shredded cheddar cheese
4 large eggs, cracked into a bowl

1 tbsp chopped scallions
Salt and black pepper to taste
2 cups water

Directions

Grease a large ramekin with cooking spray and lay in ingredients in this order: sausages, hash browns, and cheddar cheese. Create a hole in the center and pour in eggs. Scatter scallions on top and season with salt and pepper.

Pour water into inner pot and fit in a trivet. Place ramekin on trivet, seal the lid, select Manual/Pressure Cook on Low, and set cooking time to 2 minutes. When done, perform quick pressure release and unlock the lid. Carefully remove ramekin and serve for breakfast.

Guacamole Stuffed Eggs

Total Time: 20 minutes | **Servings**: 4 | **Per Serving**: Kcal 227; Carbs 8g; Fat 17g; Protein 13g

Ingredients

8 eggs
1 cup guacamole
Salt and black pepper to taste

A pinch paprika, for garnish
Cilantro, chopped for garnish

Directions

Pour 1 cup of water into the pot and fit in a trivet. Place the eggs on the trivet. Seal the lid, select Manual/Pressure Cook mode on High, and cook for 6 minutes. When done, perform a quick pressure release to let out the remaining steam. Unlock the lid and cool the eggs in ice water.

Peel the cold eggs and slice them in half, lengthwise. Scoop out the yolks into a mixing bowl. Mash with a fork and add in guacamole; stir until smooth. Season to taste. Stuff the white halves eggs with the guacamole mixture. Sprinkle with paprika and cilantro to serve.

Kale-Sausage Egg Scramble

Total Time: 15 minutes | **Servings**: 2 | **Per Serving**: Kcal 192; Carbs 7g; Fat 14g; Protein 9g

Ingredients

¼ cup Italian sausage, casing removed
½ cup finely chopped kale
4 large eggs
3 tbsp milk

½ tsp chopped thyme
Salt and black pepper to taste
A pinch of red pepper flakes

Directions

Set your Instant Pot to Sauté and adjust to medium heat. Add sausage to inner pot and cook with frequent stirring while breaking into small pieces until brown, 5 minutes. Top with kale and cook until wilted, 3 minutes.

Meanwhile, beat eggs with milk. Pour onto kale mixture and scramble until eggs solidify, 1 minute. Turn Instant Pot off and season eggs with thyme, salt, black pepper, and red chili flakes. Plate and serve immediately for breakfast.

Mozzarella & Kale Frittata

Total time: 30 minutes | **Servings:** 4 | **Per Serving:** Kcal 291; Carbs 11g; Fat 17g; Protein 25g

Ingredients

2 cups kale
2 tbsp olive oil
1 onion, chopped
2 garlic cloves, minced
8 large eggs

2 cups shredded mozzarella cheese, divided
2 tomatoes, chopped
¼ cup milk
Salt and black pepper to taste
1 cup water

Directions

Line a baking dish with aluminium foil and grease with cooking spray. Set your Instant Pot to Sauté mode and heat the olive oil. Cook the onion, kale, and garlic for 3 minutes until the onion is translucent and the kale soft. Remove to a bowl. Stir in the eggs, 1 cup of cheese, tomatoes, milk, salt, and pepper. Mix until well combined.

Spoon the egg mixture into the baking dish and cover with aluminium foil. Add the water to the pot and fit in a trivet. Lay the dish on top. Seal the lid, select Manual/Pressure Cook mode on High, and set time to 5 minutes.

After cooking, perform natural pressure release for 10 minutes, then a quick pressure release to let out the remaining steam and remove the lid. Scatter the remaining cheese over the top of the frittata. Slice into wedges to serve.

Mushroom Frittata

Total Time: 30 minutes | **Servings:** 4 | **Per Serving:** Kcal 306; Carbs 5g; Fat 25g; Protein 15g

Ingredients

2 tbsp butter
1 cup sliced cremini mushrooms
Salt and black pepper to taste
2 cups water

8 large eggs
½ cup half and half
1 tsp dried thyme
1 cup shredded asiago cheese

Directions

Set your Instant Pot to Sauté and adjust to medium heat. Melt butter in inner pot and sauté mushrooms until softened, 5 minutes. Season with salt and black pepper, and transfer to a plate. Clean inner pot, return to base, pour in water, and fit in a trivet. Also, grease a 7-inch springform pan with cooking spray and set aside.

In a medium bowl, beat eggs with half and half, salt, black pepper, and thyme. Pour mixture into springform pan, sprinkle with asiago cheese, cover with aluminum foil, and place on trivet.

Seal the lid, select Manual/Pressure Cook on High, and set cooking time to 5 minutes. After cooking, do a natural pressure release for 10 minutes, then quick pressure to release remaining steam. Unlock the lid, take out pan, uncover, and transfer frittata onto a wide plate. Slice and serve warm.

Savory Spinach Egg Bites

Total Time: 30 minutes | **Servings:** 2 | **Per Serving:** Kcal 640; Carbs 11g; Fat 55g; Protein 26g

Ingredients

5 bacon slices, chopped
4 large eggs
¼ cup coconut cream
¼ cup chopped spinach

¾ cup grated Parmesan cheese
Salt and black pepper to taste
2 cups water

Directions

Set your Instant Pot to Sauté and adjust to medium heat. Add in bacon pieces and fry until brown and crispy, 5 minutes. Transfer to a paper towel-lined plate to drain grease and set aside. Clean inner pot and return to base.

In a medium bowl, beat eggs with coconut cream and fold in spinach, Parmesan cheese, salt, and black pepper. Fill a silicone muffin tray (two-thirds way up) with the mixture, cover with aluminum foil, and set aside.

Pour water into inner pot, fit in a trivet, and place muffin tray on top. Seal the lid, select Manual/Pressure Cook on High, and set time to 10 minutes. After cooking, perform a natural pressure release for 10 minutes. Unlock the lid, remove, and uncover muffin mold. Invert tray onto a plate to release egg bites and serve with hot sauce or butter.

Asparagus-Spinach Baked Eggs

Total Time: 15 minutes | **Servings**: 2 | **Per Serving**: Kcal 194; Carbs 9g; Fat 13g; Protein 11g

Ingredients

½ cup finely chopped broccoli
½ cup chopped asparagus
½ cup finely chopped spinach
½ tsp onion powder
½ tsp garlic powder

4 large eggs, beaten
¼ cup crumbled ricotta cheese
1 tbsp chopped scallions
Salt and black pepper to taste
2 cups water

Directions

Grease a large ramekin with cooking spray. Lay ingredients in the following way: broccoli, asparagus, and spinach. Sprinkle with onion and garlic powders and create a hole in the center of the greens. Pour over the eggs and top with ricotta cheese. Season with salt and black pepper.

Pour water into inner pot, fit in a trivet, and place ramekin on top. Seal the lid, select Manual/Pressure Cook on High, and set cooking time to 5 minutes. After cooking, perform a quick pressure release to let out steam and unlock the lid. Carefully remove ramekin and serve eggs, scattered with scallions.

Ham & Egg Tortilla Wraps

Total time: 25 minutes | **Servings**: 5 | **Per Serving**: Kcal 303; Carbs 41g; Fat 12g; Protein 10g

Ingredients

½ cup diced ham
1 ¼ cups frozen hash browns
3 large eggs
2 tbsp milk
3 tbsp crème fraîche

¼ cup shredded cheddar cheese
Salt and black pepper to taste
1 cup water
5 flour tortillas
2 tbsp cilantro, chopped for garnish

Directions

Pour the water in your Instant Pot and set in a trivet with slings. Place the hash browns in a greased baking dish and top with ham. Combine eggs, milk, crème fraîche, cheddar cheese, salt, and pepper.

Top the hash browns with this mixture and cover tightly with foil. Seal the lid, select Manual/Pressure Cook mode on High, and set time to 10 minutes.

When done cooking, perform natural pressure release for 10 minutes, then a quick pressure release to let out the remaining steam. Remove the aluminium foil and stir the mixture. Warm the tortillas for a few seconds in the microwave. Divide the egg mixture between the tortillas, top with cilantro and roll up to serve.

Cheese & Bacon Egg Bites

Total time: 25 minutes | **Servings:** 4 | **Per Serving:** Kcal 193; Carbs 3g; Fat 14g; Protein 14g

Ingredients

¾ cup shredded mozzarella cheese
½ cup ricotta cheese
¼ cup crumbled cooked bacon
4 large eggs

¼ cup heavy cream
½ tsp salt
1 cup water
2 tbsp parsley, chopped for garnish

Directions

Mix together the eggs, mozzarella cheese, ricotta cheese, heavy cream, and salt in a bowl. Divide the bacon among ramekins, then fill with the cheese mixture, and cover with foil. Pour the water in your Instant Pot and fit in a trivet with slings. Place the filled ramekins on the trivet.

Seal the lid, select Manual/Pressure Cook mode on High, and set time to 8 minutes. When done cooking, perform a natural pressure release for 10 minutes, then a quick pressure release to let out the remaining steam. Remove the ramekins and let sit for a few minutes, then garnish with parsley to serve.

Gruyere-Onion Egg Scramble

Total Time: 20 minutes | **Servings:** 2 | **Per Serving:** Kcal 250; Carbs 7g; Fat 21g; Protein 10g

Ingredients

1 tbsp butter
1 large yellow onion, sliced
1 tsp Worcestershire sauce
½ tsp chopped rosemary

4 large eggs
3 tbsp milk
¼ cup shredded Gruyère cheese + extra for garnishing
Salt and black pepper to taste

Directions

Melt butter in inner pot on Sauté, and stir-fry onion until caramelized and brown, 15 minutes. Season with Worcestershire sauce and rosemary. Beat eggs with milk and pour them into onion mixture. Scramble immediately until eggs solidify.

Turn Instant Pot off and add Gruyere cheese; stir mixture until cheese melts and then, season with salt and black pepper. Plate eggs, garnish with some more cheese, and serve immediately.

Cheesy Prosciutto Egg Bake

Total Time: 35 minutes | **Servings:** 4 | **Per Serving:** Kcal 297; Carbs 6g; Fat 18g; Protein 27g

Ingredients

4 eggs
1 cup whole milk
Salt and black pepper to taste

1 cup shredded Monterey Jack cheese
1 orange bell pepper, chopped
8 oz prosciutto, chopped

Directions

Break the eggs into a bowl, pour in the milk, salt, and black pepper and whisk until combined. Stir in the cheese. Arrange the bell pepper and prosciutto on a greased cake pan. Pour over the egg mixture, cover the pan with foil.

Put a trivet in the Instant Pot and pour in 1 cup of water. Lay the pan on top. Seal the lid, select Manual/Pressure Cook on High, and set the time to 20 minutes. When done cooking, do a quick pressure release. Serve warm.

Gyeran-Jjim (Korean Steamed Egg Custard)

Total Time: 25 minutes | **Servings**: 2 | **Per Serving**: Kcal 112; Carbs 2g; Fat 9g; Protein 6g

Ingredients

4 large eggs
2 tbsp sesame oil

¾ tsp fish sauce
2 chopped green onions

Directions

Beat eggs in a bowl until very smooth. Mix in fish sauce, 1 green onion, and 1 cup of water. Pour mixture into a ramekin and cover with foil. Pour 1 cup of water in your Instant Pot and fit in a trivet.

Put the ramekin on the trivet. Seal the lid, select Manual/Pressure Cook on Low, and set time to 7 minutes. After cooking, perform natural pressure release for 10 minutes. Unlock the lid, carefully remove ramekin, top with remaining green onion. Drizzle with sesame oil to serve.

Eggs in Avocados with Herbs

Total Time: 10 minutes | **Servings**: 2 | **Per Serving**: Kcal 233; Carbs 7g; Fat 17g; Protein 15g

Ingredients

1 cup water
2 large ripe avocados, halved and pitted
4 small eggs

Salt and black peppers
1 ½ tsp dried Italian herb mix
½ cup Mexican four-cheese blend

Directions

Pour water in inner pot. Spoon out half of avocado flesh to make way for eggs and place in a steamer basket. Fill each hole with an egg, sprinkle with salt, black pepper, herb mix, and cheese blend.

Carefully lower steamer basket into inner pot, Seal the lid, select Manual/Pressure Cook on High, and set time to 4 minutes. After cooking, do a quick pressure release to release. Serve immediately with arugula and toasts.

Broccoli-Pepper Scrambled Eggs

Total Time: 20 minutes | **Servings**: 2 | **Per Serving**: Kcal 232; Carbs 8g; Fat 18g; Protein 10g

Ingredients

2 tsp olive oil
½ cup finely chopped broccoli
1 orange bell pepper, deseeded and diced
1 garlic clove, minced
4 large eggs

3 tbsp milk
¼ cup crumbled goat cheese + extra for garnishing
½ tsp dried oregano
Salt and black pepper to taste

Directions

Set your Instant Pot to Sauté and adjust to medium heat. Heat olive oil and sauté broccoli and bell pepper until softened, 4 minutes. Add garlic and keep cooking until fragrant, 1 minute.

Meanwhile, beat the eggs with milk and pour mixture onto the vegetables. Using a spatula, begin scrambling the eggs immediately until set and soft, 2 minutes.

Press Cancel and mix in goat cheese, oregano, salt, and black pepper until well-combined. Transfer scrambled eggs to serving plates and serve warm for breakfast.

Balsamic Fennel with White Beans

Total Time: 50 minutes | **Servings**: 4 | **Per Serving**: Kcal 162; Carbs 21g; Fat 7g; Protein 5g

Ingredients

2 tbsp olive oil
1 fennel bulb, thinly sliced
1 small red onion, chopped
1 cup dry white beans, soaked and rinsed

3 cups vegetable broth
2 tbsp balsamic vinegar
2 tsp freshly squeezed lemon juice

Directions

Set your Instant Pot to Sauté mode and adjust to medium heat. Heat olive oil in inner pot and sauté onion and fennel, until softened, 3 minutes. Add white beans, vegetable broth, and balsamic vinegar.

Seal the lid, select Bean/Chili mode, and set cooking time to 30 minutes. After cooking, do a quick pressure release to let out steam, and unlock the lid. Stir food, dish into serving plates, and drizzle with lemon juice. Serve.

Potato Carrot Medley

Total Time: 20 minutes | **Servings**: 4 | **Per Serving**: Kcal 120; Carbs 14g; Fat 7g; Protein 2g

Ingredients

2 tbsp olive oil
1 cup potatoes, peeled and chopped
3 carrots, peeled and chopped
3 garlic cloves, minced
1 cup vegetable broth

1 tsp Italian seasoning
Salt and black pepper to taste
1 tbsp chopped parsley
1 tbsp chopped oregano

Directions

Set your Instant Pot to Sauté mode and heat olive oil. Sauté potatoes and carrots until sweaty, 5 minutes. Add garlic and cook until fragrant, 30 seconds. Pour in vegetable broth, season with Italian seasoning, salt, and black pepper. Seal the lid, select Manual/Pressure Cook on High, and set time to 5 minutes

After cooking, do a quick pressure release to let out steam, and unlock the lid. Spoon carrots and potatoes into a serving bowl and mix in parsley and oregano. Serve warm.

Hot Broccoli & Mushroom Side

Total Time: 15 minutes | **Servings**: 4 | **Per Serving**: Kcal 76; Carbs 2g; Fat 7g; Protein 1g

Ingredients

1 large head broccoli, cut into bite-size pieces
2 tbsp olive oil
1 cup chopped mixed mushrooms

2 tsp hot sauce
Salt and black pepper to taste
2 tbsp chopped almonds

Directions

Pour 1 cup of water into inner pot, fit in a steamer basket, and put in broccoli. Seal the lid, select Manual/Pressure Cook mode on High, and set cooking time to 2 minutes. After cooking, do a quick pressure release to let out steam, and unlock the lid. Transfer broccoli to a bowl and empty inner pot.

Wipe clean with a clean napkin and set the pot to Sauté. Heat olive oil and sauté mushrooms until softened, 5 minutes. Add broccoli, hot sauce, salt, and pepper. Sauté until well coated in hot sauce. Stir in almonds. Serve.

Tangy Green Beans with Peanuts

Total Time: 10 minutes | **Servings**: 4 | **Per Serving**: Kcal 134; Carbs 9g; Fat 10g; Protein 4g

Ingredients

1 lb green beans, trimmed
1 lemon, juiced
2 tbsp olive oil

Salt and black pepper to taste
2 tbsp toasted peanuts

Directions

Pour 1 cup of water into inner pot, fit in a steamer basket, and arrange green beans on top. Seal the lid, select Manual/Pressure Cook mode on High, and set cooking time to 1 minute.

After cooking, do a quick pressure release to let out steam, and unlock the lid. Remove green beans onto a plate and mix in lemon juice, olive oil, salt, black pepper, and toasted peanuts. Serve immediately.

Mixed Vegetable Soup

Total Time: 20 minutes | **Servings**: 4 | **Per Serving**: Kcal 273; Carbs 53g; Fat 3g; Protein 6g

Ingredients

3 cups vegetable broth
1 ½ cups water
4 garlic cloves, minced
1 medium sweet onion
5 Yukon gold potatoes, peeled and diced
4 celery stalks, chopped
4 medium carrots, peeled and chopped

1 cup chopped tomatoes
1 tsp dried oregano
1 tsp dried thyme
2 bay leaves
1 bunch parsley, chopped
Salt and black pepper to taste

Directions

In inner pot, add vegetable broth, water, garlic, onion, potatoes, celery, carrots, tomatoes, oregano, thyme, bay leaves, parsley, salt, and black pepper.

Seal the lid; select Manual/Pressure Cook on High, and set cooking time to 10 minutes. After cooking, do a quick pressure release to let out steam, and unlock the lid. Stir and adjust taste with salt and black pepper. Dish and serve.

Steamed Winter Vegetables with Miso Dressing

Total Time: 15 minutes | **Servings**: 4 | **Per Serving**: Kcal 154; Carbs 14g; Fat 11g; Protein 3g

Ingredients

1 cup Brussels sprouts, trimmed and halved lengthwise
1 head cauliflower, cut into bite-size pieces
1 sweet potato, peeled and cut in ½-inch cubes
1 tbsp olive oil

Salt and black pepper to taste
1 ½ tsp yellow miso paste
½ lemon, juiced
2 tbsp peanut oil

Directions

Pour 1 cup of water into inner pot, fit in a steamer basket, and place in Brussels sprouts, cauliflower, and sweet potato. Seal the lid, select Manual/Pressure Cook mode on High, and set cooking time to 8 minutes.

After cooking, do a quick pressure release to let out steam, and unlock the lid. Meanwhile, in a large bowl, whisk olive oil, salt, black pepper, miso paste, lemon juice, and peanut oil. Toss vegetable in dressing and serve after.

Vegetable Tart

Total Time: 25 minutes | **Servings**: 4 | **Per Serving**: Kcal 493; Carbs 38g; Fat 30g; Protein 17g

Ingredients

2 cups broccoli, grated
1 onion, diced
3 large zucchini, grated and drained
6 large carrots, grated
5 eggs, beaten
Salt and black pepper to taste

½ cup panko breadcrumbs
½ cup plain flour
½ tsp baking powder
½ cup grated cheddar cheese
5 tbsp olive oil

Directions

Pour 1 cup of water in inner pot and fit in a trivet. Also, lightly grease a springform pan with cooking spray and set aside. In a large bowl, mix broccoli, onion, zucchini, carrots, eggs, salt, black pepper, panko breadcrumbs, flour, baking powder, and cheddar cheese. Pour vegetable mixture into the pan, cover with foil, and place on the trivet.

Seal the lid, select Manual/Pressure Cook on High, and set cooking time to 10 minutes. After cooking, do a quick pressure release to let out steam, and unlock the lid. Carefully remove the pan, take off the foil, and allow cooling to firm up the cake. Release the pan, slice the cakes, and serve warm.

Steamed Cabbage with Spicy Lemon Dressing

Total Time: 5 minutes | **Servings**: 10 | **Per Serving**: Kcal 142; Carbs 22g; Fat 6g; Protein 4g

Ingredients

1 large cabbage, cut into wedges
2 tbsp butter, melted
Salt and black pepper to taste

1 lemon, juiced
¼ tsp red chili flakes

Directions

Pour 1 cup of water into inner pot, fit in a trivet, and place cabbage on top. Seal the lid, select Manual/Pressure Cook mode on High, and set cooking time to 2 minutes.

After cooking, do a quick pressure release to let out steam, and unlock the lid. Place cabbage on a plate. In a small bowl, whisk butter, salt, black pepper, lemon juice, and chili flakes. Drizzle mixture all over cabbage and serve.

Thai-Style Brussels Sprouts

Total Time: 15 minutes | **Servings**: 4 | **Per Serving**: Kcal 275; Carbs 63g; Fat 28g; Protein 14g

Ingredients

3 tbsp sesame oil
1 ½ lb Brussels sprouts, halved
2 tbsp fish sauce

½ cup chicken stock
½ cup chopped roasted peanuts

Directions

Set your Instant Pot to Sauté mode and adjust to medium heat. Warm sesame oil in inner pot and fry Brussels sprouts until golden around edges, 5 minutes. Mix in fish sauce and chicken stock.

Seal the lid, select Manual/Pressure Cook on High, and set cooking time to 3 minutes. After cooking, do a quick pressure release to let out steam, and unlock the lid. Mix in peanuts, dish and serve.

Mexican Fajita Bell Pepper Mix

Total Time: 15 minutes | **Servings**: 4 | **Per Serving**: Kcal 153; Carbs 27g; Fat 5g; Protein 4g

Ingredients

4 large mixed bell peppers, sliced into strips
1 (15 oz) can tomato sauce
2 tsp chili powder
2 large white onions, sliced

½ tsp Mexican seasoning
½ tsp garlic powder
Salt and black pepper to taste

Directions

In inner pot, mix bell peppers, tomato sauce, chili powder, onions, Mexican seasoning, garlic powder, salt, and black pepper. Seal the lid, select Manual/Pressure Cook on High, and set cooking time to 5 minutes. After cooking, do a quick pressure release, and unlock the lid. Stir well and serve warm.

Cheesy Baked Potatoes with Broccoli

Total time: 25 minutes | **Servings**: 4 | **Per Serving**: Kcal 553; Carbs 33g; Fat 35g; Protein 28g

Ingredients

1 head broccoli, cut into florets
4 small russet potatoes
¾ cup half and half
1 tbsp butter

2 cups Gruyere cheese, grated
1 tsp cornstarch
4 bacon slices, cooked and crumbled
¼ cup chopped fresh chives

Directions

Pour 1 cup of water in your Instant Pot and fit in a steamer basket. Place in the broccoli. Seal the lid, select Manual/Pressure Cook mode on Low and set time to 1 minute. When done, perform a quick pressure to let out steam. Unlock the lid and remove the broccoli to a bowl.

In the steamer basket, add in the potatoes. Seal the lid again, select Manual/Pressure Cook mode on High, and set time to 15 minutes. When done, perform a quick pressure release to let out the steam. Let the potatoes cool.

Take out the trivet and discard the water. Press Sauté and warm half and half and butter. In a bowl, mix the cheese with cornstarch and pour it into the pot. Stir until the cheese melts. Toss broccoli with cheese sauce. Cut a slit into each potato and stuff with the broccoli mixture. Scatter with bacon and chives. Serve warm.

Maple Cinnamon Coated Squash

Total Time: 10 minutes | **Servings**: 4 | **Per Serving**: Kcal 71; Carbs 18g; Fat 0.12g; Protein 1g

Ingredients

1 acorn squash, deseeded, cut into 1-inch slices
2 tbsp maple syrup

1 tsp cinnamon powder

Directions

Pour 1 cup of water into inner pot, fit in a steamer basket, and put in acorn squash. Seal the lid, select Manual/Pressure Cook mode on High, and set cooking time to 2 minutes.

After cooking, do a quick pressure release to let out steam, and unlock the lid. Transfer to a plate and set aside. Combine maple syrup and cinnamon powder in a deep plate and coat each squash slice in syrup mixture. Plate and serve as a snack.

Hot Beans with Sweet Potatoes

Total time: 1 hour | **Servings**: 4 | **Per Serving**: Kcal 170; Carbs 14g; Fat 12g; Protein 4g

Ingredients

2 tbsp olive oil
8 oz dried kidney beans
3 ½ cups vegetable broth
1 onion, quartered
1 garlic clove, minced
2 tsp chili powder

Salt to taste
¼ tsp cayenne pepper
4 sweet potatoes, scrubbed
½ cup crème fraîche
3 spring onions, chopped

Directions

Set your Instant Pot to Sauté mode and heat the olive oil. Cook the onion and garlic for 3 minutes, until tender. Stir in the chili powder, cayenne pepper, and salt. Mix in the beans with 3 cups of broth. Seal the lid, select Manual/Pressure Cook mode on High, and set time to 15 minutes.

When done, perform a natural pressure release for 10 minutes, then a quick pressure release to let out the remaining steam and unlock the lid. Add in a tall trivet, and arrange the potatoes on the trivet. Lock the lid again; select Manual/Pressure Cook mode on High, and set time to 10 minutes.

When done, perform a natural pressure release for 8 minutes, then a quick pressure release to let out the remaining steam. Remove the potatoes and let cool for a few minutes. To serve, make a hole in the middle of each potato and stuff with bean mixture; top with crème fraîche and spring onions.

Bacon-Ham Pea Mix

Total Time: 15 minutes | **Servings**: 2 | **Per Serving**: Kcal 220; Carbs 16g; Fat 12g; Protein 14g

Ingredients

2 bacon slices, chopped
3 ham slices, chopped
½ cup chicken broth
1 cup frozen peas

1 tsp garlic powder
1 tsp onion powder
Salt and black pepper to taste
1 tbsp chopped parsley

Directions

Set your Instant Pot to Sauté mode and adjust to medium heat. Add bacon and cook until brown and crispy, 5 minutes. Mix in ham and heat through, 1 minute. Top with chicken broth, frozen peas, garlic powder, onion powder, salt, and black pepper.

Seal the lid, select Manual/Pressure Cook mode on High, and set cooking time to 1 minute. After cooking, do a quick pressure release to let out steam, and unlock the lid. Dish food, garnish with parsley and serve warm.

Cauliflower Tots

Total Time: 40 minutes | **Servings**: 4 | **Per Serving**: Kcal 351; Carbs 4g; Fat 29g; Protein 19g

Ingredients

1 large cauliflower
1 egg, beaten
1 cup almond meal
2 garlic cloves, minced

1 cup grated Gruyere cheese
3 tbsp olive oil
1 cup grated Parmesan cheese
Salt to taste

Directions

Pour 1 cup of water in inner pot, fit in a trivet, and place cauliflower on top. Seal the lid, select Manual/Pressure Cook on High, and set cooking time to 3 minutes. After cooking, do a quick pressure release to let out steam, and unlock the lid. Remove cauliflower to a food processor and blend until rice-like. Pour cauliflower into a large bowl.

Add in egg, almond meal, garlic, cheeses, and salt. Form 2-inch oblong balls out of the mixture, place on a baking sheet, and chill for 20 minutes. Set the pot to Sauté mode. Heat olive oil, remove tots from refrigerator and fry in the oil on all sides (in batches) until golden brown. Place on a paper towel-lined plate to drain grease and serve warm.

Swiss Cheese & Mushroom Tarts

Total Time: 45 minutes | **Servings**: 4 | **Per Serving**: Kcal 378; Carbs 37g; Fat 21g; Protein 15g

Ingredients

2 tbsp melted butter, divided
1 small white onion, sliced
5 oz oyster mushrooms, sliced
Salt and black pepper to taste

¼ cup dry white wine
1 sheet puff pastry, thawed
1 cup shredded Swiss cheese
1 tbsp thinly sliced green onions

Directions

Select Sauté to preheat your Instant Pot. Add in 1 tbsp of butter, onion, and mushrooms and sauté for 5 minutes or until the vegetables are tender. Season with salt and black pepper, pour in the white wine and cook until evaporated, about 2 minutes. Set aside.

Unwrap the puff pastry and cut into 4 squares. Pierce the dough with a fork and brush both sides with the remaining oil. Share half of the Swiss cheese evenly over the puff pastry squares. Also, share the mushroom mixture over the pastry squares and top with the remaining cheese. Place in a baking pan.

Pour 1 cup of water in your Instant Pot and place a trivet. Lay the pan on top of the trivet. Lock lid in place, select Manual/Pressure Cook on High, and set the cooking time to 20 minutes.

After cooking, do a natural pressure release for 10 minutes, then a quick pressure release to let out the remaining steam. Take the tart out of the pot and transfer to a plate. Garnish with the green onions and serve.

Spaghetti a la Puttanesca

Total time: 20 minutes | **Servings**: 5 | **Per Serving**: Kcal 266; Carbs 31g; Fat 12g; Protein 11g

Ingredients

2 tbsp olive oil
1 pound dried spaghetti
3 garlic cloves, minced
1 (32-oz) jar pasta sauce
3 cups water
1 tsp crushed chilies

1 tbsp capers
½ cup pitted black olives, sliced
Salt and black pepper to taste
2 tsp grated lemon zest
Grated Grana Padano cheese, to serve

Directions

In your Instant Pot, mix spaghetti and water. Seal the lid, select Manual/Pressure Cook on High, and set time to 5 minutes. When done, perform a quick pressure to let out steam and remove the lid. Drain the spaghetti and set aside.

Set the pot to Sauté and add in the olive oil. Cook the garlic, chilies, capers, and olives for 2 minutes. Pour in the pasta sauce and stir. Once the sauce is ready, adjust the seasoning with salt and pepper. Add in the spaghetti and toss to coat in the sauce. Divide between plates and sprinkle the Grana Padano cheese and lemon zest, to serve.

Tangy Risotto & Roasted Bell Peppers

Total Time: 30 minutes | **Servings**: 4 | **Per Serving**: Kcal 441; Carbs 52g; Fat 25g; Protein 21g

Ingredients

2 tbsp ghee, divided
1 garlic clove, minced
5 cups vegetable stock
¼ cup freshly squeezed lemon juice
1 tsp grated lemon zest

2 cups Carnaroli rice
Salt and black pepper to taste
4 mixed bell peppers, chopped diagonally
2 tbsp butter
1 ½ cups grated Parmesan cheese + for garnish

Directions

Melt the ghee on Sauté and cook the garlic until fragrant, about 1 minute. Stir in the vegetable stock, lemon juice, lemon zest, salt, and rice. Seal the lid, select Manual/Pressure Cook on High, and set the cooking time to 7 minutes.

In a bowl, toss the bell peppers with the remaining ghee, salt, and black pepper. When the timer has ended, do a natural pressure release for 10 minutes, then a quick pressure release. Stir the butter into the rice until adequately mixed. Arrange the bell peppers on top of rice and cook on Sauté for 5 minutes. Stir in the Parmesan cheese to serve.

Super Green Mash

Total Time: 15 minutes | **Servings**: 4 | **Per Serving**: Kcal 190; Carbs 9g; Fat 17g; Protein 3g

Ingredients

1 medium broccoli, cut into florets
2 cups spinach
½ cup vegetable broth
2 avocados, halved, pitted, and peeled
2 tbsp butter

2 tbsp chopped parsley
Salt and black pepper to taste
3 tbsp Greek yogurt
2 tbsp toasted pine nuts for topping

Directions

In inner pot, add broccoli, spinach, and vegetable broth. Seal the lid, select Manual/Pressure Cook mode on High, and set cooking time to 3 minutes. After cooking, do a quick pressure release to let out steam, and unlock the lid. Add avocado, butter, parsley, salt, black pepper, and Greek yogurt.

Using an immersion blender, puree ingredients until smooth. Spoon into serving bowls and top with pine nuts.

Pesto Minestrone with Cheesy Bread

Total Time: 35 minutes | **Servings**: 4 | **Per Serving**: Kcal 379; Carbs 30g; Fat 25g; Protein 12g

Ingredients

3 tbsp vegetable oil
1 red onion, chopped
1 celery stalk, chopped
1 large carrot, chopped
1 small yellow squash, chopped
1 (14-oz) can chopped tomatoes
1 (27-oz) can cannellini beans, drained
1 cup chopped zucchini
1 bay leaf
1 tsp mixed herbs

¼ tsp cayenne pepper powder
Salt to taste
1 rind of Pecorino Romano cheese
3 tbsp butter, at room temperature
¼ cup shredded Pecorino Romano cheese
1 garlic clove, minced
4 slices white bread
¼ cup pesto

Directions

Select Sauté to preheat your Instant Pot. Heat vegetable oil and sauté onion, celery, and carrot for 5 minutes, until softened. Stir in the yellow squash, tomatoes, beans, 4 cups of water, zucchini, bay leaf, mixed herbs, cayenne pepper, salt, and Pecorino Romano rind. Seal the lid, select Manual/Pressure Cook on High, and set the cooking time to 4 minutes.

Meanwhile, in a bowl, mix the butter, shredded cheese, and garlic. Spread the mixture on the bread slices. Place under the broiler for 4 minutes on high.

After cooking the soup, perform a natural pressure release for 10 minutes, then a quick pressure release and unlock the lid. Adjust the taste with salt and black pepper, and remove the bay leaf. Ladle the soup into serving bowls and drizzle the pesto over. Serve with the garlic toasts.

Mushroom Risotto with Swiss Chard

Total Time: 20 minutes | **Servings**: 4 | **Per Serving**: Kcal 295; Carbs 43g; Fat 11g; Protein 5g

Ingredients

3 tbsp olive oil
1 small bunch Swiss chard, chopped
1 cup short-grain rice
½ cup white wine
2 cups vegetable stock

Salt to taste
½ cup mushrooms, sliced
½ cup caramelized onions
½ cup grated Pecorino Romano cheese

Directions

Heat olive oil on Sauté and stir-fry mushrooms for 5 minutes. Add in and cook Swiss chard for 2 minutes or until wilted. Spoon into a bowl and set aside. Stir in the rice and cook for about 1 minute. Add the white wine and cook for 2 to 3 minutes, with occasional stirring until the wine has evaporated. Add in stock and salt; stir to combine.

Seal the lid, select Manual/Pressure Cook on High, and set the cooking time to 8 minutes. When done, perform a quick pressure release and unlock the lid. Stir in mushroom-Swiss chard mixture, and onions and cook for 1 minute on Sauté. Mix the cheese into the rice until melted and adjust the taste. Serve immediately.

Rice Stuffed Zucchini Boats

Total Time: 30 minutes | **Servings**: 4 | **Per Serving**: Kcal 267; Carbs 21g; Fat 17g; Protein 10g

Ingredients

2 small zucchinis
½ cup cooked white short-grain rice
½ cup canned white beans, drained and rinsed
½ cup chopped tomatoes

½ cup chopped toasted cashew nuts
½ cup grated Parmesan cheese, divided
2 tbsp melted butter, divided
Salt and black pepper to taste

Directions

Cut each zucchini in half, lengthwise and scoop out the pulp. Chop the pulp and set aside.

In a bowl, combine the rice, beans, tomatoes, cashew nuts, half of Parmesan cheese, 1 tbsp of melted butter, salt, and black pepper. Spoon the mixed ingredients into the zucchini boats and arrange the stuffed zucchinis in a single layer in your Instant Pot. Pour in ½ cup of water and the remaining butter.

Seal the lid, select Manual/Pressure Cook on High, and set the cooking time to 6 minutes. After cooking, perform natural pressure release for 10 minutes, then a quick pressure release to let out the remaining steam. Remove the zucchinis onto a plate, top with the remaining Parmesan cheese and serve.

Roasted Squash & Rice with Tofu

Total Time: 16 minutes | **Servings**: 4 | **Per Serving**: Kcal 256; Carbs 20g; Fat 18g; Protein 15g

Ingredients

1 small butternut squash, chopped
2 tbsp melted butter, divided
Salt and black pepper to taste
1 tbsp coconut aminos

15 oz extra-firm tofu, drained and cubed
2 tsp arrowroot starch
1 cup jasmine rice

Directions

Pour the rice, salt, pepper, and 2 cups of water into the pot and mix well. Put in a trivet. In a bowl, toss the butternut squash with 1 tbsp of melted butter and season with salt and pepper. Transfer to a baking pan.

In another bowl, mix the remaining butter with coconut aminos and toss tofu in the mixture. Pour arrowroot starch over tofu. Put over the squash. Place the pan on the trivet. Seal the lid, select Manual/Pressure Cook on High, and set time to 6 minutes. When done, perform a quick pressure release. Fluff the rice and top with tofu and squash to serve.

Asparagus with Parmesan

Total Time: 15 minutes | **Servings**: 4 | **Per Serving**: Kcal 122; Carbs 7g; Fat 10g; Protein 4g

Ingredients

1 tbsp olive oil
1 lb asparagus, chopped
2 garlic cloves, minced
2 tbsp butter, softened

Salt and black pepper to taste
½ lemon, juiced
2 tbsp grated Parmesan cheese

Directions

In inner pot, pour 1 cup of water and fit in a trivet. Cut out a foil sheet, place asparagus on top as well as garlic and butter. Season with salt and black pepper. Wrap foil and place asparagus packet on the trivet.

Seal the lid, select Manual/Pressure Cook on High, and set time to 8 minutes. Do a quick pressure release. Remove foil pack, put asparagus onto a platter, drizzle with lemon juice, and top with Parmesan cheese to serve.

Cherry Stuffed Pumpkin

Total time: 35 minutes | **Servings**: 4 | **Per Serving**: Kcal 370; Carbs 22g; Fat 28g; Protein 12g

Ingredients

5 toasted bread slices, cubed
2 tbsp olive oil
1 cup water
1 ½ cups vegetable broth
1 tsp dried parsley

1 (2-pound) pumpkin, halved lengthwise, stems trimmed
1 tsp onion powder
Salt and black pepper to taste
½ cup dried cherries
½ cup chopped pecans

Directions

Brush the pumpkin with 1 tbsp of oil. Pour the water in your Instant Pot and fit in a trivet. Place the pumpkin, skin-side down, on top of the trivet. Seal the lid, select Manual/Pressure Cook mode on High, and set time to 15 minutes.

Do a quick pressure release. Remove the pumpkin and water. Press Sauté, pour in the remaining ingredients, and cook until the liquid is reduced by half. Divide the filling between pumpkin halves and top with pecans.

Stocks & Sauces

Chicken Bone Stock

Total Time: 50 minutes | **Servings**: 6 | **Per Serving**: Kcal 142; Carbs 2g; Fat 2g; Protein 5g

Ingredients

2 lb roasted chicken carcasses
1 large yellow onion, roughly chopped
6 celery stalks, roughly chopped
4 large carrots, roughly chopped
4 cloves garlic, smashed

6 sprigs thyme
6 sprigs rosemary
1 tbsp whole black peppercorns
2 tbsp white vinegar
4 cups water

Directions

In inner pot, add chicken carcasses, onion, celery, carrots, garlic, thyme, rosemary, black peppercorns, vinegar, and water. Seal the lid, select Soup/Broth on Low and set cooking time to 30 minutes.

After cooking, perform a natural pressure release for 10 minutes, then a quick pressure release to let out remaining steam. Unlock the lid and strain stock through a fine-mesh into a clean bowl.

Discard solids and pour liquid into jars. Cover and allow cooling. Refrigerate and use for up to 3 months.

Beef Bone Stock

Total Time: 100 minutes | **Servings**: 6 | **Per Serving**: Kcal 146; Carbs 2g; Fat 2g; Protein 5g

Ingredients

2 lb beef bones
1 large yellow onion, roughly chopped
2 celery stalks, roughly chopped
2 large carrots, peeled and roughly chopped
4 cloves garlic, smashed

6 sprigs thyme
6 sprigs rosemary
1 tbsp whole black peppercorns
2 tbsp white vinegar
4 cups water

Directions

Preheat oven to 380 F.

In a baking sheet, spread beef bones, onion, celery, carrots, garlic, and spray with cooking spray. Roast in the oven until browned, 45 minutes.

Transfer beef mixture to inner pot and top with thyme, rosemary, peppercorns, vinegar, and water.

Seal the lid, select Soup/Broth on High and set cooking time to 40 minutes. After cooking, perform a natural pressure release for 10 minutes, then a quick pressure release to let out remaining steam.

Unlock the lid and strain stock through a fine-mesh into a clean bowl. Discard solids and pour liquid into jars. Cover, allow cooling and discard fat layer. Refrigerate and use for up to 3 months.

Super Green Stock

Total Time: 30 minutes | **Servings**: 6 | **Per Serving**: Kcal 89; Carbs 16g; Fat 2g; Protein 3g

Ingredients

1 large yellow onion, roughly chopped
6 celery stalks, roughly chopped
1 leek stalk, roughly chopped
1 cup spinach
4 large carrots, roughly chopped
4 cloves garlic, smashed
1 bay leaf

6 sprigs thyme
1 small bunch parsley
1 small bunch tarragon
1 tbsp whole black peppercorns
2 tbsp white wine vinegar
4 cups coconut water
6 cups water

Directions

In inner pot, add onion, celery, leek, spinach, carrots, garlic, bay leaf, thyme, parsley, tarragon, peppercorns, white wine vinegar, coconut water, and water. Seal the lid, select Soup/Broth on High and set cooking time to 10 minutes.

After cooking, perform a natural pressure release for 10 minutes, then a quick pressure release to let out remaining steam. Unlock the lid and strain stock through a fine-mesh into a clean bowl. Discard solids and pour liquid into jars. Cover and allow cooling. Refrigerate and use for up to 1 month.

Tomato Basil Stock

Total Time: 30 minutes | **Servings**: 4 | **Per Serving**: Kcal 125; Carbs 23g; Fat 3g; Protein 3g

Ingredients

1 large yellow onion, roughly chopped
6 celery stalks, roughly chopped
4 large tomatoes
4 large carrots, roughly chopped
4 cloves garlic, smashed
1 bay leaf

6 sprigs fresh oregano
1 small bunch basil leaves
1 tbsp whole black peppercorns
2 tbsp apple cider vinegar
6 cups chicken broth
2 cups water

Directions

In inner pot, add onion, celery, tomatoes, carrots, garlic, bay leaf, oregano, basil, peppercorns, apple cider vinegar, chicken broth, and water. Seal the lid, select Soup/Broth on High and set cooking time to 10 minutes.

After cooking, perform a natural pressure release for 10 minutes, then a quick pressure release to let out remaining steam. Unlock the lid and strain stock through a fine-mesh into a clean bowl. Discard solids and pour liquid into jars. Cover and allow cooling. Refrigerate and use for up to 2 months.

Mushroom Seafood Stock

Total Time: 40 minutes | **Servings**: 4 | **Per Serving**: Kcal 275; Carbs 13g; Fat 13g; Protein 25g

Ingredients

2 tbsp olive oil
1 lb shrimp shells and heads
2 large yellow onions, roughly chopped
6 celery stalks, roughly chopped
2 cups sliced mixed mushrooms
4 large carrots, roughly chopped

4 cloves garlic, smashed
1 bay leaf
6 sprigs thyme
1 tbsp whole black peppercorns
½ cup white wine
8 cups water

Directions

Set your Instant Pot to Sauté. Heat olive oil and brown shrimp shells and heads, onions, garlic, celery, mushrooms, and carrots, 5 minutes. Top with bay leaf, thyme, peppercorns, white wine, and water.

Seal the lid, select Soup/Broth on High and set time to 30 minutes. After cooking, perform a natural pressure release for 10 minutes.

Unlock the lid and strain stock through a fine-mesh into a clean bowl. Discard solids and pour liquid into jars. Cover and allow cooling. Refrigerate and use for up to 3 months.

Thai Carrot-Coconut Stock

Total Time: 50 minutes | **Servings**: 6 | **Per Serving**: Kcal 116; Carbs 21g; Fat 2g; Protein 4g

Ingredients

1 large yellow onion, roughly chopped
8 large carrots, roughly chopped
4 cloves garlic, smashed
1 lemongrass stalk, roughly chopped
8 cilantro sprigs

1 tbsp whole black peppercorns
2 tbsp white wine vinegar
6 cups coconut water
2 cups water

Directions

In inner pot, add onion, carrots, garlic, lemongrass, cilantro, peppercorns, vinegar, coconut water, and water. Seal the lid, select Soup/Broth on Low and set cooking time to 30 minutes.

After cooking, perform a natural pressure release for 10 minutes, then a quick pressure release to let out remaining steam. Unlock the lid and strain stock through a fine-mesh into a clean bowl.

Discard solids and pour liquid into jars. Cover and allow cooling. Refrigerate and use for up to 1 month.

Ginger Masala Broth

Total Time: 50 minutes | **Servings**: 4 | **Per Serving**: Kcal 173; Carbs 33g; Fat 5g; Protein 7g

Ingredients

2 tbsp black peppercorns
1 tbsp cumin seeds
2 tbsp coriander seeds
1 tbsp turmeric
15 curry leaves, torn into pieces
1-inch finger ginger, sliced

2 green chilies, chopped
2 medium yellow onions, chopped
6 garlic cloves peeled and smashed
¼ cup white vinegar
6 cups chicken broth
2 cups water

Directions

Set your Instant Pot to Sauté mode and adjust to medium heat. Add peppercorns, cumin seeds, coriander seeds, turmeric, curry leaves. Toast for 1 to 2 minutes or until fragrant.

Stir in ginger, green chilies, onions, garlic, white vinegar, chicken broth, and water. Seal the lid, select Soup/Broth on High and set cooking time to 30 minutes.

After cooking, perform a natural pressure release for 10 minutes, then a quick pressure release to let out remaining steam. Unlock the lid and strain stock through a fine-mesh into a clean bowl. Discard solids and pour liquid into jars. Cover and allow cooling. Refrigerate and use for up to 3 months.

Chinese Vegetable Stock

Total Time: 30 minutes | **Servings:** 6 | **Per Serving:** Kcal 46; Carbs 6g; Fat 2g; Protein 1g

Ingredients

1 tbsp olive oil
1 white onion, diced
1 knob ginger, washed and sliced
10 garlic cloves, crushed
5 celery stalks, chopped

3 carrots, peeled and sliced
10 scallions, cut into thirds
1 tbsp salt
1 bunch cilantro
8 cups water

Directions

Set your Instant Pot to Sauté and heat olive oil. Brown onion, ginger, garlic, celery, and carrots, 10 minutes. Add scallions, salt, cilantro, and water. Seal the lid, select Soup/Broth on High and set cooking time to 10 minutes.

After cooking, perform a natural pressure release for 10 minutes. Strain stock through a fine-mesh into a clean bowl. Discard solids and pour liquid into jars. Cover and allow cooling. Refrigerate and use for up to 3 months.

Pork Stock

Total Time: 60 minutes | **Servings:** 6 | **Per Serving:** Kcal 272; Carbs 2g; Fat 18g; Protein 24g

Ingredients

2 lb pork leg bones, rinsed well
1 finger ginger, sliced

½ cup white wine
8 cups water

Directions

In inner pot of your Instant Pot, add pork leg bones, ginger, white wine, and water.

Seal the lid, select Soup/Broth on High and set time to 40 minutes. After cooking, perform a natural pressure release for 10 minutes. Unlock the lid and strain stock through a fine-mesh into a clean bowl.

Discard solids and pour liquid into jars. Cover and allow cooling. Refrigerate and use for up to 2 months.

Speedy White Sauce with Yogurt

Total Time: 10 minutes | **Servings:** 4 | **Per Serving:** Kcal 180; Carbs 10g; Fat 14g; Protein 5g

Ingredients

1 tbsp olive oil
2 tbsp butter
2 tbsp flour
1 egg yolk
½ cup chicken broth

Salt and black pepper to taste
1 ½ cups yogurt
2 tbsp lemon juice
2 tbsp dill, chopped

Directions

In a bowl, combine yogurt and egg yolk until well mixed; set aside. Set your Instant Pot to Sauté and heat olive oil and butter. Add flour and stir constantly until well combined, 1 minute.

Pour in chicken broth and continue stirring until uniform. Season with salt and pepper. Transfer to a bowl and slowly mix in yogurt mixture. Return to the pot and stir until just heated. Spoon into bowl, drizzle with lemon juice and sprinkle with dill to serve.

Orange-Cranberry Sauce

Total Time: 25 minutes | **Servings**: 6 | **Per Serving**: Kcal 108; Carbs 27g; Fat 0.18g; Protein 0g

Ingredients

2 cups fresh cranberries

½ cup squeezed orange juice

1 tsp grated orange zest

½ cup agave syrup

Directions

In inner pot, add cranberries, orange juice, orange zest, and agave syrup. Seal the lid, select Manual/Pressure Cook mode on High, and set cooking time to 5 minutes. After cooking, perform natural pressure release for 10 minutes.

Unlock the lid, stir and mash cranberries to make a smoother sauce. Spoon into jars, allow cooling, and store in refrigerator. Use for up to 1 week.

Chili Marinara Sauce

Total Time: 45 minutes | **Servings**: 6 | **Per Serving**: Kcal 244; Carbs 26g; Fat 15g; Protein 5g

Ingredients

4 tbsp olive oil

1 small white onion, chopped

5 garlic cloves, minced

8 cups tomatoes, crushed

4 tbsp tomato paste

½ cup red wine

½ cup water

Salt and black pepper to taste

2 tsp dried basil

2 tsp dried oregano

2 tbsp dried parsley

2 tbsp Italian seasoning

1 tsp granulated sugar

1 tsp red chili powder

Directions

Set your Instant Pot to Sauté mode and adjust to medium heat. Heat olive oil in inner pot and sauté onion until softened, 3 minutes. Stir in garlic and cook until fragrant, 30 seconds. Add tomatoes, tomato paste, red wine, water, salt, black pepper, basil, oregano, parsley, Italian seasoning, sugar, and chili powder.

Seal the lid, select Manual/Pressure Cook mode on High, and set cooking time to 25 minutes. After cooking, perform a natural pressure release for 10 minutes, then a quick pressure release to let out remaining steam. Unlock the lid. Stir sauce, turn Instant Pot off and allow cooling. Spoon into jars, cover, and refrigerate. Use for up to 5 days.

Classic Pizza Sauce

Total Time: 25 minutes | **Servings**: 8 | **Per Serving**: Kcal 109; Carbs 23g; Fat 11g; Protein 15g

Ingredients

2 lb tomatoes crushed with juice

4 tbsp tomato paste

½ cup chicken broth

3 tsp dried oregano

Salt and black pepper to taste

Directions

In inner pot, add tomatoes, tomato paste, chicken broth, oregano, salt, and black pepper. Seal the lid, select Manual/Pressure Cook mode on High, and set cooking time to 5 minutes.

After cooking, perform a natural pressure release for 10 minutes. Unlock the lid. Stir sauce, turn Instant Pot off and allow cooling. Spoon into jars, cover, and refrigerate. Use for up to 5 days.

Pop's BBQ Sauce

Total Time: 25 minutes | **Servings:** 4 | **Per Serving:** Kcal 357; Carbs 65g; Fat 12g; Protein 5g

Ingredients

3 tbsp olive oil
1 medium brown onion, finely chopped
6 garlic cloves, minced
2 cups ketchup
½ cup brown sugar

2 tbsp chili powder
½ cup apple cider vinegar
4 tbsp Worcestershire sauce
Salt and black pepper to taste

Directions

Set your Instant Pot to Sauté mode. Heat olive oil in inner pot and sauté onion until softened, 3 minutes. Stir in garlic and cook until fragrant, 30 seconds.

Add in ketchup, brown sugar, chili powder, vinegar, Worcestershire sauce, salt, and black pepper, and cook for 15 minutes, until sticky, stirring occasionally. Let cool. Spoon sauce into jars, cover, and refrigerate for up to 5 days.

Tomato Pasta Sauce

Total Time: 45 minutes | **Servings:** 6 | **Per Serving:** Kcal 251; Carbs 30g; Fat 13g; Protein 5g

Ingredients

2 tbsp olive oil
2 tbsp butter
1 lb ground beef
1 small white onion, chopped
5 garlic cloves, minced
6 cups chopped tomatoes
4 tbsp tomato paste
2 cups tomato ketchup

½ cup red wine
½ cup water
2 bay leaves
2 tsp dried oregano
2 tbsp dried parsley
2 tbsp Italian seasoning
Salt and black pepper to taste
2 tbsp maple syrup

Directions

Set your Instant Pot to Sauté mode. Heat olive oil and butter and cook beef until brown, 5 minutes. Add and sauté onion until softened, 3 minutes. Stir in garlic and cook until fragrant, 30 seconds. Add tomatoes, tomato paste, tomato ketchup, red wine, water, bay leaves, oregano, parsley, Italian seasoning, salt, black pepper, and maple syrup.

Seal the lid, select Manual/Pressure Cook mode on High, and set cooking time to 25 minutes. After cooking, perform a natural pressure release for 10 minutes, then a quick pressure release to let out remaining steam. Unlock the lid. Stir sauce, turn Instant Pot off and allow cooling. Spoon into jars, cover, and refrigerate. Use for up to 5 days.

Mushroom Sauce

Total Time: 35 minutes | **Servings:** 6 | **Per Serving:** Kcal 192; Carbs 15g; Fat 12g; Protein 8g

Ingredients

5 cups mushrooms, chopped
2 yellow onions, chopped
4 garlic cloves, minced
½ cup chicken broth
1 tsp dried mixed herbs
¼ tsp red chili flakes

1 tsp dried thyme
Salt and black pepper to taste
2 tbsp cornstarch

Directions

In inner pot, combine mushrooms, onions, garlic, chicken broth, mixed herbs, chili flakes, thyme, salt, and black pepper. Seal the lid, select Manual/Pressure Cook mode on High, and set cooking time to 10 minutes. After cooking, perform a natural pressure release for 10 minutes, then a quick pressure release to let out remaining steam.

Unlock the lid and set to Sauté mode. Using an immersion blender, puree ingredients until smooth. Stir in cornstarch and allow thickening for 2 to 3 minutes. Spoon soup into bowls and serve.

Homemade Ketchup Sauce

Total Time: 25 minutes | **Servings**: 4 | **Per Serving**: Kcal 57; Carbs 12g; Fat 1g; Protein 2g

Ingredients

1 ½ lb tomatoes, quartered
1 cup chicken broth
¼ tsp cinnamon powder
1 tbsp paprika
1 tbs salt
¼ tsp clove powder
¼ tsp garlic powder

½ tsp Dijon mustard
¼ tsp celery seeds
1 tbsp honey
¼ cup raisins
1 onion, cut into wedges
6 tbsp apple cider vinegar
1 tbsp cornstarch mixed with 1 tbsp water

Directions

In inner pot, add tomatoes, chicken broth, cinnamon powder, paprika, salt, clove powder, garlic powder, Dijon mustard, celery seeds, honey, raisins, onion, and apple cider vinegar. Using an immersion blender, puree the ingredients.

Seal the lid, select Manual/Pressure Cook mode on High, and set cooking time to 5 minutes.

After cooking, perform a quick pressure release to let out steam, and unlock the lid. Select Sauté, mix in cornstarch and cook until thickened, 5 minutes. Spoon ketchup into storage jars, allow cooling, and preserve in refrigerator for a week.

Chinese Black Bean Sauce

Total Time: 45 minutes | **Servings**: 4 | **Per Serving**: Kcal 113; Carbs 10g; Fat 7g; Protein 3g

Ingredients

2 tbsp coconut oil
4 garlic cloves, minced
2 tbsp ginger paste
2 scallions, chopped
1 ½ cups chicken broth
1 cup black beans, soaked for 1 hour, drained

2 tbsp rice wine
1 tbsp tamarind sauce
1 tsp brown sugar
½ tsp rice vinegar
1 ½ tsp cornstarch, dissolved in 3 tbsp of water

Directions

Set your Instant Pot to Sauté. Heat coconut oil in inner pot and sauté garlic, scallions, and ginger until fragrant, 2 minutes. Stir in chicken broth, black beans, rice wine, tamarind sauce, brown sugar, and rice vinegar.

Seal the lid, select Manual/Pressure Cook mode on High, and set cooking time to 25 minutes.

After cooking, perform natural pressure release for 10 minutes, then a quick pressure release to let out remaining steam. Unlock the lid and using an immersion blender, puree ingredients until smooth. Press Sauté and stir in the slurry, until thickened, 2 minutes. After, spoon sauce into a bowl to serve.

Green Pea-Lime Butter Sauce

Total Time: 20 minutes | **Servings**: 4 | **Per Serving**: Kcal 285; Carbs 2g; Fat 31g; Protein 12g

Ingredients

2 tbsp unsalted butter
1 garlic clove, minced
¼ cup chopped cilantro
1 cup green peas

½ cup chicken broth
¼ cup squeezed lime juice
Salt and black pepper to taste

Directions

Set your Instant Pot to Sauté and melt butter. Sauté garlic and cilantro until fragrant, 1 minute. Add in peas and broth. Seal the lid, select Manual/Pressure Cook on High, and set time to 3 minutes.

After cooking, perform a natural pressure release for 10 minutes. Unlock the lid. Spoon mixture into a blender and top with lime juice, salt, and black pepper. Process until smooth. Pour into a bowl to serve.

Red Wine Onion Gravy

Total Time: 25 minutes | **Servings**: 4 | **Per Serving**: Kcal 192; Carbs 3g; Fat 6g; Protein 2g

Ingredients

2 tbsp butter
1 shallot, finely chopped
1 tsp plain flour
1 tbsp red wine vinegar
2 cups red wine

1 cup thinly sliced red onion
1 cup chicken stock
1 tsp dried oregano
1 tbsp Dijon mustard

Directions

Set your Instant Pot to Sauté and melt half of butter in inner pot, sauté shallots until softened, 2 minutes, and stir in flour until a sand-like consistency forms. Mix in vinegar until thick paste forms and stir in red wine while scraping the stuck bits at the bottom of the pot. Stir in onion, chicken stock, oregano, and mustard.

Seal the lid, select Manual/Pressure Cook on High, and set time to 2 minutes. After cooking, perform a natural pressure release for 10 minutes. Select Sauté. Mix in remaining butter and pour into sauce cups.

Alfredo Sauce

Total Time: 20 minutes | **Servings**: 4 | **Per Serving**: Kcal 459; Carbs 11g; Fat 42g; Protein 13g

Ingredients

½ cup chicken broth
4 garlic cloves, minced
4 leaves basil, chopped
¼ cup chopped parsley

4 tbsp butter
2 cups heavy cream
8 oz cream cheese, softened
1 cup grated Parmesan cheese

Directions

Into inner pot, add chicken broth, garlic, basil, and parsley. Seal the lid, select Manual/Pressure Cook mode on High, and set cooking time to 1 minute. After cooking, perform a quick pressure release to let out steam.

Unlock the lid and select Sauté mode. Vigorously whisk in butter, heavy cream, and cream cheese until melted and well-combined, 3 minutes. Mix in Parmesan cheese to melt and turn Instant Pot off. Spoon into bowls and serve.

Bread Sauce

Total Time: 20 minutes | **Servings**: 6 | **Per Serving**: Kcal 196; Carbs 18g; Fat 11g; Protein 4g

Ingredients

1 medium onion, chopped
12 garlic cloves, minced
1 bay leaf
½ cup chicken broth
6 black peppercorns
1 cup whole milk

¼ cup white breadcrumbs
2 tbsp butter
2 tbsp heavy cream
A pinch nutmeg powder
Salt and black pepper to taste

Directions

Combine onion, garlic, bay leaf, chicken broth, and peppercorns in inner pot. Seal the lid, select Manual/Pressure Cook mode on High, and set cooking time to 3 minutes. After cooking, perform a quick pressure release. Unlock the lid and set to Sauté mode. Strain mixture through a colander and return warm liquid to inner pot.

Stir in milk and breadcrumbs and continue cooking for 4 to 5 minutes. Whisk in butter, heavy cream, nutmeg, salt, and black pepper. Spoon into sauce cups and serve immediately.

Velouté Sauce

Total Time: 10 minutes | **Servings**: 4 | **Per Serving**: Kcal 97; Carbs 6g; Fat 8g; Protein 1g

Ingredients

2 tbsp unsalted butter
2 tbsp all-purpose flour
1 cup chicken broth, warmed

3 tbsp heavy cream
2 tbsp squeezed lemon juice
Salt and black pepper to taste

Directions

Set your Instant Pot to Sauté mode and adjust to medium heat. Melt butter in inner pot and whisk in flour. Cook until golden, 1 minute. Stir in chicken stock until smooth; cook further for 2 to 3 minutes. Turn Instant Pot off. Whisk in heavy cream, lemon juice, salt, and black pepper.

Teriyaki Sauce

Total Time: 15 minutes | **Servings**: 4 | **Per Serving**: Kcal 254; Carbs 33g; Fat 12g; Protein 5g

Ingredients

1 cup soy sauce
1 cup pineapple juice
2 tbsp mirin
3 tbsp water
3 tbsp brown sugar

1 clove garlic, minced
1 tsp ginger paste
Black pepper to taste
2 tsp cornstarch

Directions

In inner pot, mix soy sauce, pineapple juice, mirin, water, brown sugar, garlic, ginger, and black pepper, until well combined. Seal the lid, select Manual/Pressure Cook mode on High, and set cooking time to 1 minute.

After cooking, perform a quick pressure release to let out steam. Unlock the lid and select Sauté mode. Stir in cornstarch until dissolved. Cook sauce until thickened, 1 minute. Spoon into jars, cover, and allow cooling.

Pineapple Sauce

Total Time: 30 minutes | **Servings**: 4 | **Per Serving**: Kcal 251; Carbs 60g; Fat 1g; Protein 4g

Ingredients

2 cups chopped pineapples
3 garlic cloves, minced
½ cup pineapple juice
½ lemon, zested and juiced
¼ cup white vinegar

1 cup maple syrup
2 tsp red chili flakes
1 tsp salt
3 tbsp cornflour mixed with ¼ cup water

Directions

Add pineapples and garlic to a blender, and process until coarsely mixed. Pour into inner pot and top with pineapple juice, lemon zest, lemon juice, white vinegar, maple syrup, chili flakes and salt. Seal the lid, select Manual/Pressure Cook mode on High, and set cooking time to 1 minute.

After cooking, perform natural pressure release for 10 minutes, then quick pressure release to let out the remaining steam. Unlock the lid and select Sauté mode, and stir in cornflour mixture. Cook until sauce thickens, 2 to 3 minutes. Turn Instant Pot off and spoon sauce into a glass jar. Cover and refrigerate. Use for up to a week.

Enchilada Sauce

Total Time: 15 minutes | **Servings**: 4 | **Per Serving**: Kcal 169; Carbs 15g; Fat 12g; Protein 3g

Ingredients

3 tbsp olive oil
3 tbsp all-purpose flour
¼ tsp dried oregano
½ tsp garlic powder
2 tsp chili powder

1 tsp cumin powder
Salt and black pepper to taste
2 tbsp unsweetened tomato paste
2 cups vegetable broth
1 tsp white vinegar

Directions

Set your Instant Pot to Sauté mode and adjust to medium heat. Heat olive oil in inner pot and mix in all-purpose flour; cook until golden, 1 minute. Add oregano, garlic powder, chili powder, cumin powder, salt, and black pepper. Stir and cook until fragrances release, 1 minute. Mix in tomato paste and vegetable broth.

Seal the lid, select Manual/Pressure Cook mode on High, and set cooking time to 1 minute. After cooking, do a quick pressure release to let out steam and unlock the lid. Stir in white vinegar and turn Instant Pot off. Pour into jars, cover and cool.

Simple Buffalo Sauce

Total Time: 10 minutes | **Servings**: 4 | **Per Serving**: Kcal 78; Carbs 3g; Fat 16g; Protein 2g

Ingredients

1 cup hot sauce
½ cup unsalted butter

¼ tsp Worcestershire sauce
1 ½ tbsp white vinegar

Directions

Set your Instant Pot to Sauté mode and adjust to medium heat. In inner pot, combine hot sauce, butter, Worcestershire sauce, and white vinegar. Allow cooking until bubbling, 7 to 10 minutes. Spoon into jars or serve.

Basil-Mascarpone & Blue Cheese Sauce

Total Time: 8 minutes | **Servings**: 4 | **Per Serving**: Kcal 268; Carbs 2g; Fat 23g; Protein 13g

Ingredients

1 cup heavy cream

1 ½ cups mascarpone cheese

1 cup crumbled blue cheese

2 tbsp butter

1 tsp dried basil

Salt and black pepper to taste

Directions

Select Sauté mode and boil heavy cream until thickened, while occasionally stirring. Whisk in mascarpone cheese, blue cheese, and butter, to melt for 2 minutes. Stir in basil, salt, and black pepper. Turn Instant Pot off. Spoon sauce into serving cups and use.

Black Peppercorn Sauce

Total Time: 10 minutes | **Servings**: 4 | **Per Serving**: Kcal 160; Carbs 7g; Fat 12g; Protein 4g

Ingredients

3 tbsp black peppercorns, finely crushed

2 tsp smoked paprika

1 tsp Dijon mustard

3 tbsp butter

1 shallot, minced

½ cup brandy

1 cup beef stock

¼ cup heavy cream

Salt to taste

Directions

Set your Instant Pot to Sauté mode and adjust to medium heat. Toast peppercorns in inner pot until fragrant, 1 minute. Add butter to melt. Stir in paprika and shallot, and cook for 2-3 minutes. Pour in brandy and beef stock.

Seal the lid, select Manual/Pressure Cook mode on High, and set cooking time to 5 minutes. After cooking, do a quick pressure release to let out steam and unlock the lid. Whisk in heavy cream and Dijon mustard until well combined and heated through. Adjust taste with salt and spoon into sauce cups.

Spicy Zucchini Sauce

Total Time: 15 minutes | **Servings**: 4 | **Per Serving**: Kcal 244; Carbs 3g; Fat 25g; Protein 2g

Ingredients

6 tbsp olive oil

2 zucchinis, sliced into ribbons

3 garlic cloves, minced

2 red chilies, minced

3 tbsp chopped basil

½ cup chicken broth

1 lemon, juiced

Salt and black pepper to taste

½ cup heavy cream

4 tbsp grated Parmesan cheese

Directions

Set your Instant Pot to Sauté mode. Heat olive oil in inner pot and sauté zucchinis until softened, 3 minutes. Stir in garlic and cook until fragrant, 30 seconds. Mix in chilies, basil, chicken broth, lemon juice, salt, and black pepper. Seal the lid, select Manual/Pressure Cook mode on High, and set cooking time to 5 minutes.

After cooking, do a quick pressure release to let out steam and unlock the lid. Using an immersion blender, puree ingredients until smooth. Select Sauté mode and stir in heavy cream and Parmesan cheese until the cheese melts. Spoon sauce into bowls to serve.

Caribbean Hot Sauce

Total Time: 25 minutes | **Servings**: 4 | **Per Serving**: Kcal 59; Carbs 14g; Fat 0.23g; Protein 2g

Ingredients

8 cups habanero peppers, heads removed
3 tbsp salt
1 ¼ cups water
6 garlic cloves, crushed

¼ cup tequila
¼ cup agave nectar
¼ cup apple cider vinegar

Directions

Add habanero peppers, salt, water, and garlic to inner pot. Seal the lid, select Manual/Pressure Cook on High, and set time to 2 minutes. After cooking, perform natural pressure release for 10 minute.

Unlock the lid and stir in tequila, agave nectar, and vinegar. Using an immersion blender, process ingredients until smooth. Spoon into jars, cover, and refrigerate. Use for up to 2 months.

Sweet & Sour Sauce

Total Time: 20 minutes | **Servings**: 4 | **Per Serving**: Kcal 152; Carbs 25g; Fat 6g; Protein 1g

Ingredients

3 tbsp rice vinegar
1 tbsp light soy sauce
2 tbsp granulated sugar
1 tbsp ketchup
1 ½ tbsp olive oil
1 small white onion, quartered

1 small carrot, peeled and chopped
1 green bell pepper, deseeded and chopped
1 garlic clove, minced
1 tsp ginger paste
1 cup pineapple chunks
1 cup vegetable broth

Directions

In a medium bowl, combine rice vinegar, soy sauce, sugar, and ketchup. Set your Instant Pot to Sauté mode and adjust to medium heat. Heat olive oil and sauté onion, carrot, and bell pepper until softened, 5 minutes. Stir in garlic, ginger and sauté until fragrant, 1 minute. Stir in vinegar mixture, pineapples, and vegetable broth.

Seal the lid, select Manual/Pressure Cook on High, and set time to 2 minutes. After cooking, do a quick pressure release. Stir and turn Instant Pot off. Spoon into serving bowls and serve right away.

Orange-Apple Sauce

Total Time: 20 minutes | **Servings**: 4 | **Per Serving**: Kcal 111; Carbs 19g; Fat 4g; Protein 1g

Ingredients

1 large orange, zested
1 cup squeezed orange juice
1 cup apple juice

2 cinnamon sticks
2 tbsp honey
½ lemon, juiced

Directions

In inner pot, add orange zest, orange juice, apple juice, and cinnamon sticks. Seal the lid, select Manual/Pressure Cook mode on High, and set cooking time to 4 minutes.

After cooking, perform a natural pressure release for 10 minutes, then a quick pressure release to let out remaining steam, and unlock the lid. Remove and discard cinnamon sticks. Mix in honey and add lemon juice. Serve warm.

French Chocolate Sauce

Total Time: 15 minutes | **Servings**: 4 | **Per Serving**: Kcal 280; Carbs 15g; Fat 23g; Protein 2g

Ingredients

2 cups heavy cream
¼ cup plain chocolate, chopped

2 tbsp brandy

Directions

Add heavy cream to inner pot. Select Sauté mode and cook heavy cream until thickened while occasionally stirring, 3-4 minutes. Whisk in chocolate and brandy until chocolate melts.

Turn Instant Pot off and spoon sauce into serving cups. Serve immediately.

Arrabbiata Sauce

Total Time: 20 minutes | **Servings**: 4 | **Per Serving**: Kcal 87; Carbs 6g; Fat 7g; Protein 1g

Ingredients

2 tbsp olive oil
1 red serrano chili pepper, minced
2 garlic cloves, minced
1 lb ripe tomatoes, peeled and chopped
1 tbsp tomato paste

1 tbsp zested lemon
½ cup water
A pinch granulated sugar
1 tbsp balsamic vinegar
1 tsp dried marjoram

Directions

Set your Instant Pot to Sauté mode. Heat olive oil and sauté serrano chili and garlic until fragrant, 1 minute. Stir in tomatoes, tomato paste, lemon zest, water, and sugar.

Seal the lid, select Manual/Pressure Cook on High, and set cooking time to 3 minutes. After cooking, perform a natural pressure release for 10 minutes, then a quick pressure release to let out remaining steam. Unlock the lid.

Using an immersion blender, puree ingredients until almost smooth. Stir in balsamic vinegar and marjoram. Spoon sauce into glass jars and serve right away. Preserve extra in refrigerator and use for up to 1 week.

Gorgonzola Sauce

Total Time: 15 minutes | **Servings**: 6 | **Per Serving**: Kcal 443; Carbs 9g; Fat 37g; Protein 19g

Ingredients

2 tbsp butter
1 cup heavy cream
2 tbsp dry white wine
2 cups crumbled Gorgonzola cheese

1 tsp cornflour
2 tsp chopped sage
Salt and white pepper to taste

Directions

Set your Instant Pot to Sauté mode and adjust to medium heat. Melt butter in inner pot and stir in heavy cream and white wine. Seal the lid, select Manual/Pressure Cook mode on High, and set cooking time to 1 minute. After cooking, do a quick pressure release to let out steam and unlock the lid.

Select Sauté mode and keep boiling heavy cream until thickened like white sauce; occasionally stir. Whisk in Gorgonzola cheese until melted, and stir in cornstarch; cook until thickened, 1 to 2 minutes. Stir in sage, salt, and white pepper. Cook further for 1 minute and turn Instant Pot off. Spoon into cups to serve.

Almond Satay Sauce

Total Time: 15 minutes | **Servings**: 4 | **Per Serving**: Kcal 234; Carbs 12g; Fat 19g; Protein 8g

Ingredients

4 scallions, roughly chopped
2 garlic cloves, minced
2 tsp ginger paste
2 tsp brown sugar
½ cup almond butter
1 tsp fish sauce

2 tbsp soy sauce
1 tsp squeezed lemon juice
1 tbsp Sriracha sauce
Salt to taste
2 tbsp chopped almonds to garnish

Directions

In a blender, add scallions, garlic, ginger, brown sugar, almond butter, fish sauce, soy sauce, lemon juice, and Sriracha sauce. Process until smooth. Pour blended ingredients into inner pot.

Select Sauté mode, and cook the sauce until thickened, 3-5 minutes. Stir and adjust the taste with salt. Spoon sauce into serving bowls, garnish with almonds and serve.

Vanilla Toffee Sauce

Total Time: 15 minutes | **Servings**: 4 | **Per Serving**: Kcal 239; Carbs 26g; Fat 14g; Protein 2g

Ingredients

4 tbsp butter
4 tbsp brown sugar
2 tbsp maple syrup
2 tbsp agave syrup
2 tbsp water

1 cup condensed milk
1 tsp vanilla extract
½ tsp cinnamon powder
1 tbsp rum

Directions

Melt butter on Sauté mode and whisk in brown sugar, maple syrup, agave syrup, water, condensed milk, vanilla, and cinnamon until sugar dissolves and ingredients are combined, 4 minutes. Mix in rum. Stir, and cook until thickened, 3 minutes. Transfer sauce to a jug and serve.

Nutty Butterscotch Sauce

Total Time: 15 minutes | **Servings**: 4 | **Per Serving**: Kcal 292; Carbs 15g; Fat 25g; Protein 2g

Ingredients

¼ cup brown sugar
3 tbsp water
1 tbsp rum

3 tbsp unsalted butter
1 ½ cups heavy cream
2 tbsp chopped walnuts

Directions

Set your Instant Pot to Sauté mode and adjust to medium heat. Mix brown sugar and water in inner pot and cook until dissolved while continuously stirring, 3 minutes. Allow bubbling for 3 to 4 more minutes.

Stir in rum and cook further for 1 minute. Turn Instant Pot off. Whisk in butter and heavy cream. Fold in walnuts and spoon sauce into serving bowls to cool before serving.

Custard Sauce

Total Time: 15 minutes | **Servings:** 4 | **Per Serving:** Kcal 80; Carbs 13g; Fat 3g; Protein 2g

Ingredients

1 tbsp cornflour
1 cup whole milk
1 egg, cracked into a bowl

2 tbsp granulated sugar
½ tsp vanilla extract

Directions

In a bowl, mix cornflour with 3 tablespoons of milk until smooth, and set aside. Pour the remaining milk into inner pot. Seal the lid, select Manual/Pressure Cook mode on High, and set cooking time to 1 minute. After cooking, perform a quick pressure release to let out steam, and unlock the lid.

Meanwhile, in a food processor, blend egg, sugar, and vanilla. Whisk hot milk into cornflour mixture until smoothly combined and pour back into inner pot. Cook on Sauté mode with continuous stirring for 2 more minutes. Pour milk mixture into food processor and blend with sugar mixture until smoothly mixed. Transfer to a serving jug and serve.

White Chocolate Fudge Sauce

Total Time: 15 minutes | **Servings:** 4 | **Per Serving:** Kcal 357; Carbs 14g; Fat 33g; Protein 2g

Ingredients

2 cups heavy cream
3 tbsp granulated sugar
4 tbsp unsalted butter

¼ cup white chocolate, chopped
2 tbsp brandy

Directions

In inner pot, add heavy cream, sugar, butter, and white chocolate. Seal the lid, select Manual/Pressure Cook mode on High, and set cooking time to 4 minutes.

After cooking, perform a quick pressure release to let out steam, and unlock the lid. Whisk brandy into mixture and pour into a serving jar. Serve right away.

Sweets & Desserts

White Chocolate Oreo Cake

Total Time: 60 minutes + cooling time | **Servings**: 6 | **Per Serving**: Kcal 534; Carbs 57g; Fat 27g; Protein 17g

Ingredients

12 Oreo cookies, smoothly crushed
2 tbsp salted butter, melted
16 oz cream cheese, softened
½ cup granulated sugar
2 large eggs, room temperature
1 tbsp plain flour

¼ cup heavy cream
2 tsp vanilla extract
16 whole Oreo cookies, coarsely crushed
1 cup whipped cream
2 tbsp chocolate sauce for topping

Directions

Line the bottom of a 7-inch springform pan with foil, grease lightly with cooking spray, and set aside.

In a medium bowl, combine smoothly crushed Oreo cookies with butter and press into bottom of pan. Freeze for 10 to 15 minutes. In another bowl, add cream cheese, and beat using a mixer until smooth. Add sugar, whisk further until homogeneous. Beat in eggs one by one, until well-mixed. Whisk in flour, heavy cream, and vanilla until adequately combined.

Fold in 8 coarsely crushed cookies and pour mixture onto crust in springform pan. Cover pan tightly with foil. Pour 1 ½ cups of water in inner pot and set to a trivet with slings. Place pan on trivet. Seal the lid, set to Manual/Pressure Cook mode on High, and set cooking time to 35 minutes.

After cooking, perform a natural pressure release for 10 minutes. Holding slings, remove trivet with cake pan onto a flat surface. Take off foil and transfer cake to a cooling rack. Allow chilling. Transfer to refrigerator for 8 hours. After, top with whipped cream, remaining 8 Oreo cookies, and swirl with chocolate sauce. Slice and serve.

Chocolate Crème de Pot

Total Time: 40 minutes + chilling time | **Servings**: 6 | **Per Serving**: Kcal 369; Carbs 27g; Fat 27g; Protein 6g

Ingredients

½ cup whole milk
1 ½ cups heavy cream
5 large egg yolks
¼ cup caster sugar

A pinch of salt
¼ cup bittersweet chocolate, melted
Whipped cream for topping
1 tbsp chocolate sprinkles for topping

Directions

Set your Instant Pot to Sauté mode. Mix milk and heavy cream in inner pot, and allow boiling. In a medium bowl, beat egg yolks, sugar, and salt until well combined. Gradually, whisk egg mixture into cream until well mixed. Also, mix in melted chocolate; cook until thickened, 2 to 3 minutes. Spoon mixture into 6 custard cups and clean inner pot.

Pour 1 cup of water in inner pot, fit in a trivet with slings, and arrange 3 cups on top. Stand the other cups on the touching rims of the other cups. Seal the lid, set to Manual/Pressure Cook on High, and cook for 6 minutes. After cooking, perform a natural pressure release for 10 minutes, then a quick pressure release to let out remaining steam.

Carefully remove cups onto a flat surface and allow cooling. Chill further in refrigerator for at least 6 hours. When ready to serve, remove from refrigerator, swirl the top with whipping cream, and decorate with chocolate sprinkles.

Apple Crisps

Total Time: 25 minutes | **Servings**: 4 | **Per Serving**: Kcal 299; Carbs 65g; Fat 10g; Protein 5g

Ingredients

5 Granny Smith apples, chopped
½ tsp nutmeg powder
2 tsp cinnamon powder
1 tbsp honey
½ cup water
4 tbsp unsalted butter, melted

¾ cup old fashioned rolled oats
¼ cup plain flour
½ tsp salt
¼ cup brown sugar
1 cup vanilla ice cream for topping

Directions

In inner pot, mix apples, nutmeg, cinnamon, honey, and water. In a medium bowl, combine butter, rolled oats, flour, salt, and brown sugar. Drop tablespoons of the mixture all over the apples.

Seal the lid, set to Manual/Pressure Cook on High, and cook for 5 minutes. After cooking, perform a natural pressure release for 10 minutes. Spoon dessert into serving bowls, top with vanilla ice cream and serve immediately.

Coconut Rice Pudding with Blueberries

Total Time: 25 minutes | **Servings**: 4 | **Per Serving**: Kcal 248; Carbs 36g; Fat 12g; Protein 8g

Ingredients

1 cup jasmine rice
½ tsp nutmeg powder
1 tsp cinnamon powder + extra for topping
1 tbsp unsalted butter

2 cups coconut milk
¼ cup granulated sugar
A pinch of salt
½ cup blueberries for topping

Directions

In inner pot, combine rice, nutmeg, cinnamon, butter, coconut milk, salt, and sugar. Seal the lid, set to Manual/Pressure Cook mode on High, and set cooking time to 5 minutes.

After cooking, perform a natural pressure release for 10 minutes. Stir and adjust taste with sugar. Spoon into serving bowls, top with blueberries, and sprinkle with more cinnamon. Serve warm or chilled.

Caramel Corns

Total Time: 20 minutes | **Servings**: 4 | **Per Serving**: Kcal 168; Carbs 14g; Fat 13g; Protein 2g

Ingredients

4 tbsp butter
1 cup sweet corn kernels

3 tbsp brown sugar
¼ cup whole milk

Directions

Set your Instant Pot to Sauté mode. Melt butter and mix in corn kernels. Once heated and started popping, cover the top with a clear instant pot safe lid, and continue cooking until corn stops popping, for 2 to 3 minutes. After, carefully open the lid and transfer popcorns to a large bowl. Press Cancel and wipe inner pot clean.

Select Sauté mode. Combine brown sugar and milk in inner pot and cook with frequent stirring until sugar dissolves and sauce coats the back of the spoon, 3 to 4 minutes. Turn Instant Pot off. Drizzle caramel sauce all over corns and toss to coat thoroughly. Allow cooling and serve.

Molten Brownie Pudding

Total Time: 45 minutes | **Servings:** 6 | **Per Serving:** Kcal 297; Carbs 33g; Fat 18g; Protein 4g

Ingredients

1 ½ cups water
7 tbsp butter, melted and divided
1 cup caster sugar
2 eggs, cracked into a bowl
¼ cup plain flour

¼ cup unsweetened cocoa powder
1 tsp vanilla extract
¼ cup semisweet chocolate chips
¼ cup milk chocolate chip
Vanilla ice cream for serving

Directions

Pour 1 ½ cups of water in inner pot and fit in a trivet with slings. Grease the inner parts of a 7-inch baking dish with 1 tablespoon of butter and set aside.

In a medium bowl, using an electric hand mixer, whisk sugar and eggs. In another bowl, combine flour and cocoa powder. Pour into wet ingredients and mix until well combined. Add remaining butter and vanilla. Mix again. Pour mixture into a baking dish and sprinkle the top with the two types of chocolate chips. Place on trivet.

Seal the lid, set to Manual/Pressure Cook mode on High, and set cooking time to 30 minutes. After cooking, perform a quick pressure release to let out steam, and unlock the lid. Carefully take out baking dish and scoop fudge into dessert cups. Top with vanilla ice cream and serve.

French Apricot Cobbler

Total Time: 50 minutes | **Servings:** 4 | **Per Serving:** Kcal 656; Carbs 72g; Fat 22g; Protein 12g

Ingredients

4 cups sliced apricots
½ cup + ¼ cup brown sugar, divided
2 tbsp + ¾ cup plain flour, divided
½ tsp cinnamon powder
¼ tsp nutmeg powder
1 ½ tsp salt, divided

1 tsp vanilla extract
¼ cup water
½ tsp baking powder
½ tsp baking soda
3 tbsp butter, melted

Directions

In a 7-inch heatproof bowl, mix apricots, ½ cup of brown sugar, 2 tbsp of flour, cinnamon, nutmeg, ½ tsp of salt, vanilla, and water. Set aside. In another bowl, mix the remaining flour, salt and brown sugar, the baking powder, baking soda, and butter. Spoon mixture over apricot mixture and spread to cover.

Pour 1 cup of water in inner pot, fit in a trivet with slings, and place heatproof bowl on top. Seal the lid, select Manual/Pressure Cook mode on High, and set cooking time to 25 minutes. After cooking, perform a natural pressure release for 10 minutes. Unlock the lid. Take out bowl and serve after.

Steamed Yogurt Pudding with Nuts

Total Time: 40 minutes | **Servings:** 4 | **Per Serving:** Kcal 175; Carbs 10g; Fat 11g; Protein 11g

Ingredients

2 cups sweetened condensed milk
1 ½ cups Greek yogurt
1 tsp cocoa powder

1 tsp cardamom powder
¼ cup mixed nuts, chopped

Directions

Lightly grease 4 medium ramekins with cooking spray. Set aside. In a bowl, combine condensed milk, Greek yogurt, cocoa powder, and cardamom powder. Pour mixture into ramekins and cover with foil.

Pour 1 cup of water into the pot, fit in trivet, and place ramekins on top. Seal the lid, select Manual/Pressure Cook on High, and set time to 15 minutes. After cooking, perform a natural pressure release for 15 minutes. Unlock the lid, remove ramekins, take off foil, and cool slightly. Top with nuts and serve immediately.

Sticky Bourbon Pudding Cake

Total Time: 50 minutes | **Servings:** 4 | **Per Serving:** Kcal 267; Carbs 41g; Fat 8g; Protein 6g

Ingredients

½ tsp baking soda
½ tsp cinnamon powder
¼ tsp cloves powder
¼ tsp allspice
¼ tsp salt
¾ cup plain flour
1 tsp baking powder

6 tbsp hot water
2 tbsp bourbon
3 tbsp unsalted butter, melted
2 tbsp whole milk
1 egg, lightly beaten
½ cup chopped dates
½ cup salted caramel sauce for topping

Directions

In a medium bowl, combine baking soda, cinnamon, cloves, allspice, salt, flour, and baking powder. In another bowl, mix hot water, bourbon, butter, and milk. Pour into dry ingredients and mix until well-mixed. Whisk in egg and then fold in the dates.

Lightly grease 4 medium ramekins with cooking spray, divide mixture among them, and cover with foil. Pour 1 cup of water in inner pot, fit in a trivet with slings, and place ramekins on top. Seal the lid, select Manual/Pressure Cook mode on High, and set cooking time to 25 minutes.

After cooking, perform a natural pressure release for 10 minutes, then a quick pressure release to let out the steam. Unlock the lid and carefully remove ramekins, invert onto dessert plates, and drizzle caramel sauce on top. Serve.

Pecan Monkey Bread

Total Time: 50 minutes + overnight rising | **Servings:** 6 | **Per Serving:** Kcal 379; Carbs 61g; Fat 14g; Protein 7g

Ingredients

16 frozen unbaked dinner rolls, thawed
¼ cup light brown sugar
1 ½ cinnamon powder
¼ cup toasted pecans, chopped

½ cup butter, melted
½ cup powdered sugar
2 tsp whole milk

Directions

Grease a bundt pan with cooking spray and set aside. Divide each dinner roll into half. Set aside. In a shallow plate, mix sugar, cinnamon, and pecans. Coat bread rolls in sugar mixture, in butter, and then place in bundt pan, making sure to build layers. Cover pan with foil and allow rising overnight on the counter.

The next morning, pour 1 cup of water into inner pot, fit in trivet, and place bundt pan on top. Seal the lid, select Manual/Pressure Cook on High, and set cooking time to 25 minutes. After cooking, perform a natural pressure release for 10 minutes. Unlock the lid, remove pan, take off foil, and allow complete cooling. In a bowl, whisk sugar with milk until smooth. Invert bread onto a serving platter and drizzle with sugar glaze. Slice and serve.

Lemon Pudding

Total Time: 25 minutes + chilling time | **Servings**: 4 | **Per Serving**: Kcal 355; Carbs 51g; Fat 12g; Protein 9g

Ingredients

2 ½ cups whole milk
2 lemons, zested + ¼ cup lemon juice
¼ cup cornstarch
¼ tsp salt

1 cup granulated sugar
2 eggs
2 egg yolks
1 tbsp butter, melted

Directions

In a medium pot, combine milk, lemon zest, cornstarch, salt, and sugar. Place over medium heat on a stovetop until boiling, 2 minutes. Turn off heat. In a medium bowl, beat eggs and egg yolks. Slowly whisk in milk mixture until well combined. Mix in butter and then, lemon juice. Pour mixture into 4 medium ramekins and cover with foil.

Pour 1 cup of water into inner pot, fit in trivet, and place ramekins on top. Seal the lid, select Manual/Pressure Cook on High, and set cooking time to 5 minutes. After cooking, perform a quick pressure to let out steam. Unlock the lid, remove ramekin onto a flat surface, take off foil, and allow complete cooling. Chill in refrigerator before serving.

Dulce de Leche with Apricots

Total Time: 45 minutes | **Servings**: 6 | **Per Serving**: Kcal 108; Carbs 14g; Fat 4g; Protein 4g

Ingredients

2 cups sweetened condensed milk

4 apricots, halved, cored, and sliced

Directions

Pour 5 cups of water in inner pot and fit in a trivet with slings. Divide condensed milk into 6 medium canning jars and close with lids but not tight. Place jars on trivet. Seal the lid, set to Manual/Pressure Cook mode on High, and set cooking time to 25 minutes.

After cooking, perform a natural pressure release for 10 minutes. Unlock the lid. Allow jars and water in pot to cool completely before lifting the jars out to avoid the jars from breaking. Open lids and use a fork to whisk caramel well until creamy. Serve with sliced apricots and reserve extras in refrigerator.

Stuffed Baked Apples

Total Time: 20 minutes | **Servings**: 6 | **Per Serving**: Kcal 235; Carbs 35g; Fat 12g; Protein 2g

Ingredients

2 tbsp brown sugar
¼ cup toasted pecans, chopped
¼ cup sultanas
½ cup dates, chopped

1 tbsp cinnamon powder
4 tbsp butter
6 red apples, whole and cored
4 tbsp chocolate sauce for topping

Directions

In a medium bowl, mix brown sugar, pecans, sultanas, dates, cinnamon, and butter. Stuff apples with mixture. Pour 1/3 cup of water in inner pot and place stuffed apples in water. Seal the lid, select Manual/Pressure Cook mode on Low and set cooking time to 3 minutes.

After cooking, perform natural pressure release to let out steam and then, a quick pressure release to let out remaining steam. Unlock the lid and carefully remove apples onto serving plates, drizzle with chocolate sauce, and serve.

Mango Rice Pudding

Total Time: 35 minutes | **Servings**: 4 | **Per Serving**: Kcal 282; Carbs 45g; Fat 12g; Protein 8g

Ingredients

1 cup jasmine rice
½ tsp nutmeg powder
1 tsp vanilla extract
1 tbsp unsalted butter

2 cups whole milk
1 mango, chopped into small bits
A pinch of salt
¼ cup granulated sugar

Directions

In inner pot, combine jasmine rice, nutmeg, vanilla, butter, milk, mango, salt, and sugar. Seal the lid, set to Manual/Pressure Cook on High and set cooking time to 5 minutes.

After cooking, perform a natural pressure release for 10 minutes, then a quick pressure release to let out remaining steam. Unlock the lid and stir and adjust taste with sugar. Spoon into serving bowls. Serve warm or chilled.

Japanese Cheesecake

Total Time: 45 minutes + cooling time | **Servings**: 4 | **Per Serving**: Kcal 275; Carbs 14g; Fat 20g; Protein 9g

Ingredients

4 large eggs, separated into yolks and whites
½ cup cream cheese, softened

½ cup white chocolate chips, melted

Directions

Line a 7-inch springform pan with parchment paper and set aside. Pour egg whites into a dry bowl, making sure not to have any contact with water or oil. Cover with plastic wrap and place in refrigerator.

In a medium bowl, whisk cream cheese and white chocolate chips until smooth. Beat in egg yolks until smooth. Remove egg whites from refrigerator and beat on high speed using an electric mixer until stiff, glossy peak forms. Fold into chocolate mixture one tablespoon at a time until evenly combined. Pour mixture into cake pan.

Pour 1 cup of water in inner pot, fit in a trivet with slings, and place pan on top. Seal the lid, select Manual/Pressure Cook on High, and set time to 17 minutes. After cooking, perform a natural pressure release for 10 minutes. Unlock the lid and carefully remove cake pan and allow cooling for 3 hours. Release cake pan, slice cake, and serve.

Yellow Cake Pineapple Upside Down

Total Time: 50 minutes | **Servings**: 4 | **Per Serving**: Kcal 487; Carbs 78g; Fat 13g; Protein 7g

Ingredients

1 (18.5-oz) box yellow cake mix
2 tbsp butter, melted

¼ cup brown sugar
1 cup pineapple slices

Directions

In a medium bowl, prepare cake mix according to instruction on box. Set aside. Grease a 7-inch springform pan with butter, sprinkle brown sugar at bottom of pan and arrange pineapple slices on top. Pour cake batter all over and cover pan with foil. Pour 1 cup of water in inner pot, fit in a trivet, and place cake pan on top.

Seal the lid, select Manual/Pressure Cook on High, and set time to 18 minutes. After cooking, perform natural pressure release for 10 minutes, then a quick pressure release to let out remaining steam. Unlock the lid and carefully remove cake pan. Take off foil and allow cooling for 10 minutes. Turn cake over onto a plate, slice, and serve.

Raspberry Cheesecake

Total Time: 70 minutes + cooling time | **Servings**: 4 | **Per Serving**: Kcal 663; Carbs 47g; Fat 48g; Protein 12g

Ingredients

12 graham crackers

2 tbsp melted butter

16 oz cream cheese, softened

1 cup granulated sugar

1 tsp vanilla extract

12 large raspberries + more for garnishing

3 tbsp maple syrup

2 eggs

2 tsp cinnamon powder

½ cup heavy cream

Directions

Pour graham crackers in a plastic bag and gently break into crumbs by pounding with a rolling pin. Transfer biscuit to a bowl and mix in butter. Pour mixture into a 7-inch springform pan and press to fit with a spoon. Set aside in refrigerator to compact while you prepare the remaining ingredients.

In a large bowl, using an electric hand mixer, whisk cream cheese and sugar until smooth. Add vanilla, raspberries, maple syrup, eggs, cinnamon powder, and heavy cream, and mix until well combined.

Remove cake pan from refrigerator and pour cream cheese mixture on top. Spread evenly using a spatula and cover pan with foil. Pour 1 cup of water in inner pot, fit in a trivet, and place cake pan on top. Seal the lid, select Manual/ Pressure Cook on High, and set cooking time to 40 minutes. After cooking, perform a natural pressure release for 10 minutes, and then a quick pressure release.

Unlock the lid and carefully remove cake pan. Allow cooling for 10 minutes and chill in refrigerator for 3 hours. Release cake pan, garnish with 3 to 4 raspberries, slice, and serve.

Super Easy Soda Cake

Total Time: 35 minutes + cooling time | **Servings**: 6 | **Per Serving**: Kcal 389; Carbs 82g; Fat 5; Protein 5g

Ingredients

1 ½ cups orange soda

1 (15.25 oz) box orange cake mix

1 tbsp caster sugar for decorating

Directions

Lightly grease a bundt pan with cooking spray and set aside. In a bowl, mix orange soda and orange cake mix until well combined. Pour into bundt pan, cover with a paper towel, and then with a foil.

Pour 1 cup of water in inner pot, fit in a trivet, and place pan on top. Seal the lid, select Manual/Pressure Cook on High, and set time to 30 minutes. After cooking, do a quick pressure release to let out the steam. Remove pan, take off foil and paper towel, and allow cooling. Turn over onto a platter, decorate with caster sugar, slice, and serve.

New York Style Cheesecake

Total Time: 65 minutes + cooling time | **Servings**: 4 | **Per Serving**: Kcal 608; Carbs 42g; Fat 44g; Protein 13g

Ingredients

12 graham crackers

2 tbsp melted salted butter

1 ½ tbsp brown sugar

16 oz cream cheese, softened

1 cup granulated sugar

1 tsp vanilla extract

2 eggs

½ cup sour cream

2 tbsp cornstarch

2 pinches salt

Directions

Pour graham crackers into a plastic bag and gently break into crumbs by pounding a rolling pin on top. Transfer biscuit to a bowl and mix in butter and brown sugar. Pour mixture into a 7-inch springform and use a spoon to press to fit. Set aside in refrigerator to harden.

Meanwhile, in a large bowl, using an electric hand mixer, whisk cream cheese and sugar until smooth. Add vanilla, eggs, sour cream, cornstarch, and salt. Remove cake pan from refrigerator and pour cream cheese mixture on top. Spread evenly using a spatula and cover pan with foil. Pour 1 cup of water in inner pot, fit in a trivet, and place cake pan on top.

Seal the lid, select Manual/Pressure Cook on High, and set cooking time to 40 minutes. After cooking, perform natural pressure release for 10 minutes, then a quick pressure release. Unlock the lid and carefully remove cake pan. Allow cooling for 10 minutes and chill in refrigerator for 3 hours. Remove from refrigerator; slice and serve.

Lemon Berry Pudding

Total Time: 50 minutes + 4 hours | **Servings**: 4 | **Per Serving**: Kcal 277; Carbs 32g; Fat 15g; Protein 6g

Ingredients

1 tsp melted butter, for greasing
3 tbsp butter, room temperature
½ cup caster sugar
½ cup plain flour
A pinch of salt

1 cup milk
1 lemon, zested and juiced
2 eggs, beaten
1 ½ cups strawberries and raspberries, mashed

Directions

Grease 4 medium ramekins with melted butter and set aside. Put softened butter in a medium bowl and whisk with an electric hand mixer until creamy. Add sugar, flour, salt, and continue whisking until smooth. Beat in milk, lemon zest, and lemon juice until well-combined. While still whisking, add eggs gradually until smoothly mixed. Fold in berries, divide mixture into ramekins, and cover with foil.

Pour 1 cup of water in inner pot, fit in a trivet, and place ramekins on top. Seal the lid, select Manual/Pressure Cook and set cooking time to 20 minutes. After cooking, perform a quick pressure release to let out steam, and unlock the lid. Carefully remove ramekins, allow cooling, and chill in refrigerator for at least 4 hours. Serve when ready to enjoy.

Chocolate Pudding in a Jar

Total Time: 30 minutes + chilling time | **Servings**: 4 | **Per Serving**: Kcal 350; Carbs 47g; Fat 13g; Protein 11g

Ingredients

3 ¼ cups whole milk
¼ cup maple syrup
1 ½ tbsp vanilla extract
1 tbsp coconut oil

3 medium eggs, cracked
4 tbsp cocoa powder
1 ¼ tsp gelatin
¼ cup collagen

Directions

In a blender, add milk, maple syrup, vanilla, coconut oil, eggs, and cocoa powder. Process until smoothly combined. Add gelatin and collagen; blend again until smooth. Pour mixture into 4 large mason jars and cover. Pour 1 cup of water in inner pot, fit in a trivet, and stand mason jars on top.

Seal the lid, select Manual/Pressure Cook on High, and set cooking time to 5 minutes. After cooking, perform a natural pressure release for 10 minutes, then a quick pressure release to let out remaining steam, and unlock the lid. Carefully remove jars and allow cooling. Chill in refrigerator overnight and serve when ready to enjoy.

Caramel Cheesecake

Total Time: 70 minutes + cooling time | **Servings**: 4 | **Per Serving**: Kcal 652; Carbs 31g; Fat 53g; Protein 14g

Ingredients

2 cups graham crackers
3 tbsp brown sugar
¼ cup butter, melted
2 (8 oz) cream cheese, softened
½ cup granulated sugar

2 tbsp plain flour
1 tsp vanilla extract
3 eggs
1 cup caramel sauce

Directions

Pour graham crackers in a plastic bag and crush biscuits with a rolling pin. Pour into a bowl and mix in brown sugar and butter. Spread mixture at the bottom of a 7-inch springform pan and use a spoon to press to fit. Freeze in refrigerator to compact for 10 minutes.

In a large bowl, using an electric hand mixer, whisk cream cheese and sugar until smooth. While mixing, add flour gradually and vanilla until well combined. Beat in eggs on low speed until blended. Remove pan from oven and pour mixture over crust; cover pan with foil.

Pour 1 cup of water in inner pot, fit in a trivet, and place cake pan on top. Seal the lid, select Manual/Pressure Cook on High, and set cooking time to 40 minutes.

After cooking, perform natural pressure release for 10 minutes, then a quick pressure release to let out remaining steam. Unlock the lid, carefully remove cake pan, and take off foil. Allow cooling for 10 minutes, pour caramel sauce all over cake, and chill in refrigerator for 3 hours. Remove and release cake pan, slice, and serve.

Homemade Apricot Yogurt

Total Time: 8 hours 20 minutes | **Servings**: 4 | **Per Serving**: Kcal 303; Carbs 43g; Fat 8g; Protein 16g

Ingredients

4 cups whole milk
2 packets yogurt starter

4 tsp apricot spread

Directions

Set your Instant Pot to Sauté, pour in the milk, and bring to a boil. Remove to a heat-proof bowl and cool until a thermometer has reached a temperature of 110°F. Clean the inner pot.

In a small bowl, pour 1 cup of the cooled milk and mix in yogurt starter. Return to the pot and add in the remaining cooled milk; stir to combine. Seal the lid, select Yogurt, and cook for 8 hours.

When done, perform a quick pressure release to let out the steam. Unlock the lid and gently stir the yogurt. Divide the apricot spread between jars, top with yogurt, and let it sit for 6 hours to thicken. Chill in the fridge and serve.

Sugar Cookie Fudge

Total Time: 20 minutes + chilling time | **Servings**: 6 | **Per Serving**: Kcal 360; Carbs 50g; Fat 16g; Protein 5g

Ingredients

1 ½ cups bags white chocolate chips
2 cups sweetened condensed milk
1 ¼ cups sugar cookie mix
2 tbsp butter

1 tsp almond extract

Directions

Set your Instant Pot to Sauté mode. Put in white chocolate chips, condensed milk, almond extract, sugar cookie mix, and butter. Melt chocolate fully while continuously stirring, 10 minutes. Pour mixture into cake pan and refrigerate for 2 hours. Remove and release pan after. Slice fudge into squares and serve.

Crème Brulee

Total Time: 40 minutes + cooling time | **Servings**: 4 | **Per Serving**: Kcal 523; Carbs 37g; Fat 25g; Protein 13g

Ingredients

For crust:

2 cups graham crackers

3 tbsp brown sugar

¼ cup butter, melted

A pinch salt

For filling:

2 (8 oz) cream cheese, softened

½ cup granulated sugar

2 large eggs

2 tsp vanilla extract

½ cup sour cream, room temperature

2 tbsp cornstarch

For crack-able caramel:

4 tsp white sugar

Directions

Crush graham crackers in a plastic bag using a rolling pin and pour biscuits into a medium bowl. Mix in brown sugar, butter, and salt. Spoon mixture into 4 medium ramekins. Place in refrigerator to harden crust.

In a large bowl, using an electric hand mixer, whisk cream cheese and sugar until smooth. Beat in eggs and vanilla until smooth. Fold in sour cream, while adding cornstarch gradually until adequately blended.

Remove ramekins, pour in filling, and cover with foil. Pour 1 cup of water in inner pot, fit in a trivet, and place cups on top. Seal the lid, select Manual/Pressure Cook on High, and set cooking time to 10 minutes. After cooking, perform natural pressure release for 10 minutes, and then a quick pressure release to let out the steam. Unlock the lid, carefully remove ramekins and take off foil.

Allow cooling for 10 minutes and then chill dessert further for 2 hours. When ready to serve, take out crème brulee cups and sprinkle 1 teaspoon of sugar on each dessert. Using a torch, caramelize sugar until toffee brown in color. Serve immediately.

Strawberry Pancake Bites

Total Time: 30 minutes | **Servings**: 4 | **Per Serving**: Kcal 281; Carbs 26g; Fat 16g; Protein 8g

Ingredients

1 cup pancake mix

¾ cup water

2 large eggs

½ cup fresh strawberries, chopped

¼ cup olive oil

Directions

In a medium bowl, combine pancake mix, water, eggs, strawberries, and olive oil. Spoon mixture into 4 large silicone muffin cups and cover with foil. Pour 1 cup of water in inner pot, fit in a trivet, and place muffin cups on top. Seal the lid, select Manual/Pressure Cook on High, and set cooking time to 10 minutes.

After cooking, perform natural pressure release for 10 minutes, and then a quick pressure release to let out the remaining steam. Unlock the lid, carefully remove cups, and take off foil. Empty pancake bites onto plates and serve.

White Chocolate Blueberry Minis

Total Time: 45 minutes + cooling time | **Servings**: 4 | **Per Serving**: Kcal 657; Carbs 36g; Fat 54g; Protein 9g

Ingredients

2 cups graham crackers
4 tbsp butter, melted
2 (8 oz) cream cheese, softened
½ cup caster sugar
½ tsp vanilla extract

1 tbsp honey
1 egg
¼ cup grated white chocolate
½ cup blueberries, mashed + extra for garnishing
2 tbsp heavy cream

Directions

Crush graham crackers in a plastic bag using a rolling pin and transfer to a medium bowl. Mix in butter and pour mixture into 4 medium ramekins that have been greased with cooking spray. Press with a spoon fit and freeze crust in refrigerator while you prepare the filling.

In a large bowl, whisk cream cheese and sugar until smooth. While mixing, add vanilla, honey, and egg until well blended. Mix in chocolate, blueberries, and heavy cream. Remove ramekins from refrigerator and pour in filling; cover ramekins with foil.

Pour 1 cup of water in inner pot, fit in a trivet, and place cake pan on top. Seal the lid, select Manual/Pressure Cook on High, and set time to 25 minutes. After cooking, perform a natural pressure release for 10 minutes. Unlock the lid, carefully remove ramekins, and take off foil. Allow cooling for 10 minutes and then chill cake in refrigerator for 2 hours. When ready to serve, garnish with blueberries and enjoy.

Blackberry Yogurt Jars

Total Time: 8 hrs 40 min + cooling time | **Servings**: 4 | **Per Serving**: Kcal 418; Carbs 29g; Fat 16g; Protein 16g

Ingredients

8 cups whole milk
½ cup plain yogurt

2 tbsp vanilla bean paste
1 cup blackberries

Directions

Pour milk into inner pot. Seal the lid, select Yogurt mode, and press Adjust until display shows "Boil." When done, turn the pot off and unlock the lid. Stir milk, remove inner pot and allow cooling up to 100°F. Check the temperature with a food thermometer.

Whisk in yogurt and vanilla bean paste. Return inner pot to Instant Pot. Seal the lid, select Yogurt mode, and set cooking time to 8 hours. After cooking, the display will show "Yogt." Refrigerate the yogurt for a few hours.

Meanwhile, mash blackberries in a bowl using a fork. Divide blackberries into mason jars and divide yogurt on top.

Coconut Pudding

Total Time: 25 minutes + cooling time | **Servings**: 4 | **Per Serving**: Kcal 232; Carbs 25g; Fat 12g; Protein 6g

Ingredients

¼ cup granulated sugar
2 egg yolks
2 cups coconut milk
2 tbsp coconut cream
2 tbsp flour

1 tbsp cornstarch
Pinch of salt
1 tsp vanilla extract
½ cup sweetened coconut flakes, toasted

Directions

In a medium bowl, whisk sugar and eggs until smoothly combined; set aside. Set your Instant Pot to Sauté and adjust to medium heat. Warm coconut milk and coconut cream in inner pot until liquid starts to scald. Set aside.

In a bowl, beat egg yolks with sugar and add flour, cornstarch, and salt and whisk until smooth. Put 1 tbsp of coconut milk mixture into egg mixture and whisk again. Pour mixture into inner pot. Mix in vanilla extract.

Seal the lid, select Manual/Pressure Cook on High, and set cooking time to 2 minutes. After cooking, perform a quick pressure release and unlock the lid. Stir and spoon pudding into dessert bowls. Allow complete cooling and chill in refrigerator for at least 1 hour. To serve, top pudding with coconut flakes.

Key Lime Pie

Total Time: 80 minutes + cooling time | **Servings**: 4 | **Per Serving**: Kcal 296; Carbs 25g; Fat 20g; Protein 7g

Ingredients

1 cup graham crackers
4 tbsp unsalted butter, melted
3 large egg yolks
2 tbsp granulated sugar
9 key limes, juiced
1 tbsp zested key lime

1 (14 oz) can sweetened condensed milk
For topping:
½ cup heavy cream
¼ cup granulated sugar
1 tsp zested key lime

Directions

Pour graham crackers in a plastic bag and gently crush using a rolling pin. Pour biscuit into a bowl and mix in butter. Pour mixture into a greased 7-inch springform and use a spoon to press to fit. Freeze in refrigerator to compact.

In a large bowl, using an electric hand mixer, whisk egg yolks and sugar until yolk is pale yellow and thickened. While mixing, add lime juice, lime zest, and condensed milk. Remove cake pan from refrigerator and pour in lime juice mixture. Cover pan with foil. Pour 1 cup of water in inner pot, fit in a trivet, and place cake pan on top.

Seal the lid, select Manual/Pressure Cook on High, and set cooking time to 40 minutes. After cooking, perform natural pressure release for 10 minutes, then a quick pressure release to let out remaining steam. Unlock the lid and carefully remove cake pan. Allow cooling for 10 minutes.

For topping, whisk heavy cream in a bowl, while slowly adding sugar until stiff. Spoon mixture into a piping bag and press decorative mounds on cake. Sprinkle with lime zest and chill cake in refrigerator for 3 hours. Slice and serve.

Tapioca Pudding

Total Time: 65 minutes + chilling time | **Servings**: 4 | **Per Serving**: Kcal 277; Carbs 32g; Fat 15g; Protein 6g

Ingredients

1 cup tapioca pearls
3 cups whole milk
¼ tsp salt

2 eggs
½ cup granulated sugar
1 tsp vanilla extract

Directions

In inner pot, add tapioca, milk, and salt. Seal the lid, select Manual/Pressure Cook on High, and set cooking time to 15 minutes. After cooking, perform a natural pressure release for 20 minutes. Unlock lid and select Sauté.

Beat eggs in a bowl and mix in 2 tbsp of tapioca liquid until well combined. Pour mixture into tapioca along with sugar and vanilla. Mix until adequately combined. Cook in the Instant Pot for 5 to 10 minutes on Sauté. Dish tapioca into dessert bowls, allow complete cooling and chill for 1 hour. Serve after.

Sticky Toffee Dessert

Total Time: 45 minutes | **Servings**: 4 | **Per Serving**: Kcal 295; Carbs 35g; Fat 15g; Protein 7g

Ingredients

¼ cup butter
¼ cup granulated sugar
1 tbsp cocoa powder
½ tsp ginger powder

2 medium eggs
1 cup self-rising flour
2 tbsp whole milk
½ cup caramel sauce

Directions

In a medium bowl, cream butter and sugar until light and fluffy. Mix in cocoa powder and ginger powder until well combined. Beat in eggs, while adding flour a little at a time, until properly mixed and then, whisk in milk.

Pour half of the mixture into a large ramekin bowl, top with caramel sauce, and cover with remaining batter. Cover bowl with foil. Pour 1 cup of water in inner pot, fit in a trivet, and place bowl on top.

Seal the lid, select Manual/Pressure Cook on High, and set cooking time to 15 minutes. After cooking, perform a natural pressure release for 10 minutes, and then a quick pressure release. Unlock the lid, carefully remove bowl, and take off foil. Allow pudding to sit for 5 minutes before serving.

Banana Pudding

Total Time: 35 minutes + 1 hour chilling | **Servings**: 4 | **Per Serving**: Kcal 604; Carbs 88g; Fat 26g; Protein 10g

Ingredients

1 cup whole milk
2 cups half-and-half
¾ cup + 1 tbsp granulated sugar, divided
¼ tsp salt
4 egg yolks

3 tbsp cornstarch
2 tbsp cold butter, cut into 4 pieces
1 tsp vanilla extract
2 medium banana, peeled and sliced
1 cup heavy cream

Directions

Set your Instant Pot to Sauté mode. In inner pot, mix milk, half-and-half, ½ cup of sugar, and salt. Heat while occasionally stirring until sugar dissolves, 3 minutes. Beat egg yolks in a medium bowl and add ¼ cup of sugar. Whisk until well combined. Add cornstarch and mix well. Scoop ½ cup of milk mixture into egg mix and whisk again until smooth. Pour mixture into inner pot.

Seal the lid, select Manual/Pressure Cook on High, and set cooking time to 2 minutes. After cooking, perform a quick pressure release to let out steam and unlock the lid. Turn Instant Pot off and stir in butter and vanilla until butter melts. Lay banana pieces into 4 dessert cups and top with pudding. In a medium bowl, whisk heavy cream with remaining sugar and spoon mixture on top of pudding. Chill dessert for 1 hour and serve after.

Mini Biscuit Cheesecakes

Total Time: 60 minutes | **Servings**: 12 | **Per Serving**: Kcal 124; Carbs 11g; Fat 8g; Protein 3g

Ingredients

8 oz cream cheese, softened
¼ cup granulated sugar
2 tbsp sour cream
¼ tsp vanilla extract

1 egg
7 Oreo cookies, broken into little pieces
2 cup water

Directions

In a medium bowl, whisk cream cheese, sugar, sour cream, and vanilla until smooth. Pour in eggs and beat until well combined. Fold in Oreo biscuits. Lightly grease a 12-holed silicone egg bite tray with cooking spray and fill with Oreo mixture. Cover tray with foil. Pour 1 cup of water in inner pot, fit in a trivet, and place egg bite tray on top.

Seal the lid, select Manual/Pressure Cook on High, and set time to 20 minutes. After cooking, perform a natural pressure release for 10 minutes, then a quick pressure release to let out remaining steam. Unlock the lid and remove tray, take off foil, allow cooling for 10 minutes, and pop out cake bites. Serve immediately or chill for later use.

Chocolate Fudge

Total Time: 50 minutes + cooling time | **Servings**: 4 | **Per Serving**: Kcal 456; Carbs 63g; Fat 32g; Protein 9g

Ingredients

1 (16 oz) box brownie mix
¼ cup olive oil
2 eggs
1 ½ cups chocolate chips

¼ cup chocolate syrup
3 tbsp whole milk
5 tbsp heavy cream
4 tbsp sprinkles

Directions

In a medium bowl, combine brownie mix, olive oil, eggs, ½ cup of chocolate chips, chocolate syrup, and milk. Lightly grease a silicone egg bite tray with cooking spray and fill with chocolate mixture two-thirds way up. Cover muffin tray loosely with foil.

Pour 1 cup of water in inner pot, fit in a trivet, and place egg bite tray on top. Seal the lid, select Manual/Pressure Cook on High, and set cooking time to 20 minutes. After cooking, perform a natural pressure release for 10 minutes, then a quick pressure release to let out remaining steam, and unlock the lid.

Carefully remove tray, take off foil, allow cooling for 5 minutes, and pop out dessert bites. While dessert cools, empty and clean inner pot, and select Sauté mode. Add remaining chocolate chips and heavy cream to inner pot and cook with continuous stirring until chocolate chips melt and well mixed with heavy cream, 5 minutes.

Pour mixture into a bowl and roll in dessert bites until well coated. Drizzle sprinkles on top and cool in refrigerator for 20 to 30 minutes. Serve.

Tasty Nutella Cakes

Total Time: 35 minutes | **Servings**: 4 | **Per Serving**: Kcal 335; Carbs 45g; Fat 15g; Protein 5g

Ingredients

1 cup Nutella
2 large eggs

¼ cup plain flour
14 blueberries + extra for serving

Directions

In a medium bowl, whisk Nutella and eggs until smoothly combined. Add flour and mix well. Grease 7 holes of a silicone egg bite tray with cooking spray and fill halfway with Nutella mixture. Drop two blueberries into each hole and cover with remaining Nutella mixture. Wrap muffin tray with foil.

Pour 1 cup of water in inner pot, fit in a trivet, and place egg bite tray on top. Seal the lid, select Manual/Pressure Cook mode on High, and set cooking time to 18 minutes.

After cooking, perform a quick pressure release to let out steam, and unlock the lid. Carefully remove tray, take off foil, allow cooling for 10 minutes, and pop out dessert bites. Serve immediately or chill for later use.

Churro Bites

Total Time: 25 minutes | **Servings**: 4 | **Per Serving**: Kcal 353; Carbs 37g; Fat 25g; Protein 11g

Ingredients

1 (21 oz) box cinnamon swirl crumb cake & muffin mix
1 brown sugar packet (included in cake mix box)
1 tsp cinnamon powder
2 eggs

1 cup heavy cream
4 tbsp brown sugar
1 tbsp granulated sugar

Directions

In a medium bowl, whisk muffin mix, brown sugar mix, ½ teaspoon of cinnamon powder, eggs, and heavy cream until smoothly combined. Lightly grease a silicone egg bite tray with cooking spray and fill with cinnamon mixture two-thirds way up. Cover muffin tray with foil.

Pour 1 cup of water in inner pot, fit in a trivet, and place egg bite tray on top. Seal the lid, select Manual/Pressure Cook mode on High, and set cooking time to 12 minutes. After cooking, perform a quick pressure release to let out steam, and unlock the lid. Carefully remove tray, take off foil, allow cooling for 5 minutes, and pop out dessert bites.

Pour brown sugar onto a plate and lightly roll in warm churro bites. In another plate, mix remaining cinnamon powder with granulated sugar and roll in churro bites a second time. Serve.

White Chocolate-Milk Faux Muffins

Total Time: 25 minutes | **Servings**: 4 | **Per Serving**: Kcal 320; Carbs 24g; Fat 12g; Protein 2g

Ingredients

1 (36 oz) white chocolate chip, melted

½ cup whole milk

Directions

In a medium bowl, mix white chocolate with milk until well combined. Lightly grease a silicone egg bite tray with cooking spray and fill with chocolate mixture two-thirds way up. Cover egg tray loosely with foil.

Pour 1 cup of water in inner pot, fit in a trivet, and place egg bite tray on top. Seal the lid, select Manual/Pressure Cook on High, and set time to 12 minutes. After cooking, perform a quick pressure release to let out steam, and unlock the lid. Carefully remove tray, take off foil, allow cooling for 5 minutes, and pop out dessert bites. Serve.

Coconut Rice Dessert Cups

Total Time: 35 minutes | **Servings**: 6 | **Per Serving**: Kcal 225; Carbs 29g; Fat 12g; Protein 7g

Ingredients

1 cup rice
3 cups milk
¼ cup water
1 tsp vanilla extract

¼ tsp ground cinnamon
A pinch of salt
¼ cup sugar
1 cup coconut flakes

Directions

Place the rice, milk, water, and salt into inner pot and stir to combine. Seal the lid, select Rice, and set time to 12 minutes on High. When done, perform a natural pressure release for 10 minutes and remove the lid. Stir in the vanilla extract and cinnamon to blend. Spoon the dessert into cups and top with the coconut flakes. Serve chilled.

Traditional Crema Catalana

Total Time: 2 hours | **Servings**: 2 | **Per Serving**: Kcal 169; Carbs 16g; Fat 9g; Protein 7g

Ingredients

2 egg yolks, room temperature
3 tsp sugar
1 cup milk
1 cinnamon stick

1 strip lemon peel
½ tbsp cornstarch
1 tbsp superfine sugar for topping

Directions

Warm the milk, cinnamon, and lemon peel in your Instant Pot on Sauté. When everything is heated, remove to a bowl and allow to infuse, about 30 minutes. Then, remove the cinnamon and lemon peel.

In a bowl, beat the eggs with the sugar and cornstarch until the sugar dissolves. Slowly add the egg mixture into the milk and gently stir until everything is well mixed. Divide the mixture between ramekins and cover with foil.

Pour 1 cup of water in your Instant Pot and fit in a trivet. Place the ramekins on the trivet. Seal the lid, select Steam, and set cooking time to 20 minutes.

When done, perform a natural pressure release for 6 minutes, then a quick pressure release to let out the remaining steam. Unlock the lid and take out the ramekins and remove the foil. Let cool for 30 minutes, then, refrigerate for 30 minutes. Sprinkle sugar on top of each ramekin and place under the broiler until the sugar is caramelized, and serve.

Baileys Hot Chocolate

Total Time: 20 minutes | **Servings**: 4 | **Per Serving**: Kcal 406; Carbs 38g; Fat 24g; Protein 7g

Ingredients

2 cups whole milk
½ cup heavy cream
4 ounces dark chocolate bar, chopped
1 tbsp sugar

1 tbsp cocoa powder
4 tbsp Baileys
A pinch salt
Mini marshmallows, to serve

Directions

Set your Instant Pot to Sauté and place in all the ingredients, except for the Baileys and marshmallows. Stir to combine. Bring to a boil for 10 minutes. Stir in Baileys and ladle into cups. Serve topped with some mini marshmallows.

Blueberry & Walnut Oatmeal Porridge

Total time: 25 minutes | **Servings**: 4 | **Per Serving**: Kcal 246; Carbs 33g; Fat 15g; Protein 8g

Ingredients

1 cup steel-cut oats
Salt to taste
½ tsp ground nutmeg

3 ½ cups water
1 cup blueberries
1 cup walnuts, chopped

Directions

Pour oats, nutmeg, and water in your Instant Pot and stir until well mixed. Seal the lid, select Manual/Pressure Cook mode on High, and set time to 10 minutes.

After cooking, perform natural pressure release for 10 minutes, then a quick pressure release to let out the remaining steam. Unlock the lid, stir, and spoon oatmeal into serving bowls. Top with blueberries and walnuts and serve.

Vanilla Liqueur Banana Bread

Total time: 70 minutes | **Servings:** 4 | **Per Serving:** Kcal 423; Carbs 52g; Fat 21g; Protein 12g

Ingredients

4 bananas, mashed
6 tbsp butter, melted
2 small eggs, beaten
1 tbsp vanilla-flavored liqueur

½ cup sugar
1 tsp baking powder
2 cups flour
1 cup water

Directions

Grease a cake pan with cooking spray and set aside. In a bowl, combine the butter, eggs, mashed bananas, and vanilla-flavored liqueur. Whisk in the sugar, baking powder and flour until well combined. Pour the mixture in the prepared pan and cover with aluminium foil.

Pour water in your Instant Pot and fit in a trivet, and place the pan on top. Seal the lid, select Manual/Pressure Cook on High, and set time to 50 minutes.

When done cooking, perform a natural pressure release for 5 minutes, then a quick pressure release. Remove the bread from the pan and let to cool. Cut into slices and serve.

Mascarpone Cake with Berries

Total time: 65 minutes | **Servings:** 8 | **Per Serving:** Kcal 436; Carbs 38g; Fat 28g; Protein 12g

Ingredients

1 large egg
1 cup butter, soften
16 oz mascarpone cheese
2 cups flour
2 tsp baking soda

1 tsp salt
¾ cup sugar
¾ cup milk
3 cups fresh berries
1 cup water

Directions

In a medium bowl, mix the mascarpone cheese, flour, baking soda, and salt. In a separate bowl, beat the butter, sugar, and egg using an electric mixer, until creamy. Add to the flour mixture, and stir in the milk and berries. Pour into a greased baking pan and cover with foil.

Pour water in your Instant Pot and fit in a trivet with slings. Place the pan on the trivet. Seal the lid, select Manual/Pressure Cook on High, and set time to 35 minutes.

When done cooking, perform natural pressure release for 10 minutes, then a quick pressure release to let out the remaining steam. Remove the aluminium foil and allow cooling for 10 minutes before slicing and serving.

Plum Breakfast Clafoutis

Total Time: 30 minutes | **Servings:** 4 | **Per Serving:** Kcal 256; Carbs 46g; Fat 6g; Protein 5g

Ingredients

2 tsp butter, softened
1 cup plums, chopped
1 cup whole milk
¼ cup half and half
¼ cup sugar

½ cup flour
2 large eggs
¼ tsp cinnamon
½ tsp vanilla extract
2 tbsp confectioners' sugar

Directions

Grease four ramekins with the butter and divide the plums among them. Set aside.

Pour the milk, half and half, sugar, flour, eggs, cinnamon, and vanilla in a bowl. Use a hand mixer to whisk the ingredients until the batter is smooth, about 2 minutes. Pour the mixture over the plums two-thirds way up.

Pour 1 cup of water into the pot. Fit in a trivet and put the ramekins on top. Lay a square of foil on the ramekins but don't crimp. Seal the lid, select Manual/Pressure Cook on High, and set the cooking time to 11 minutes. When ready, perform a quick pressure release and unlock the lid. Use tongs to remove the foil. Remove the ramekins onto a flat surface. Cool for 5 minutes, and then dust with the confectioners' sugar. Serve warm.

Orange French Toast

Total time: 40 minutes | **Servings:** 4 | **Per Serving:** Kcal 215; Carbs 33g; Fat 5g; Protein 8g

Ingredients

6 bread slices, cubed
2 large eggs
1 cup milk
2 tsp vanilla extract

1 tsp ground cinnamon
Zest from 1 orange
1 cup water
Maple syrup for topping

Directions

Beat the eggs with the milk, vanilla extract, cinnamon and orange zest in a mixing bowl. Add in the bread cubes and mix to coat. Pour this mixture into a previously greased pan and cover with aluminium foil. Pour the water into your Instant Pot and fit in a trivet. Place the covered pan on top.

Seal the lid, select Manual/Pressure Cook on High, and set time to 15 minutes. After cooking, perform a natural pressure release for 5 minutes. Unlock the lid, remove the pan, and take off the foil. Allow cooling for 5 minutes. Drizzle with maple syrup to serve.

Strawberry Bread French Toast

Total Time: 50 minutes | **Servings:** 4 | **Per Serving:** Kcal 233; Carbs 18g; Fat 14g; Protein 9g

Ingredients

3 eggs
¼ cup milk
1 tbsp sugar
1 tsp vanilla extract
1 tsp cinnamon powder
6 slices brioche, cubed

3 strawberries, sliced, divided
2 tbsp brown sugar, divided
¼ cup ricotta cheese
2 tbsp firm butter, sliced
¼ cup chopped almonds
2 tbsp maple syrup

Directions

Put the eggs into a bowl and whisk with the milk, sugar, vanilla, and cinnamon. Set aside.

Grease a baking dish with cooking spray and in a single layer, spread in half of the brioche cubes. Lay half of the strawberry slices on the bread and dust with 1 tablespoon of brown sugar. Spoon and spread the ricotta cheese on top of the strawberries. Make another layer of bread, strawberries, sugar, and ricotta cheese. Pour the egg mixture all over the layered ingredients, ensuring to give the bread a good coat.

Pour 1 cup of water into the pot and fit a trivet. Fix the pan on top. Seal the lid, select Manual/Pressure Cook on High and the cooking time to 20 minutes. Once ready, perform a quick pressure release, and unlock the lid. Top the toast with the sliced butter, almonds, and maple syrup, and serve.

Wheat Flour Cinnamon Balls

Total Time: 50 minutes | **Servings**: 8 | **Per Serving**: Kcal 160; Carbs 23g; Fat 7g; Protein 3g

Ingredients

¼ cup whole-wheat flour

½ cup all-purpose flour

½ tsp baking powder

3 tbsp sugar, divided

¼ tsp ground cinnamon + plus ½ tbsp

¼ tsp sea salt

2 tbsp cold butter, cubed

1/3 cup whole milk

Directions

Mix the whole-wheat flour, all-purpose flour, baking powder, 1 tbsp of sugar, ¼ tsp of cinnamon, and salt in a medium bowl. Add the butter and use a pastry cutter to cut into butter, breaking it into little pieces until resembling cornmeal. Pour in the milk and mix until the dough forms into a ball.

Knead the dough on a flat surface. Divide the dough into 8 pieces and roll each piece into a ball. Put the balls in a greased baking pan with space in between each ball and oil the balls. Pour 1 cup of water into the inner pot. Put in a trivet and place the pan on top. Seal the lid, select Manual/Pressure Cook on High, and set the time to 20 minutes.

After cooking, perform a natural pressure release for 5 minutes. In a medium mixing bowl, combine the remaining sugar and cinnamon. Toss the dough balls in the cinnamon and sugar mixture to serve.

Raspberry Crumble

Total Time: 40 minutes | **Servings**: 6 | **Per Serving**: Kcal 354; Carbs 25g; Fat 11g; Protein 3g

Ingredients

2 cups raspberries

2 tbsp arrowroot starch

1 tsp lemon juice

5 tbsp sugar

½ cup flour

¼ cup brown sugar

½ cup rolled oats

¼ cup cold butter, cut into pieces

1 tsp cinnamon powder

Directions

In a small bowl, combine the arrowroot starch, 1 tbsp of water, lemon juice, and 3 tbsp of sugar. Mix in the raspberries, and toss well. Pour the mixture in a baking pan.

In a separate bowl, mix the flour, brown sugar, oats, butter, cinnamon, and remaining sugar, and form crumble. Spread the crumble evenly on the raspberries.

Put a trivet in the pot. Cover the pan with foil and pour half cup of water into the pot. Put the pan on top. Seal the lid, select Manual/Pressure Cook on High, and set the cooking time to 20 minutes. When done, do a quick release and unlock the lid. Remove the foil and serve.

Apple Vanilla Hand Pies

Total Time: 60 minutes | **Servings**: 8 | **Per Serving**: Kcal 294; Carbs 39g; Fat 15g; Protein 2g

Ingredients

2 apples, chopped

3 tbsp sugar

1 lemon, juiced

A pinch of salt

1 tsp vanilla extract

1 tsp cornstarch

1 (2-crust) box refrigerated pie crusts

Directions

In a large mixing bowl, combine the apples, sugar, lemon juice, salt, and vanilla. Allow the mixture to stand for 10 minutes, then drain and reserve 1 tbsp of the liquid.

In a bowl, whisk the cornstarch into the reserved liquid and mix with the apple mixture. Put the piecrusts on a lightly floured surface and cut into 8 circles. Spoon a tbsp of apple mixture in the center of the circle. Brush the edges with some water and fold the dough over the filling. Press the edges with a fork to seal. Cut 3 small slits on top of each pie and grease with cooking spray. Arrange the cakes in a single layer in a greased baking pan.

Pour 1 cup of water into the inner pot. Fit in a trivet, and place the pan on top. Seal the lid, select Manual/Pressure Cook on High, and set the cooking time to 30 minutes. After cooking, perform a natural pressure release for 10 minutes, then a quick pressure release, and unlock the lid. Serve.

Simple Vanilla Cheesecake

Total Time: 2 hours + chilling time | **Servings**: 6 | **Per Serving**: Kcal 451; Carbs 28g; Fat 34g; Protein 9g

Ingredients

1 ½ cups finely crushed graham crackers
2 tbsp sugar
4 tbsp butter, melted
16 oz cream cheese, at room temperature
½ cup brown sugar

¼ cup sour cream
1 tbsp all-purpose flour
1 ½ tsp vanilla extract
½ tsp salt
2 eggs

Directions

Grease a springform pan with cooking spray, then line the pan with parchment paper, grease with cooking spray again, and line with aluminium foil.

In a bowl, mix the cracker crumbs, sugar, and butter. Spoon the mixture into the pan and press firmly with a spoon. In a deep bowl and with a hand mixer, beat the cream cheese and brown sugar. Whisk in the sour cream to be smooth and stir in the flour, vanilla, and salt.

Crack in the eggs and beat but not to be overly smooth. Pour the mixture over the crumbs. Pour 1 cup of water into the pot and place a trivet. Put the springform pan on top. Seal the lid, select Manual/Pressure Cook on High, and set the cooking time to 35 minutes.

Once done, perform a natural pressure release for 10 minutes, then a quick pressure release to let out any remaining pressure. Unlock the lid. Remove the pan from the trivet and allow the cheesecake to cool for 1 hour. Cover the cheesecake with foil and chill in the refrigerator for 4 hours.

Coconut Salted Caramel Cup

Total Time: 15 minutes | **Servings**: 1 | **Per Serving**: Kcal 258; Carbs 50g; Fat 6g; Protein 4g

Ingredients

25 soft caramels, unwrapped
¼ cup coconut milk

¼ cup mini marshmallows
A pinch of salt

Directions

Set your Instant Pot to Sauté and place in the caramels, coconut milk, and marshmallows. Cook for 3-5 minutes until the caramels and marshmallows melt, stirring often. Season with salt. Remove into a jar and leave to cool. Serve with strawberries or chocolate.

Mixed Berry Cobbler

Total Time: 35 minutes | **Servings**: 4 | **Per Serving**: Kcal 463; Carbs 39g; Fat 6g; Protein 5g

Ingredients

2 bags frozen mixed berries, defrosted
3 tbsp arrowroot starch

1 cup sugar

For the topping

1 cup self-rising flour
¼ tsp cinnamon powder
5 tbsp powdered sugar

1 cup crème fraiche
1 tbsp melted butter
1 tbsp whipping cream

Directions

Pour the mixed berries into your Instant Pot along with the arrowroot starch and sugar. Mix to combine. Select Sauté and cook for 3 minutes.

In a small bowl, whisk the flour, cinnamon powder, and sugar. In a separate small bowl, whisk the crème fraiche with the melted butter. Pour the cream mixture over the dry ingredients and combine evenly. Spread the dough over the berries. Brush the topping with the whipping cream.

Seal the lid, select Manual/Pressure Cook on High, and set the cooking time to 10 minutes. When ready, perform a natural pressure release for 10 minutes, then a quick pressure release to let out any remaining pressure. Allow cooling before slicing. Serve warm.

Chocolate Vanilla Swirl Cheesecake

Total Time: 90 minutes + chilling time | **Servings**: 8 | **Per Serving**: Kcal 365 ; Carbs 26g; Fat 26g; Protein 6g

Ingredients

4 oz chocolate wafer cookies, crushed
2 tbsp butter, melted
16 oz cream cheese, at room temperature
½ cup sugar
2 tbsp heavy cream

2 tsp vanilla extract
2 tbsp sour cream
2 large eggs
3 oz sweet chocolate chips, melted

Directions

In a bowl, mix cookie crumbs and butter. Spoon into a greased springform pan and press all around with a spoon.

In a separate bowl and using a hand mixer, beat the cream cheese until smooth, add the sugar, and beat further until smooth. Pour in the heavy cream, vanilla extract, and sour cream. Whisk again and crack the eggs into the bowl one after the other, while whisking after each egg is added.

Spoon ½ cup of the cream mixture into a bowl and mix in the chocolate chips. Pour the remaining cream mixture over the prepared crust and top with the chocolate mixture. Cover the filling with aluminium foil.

Pour 1 cup of water into the inner pot. Fix in a trivet and put the springform pan on top. Seal the lid, select Manual/Pressure Cook on High, and set the cooking time to 15 minutes.

After cooking, do a natural pressure release for 10 minutes, and then a quick pressure release to let out any remaining pressure. Unlock the lid and remove the cheesecake from the pot. Take off the foil.

Let the cheesecake rest for 15 to 20 minutes and then refrigerate the cooled cake for 3 to 4 hours to chill through.

Made in the USA
Monee, IL
16 November 2019